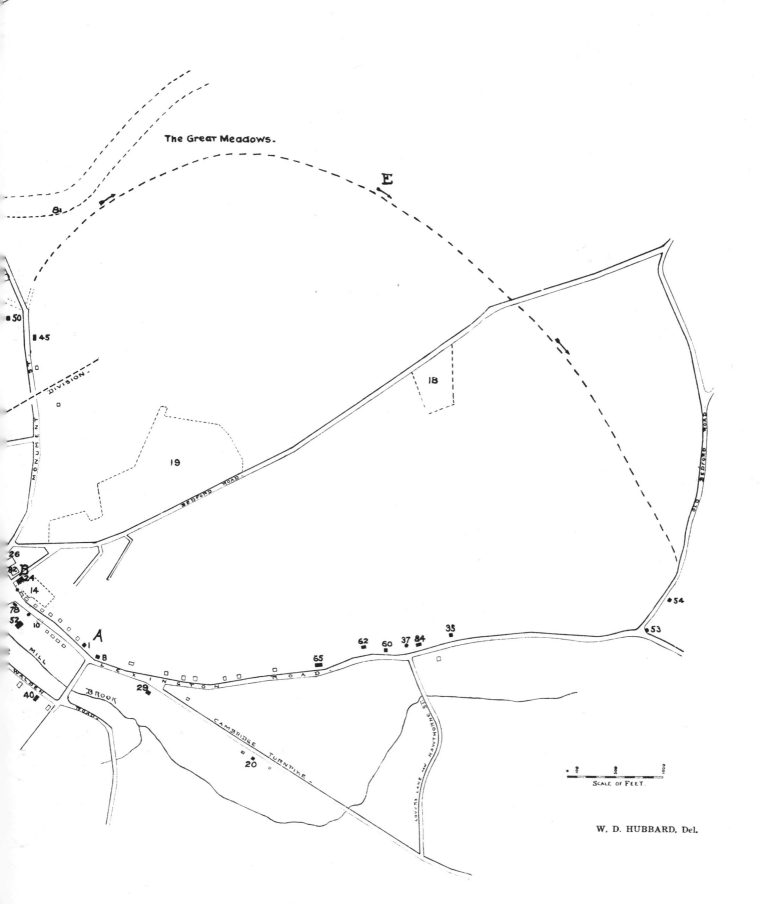

The Great Meadows.

W. D. HUBBARD, Del.

SCALE OF FEET.

The American Renaissance in New England

Map of New England.

Dictionary of Literary Biography • Volume One

The American Renaissance in New England

Edited by Joel Myerson
University of South Carolina

A Bruccoli Clark Book
Gale Research Company • Book Tower • Detroit, Michigan 48226
1978

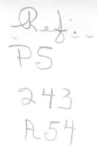
Planning Board for
DICTIONARY OF LITERARY BIOGRAPHY

John Baker
William Emerson
Orville Prescott
Vernon Sternberg
Alden Whitman

Matthew J. Bruccoli, *Editorial Director*
C. E. Frazer Clark, Jr., *Managing Editor*
Richard Layman, *Project Editor*
Joel Myerson, *Series Editor*

Copyright © 1978

GALE RESEARCH COMPANY

Library of Congress Cataloging in Publication Data

Main entry under title:

The American renaissance in New England.

(Dictionary of literary biography ; v. 1)
"A Bruccoli Clark book."
Bibliography: p.
1. American literature--New England--Bio-bibliography.
2. American literature--19th century--Bio-bibliography.
3. New England--Biography. I. Myerson, Joel.
II. Series.
PS243.A54   810'.9'003 [B]   77-82803
ISBN 0-8103-0913-0

Plan of the Work

. . . almost the most prodigious asset of a country, and perhaps its most precious possession is its native literary product—when that product is fine and noble and enduring.

Mark Twain*

The advisory board, the editors, and the publisher of the *Dictionary of Literary Biography* are joined in endorsing the truth expressed in Mark Twain's observation. The literature of a nation represents an inexhaustible resource of permanent worth. It is our expectation that this work will make the American achievement in literature better understood and more accessible to students and to the literate public, while serving the needs of scholars.

The final plan for *DLB* resulted from two years of preparation. The project was proposed to Bruccoli Clark by Frederick G. Ruffner, president of the Gale Research Company, in November 1975. After specimen entries were written and typeset, an advisory board was formed to plan and develop the series. In meetings held in New York during 1976, the publisher, series editors, and advisory board developed the scheme for a comprehensive biographical dictionary of persons who have contributed to North American literature. Editorial work on the first volume began in January 1977.

Entries range from brief notices of secondary figures (200 to 600 words) to comprehensive treatments (up to 15,000 words) of major figures. The major entries are written by authorities in their fields and intended as permanent contributions to literary history. The purpose of *DLB* is not only to provide reliable information in a clear format, but also to place literary figures in the larger perspective of North American literary history and to offer appraisals of their accomplishments by qualified scholars.

We define literature as *the intellectual commerce of a nation*: not merely as belles lettres, but as that ample and complex process by which ideas are generated, shaped, and communicated. Accordingly, entries in *DLB* will not be limited to "creative writers," but will extend to others who in their time and in their way contributed to our literature. By this means readers of *DLB* may be brought to see literature not as cult scripture in the keeping of high priests, but as at the very center of a nation's life.

DLB will include all of the major North American writers and those standing in the ranks immediately behind them. The best available scholarly and critical counsel will be sought in deciding which minor figures to include and how full the entries for them should be. Whenever possible, useful references will be made to figures who do not warrant separate entries.

In order to make *DLB* more than a reference tool and to prepare volumes that individually have claim to status as literary history, it has been decided to organize individual volumes by topic or period or genre. Thus the first five volumes are: (1) *The American Renaissance in New England*; (2) *American Novelists Since World War II*; (3) *The American Renaissance in New York and the South*; (4) *American Expatriates in Paris, 1920-1940*; and (5) *American Screenwriters*. Each of these volumes will provide a biographical-bibliographical guide and overview for a particular area of North American literature. This volume plan will require many decisions about the placement and treatment of authors who might properly be included in two or three volumes. In some instances a major author will be included in separate volumes, but with different entries emphasizing the aspect of his career appropriate to that volume. Ernest Hemingway, for example, will be represented in the *Expatriates* volume by an entry focusing on his Paris apprenticeship; he will also be included in the volume planned for the novelists of the 1920-1940 period, and there the Hemingway entry will survey his entire career. In other instances the problem will be dealt with by cross-referencing. The final volume of *DLB* will be a comprehensive index to the series.

From an unpublished section of Mark Twain's autobiography, copyright © 1972 by the Mark Twain Company.

Each *DLB* volume has a volume editor responsible for planning the volume, selecting the figures for inclusion, and assigning the entries. The volume editor is also responsible for preparing, where appropriate, appendices surveying the major periodicals and literary and intellectual movements for his volume, as well as a list of further readings. Work on the series as a whole is co-ordinated at the editorial center in Columbia, South Carolina, where the editorial staff is responsible for the accuracy of the published volumes.

One feature that distinguishes *DLB* is the illustration policy—its concern with the iconography of literature. Just as an author is influenced by his surroundings, so is the reader's understanding of the author enriched by a knowledge of his environment. Therefore *DLB* volumes include not only drawings, paintings, and photographs of authors, often depicting them at various stages in their careers, but also illustrations of their spouses, published works, and places where they lived and wrote. Specimens of the writers' manuscripts are included when feasible.

A companion volume to *DLB*—tentatively entitled *A Guide, Chronology, and Glossary for North American Literature*—will provide a sense of the frame of North American literature and trace the major influences that worked on it by means of chronologies, literary affiliation charts, glossarial entries, and entries on movements or tendencies. This supplement will be a point of reference from the *DLB* volumes, conserving space and eliminating repetition in the series. It will be planned to stand on its own as a *vade mecum*.

Samuel Johnson rightly decreed that "The chief glory of every people arises from its authours." The purpose of the *Dictionary of Literary Biography* is to trace the outlines of North American literature in the surest way available to us—by comprehensive scholarly treatment of the lives and work of those who contributed to it.

Editor's Note

The American Renaissance in New England contains biographical sketches of ninety-eight authors who participated in the American Renaissance. Authors are included who wrote or began publishing their major works during this time. The scope is wide: represented are writers of short stories, juvenile literature, sermons, and popular literature, as well as novelists, poets, essayists, editors, humorists, translators, compilers, journalists, reformers, abolitionists, scientists, and lexicographers. Special attention has been given to the Transcendental authors, headed by Emerson and Thoreau, because of the importance of this literary movement.

The American Renaissance in New England, between 1830 and 1860, was a time of spirited and original literary activity. During this time, the population of the United States grew from seven million to twelve million persons, the number of newspapers increased from 850 to 4,000, and the advent of Jacksonian democracy brought the rise of the common man. More people of varied backgrounds provided a larger audience for literary productions, and, while businessmen mined America's natural resources for material profit, writers turned to American sources with equally successful artistic results. This was the first period in American literary history when authors utilized native sources and concerns in their ever-increasing number of publications.

New England maintained cultural prominence because of its historic association with book publishing; Stephen Daye had set up the first printing press in America at Cambridge, Massachusetts, near Boston, in 1639. In the nearly two centuries that followed, only Philadelphia and New York approached Boston as a center of literary and publishing activity. Some authors of the American Renaissance—such as Cooper, Melville, Poe, and Whitman—lived much or all of their lives outside New England. But the core of New England authors, led by Emerson, Hawthorne, and Thoreau, constitute a major force in American literary history.

The influence of the major New England American Renaissance writers upon other writers and movements was enormous. Henry James, Melville, and the American short story were profoundly affected by Hawthorne; William James, E. A. Robinson, Robert Frost, and Wallace Stevens all drew upon Emerson for their works; Mahatma Gandhi and Martin Luther King both used Thoreau's "Civil Disobedience" in formulating their social movements; and all nature writers are indebted to *Walden*. The Transcendental movement as a whole strongly affected the Brook Farm and Fruitlands communities, changed the direction of American Unitarianism, influenced the concept of individual freedom in American thought, and greatly impressed nearly all the major figures of the day. Indeed, not only is Transcendentalism notable for developing certain unique aspects of American life, but also, in doing so, for drawing upon the religions and literature of other nations, and for passing on its own legacy to future generations.

Entries are divided into two types: extended factual and evaluative essays on major figures; and shorter essays on less important figures. Appendices include a glossary of terms, accounts of communal experiments, descriptions of the major periodicals of the time, and a list of supplementary readings. All entries are evaluative and provide bibliographical information. Because illustrations help bring biographical subjects to life, this work includes nearly 150 photographs of writers, their books, and their environment.

There are eleven entries on figures of major importance (Brownson, Dickinson, Emerson, Fuller, Hawthorne, Holmes, Longfellow, Lowell, Parker, Thoreau, and Whittier), each divided into three sections: The first section is a brief career chronology and list of significant publications for easy reference. The second section is a chronologically-arranged personal and career summary with discussion of all major works; it begins with a summary statement of the figure's importance and traces the critical and popular reputation, indicating the author's relationship to the social concerns and literary movements of the time. Finally, there is a bibliography of significant works by and about the subject.

All other entries deal with the subject's life, major works, and critical reputation in one section.

The editor would like to thank the staffs of the following libraries for their assistance: Harvard University, University of North Carolina, University of South Carolina, and University of Virginia. The University of South Carolina has, as usual, provided generous support and thanks are due William H. Nolte, Head, Department of English. Special thanks are due Richard Taylor for photographic work.

Contributors

Steven Allaback	*University of California at Santa Barbara*
Lawrence Buell	*Oberlin College*
Robert E. Burkholder	*University of South Carolina*
J. Wade Caruthers	*Southern Connecticut State College*
Thomas L. Connelly	*University of South Carolina*
Charles R. Crowe	*University of Georgia*
Leonard Gilhooley	*Fordham University*
Douglas Greenwood	*University of Maryland*
Walter Harding	*State University of New York, College at Geneseo*
Vivian Hopkins	*State University of New York at Albany*
Linda Maloney	*University of South Carolina*
Barry Menikoff	*University of Hawaii*
Ruth Miller	*State University of New York at Stony Brook*
Roger C. Mueller	*University of the Pacific*
Joel Myerson	*University of South Carolina*
Natalie A. Naylor	*Hofstra University*
Margaret Neussendorfer	*University of Texas at Permian Basin*
Raymond K. O'Cain	*University of South Carolina*
David Robinson	*Oregon State University*
Madeleine B. Stern	*Leona Rostenberg—Rare Books*
Arlin Turner	*Duke University*
Albert J. von Frank	*University of Rochester*
Thomas Wortham	*University of California at Los Angeles*
Conrad Wright	*Harvard Divinity School*

All unsigned contributions are by *DLB* staff.

To my parents
Edward and Gwenne Myerson

The American Renaissance
in New England

Dictionary of Literary Biography

JACOB ABBOTT (14 November 1803-31 October 1879), known today primarily for his juvenile works, was born and raised in Hallowell, Maine. After graduating from Bowdoin College, he taught briefly at the Portland Academy, where Henry Wadsworth Longfellow was one of his pupils, before becoming professor of mathematics and natural philosophy at Amherst College. Abbott was interested in

Jacob Abbott

educational theory and in his classes and writings undertook to treat children as intelligent beings, not talking down to them or being patronizing. His *The Young Christian* (Boston: Peirce & Parker, 1832) and similar religious books, and the twenty-eight volume "Rollo Books" series (1834 on) are more human and

less formal than other children's literature of the day, while at the same time instructional. Abbott wrote or edited over 200 volumes before his death and became a wealthy man from them. He died at Farmington, Maine. REFERENCES: Lyman Abbott, *Silhouettes of My Contemporaries* (Garden City, N. Y.: Doubleday, Page, 1922), pp. 332-361; William W. Lawrence, "Rollo and His Uncle George," *New England Quarterly*, 18 (September 1945): 291-302.

JEAN LOUIS RODOLPHE AGASSIZ (28 May 1807-14 December 1873), known as Louis Agassiz, was a naturalist, educator, and physician whose literary significance lies in his establishment of a scientific corollary for Emerson's belief that there is a spiritual quality underlying the natural world. Born in French Switzerland, Agassiz was the descendant of a long line of Protestant ministers. Pride in his religious heritage greatly affected Agassiz the scientist, who opposed evolution because of his piety and inculcated romantic idealism into his scientific treatises, claiming that "We may . . . come to a full understanding of Nature from the very reason that we have an immortal soul." Agassiz started collecting fishes while he was still attending the gymnasium at Bienne, and at Munich in 1828 he was appointed to classify fishes collected in Brazil. This project resulted in Agassiz's first publication, *Brazilian Fishes* (Monachii: C. Wolf, 1829-1832). That same year Agassiz received his Doctor of Philosophy degree from Erlangen and in 1830 he earned a degree of Doctor of Medicine, fulfilling a promise to his father. In 1831 he went to Paris where he fell under the influence of Georges Cuvier and Alexander von Humboldt. The latter secured Agassiz a teaching position at Neuchatel, Switzerland, where he began his lifelong research into glaciation, resulting in the delineation of his theory of an "ice age." There he also continued his study of fossil fish (begun in 1829), the

findings of which were published in *Recherches sur les Poissons Fossiles* (Neuchatel: Imprimerie de Petitpierre, 1833-1844). Only a few months after Agassiz's arrival in Boston in the fall of 1846, Thoreau was sending him specimens from Concord, and contact with Agassiz apparently resulted in Thoreau's more scientific approach to nature, beginning in the early 1850s. Agassiz also had contact with other literary notables of Boston as one of the founding members of the Saturday Club in 1856, professor of natural history at Harvard College, and founder of his own school which Emerson's daughter, Ellen, attended. Agassiz intended his *Contributions to the Natural History of the United States* (Boston: Little, Brown, 1857-1862) to be his crowning achievement, but only four of the proposed ten volumes were completed before his death in Cambridge. REFERENCES: *Louis Agassiz: His Life and Correspondence*, ed. Elizabeth Cary Agassiz (Boston: Houghton, Mifflin, 1885); Edward Lurie, *Louis Agassiz: A Life in Science* (Chicago: University of Chicago Press, 1960); Lurie, *Nature and the American Mind: Louis Agassiz and the Culture of*

Science (New York: Science History Publications, 1974). —*Robert E. Burkholder*

AMOS BRONSON ALCOTT (29 November 1799-4 March 1888), educator and philosopher, was born at Spindle Hill, Connecticut. His formal schooling ended when he was thirteen, though he continued to read on his own, and he soon became a peddler. A turning point in his life came in 1822 when, while travelling in the Carolinas, he stayed at a Quaker community. Impressed by their belief in the "inner light" of man which provided a direct spiritual contact with the divinity, Alcott felt a new sense of direction and purpose, and he returned to his first love, teaching. In 1824 he began a school at Wolcott, near his home.

Alcott taught various schools in Connecticut until 1828, when he was invited by the Boston Infant School Society to take charge of their classroom. One person who supported his assignment was Abba May and she assisted him when he took up his post. Their relationship soon turned to love and they were married in 1830. The next year the Alcotts moved to the Philadelphia area, where Alcott taught various schools. In 1834 he returned to Boston with his wife and two daughters (Anna was born in 1832 and Louisa May the following year), and began a school at the Masonic Temple.

Alcott's methods at his Temple School clearly demonstrate his educational philosophy. Contrary to the reliance upon rote education at the time, Alcott attempted to make his charges aware of the divinity within them by turning their attention inward so that, having discovered their inner power, they might use it in guiding their outward lives. Education was to Alcott a joy and not an enforced labor. His classroom was distinguished by open spaces and pleasant surroundings, with art objects and books being prominently displayed. He believed in the positive influence of the home and his schoolroom attempted to recreate a homelike atmosphere. His method was inductive and Socratic: by questioning his students, he let them discover answers instead of merely being told rules. Books were supplemental to these discussions; Alcott deplored schools where learning consisted solely of memorizing texts. There was no corporal punishment at Alcott's school; problem children were merely excluded from the group until they demonstrated a desire to return by settling down. At various times Margaret Fuller and Elizabeth Peabody assisted him with the school, and Ralph

Waldo Emerson even gave cash gifts for its upkeep.

But Alcott's honest attempts to inform others of his teaching methods, as described in Peabody's *Record of a School* (1835) and his own *Conversations with Children on the Gospels* (1836-1837), were attacked by press and public alike. The public was suspicious of his educational reforms, for his desire to discuss all subjects, including religion and sex, were not shared by many at that time. Many people soon withdrew their children and all but two did so when Alcott integrated the school in 1839, leaving him without a livelihood for his wife and three daughters (Elizabeth was born in 1836). Therefore, when an opportunity opened in 1840 for Alcott to move his family to Concord and support them by farming, he did so.

In Concord, Alcott quickly renewed his friendships with Emerson, who had sponsored him for membership in the Transcendental Club, and Henry David Thoreau, who called him "the best-natured man I ever met." He also briefly became involved with the Transcendentalist periodical, the *Dial*, which was named after the heading Alcott had given a collection of thoughts assembled from his journals. With Fuller's help, Alcott published his appropriately-named "Orphic Sayings" in the July 1840 and January 1841 numbers. The public response was disastrous—nearly every review of the *Dial* ridiculed Alcott's efforts. His only other contribution was a selection from his journals in the April 1842 issue.

Fortunately, Alcott was cheered in 1842 when, with Emerson's help, he sailed to England to visit a group of Transcendentalists who had founded a community based on his precepts at Ham, Surrey. The reception was a friendly one and Alcott returned to America with Henry Wright, Charles Lane, and Lane's son.

All this support encouraged Alcott and in June 1843, the Alcott family, Lane, and a few others moved to Harvard, Massachusetts, near Concord, and established the Fruitlands community. The experiment was a failure: neither Alcott nor Lane was practical enough to be a farmer and both were away too often on reform missions to properly work the place. Fruitlands collapsed in January 1844 and Alcott returned to Concord.

The failure at Fruitlands nearly broke Alcott. Although he never gave up his idealistic aspirations, he never again ventured out with such daring. The family was uprooted much over the next decade, living in Boston and Walpole, New Hampshire, before returning permanently to Concord in 1857. Since Alcott left his physical sustenance to others—even his job as superintendent of Concord's schools failed to pay enough to live on—the family survived on the gifts of friends and the earnings of Mrs. Alcott and the children as they taught, took in work, or—in Louisa's case—wrote. This long battle with poverty did not end until 1868, with the popular and financial success of Louisa's autobiographical *Little Women*. In the mid-1850s, Alcott began a series of "Conversations" or talks which proved financially rewarding and carried him all over the midwest. In later years, as the Transcendentalists died, Alcott became an authority on them and the unofficial keeper of the flame. Even his wife's death in 1877 did not stay his activities. The series of lectures on the Transcendental philosophy he helped organize in 1879 developed into the Concord School of Philosophy. But a stroke in 1882 paralyzed Alcott and he lived, unable to write and barely able to talk, for six more years until his death at Louisa's home in Boston.

Although Alcott's works sold respectably during his life, interest in them has waned. Alcott simply could not write well. He was incapable of writing a simple, direct sentence; all his works are oracular and, at their worse, nearly impenetrable. His style was, in Emerson's words, "All stir and no go." Alcott's poetry is pleasant but suffers from the author's lack of knowledge about versification.

The Concord School of Philosophy.

Since most of Alcott's contemporary fame rested upon his conversational powers, his posthumous reputation, based on his writings, has suffered. Thus, when the critic Henry A. Beers visited Concord in 1905 and asked an innkeeper about Alcott, he received this answer: "Oh, Alcott! The best thing he ever did was his daughters."

—*Joel Myerson*

Principal Works: *Observations on the Principles and Methods of Infant Instruction* (Boston: Carter & Hendee, 1830); *Conversations with Children on the Gospels*, [ed. Elizabeth Palmer Peabody], 2 vols. (Boston: James Munroe, 1836-1837); *Emerson* (Cambridge: privately printed, 1865; later published as *Ralph Waldo Emerson. An Estimate of His Character and Genius in Prose and Verse*, Boston: A. Williams, 1882); *Tablets* (Boston: Roberts Brothers, 1868); *Concord Days* (Boston: Roberts Brothers, 1872); *Table-Talk* (Boston: Roberts Brothers, 1877); *New Connecticut. An Autobiographical Poem* (Boston: privately printed 1881; later published, ed. F. B. Sanborn, Boston: Roberts Brothers, 1887); *Sonnets and Canzonets* (Boston: Roberts Brothers, 1882).

Principal References: [Elizabeth Palmer Peabody], *Record of a School: Exemplifying the General Principles of a Spiritual Culture* (Boston: James Munroe, 1835); F. B. Sanborn and William T. Harris, *A. Bronson Alcott: His Life and Philosophy*, 2 vols. (Boston: Roberts Brothers, 1893); F. B. Sanborn, *Bronson Alcott at Alcott House, England, and Fruitlands, New England (1842-1844)* (Cedar Rapids, Iowa: Torch Press, 1908); Clara Endicott Sears, *Bronson Alcott's Fruitlands* (Boston: Houghton Mifflin, 1915); George E. Haefner, *A Critical Estimate of the Educational Theories and Practices of A. Bronson Alcott* (New York: Columbia University Press, 1937); Odell Shepard, *Pedlar's Progress: The Life of Bronson Alcott* (Boston: Little, Brown, 1937); *The Journals of Bronson Alcott*, ed. Odell Shepard (Boston: Little, Brown, 1938); Dorothy McCuskey, *Bronson Alcott, Teacher* (New York: Macmillan, 1940); Hubert H. Hoeltje, *Sheltering Tree: A Story of the Friendship of Ralph Waldo Emerson and Amos Bronson Alcott* (Durham: Duke University Press, 1943); *The Letters of A. Bronson Alcott*, ed. Richard L. Herrnstadt (Ames: Iowa State University Press, 1969); Charles Strickland, "A Transcendentalist Father: The Child-Rearing Practices of Bronson Alcott," *Perspectives in American History*, 3 (1969): 5-73; Joel Myerson, "Bronson Alcott's 'Scripture for 1840,'" *ESQ: A Journal of the American Renaissance*, 20 (Fourth Quarter 1974): 236-259.

LOUISA MAY ALCOTT (29 November 1832-6 March 1888) still retains her reputation as one of America's best-loved writers of juveniles. That reputation was established with the publication of *Little Women* (1868-1869), a domestic novel for girls primarily autobiographical in origin. Alcott was born in Germantown, Pennsylvania, the daughter of the Transcendental philosopher and educator Amos Bronson Alcott and Abigail May, and, with her three sisters, grew up in Concord, Massachusetts. Her family background of high-minded idealism coupled with often acute poverty reappears in *Little Women* as the background of the Marches. Often Louisa was the only mainstay of her family and she refused no work that would add to the family income, from sewing to domestic service, from teaching to serving as companion to an invalid on a European tour. The work she preferred, however, was writing, and she tried her ink-stained hand at a wide variety of genres for the periodical press: poetry, fairy tales, short stories of sweetness and light, realistic episodes of the Civil War based upon her brief experience as a nurse at the Union Hotel Hospital, Georgetown, D.C., and blood-and-thunder thrillers of passion and revenge published under the pseudonym of "A. M. Barnard." Her first published book, *Flower*

Fables (1855), "legends of faery land," was dedicated to Emerson's daughter Ellen and netted the author thirty-two dollars. Her first novel, *Moods* (1865), a narrative of stormy violence, death, and intellectual love, was an attempt to apply Emerson's remark: "Life is a train of moods like a string of beads." Off and on, she worked at an autobiographical, feminist novel, *Success*, subsequently renamed *Work: A Story of Experience*. In 1868 she undertook editorship of a juvenile monthly, *Merry's Museum*, and that same year Thomas Niles of Roberts Brothers, the Boston publishers, asked her to write a girls' story. By that time she had served a long literary apprenticeship and was already a professional writer. The result of Niles' request was *Little Women*. Its characters were drawn from those of Alcott's sisters, its scenes from the New England where she had grown up, and many of its episodes from those she and her family had experienced. In the creation of *Little Women*, Alcott was something of a pioneer, adapting her autobiography to the production of a juvenile novel, and achieving a realistic but wholesome picture of family life with which young readers could readily identify. The Alcott poverty was sentimentalized,

the eccentric Alcott father was an adumbrated shadow; yet, for all the glossing over, the core of the domestic drama was apparent. Reported simply and directly in a style that applied her injunction "Never use a long word, when a short one will do as well," the narrative embodied the simple facts and persons of a family and so filled a gap in the literature of adolescence. With the publication of Part II of *Little Women* in 1869, its success became apparent. The book was received with critical acclaim and popular enthusiasm. Thousands of copies were sold; a perennial bestseller had been born. Alcott's masterpiece was followed, between 1869 and her death in Roxbury in 1888, by a succession of wholesome domestic narratives, the so-called *Little Women* series. More or less autobiographical in origin, perceptive in the characterization of adolescents, all are in a sense sequels of *Little Women*, though none of them quite rises to its level. Louisa Alcott, who never married, wryly considered that she had taken her pen as a bridegroom. Her bibliography encompasses nearly 300 books, articles, novels, short stories, and poems. Despite her experimentation with a diversity of literary techniques, despite the fact that she was a complex writer drawn to a variety of themes, Louisa Alcott has inevitably achieved fame as the "Children's Friend" and the author of a single masterpiece. Thanks to its psychological perceptions, its realistic characterizations, and its honest domesticity, *Little Women* has become an embodiment of the American home at its best. As the *Boston Herald* commented after her death: "When the family history, out of which this remarkable authorship grew, shall be told to the public, it will be apparent that few New England homes have ever had closer converse with the great things of human destiny than that of the Alcotts." —*Madeleine B. Stern*

Principal Works: *Flower Fables* (Boston: George W. Briggs, 1855); *Hospital Sketches* (Boston: James Redpath, 1863); *Moods* (Boston: Loring, 1865); *Little Women or, Meg, Jo, Beth and Amy*, 2 vols. (Boston: Roberts Brothers, 1868-1869); *An Old-Fashioned Girl* (Boston: Roberts Brothers, 1870); *Little Men: Life at Plumfield with Jo's Boys* (Boston: Roberts Brothers, 1871); *Work: A Story of Experience* (Boston: Roberts Brothers, 1873); *Eight Cousins; or, The Aunt-Hill* (Boston: Roberts Brothers, 1875); *Rose in Bloom. A Sequel to "Eight Cousins"* (Boston: Roberts Brothers, 1876); *A Modern Mephistopheles* (Boston: Roberts Brothers, 1877); *Under the Lilacs* (Boston: Roberts Brothers, 1878); *Jack and Jill: A Village Story* (Boston: Roberts

Brothers, 1880); *Jo's Boys, and How They Turned Out. A Sequel to "Little Men"* (Boston: Roberts Brothers, 1886); *Behind a Mask: The Unknown Thrillers of Louisa May Alcott,* ed. Madeleine B. Stern (New York: William Morrow, 1975); *Plots and Counterplots: More Unknown Thrillers of Louisa May Alcott,* ed. Madeleine B. Stern (New York: William Morrow, 1976).

Principal References: *Louisa May Alcott Her Life, Letters and Journals,* ed. Ednah D. Cheney (Boston: Roberts Brothers, 1889); Annie M. L. Clark, *The Alcotts in Harvard* (Lancaster, Mass.: J. C. L. Clark, 1902); Lucile Gulliver, *Louisa May Alcott: A Bibliography* (Boston: Little, Brown, 1932); Cornelia Meigs, *The Story of the Author of Little Women: Invincible Louisa* (Boston: Little, Brown, 1933); Katharine Anthony, *Louisa May Alcott* (New York: Alfred A. Knopf, 1938); Madeleine B. Stern, *Louisa May Alcott* (Norman: University of Oklahoma Press, 1950); Judith C. Ullom, *Louisa May Alcott: A Centennial for Little Women. An Annotated, Selected Bibliography* (Washington: Library of Congress, 1969); *Louisa's Wonder Book—An Unknown Alcott Juvenile,* ed. Madeleine B. Stern—contains most complete Alcott bibliography (Mount Pleasant, Mich.: Central Michigan University, 1975).

WILLIAM ANDRUS ALCOTT (6 August 1798-29 March 1859), editor and educator, was born and raised in Wolcott, Connecticut. He shared the desire of his cousin, Bronson Alcott, to improve the educational methods of the day and put his ideas into action when he taught in Connecticut schools. Alcott made the classroom a bright and attractive area to study in, with good ventilation and comfortable seats, and added grammar and geography to the curriculum. Interested in his pupils' health, Alcott attended the Yale Medical School and was licensed to practice medicine in 1826. He popularized his teaching methods through books on education, health (he was a vegetarian), and for teachers, such as *Confessions of a Schoolmaster* (Andover, Mass.: Gould, Newman & Saxton, 1839), and during his editorships of the *Annals of Education, Juvenile Rambler,* and *Parley's Magazine.* He died in Newton, Massachusetts.
REFERENCES: "Dr. William A. Alcott," *American Journal of Education,* 4 (March 1858): 629-656; Louis

B. Salomon, "The Least-Remembered Alcott," *New England Quarterly,* 34 (March 1961): 87-93.

William Andrus Alcott.

WASHINGTON ALLSTON (5 November 1779-9 July 1843), artist, poet, and novelist, is an important link between neo-classical and romantic taste in America. Born in Waccamaw, South Carolina, Allston was sent to Newport, Rhode Island, at an early age, where his aristocratic family hoped the "bracing air" would discourage his artistic temperament. After graduation from Harvard College, where he was nicknamed "Count" because of his epicurean indulgences, Allston sold his patrimony and sailed for London to study painting at the Royal Academy. In 1805 he arrived in Rome where he formed important friendships with Samuel Taylor Coleridge and Washington Irving. Allston lived in England during the War of 1812 and created some of his finest work. Although he was the logical choice to succeed Benjamin West as president of the Royal

Washington Allston

Academy, Allston returned to America in 1818, settled permanently in Cambridgeport, near Boston, and there, for a variety of reasons, failed to live up to his early promise. His *Belshazzar's Feast*, which he began in England and worked on for twenty-five years, was left unfinished at his death. Allston's writings, though few, are important. *Sylphs of the Season, with Other Poems* (London: W. Pople, 1813) reflects the influence of Allston's association with Coleridge and English romanticism. The title poem is important because of its description of the empathy between nature and the poet's imagination. *Monaldi: A Tale* (Boston: Little & Brown, 1841), Allston's only novel, was written in 1821 and is loaded with the "Gothic" devices that Allston admired in the work of Ann Radcliffe, including haunted castles and bizarre murders. *Lectures on Art and Poems*, ed. Richard H. Dana, Jr. (New York: Baker & Scribner, 1850), is a posthumous collection of Allston's four discourses on art. Breaking from the neo-classical tradition, Allston stated that art was not an imitation of nature, but an original product of the artist's mind. However, unwilling to commit himself completely to the sometimes formless

originality of romanticism, Allston held that all artists must consider the tradition in which they work. Although Emerson often grumbled that Allston's paintings were not dazzling, that they were "fair, serene, but unreal," his own developing aesthetic owes a great deal to Allston's ideas on the role of originality in artistic creation.

REFERENCES: Jared B. Flagg, *The Life and Letters of Washington Allston* (New York: Scribners, 1892); Edgar Preston Richardson, *Washington Allston: A Study of the Romantic Artist in America* (Chicago: University of Chicago Press, 1948).

—*Robert E. Burkholder*

Delia Bacon

DELIA BACON (2 February 1811-2 September 1859), a leading proponent of the Baconian theory, was born in Tallmadge, Ohio. After a year in Catharine Beecher's Hartford school, Bacon taught school in Connecticut, New Jersey, and Long Island. In 1831, her first book, *Tales of the Puritans* (New Haven: A. H. Maltby), was published anonymously. She successfully conducted classes in history and literature in New Haven, Cambridge, and Boston, and she lectured to appreciative audiences in New York and Brooklyn. An unhappy love affair with a Yale Divinity School student, Alexander MacWhorter, whetted her desire to achieve fame. Her ardent study of Shakespeare led her to propose the iconoclastic theory that the *Plays* were written by a coterie of wits, with Francis Bacon the chief composer. Encouraged by Emerson, Thomas Carlyle, and Hawthorne, she pursued her study of Shakespeare in London and Stratford. Her conclusions were published as *The Philosophy of the Plays of Shakspere Unfolded* (London: Groombridge & Sons, and Boston: Ticknor & Fields, 1857). The immediate critical reaction was negative, but the Baconian theory later won some converts. Although her brother, the Reverend Leonard Bacon, pastor of the First Church in New Haven, did not believe in her theory, he came to his sister's aid on many occasions. Miss Bacon suffered a mental collapse in Stratford in June 1856 and died in Hartford three years later.

REFERENCES: Nathaniel Hawthorne, "Recollections of a Gifted Woman," *Atlantic Monthly*, 11 (January 1863): 43-58, collected in *Our Old Home* (1863); Theodore Bacon, *Delia Bacon, A Biographical Sketch* (Boston: Houghton, Mifflin, 1888); Vivian C. Hopkins, *Prodigal Puritan: A Life of Delia Bacon* (Cambridge: Harvard University Press, 1959). —*Vivian Hopkins*

GEORGE BANCROFT (3 October 1800-17 January 1891) was an important factor in the flowering of New England Romanticism in the early nineteenth century. Together with Francis Parkman, William Hickling Prescott, and others, he exemplified the New England intellectual response to the Romantic era. While Prescott fascinated readers with accounts of the Spanish empire in Latin America, and while Parkman described the conflict between France and England for North America, Bancroft applied the same narrative approach to the development of the United States. In some respects he exemplified the typical New England Brahmin. His ancestor, John Bancroft, had settled near Lynn, Massachusetts, in 1632, and his mother, Lucretia Chandler, had descended from a prominent family in Worcester County. Also, George Bancroft obtained the traditional Brahmin education. After preliminary schooling in his native Worcester, he attended Phillips Exeter Academy in New Hampshire, and at the age of thirteen was admitted to Harvard College. After his graduation in 1817, Bancroft remained for a

year at Cambridge as a graduate student, preparing for the ministry. Colleagues at Harvard saw much promise in him, and encouraged Bancroft to study abroad. In 1818 Bancroft journeyed to Europe to continue his theological training. Like other New England intellectuals, such as George Ticknor, and Edward Everett, he was attracted to the new German scholarship, and enrolled at the University of Gottingen. After he received the degrees of Doctor of Philosophy and Master of Arts in 1820, he remained in Europe for two years, concentrating most of his energies upon the new intellectual climate in Germany. The new German intellectualism was to influence greatly his future historical writing.

George Bancroft

Already Harvard College had sent many of its most gifted students to study under German thinkers such as Kant, Herder, Hegel, and Ranke. Young Bancroft was influenced especially by the German schematic philosophy of history as a guide for mankind in the future. The Christian interpretation of the past, as taught by adherents of St. Augustine, viewed history as the saga of Christ's redemption of mankind. The new German approach did not reject the divine concept, but it restructured matters to stress the evolution of the divine Idea as history's guiding force. The impact of the environment in shaping mankind had been a basic faith of eighteenth-century rationalists. The new German romanticism downplayed such an idea, and spoke of what would eventually become the "germ" theory. Hegel, Kant, and others taught their students the importance of primordial ideas, particularly of Teutonic origins, as the basis for man's development. In his studies at Gottingen, and in classes at Berlin under Hegel, Bancroft absorbed this philosophy. By the time of his return to the United States in 1822, Bancroft was committed deeply to a belief in progress, to the influence of Teutonic folkways, and to a divine influence upon history. It was soon apparent that Bancroft was not the typical Brahmin. He intended to return to the United States and become either a clergyman or high school instructor. His idealism, influenced by his German training, appeared too liberal for conservative churchmen, and his brief foray into secondary education at an experimental preparatory school, Round Hill Academy, failed to satisfy his intellectual hunger. Too, Bancroft had departed from the traditional conservative Whig demeanor of the Brahmin stereotype and had become active in the Massachusetts Democratic Party. In fact, by the early 1830s, Bancroft was considering seriously a career in politics. He was courted by Democratic officials who relished his support of the Jacksonian anti-bank philosophy and exulted at his campaign biography written for Martin Van Buren. But Bancroft was more committed to history. Already by 1823 he had begun writing reviews and essays on European history, and by the 1830s had begun work on American history. His writing on the American past was a curious mixture of the Brahmin's love for romantic, narrative history blended with German liberalism. In 1834 he published the first volume of his *History of the United States of America from the Discovery of the Continent*; nine more volumes would follow by 1874. During this long period of narrating the American past from the standpoint of a Jacksonian, Bancroft continued to participate actively in Democratic politics. In 1837 President Martin Van Buren appointed him Collector of the Port of Boston. Despite his unsuccessful campaign for governor of Massachusetts in 1844, his strong support of James K. Polk in the National Democratic Convention brought political reward. Bancroft was appointed secretary of the navy, and in 1846 was sent by Polk as ambassador to Great Britain. Upon his return to the United States in 1849, Bancroft plunged more deeply

into the narrative history of the United States, and issued four volumes between 1852 and 1858. Still his political life had not ended. A strong advocate of President Abraham Lincoln's policies, Bancroft was an advisor and speechwriter for President Andrew Johnson, and was rewarded in 1867 by an appointment as minister to Berlin. In 1891, at the age of ninety, George Bancroft died in his beloved Washington. —*Thomas L. Connelly*

Principal Work: *The History of the United States from the Discovery of the Continent*, 10 vols. (Boston: Little, Brown, 1834-1875).

Principal References: Russel Blainé Nye, *George Bancroft: Brahmin Rebel* (New York: Alfred A. Knopf, 1945); Harvey Wish, *The American Historian: A Social-Intellectual History of the Writing of the American Past* (New York: Oxford University Press, 1969); Nye, *George Bancroft* (New York: Twayne, 1964).

John Bartlett.

JOHN BARTLETT (14 June 1820-3 December 1905), lexicographer, was born in Plymouth, Massachusetts, and received a public school education. He joined the University Book Store in

Cambridge and continued his education by reading widely. Soon "Ask John Bartlett" became the standard answer to customers' questions. Bartlett kept journals in which he jotted down well-known sayings and he drew upon these for his famous *Familiar Quotations* (New York: H. M. Caldwell, 1855), a book that has gone through numerous editions and still bears Bartlett's name. He also published a phrase book and a concordance to Shakespeare's plays. He died in Cambridge. REFERENCES: M. H. Morgan, "John Bartlett," *Proceedings of the American Academy of Arts and Sciences*, 41 (July 1906): 841-846; Thomas Wentworth Higginson, *Carlyle's Laugh and Other Surprises* (Boston: Houghton Mifflin, 1909), pp. 193-199.

C. A. Bartol

CYRUS AUGUSTUS BARTOL (30 April 1813-16 December 1900), Unitarian preacher and writer, was born and grew up in Freeport, Maine. After his graduation from Bowdoin College in 1832, he attended the Harvard Divinity School, receiving his degree three years later. Following a year's apprentice preaching in Cincinnati, Bartol succeeded the Reverend Charles Lowell (James Russell Lowell's father) at the historic West Church in Boston. He served in this post until 1889. He died in Boston. Although Bartol was early attracted to the Transcendentalists, he came to dislike their radical ways and was himself always known for taking mediatory positions. He contributed to many religious journals, including the *Christian Examiner* and the *Unitarian Review*. A friend of many of the great men of the time, Bartol either reviewed their books or gave recollections of them in his published writings. In addition to numerous religious pamphlets, he published funeral sermons of Bronson Alcott, Emerson, Edward Everett, James T. Fields, Theodore Parker, Charles Sumner, and Daniel Webster; gave his opinions of contemporaries in *Principles and Portraits* (Boston: Roberts Brothers, 1880); and stated his religious views in *Discourses on the Christian Spirit and Life* (Boston: Crosby, Nichols, 1850) and *Radical Problems* (Boston: Roberts Brothers, 1872). REFERENCE: Charles G. Ames, "Cyrus Augustus Bartol," in *Heralds of a Liberal Faith*, ed. Samuel A. Eliot (Boston: American Unitarian Association, 1910), 3:17-22.

CATHARINE ESTHER BEECHER (6 September 1800-12 May 1878), author and educator, used the printed word as a weapon to advance her principles. A doer and writer, she effectively elevated the status of women, although the scope of her feminism was narrow by today's standards. Born in East Hampton, New York, the eldest child of Lyman and Roxana (Foote) Beecher, she moved with her family to Litchfield, Connecticut, in 1810. Her mother died when Catharine was sixteen, and her father's remarriage increased the already large household. Deeply attached to her father, a dynamic Congregational minister, Catharine assumed much of the responsibility for the family management. After a brief period studying at Sarah Pierce's school in Litchfield, she taught in New London, Connecticut. Her engagement to marry a Yale mathematics professor, Alexander Metcalf Fisher, ended in tragedy when he died at sea. As a result, the plain, heavy-featured, sallow-complexioned Catharine renounced worldly pursuits and devoted herself to "benevolent service." In 1823 she opened a girls' school in Hartford, later incorporated as the Hartford Female Seminary. There she inculcated her own high purposes and her belief in physical, moral and intellectual training for young women. When the family moved to Cincinnati, she established there the Western Female Institute. In 1833 she recommended McGuffey as the author of school texts for Truman and Smith, and so helped launch the famous *Reader*s. In the Panic year of 1837 her school failed. Despite delicate health and a tendency to nervous collapses, she went forth to spread her educational doctrine in lectures and writings.

Catharine Beecher.

Beecher believed in equality of education for both sexes; the establishment of normal schools; the dispatch of qualified teachers from the East to the South and West. She held that women should be educated for their "natural" sphere: homemaking, teaching young children, service to the community. "Woman's *distinctive profession*," she wrote, "includes three departments—the training of the mind in childhood, the nursing of infants and of the sick, and all the handicrafts and management of the family state." Women, she believed, were to control all aspects of household life while men controlled the political and economic spheres. Beecher was opposed to woman suffrage and feminist advocacy

of abolition, and held that women were most effective behind the scenes. Yet she fought the exploitation of women by their employers, their husbands, and the fashions of the day. Her position is succinctly expressed in a paper read at the first American Woman Suffrage Convention (1869): "The 'right object' sought is to remedy the wrongs and relieve the sufferings of great multitudes of our sex. The 'wrong mode' is that which aims to enforce by law instead of by love." Her strong will, her vigorous mind, and her earnest pen were all directed toward that "right object." Beecher's style was didactic and homiletic, but vigorous, forceful, and direct, an instrument well honed for the message she purveyed. In 1841 she published *A Treatise on Domestic Economy* and in 1846 *The Domestic Receipt Book*, for both of which she received from Harpers half the net profits. In those works she enlarged the scope of domestic economy and introduced a scientific approach previously wanting. With her more famous sister, Harriet Beecher Stowe, she revised the *Treatise on Domestic Economy* as *The American Woman's Home* (1869), a subscription book that sold nearly 50,000 copies. The annual income from her copyrights enabled her to proselytize actively for her causes. She helped found the Board of National Popular Education and in 1852 organized the American Woman's Educational Association. Toward the end of her life she moved to Elmira, New York, where she died. Beecher lacked imagination and "believed that what she could not comprehend could not exist." Her books were her missionaries. Through them as well as through her personal crusade she helped extend national literacy, elevate the educational level of the country, and advance the economic position of women.

—*Madeleine B. Stern*

Principal Works: *Lectures on the Difficulties of Religion* (Hartford, Ct.: Belknap & Hamersley, 1836); *An Essay on Slavery and Abolitionism, with Reference to the Duty of American Females* (Philadelphia: H. Perkins; Boston: Perkins & Marvin, 1837); *A Treatise on Domestic Economy for the Use of Young Ladies at Home and at School* (New York: Harpers, 1841); *The Duty of American Women to Their Country* (New York: Harpers, 1845); *The Domestic Receipt Book* (New York: Harpers, 1846); *The Evils Suffered by American Women and American Children: The Causes and the Remedy* (New York: Harpers, 1846); *The True Remedy for the Wrongs of Woman* (Boston: Phillips, Sampson, 1851); *Physiology and Calisthenics for Schools and Families* (New York: Harpers, 1856); *Common Sense Applied to Reli-*

gion; or, The Bible and the People (New York: Harpers, 1857); *The American Woman's Home* [with Harriet Beecher Stowe] (New York: J. B. Ford, 1869); *Principles of Domestic Science as Applied to the Duties and Pleasures of Home* (New York: J. B. Ford, 1870); *Woman Suffrage and Woman's Profession* (Hartford, Ct.: Brown & Gross, 1871); *Educational Reminiscences and Suggestions* (New York: J. B. Ford, 1874).

Principal References: Mae Elizabeth Harveson, *Catharine Esther Beecher, Pioneer Educator* (Philadelphia: privately printed, 1932); Lyman Beecher Stowe, *Saints, Sinners, and Beechers* (Indianapolis: Bobbs-Merrill, 1934); Kathryn Kish Sklar, *Catharine Beecher: A Study in American Domesticity* (New Haven: Yale University Press, 1973).

Harvard, Bowen travelled to Europe in 1839. Upon his return, he settled in Cambridge, Massachusetts, where he began writing books and edited, for ten years, the *North American Review*. In 1853 Harvard appointed him to a professorship that he held for thirty-six years. He died in Boston. Bowen wrote over fifteen books on subjects ranging from the Bible to the Hungarian Revolution, but is best known for his philosophical works, including *Critical Essays on a Few Subjects Connected with the History and Present Condition of Speculative Philosophy* (Boston: Williams, 1842), *Principles of Political Economy* (Boston: Little, Brown, 1856), and *Modern Philosophy: From Descartes to Schopenhauer and Hartmann* (New York: Scribner, Armstrong, 1877). He strongly supported a teleological argument that the existence of God may be inferred from the order and harmony of the universe. REFERENCE: Daniel Walker Howe, *The Unitarian Conscience: Harvard Moral Philosophy, 1805-1861* (Cambridge: Harvard University Press, 1970).

FRANCIS BOWEN (8 September 1811-21 January 1890), educator and philosopher, was born in Charlestown and brought up in the best Massachusetts fashion: after attending Phillips Exeter Academy, he went to Harvard College, graduating in 1833. Following brief stints teaching at Exeter and

CHARLES TIMOTHY BROOKS (20 June 1813-14 June 1883), poet and translator of German literature, was born in Salem, Massachusetts. He attended

12

Harvard College from 1828 to 1832 and then entered the Divinity School, graduating in 1835. Brooks supplied various pulpits for two years before being ordained in 1837. His first ministry was at Newport, Rhode Island, where he settled permanently. He married in 1837. Always somewhat sickly, Brooks served in Newport for thirty-seven years, with brief interruptions for travels to help his respiratory problems; in 1853-1854 he travelled to India; and 1865-1866 he journeyed to England and the continent. He resigned his pulpit in 1871. Always interested in German literature, Brooks contributed to the major journals of the day and published nearly a dozen translations, including Schiller's *William Tell* (Providence: B. Cranston, 1838), Goethe's *Faust* (Boston: Ticknor & Fields, 1856), and Richter's *Titan: A Romance* (Boston: Ticknor & Fields, 1862). His own poetry was undistinguished, but his translations, enthusiastic if uneven, did much to promote the study of German literature and were well-received by his contemporaries. A collection of his best verse was published two years after his death: *Poems, Original and Translated*, ed. W. P. Andrews (Boston: Roberts Brothers, 1885).

REFERENCES: Charles D. Wendte, "Memoir," *Poems* (1885), pp. 3-114; Camillo von Klenze, *Charles Timothy Brooks: Translator from the German and the Genteel Tradition* (Boston: D. C. Heath, 1937); Jacob Blanck, *Bibliography of American Literature* (New Haven: Yale University Press, 1955), 1:279-297. —*Joel Myerson*

Orestes Augustus Brownson

Leonard Gilhooley
Fordham University

BIRTH: Stockbridge, Windsor County, Vermont, 16 September 1803.

MARRIAGE: Sally Healy, Onondaga County, New York, 19 June 1827. Eight children: Orestes Augustus (1828-1892); John Healy (1829-1858); William Ignatius (1834-1864); Henry Francis (1835-1913); Sarah Nicolena (1839-1876); George (1840-1849); Edward Patrick (1843-1864); Charles Joseph (1845-1851).

DEATH: Detroit, Michigan, 17 April 1876.

MAJOR WORKS: *New Views of Christianity, Society, and the Church* (Boston: Little & Brown, 1836); *Boston Quarterly Review* (1838-1842); *Charles Elwood, or the Infidel Converted* (Boston: Little & Brown, 1840); *The Mediatorial Life of Jesus* (Boston: Little & Brown, 1842); *Brownson's Quarterly Review* (1844-1864; 1873-1875); *The Convert: or, Leaves from My Experience* (New York: D. & J. Sadlier, 1857); *The American Republic: Its Constitution, Tendencies, and Destiny* (New York: P. O'Shea, 1866; reprinted, ed. Americo Lapati, New Haven: College & University Press, 1972); *The Works of Orestes A. Brownson*, ed. Henry F. Brownson, 20 vols. (Detroit: Thorndike Nourse, 1882-1885, vols. 1-19; Detroit: Henry F. Brownson, 1887, vol. 20).

Orestes Augustus Brownson

Life and Career:

Brownson and his work have engaged so many able minds, both in his own time and today, that his comparative neglect for over sixty years after his death is at least a minor conundrum in American intellectual history. Philosopher, theologian, economist, political scientist, literary critic, historian, his polymathic range is as astonishing as it is rare. Few, if any, significant American thinkers or doers were unaware of him in his own time, nor was his work neglected in Europe. He knew—either personally or through his work or correspondence— the Emersons, the Ripleys, the Thoreaus, the Bancrofts, Poe, Lowell, Whitman, the Lord Actons, Montalembert, Donoso Cortes, as they knew and respected him; he was an American expert on the work of Immanuel Kant. He worked his way *through* the efforts of each; when he mistook the efforts of any (and he did), his error was the unintended wound of method; the scar, a mark of his fallible brilliance. He never lost, for example, his profound respect for Emerson, even if their disagreement was one of root. Brownson attempted a scan of man, and that effort was, and remains, as honest as any, as intelligent and worthy as most, perhaps more significant than those of so many fungible heroes bound to the hurrahs of a year or a decade. Straightforward, honest—always honest— blunt, lean, and vascular of style, immensely intelligent and searching, he was as free and independent a mind, perhaps, as any America had in its nineteenth century. He must be one of America's most undervalued men.

Soon after the birth of the twins, Orestes and Daphne, Sylvester Brownson, their father, who had married Relief Metcalf, died. Relief, impoverished, did what she could for her five orphans; the family moved to Royalton, Vermont, and young Orestes at the age of six was sent to board with a sympathetic family who were New England Congregationalists. Indeed, his earliest interests were in religious matters—by the age of eight he had read the Scriptures through; by fourteen, he had memorized a considerable part of them. In 1817, the Brownson family, Orestes among them, moved to Ballston Spa, Saratoga County, New York. In between stints in a print shop (he ultimately achieved status as a journeyman) he briefly attended a local school, an activity which, when ended, completed his formal education. A Presbyterian at nineteen, Brownson quickly found its Calvinist tenets neither appetizing nor, for him, true. He taught school at Stillwater, New York, and Detroit, Michigan (1823-1824),

became a Universalist in the latter year, and a minister of that sect at Jaffrey, New Hampshire, in 1825. The following year he married Sally Healy, and became editor of *The Gospel Advocate and Impartial Investigator,* at the time, perhaps, the most influential Universalist publication in the country. Brownson was moving toward a more "liberal Christianity." He became involved in social problems, which became for him political; his religious views, growing more definite as his interests widened, influenced his editorial opinions, and the process began to make his readers uneasy. By 1829 he had become disenchanted with Universalism, and, under the influence of Frances Wright and Robert Dale Owen, a separation from that religious sect was inevitable. As editor of the *Genesee Republican and Herald of Reform* he promulgated his strongly held political and social opinions: circumstance caused men to do evil; a "paradise on this earth" was possible; Progress, the "evangel of the 19th century," demanded social, religious, and political change. And Brownson was nothing if not blunt and outspoken. He became a corresponding editor of the Owenite *Free Enquirer* (formerly the *New Harmony Gazette*), and then in 1831 of the *Philanthropist,* as he labored to advance the cause of the Workingmen's Party (founded in Philadelphia in 1828), a group which was attempting to control political power in New York, and especially the New York school system.

Brownson had earlier immersed himself in William Godwin's *Political Justice;* now, under the influence of the Reverend William Ellery Channing, his "spiritual father" as he said at a somewhat later time, he became a Unitarian minister in 1832, and served at Walpole, New Hampshire, and again at Canton, Massachusetts (1834), where Henry David Thoreau was a temporary boarder at the parsonage. He thought French philosophers more influential, generally, than the Germans, and his readings in Benjamin Constant, Louis, Duc de Saint-Simon, and Victor Cousin, whose work seemed tinged with Hegelianism, gave further shape to a developing philosophical eclecticism. As a Unitarian he contributed articles to the *Christian Register,* the *Unitarian,* and the *Christian Examiner.* In 1834 he wrote *Charles Elwood* (originally called *Letters to an Unbeliever*), a work highly commended later by Edgar Allan Poe in *Graham's Magazine.* By 1836, the year Ralph Waldo Emerson brought out *Nature,* Brownson had become editor of the *Boston Reformer,* published a work at least two years in preparation, *New Views of Christianity, Society, and The Church,* and, in September, began

CHARLES ELWOOD:

OR

THE INFIDEL CONVERTED.

By O. A. BROWNSON.

————

BOSTON:
CHARLES C. LITTLE AND JAMES BROWN.
MD CCC XL.

attending the first meetings of the Transcendental Club, whose other members included Emerson, George Ripley, Frederic Henry Hedge, Convers Francis, and James Freeman Clark. Brownson, in a kind of contemporaneous New England rhythm, had moved from a strict Calvinism, through Universalism and Unitarianism, to the edge of Transcendentalism. In varying ways so had a great many of New England's leaders of thought.

Brownson shared with Emerson a strong individualistic streak (at this period he was in some ways better known than Emerson). But where Emerson tended to the visionary, the vatic, the intuitive, and the solitary, Brownson's strong weapon was the logical power and a belief in society. He began his own *Boston Quarterly Review*, publishing the first number in December 1837. It early reached a circulation of about 1,000, but there is evidence that it reached many more readers than that. Amos Bronson Alcott, Ripley, Theodore Parker, and especially Thoreau were sincerely generous in their praise of the editor's efforts— Brownson, now and throughout his ensuing career, wrote most, though not all, of each number himself.

He covered many subjects, and in most cases with an astonishing force and erudition: The American Idea, the need for a native American literature, the issue of slavery, the necessary nexus of a liberal Christianity and democracy (a "kindling truth" for him as was the Idea of Progress), the errors of John Locke, Emerson's Divinity School Address, the need for the political party of Hope (the Democratic Party), the nature of democracy, the need for radical changes in society—all these constitute merely a partial listing. A feature of every number, too, was the book reviews ("Literary Notices") he included in each issue. His most famous essays, published in 1840, were what are now called the "Laboring Classes" essays. Yet, even following those seminal efforts throughout 1841 and 1842, one finds his subjects were full-scale reviews (really articles) of Emerson's *Essays* (which included a critical examination of Transcendentalism), Theodore Parker's "Discourse of the Transient and the Permanent in Christianity," the relation of Providence to Progress, the Nature of Constitutional Government, "Reform and Conservatism," and others of similar weight and importance.

The "Laboring Classes" essays, published in two parts (July, October 1840), had, perhaps, the most far-reaching effects of any essays he ever wrote for his *Review*s. Ostensibly a review of Thomas Carlyle's *Chartism*, they were in essence a *prediction* of rather than a *demand* for a bloody class struggle between capital and labor; he indicted the wage system, excoriated social inequality, and felt that the "system" was at fault, and would be overthrown. He saw the root of the trouble not in true Christianity but in the "priesthood." He argued for the circumscribing of government by government itself, and the dissolution of all privileged monopoly together with that "anomaly," the hereditary descent of property. The origin of the right of property should be anchored in nothing else but "creation, production." The conjoining of *true* democracy and *true* Christianity could lead to Justice in the state. Brownson saw himself as Jeffersonian in his approach to these problems.

The reaction to these essays was widespread and intense. He was denounced as a wild-eyed "Jacobin"; the Democratic party was put on the defensive, and Martin Van Buren, its Presidential candidate, went down to defeat in the election of 1840. How much Brownson's essays contributed to that end is debatable; the least which may be said is that they were not without serious consequences. Slogans of "Jacobinism," refreshed in raucousness by hard cider, contributed certainly to the carnival that elevated William Henry Harrison to the Presidency.

Stunned, Brownson continued the *Boston Quarterly Review* until the October number of 1842, the last he ever published under that masthead. There is evidence that during these two years he was undergoing a profound re-examination of the bases of his thought. Philosophically, in his adoption of Pierre Leroux's doctrines of "providential men" and his theory of "Communion," Brownson was moving away from Victor Cousin, although in some ways he never lost the Frenchman's possibly Hegelian notion of the accommodation of contrarieties (liberty and order, fate and free will, human drives and divine Grace, strength of will and force of circumstance). While Brownson still held to the American Idea (Dream, Experiment, and Mission), and to Progress, he was coming to conclude that the essential Mediator of God to man was Jesus Christ, a theme most fully articulated in his pamphlet, *The Mediatorial Life of Jesus* (1842), written for William Ellery Channing.

In 1843 he joined John L. O'Sullivan's *United States Magazine and Democratic Review* (he had written an article for it in November 1842 in qualified praise of Brook Farm, which, among others, influenced Isaac Hecker); he remained with O'Sullivan throughout the year. His contributions to this journal were chiefly essays on Providence—"murky" they have been called—which gave evidence that he had lost some confidence in the American mass man considered as a democracy. He was corresponding both with friends of John C. Calhoun, and Calhoun himself, with a view to the latter's nomination for the Presidency in 1844. He was also examining the claims of the Catholic Church, and, finding them persuasive to his need, he joined that Church in October 1844.

But in January, months prior to that event, he had begun his second review, entitled *Brownson's Quarterly Review*. Severing relations with O'Sullivan's magazine in October 1843, he wanted again a vehicle for his own free expression, and, to stamp that point clearly, he felt sufficiently confident of its reception to use his surname on the masthead. His editorial procedure for the new review followed rather closely the one he used in his earlier effort. Yet part of that method has caused confusion for readers who know Brownson only from the twenty-volume compendium of his efforts, the *Works*, edited by his son, Henry F. Brownson. The *Works* contain less than half of the Brownson canon. Further, Brownson on occasion published articles by other writers, sometimes initialed, sometimes not. The

editor periodically warned his readers that he was not responsible for other men's opinions, and that in his own work, all that he had written beforehand was to be kept in mind in any new effort of his on a given subject. Again, one critic has discerned three separate rhetorical styles which Brownson employed: a lyrical rhetoric (in his essays on Emerson, for example); a severely logical approach, the one he most often used (as in the "Laboring Classes" essays); and a "philosophical style" (his essays on Kant, whose *Critique of Pure Reason* he had translated and criticized in a three-part discussion in the *Review* for 1844, and in the *American Republic*). None of these facts aids full comprehension to any running reader.

Concomitant with his conversion to "Catholicity," he had begun a study of St. Thomas Aquinas under the tutelage of Father John Bernard Fitzpatrick, later Bishop of Boston (1846). That Fitzpatrick's conservatism influenced Brownson may indeed be true; that that influence was overweening is doubtful. In any case the editor may ultimately have tired of Fitzpatrick's interference and moved *Brownson's Quarterly Review* to New York in the fall of 1855, where the redoubtable Bishop (later Archbishop) John Hughes was the spiritual leader of Catholics in that city.

Yet before and after that removal Brownson continued to examine the social, political, economic, philosophical, and—now even more intensively—theological questions of the time. He was more doubtful of Progress (especially that doctrinal part which he saw as pantheistic), saw Socialism as a Christian headstand, a heresy; religion, he thought was necessary to virtue, virtue, to democracy, and democracy, central to the American Idea. And the Republic was America's democracy; the Constitution, its guardian. Democracy itself was no religion at all. Together with all this, he noted the revolutions in Europe, and feared that in his native country revolution would smash the last, best hope of earth.

His relations with his new fellow-churchmen, especially with the immigrant Irish, were often more stormy than sunny: Brownson wanted his coreligionists to come out from behind ethnic and religious barriers and meld into the common making of a virtuous Republic; he gave his advice copiously even in the teeth of the Know-Nothing movement. Early on, Brownson was unimpressed by the developing Oxford Movement in England; he was particularly upset by John Henry Newman's "Essay on Development," although by 1854 he was somewhat more generous to Newman and the

Puseyites in his review of Newman's *Loss and Gain*. While Newman himself had initially regarded Brownson as a kind of amateur theologian, he made clear that Brownson was "the first person to whom I have applied" with an offer of a professorial Chair at Newman's contemplated Catholic University of Ireland (1853). The Chair was to be in Geography; Brownson demurred on the proposed subject; Sir John Dalberg (later Lord) Acton, who admired Brownson enormously, took part in the correspondence, and Newman finally offered Brownson the Chair of the Philosophy of Religion, a post Brownson accepted. But this idea of a University, for political and other reasons, never materialized (though Newman's famous book did), and Brownson remained in America.

His essays during these years reveal, among theological and philosophical considerations, a continuing preoccupation with constitutional government, and the history of the common law, especially as that applied to the American Republic. His emphasis on the necessary equipoise of liberty and order was a continuing staple as the clouds of

The G. P. A. Healy painting of Brownson.

armed conflict were forming. When the Civil War broke, Brownson excoriated the weakness of James Buchanan, voted hesitantly for Lincoln, urged emancipation of the slaves and, in fairness to the blacks, their colonization elsewhere (as had Madison and Jefferson before him). He was defeated for Congress (1862), was a sometime advisor to President Lincoln, became disenchanted with him, too, and, in the election of 1864, he supported John C. Fremont, a disastrous choice. While Brownson's support of the Union cause never flagged—he actually voted for Lincoln—a combination of failing health, the death of two sons in the war, internecine squabbles with his coreligionists, and physical weariness caused him to end *Brownson's Quarterly Review* with the final number of 1864.

Yet in 1866 he published his major book, *The American Republic: Its Constitution, Tendencies, and Destiny*. He borrowed the term "territorial democracy" from Benjamin Disraeli, found the state organic, and the power of the people to be delegated from God, the font of justice, acting through the *fusion* of the federated states, under the Constitution. His greatest fear was either Caesar or the anarchic mob. Through the years since its publication there have been disagreements with its parts—sometimes severe ones—but its perdurable quality seems some evidence of its worth.

Brownson spent the years 1865-1873 rusticating in a way at Elizabeth, New Jersey. He wrote, often anonymously, for such magazines as the *Catholic World* and *Ave Maria*, came more and more under the influence of the Italian theologian, Vincenzo Gioberti, and was accused of "ontologism"; some thought his writing heretical, and his work was sent to Rome for possible censure. He resumed *Brownson's Quarterly Review* in 1873 and published its final number in October 1875.

Some commentators find still in these winter years of the editor and his review the fire and force of his earlier efforts. Others do not. He became more and more an apologist, yet even in gradually failing health, he espoused his causes in the clear, if sometimes verbose, English that his readers had come to expect, and which many later students find lean and to the point. His comments on the Republic and on the American scene generally from the true beginning of American literature with Emerson's *Nature* to the very center of the Gilded Age scan with depth the range of the American Experience in the nineteenth century. As Arthur Schlesinger, Jr., has put it "Brownson's observations on society had a profundity no other American of the time approached. . . . [He] fell victim to the accidents of history and vanished from America's remembrance of her past. His extraordinary intelligence and profound honesty deserved a richer reward. . . . [Brownson] belongs to all Americans. . . . He is a part of the national heritage."

Brownson died at Detroit, Michigan, where he had gone to visit his son in November 1875, and is buried in the Brownson Memorial Chapel at the Sacred Heart Church, University of Notre Dame. A bust, executed by Samuel Kitson, which many have thought to be the most accurate likeness, is installed near the University Church, Fordham University.

It was Brownson's purpose, he once wrote, to join those "thinking men who write freely from their own rich minds and free hearts." Apparently in the American 1830s and early 1840s, such efforts were appreciated by most other thoughtful men for what they were. Brownson's escape from obscurity was, like the man, quick and decisive; by 1838 and the *Boston Quarterly Review* he was certainly well known, and his ability recognized in New England, New York, and Washington, D.C. His admission to company in the select circle of souls in Boston was achieved with an *elan* as much a credit to its author as to its observers. *New Views* spoke for many in paragraphs, at least, if not in total, precise substance. The *Boston Quarterly Review*—Hercules to the *Dial*'s Antimachus, wrote Theodore Parker—was to George Ripley "the best indication of the culture of philosophy in this country"; for Bronson Alcott, it was "the best journal now current on this side of the Atlantic." Both *Blackwood's Magazine* and the *Western Messenger* also sought Greek metaphors in its praise; in England and among French philosophers (especially Victor Cousin) many found words which approximate that judgement of a twentieth-century English commentator, Harold Laski, "astonishing." Yet it is true, in general at least, that after 1842, and surely by his conversion in 1844, Brownson had lost caste in New England, if not entirely in the country and abroad. After the Civil War, he faded gradually into an undeserved obscurity and until recently has survived for the most part in footnotes or other easy cages. However, the American twentieth century has increasingly refused to let him die. Why, then, the sudden neglect in his own time, and what appears to be the sudden resurrection a century later?

Perry Miller—and Russell Kirk with him—believes that a "tacit conspiracy" has been at work to keep Brownson from his properly important historical niche; others, that he suffered the unpopularity that his often abrasive treatment of unpopular, nervous matters dictated. There is a

Brownson as an old man.

certain misunderstanding both within and without the Catholic communion as to his sincerity (Newman underwent a similar Coventry), and there is always the matter of his imagined or real inconsistency. Again, and Lord Acton warned him on this point in 1854, besides *The American Republic*, no full, major book of Brownson's survives. His chief work was done in his *Reviews*, and neither the *Works* nor especially the *Reviews* themselves are readily accessible. Finally, until recently there has been a quantitative diminution of interest in the philosophical bases of the American Idea, a subject Brownson probed continually throughout his career. All of this serves at least partly to explain why, in 1937, when vandals knocked down his statue in Riverside Park, New York, the *New York Times* confessed confusion as to the importance he once held.

But Arthur Schlesinger's biography (1939), in aid of quiet scholars in the intervening years, began Brownson's climb back. Theodore Maynard's followed, and gradually articles in serious periodicals and doctoral dissertations began to appear. A symposium was held at Detroit in 1953 under the aegis of Peter Stanlis; since then volumes of serious examination of his thought have been published. Two symposia on Brownson's thought were held in the American Bicentennial Year—Brownson's cente-

Bust of Brownson by Kitson at Fordham University. Courtesy of Fordham University and Thomas Ryan.

nary. In that same year appeared Thomas R. Ryan's biography—an indispensable book for future studies of Brownson.

"Every man who helps me to a truth I knew not is my friend and benefactor," Brownson once wrote. The words sum up the man as well as any.

Other Writings:

Essays and Reviews, Chiefly on Theology, Politics, and Socialism (New York: D. & J. Sadlier, 1852); *The Spirit-Rapper* (Boston: Little, Brown, 1854); *Conversations on Liberalism and the Church* (New York: D. & J. Sadlier, 1870); *Literary, Scientific, and Political Views of Orestes A. Brownson*, ed. Henry F. Brownson (New York: Benziger, 1893); *Orestes Brownson: Selected Essays*, ed. Russell Kirk (Chicago: Henry Regnery, 1955); *The Brownson Reader*, ed. Alvan S. Ryan (New York: P. J. Kenedy & Sons, 1955).

Bibliographies:

There is no annotated bibliography. An excellent bibliography is that contained in Thomas R. Ryan, *Orestes A. Brownson: A Definitive Biography* (Huntington, Ind.: Our Sunday Visitor, Inc., 1976), pp. 851-863.

Biographies:

Henry F. Brownson, *Orestes A. Brownson's Early Life, From 1803-1844; Orestes A. Brownson's Middle Life, From 1845-1855; Orestes A. Brownson's Latter Life, From 1856-1876*, 3 vols. (Detroit: H. F. Brownson, 1898-1900); Arthur M. Schlesinger, Jr., *Orestes A. Brownson: A Pilgrim's Progress* (Boston: Little, Brown, 1939); Theodore Maynard, *Orestes Brownson: Yankee, Radical, Catholic* (New York: Macmillan, 1943); Americo D. Lapati, *Orestes A. Brownson* (New York: Twayne, 1965); Thomas R. Ryan, *Orestes A. Brownson: A Definitive Biography.*

Letters and Journals:

Daniel Ramon Barnes, "An Edition of the Early Letters of Orestes Brownson," Ph.D. dissertation, University of Kentucky, 1970; *The Brownson-Hecker Correspondence*, ed. Joseph F. Gower and Richard M. Leliaert (Notre Dame: University of Notre Dame Press, forthcoming).

Criticism:

Octavius Brooks Frothingham, *Transcendentalism in New England* (New York: Putnam's, 1876); Thomas I. Cook and Arnaud B. Leavelle, "Orestes Brownson's *The American Republic*," *Review of Politics*, 4 (January, April 1942): 77-90, 173-193; Rene Wellek, "The Minor Transcendentalists and German Philosophy," *New England Quarterly*, 15 (December 1942): 652-680; Ross J. S. Hoffman, "The American Republic and Western Christendom," *Historical Records and Studies*, 35 (1945): 3-17; A. R. Caponigri, "Brownson and Emerson: Nature and History," *New England Quarterly*, 18 (September 1945): 368-390; Thomas R. Ryan, *The Sailor's Snug Harbor: Studies in Brownson's Thought* (Westminster, Md.: Newman Press, 1952); Lawrence Roemer, *Brownson, Democracy, and the Trend Toward Socialism* (New York: Philosophical Library, 1953); Carroll Hollis, "The Literary Criticism of Orestes Brownson," Ph.D. dissertation, University of Michigan, 1954; M. A. Fitzsimmons, "Brownson's Search for the Kingdom of God: The Social Thought of an American Radical," *Review of Politics*, 16 (January 1954): 22-36; R. W. B. Lewis, *The American Adam: Innocence, Tragedy, and Tradition in the Nineteenth Century* (Chicago:

University of Chicago Press, 1955); Aaron I. Abell, "Brownson's 'The American Republic': The Political Testament of a Reluctant Democrat," *Records of the American Catholic Historical Society of Philadelphia*, 63 (1955): 118-172; Perry Miller, *The American Transcendentalists, Their Prose and Poetry* (New York: Doubleday, 1957); Alvan S. Ryan, "Orestes Brownson: The Critique of Transcendentalism," in *American Classics Reconsidered*, ed. Harold Gardiner (New York: Scribners, 1958); Allen Guttmann, *The Conservative Tradition in America* (New York: Oxford University Press, 1967); Daniel R. Barnes, "Brownson and Newman: The Controversy Re-examined," *Emerson Society Quarterly*, No. 50 (I Quarter 1968): 9-20; Hugh Marshall, *Orestes Brownson and the American Republic* (Washington, D.C.: Catholic University of America Press, 1971); Per Sveino, *Orestes A. Brownson's Road to Catholicism* (New York: Humanities Press, 1971); Leonard Gilhooley, *Contradiction and Dilemma: Orestes Brownson and the American Idea* (New York: Fordham University Press, 1972); Peter J. Stanlis, "Orestes A. Brownson: The American Republic," *The University Bookman*, 13 (1973): 52-60; Russell Kirk, *The Roots of American Order* (LaSalle, Ill.: Open Court Publishing Co., 1975); Robert E. Moffit, "Metaphysics and Constitutionalism: The Political Theory of Orestes Brownson," Ph.D. dissertation, University of Arizona, 1975.

Papers:

The Brownson Papers are in the Archives, University of Notre Dame. A twenty-roll microfilm is available; see the pamphlet, *A Guide to the Microfilm Edition of the Orestes Augustus Brownson Papers* (Notre Dame: University of Notre Dame, 1966). Other Brownson holdings are in the Archives of the Paulist Fathers, St. Paul's Church, New York City; Library of Congress; Harvard University Libraries; Birmingham Oratory, Birmingham, England; Pius XII Memorial Library, St. Louis, Missouri.

GEORGE HENRY CALVERT (2 June 1803-24 May 1889), editor, essayist, dramatist, poet, and biographer, grew up on his family's estate in Riverdale, Maryland. Upon graduation from Harvard College in 1823, he travelled to Europe, where he studied in German universities and met Goethe. He returned to Baltimore, married, and

edited the Baltimore *American*. In 1840 he returned to Europe, visiting William Wordsworth before his return to Newport, Rhode Island, where he settled permanently in 1843. Calvert wrote nearly forty books in over fifty years, well-read in their time but too dated to have merit today. His most famous work, *Scenes and Thoughts in Europe* (New York: Wiley & Putnam, 1846), describes continental life in the mid-century. A proponent of phrenology and the water cure, Calvert also supported German and English literature, and wrote biographies of Samuel Taylor Coleridge, Goethe, Shakespeare, Percy Bysshe Shelley, and Wordsworth. REFERENCES: Ida G. Everson, *George Henry Calvert: American Literary Pioneer*—includes bibliography (New York: Columbia University Press, 1944); Jacob Blanck, *The Bibliography of American Literature* (New Haven: Yale University Press, 1957), 2:15-24.

EDWARD TYRRELL CHANNING (12 December 1790-8 February 1856), educator and younger brother of the Reverend William Ellery Channing, was born in Newport, Rhode Island. He took a law

Edward Tyrrell Channing.

degree from Harvard University but soon quit his practice to pursue literary endeavors. Channing edited the *North American Review* from 1818 to 1819, then accepted the post of Boylston Professor of Rhetoric and Oratory at Harvard. During thirty-two years there, he taught his students, including Emerson, Oliver Wendell Holmes, James Russell Lowell, and Thoreau, to write in a natural yet lucid style. He also moved away from classical theories of rhetoric towards more modern ones. His *Lectures Read to the Seniors in Harvard College* (Boston: Ticknor & Fields, 1856), edited by Richard Henry Dana, Jr., contains the essence of his courses. He died in Cambridge. REFERENCE: Dorothy I. Anderson and Waldo W. Braden, "Introduction," Channing, *Lectures Read to the Seniors in Harvard College* (Carbondale: Southern Illinois University Press, 1968), pp. ix-lii.

WILLIAM ELLERY CHANNING (7 April 1780-2 October 1842), the leading spokesman for liberal religion of his generation in New England, helped to prepare the way for Transcendentalism. He was born in Newport, Rhode Island, the son of a lawyer and public official, and the grandson of a signer of the Declaration of Independence. He graduated from Harvard in 1798, and in due course prepared for the ministry. From 1803 until his death he was the minister of the Federal Street Church in Boston. At the time of his ordination, the congregational churches of New England were still one body; but in the next thirty years, a period marked by bitter controversy, a division occurred between the liberal Christians, or Unitarians, and the orthodox or Trinitarian congregationalists. Although a reluctant controversialist, Channing belonged with the liberals, and a sermon preached at Baltimore in 1819 at the ordination of Jared Sparks attracted widespread attention as a statement of the Unitarian position.

At a time when eloquence in public address was much admired, Channing's sermons, preached with glowing intensity, won for him a wide hearing. In the 1820s, he achieved something of an international reputation as a critic, on the basis of ambitious reviews of the lives and characters of Milton, Napoleon, and Fenelon, written in the magisterial style of the *Edinburgh Review*. In 1830, his essay on a national literature anticipated some of the themes of Emerson's *American Scholar* (1837). In the 1830s, he played a prominent role as an anti-slavery pamphleteer; though not a radical abolitionist, his little book called *Slavery* (1835) had a notable impact on opinion. Throughout his career, it was the element of moral passion and the concern for human freedom and dignity, rather than any extraordinary stylistic quality, that gave his writings their special claim to distinction. He died at Bennington, Vermont.

Channing's continuing reputation—apart from his very real importance in the history of American theology—derives from the fact that, though not himself one of them, he greatly influenced the Transcendentalists. Elizabeth Peabody said that he was "a fixed centre, around which was much revolution of thought in Massachusetts." Emerson, too, testified as to his importance. Emerson was present, as a young man, at Channing's Dudleian Lecture at Harvard in 1821, and remembered the occasion vividly two years later when Channing returned to the same topic in a Sunday sermon. "I heard Dr. Channing deliver a discourse upon Revelation as standing in comparison with Nature," he wrote in his Journal. "I have heard no sermon approaching in excellence to this, since the Dudleian Lecture." At this time, Emerson's

breaking point, so that those who burst through them and went beyond him were always conscious of their indebtedness. If Emerson was the sun of the New England renaissance, Dr. Channing was the morning star. —*Conrad Wright*

Principal Works: *Discourses, Reviews, and Miscellanies*—includes polemical writings such as the Baltimore Sermon, and the essays on Milton, Napoleon, and Fenelon (Boston: Carter & Hendee, 1830); *Likeness to God*—ordination sermon for Frederick A. Farley (Boston: Bowles & Dearborn, 1829); "Importance and Means of a National Literature," *Christian Examiner*, 7 (January 1830): 269-295; *Slavery* (Boston: James Munroe, 1835).

Principal References: William Henry Channing, *Memoir of William Ellery Channing*, 3 vols. (Boston: Crosby & Nichols, 1851); John White Chadwick, *William Ellery Channing: Minister of Religion* (Boston: Houghton, Mifflin, 1903); David P. Edgell, *William Ellery Channing: An Intellectual Portrait* (Boston: Beacon, 1955).

Transcendentalism was yet to come; he still accepted the traditional view of Christianity as a revealed religion attested by the miracles recorded in the gospels. Later he would ground religious truth on inner consciousness, on intuition, rather than on historic evidences. Then he would say: "Once Dr. Channing filled our sky. Now we become so conscious of his limits and of the difficulty attending any effort to show him our point of view that we doubt if it be worth while. Best amputate."

Emerson was thus conscious of Channing's limits, yet it was the Unitarianism of which Channing was the most distinguished exponent that brought the religious and literary culture of New England to those boundaries, and thereby enabled the Transcendentalists to go beyond them. In terms of formal theology, Channing never gave up the belief that Christ was a superangelic being who pre-existed the world, or abandoned the concept of the Christian revelation as dependent for proof on the historic miracles. But his preaching was not directed toward such traditional doctrines, but rather was suffused with the concept of the limitless spiritual capacities of human nature. He stretched the traditional theological categories almost to the

WILLIAM ELLERY CHANNING II (29 November 1817-23 December 1901), in his youth known as a Transcendental poet, is today best remembered as Thoreau's first biographer. He was born at Boston into a well-connected family: his uncles included Washington Allston and the Reverend William Ellery Channing, and his father became dean of the Harvard Medical School. But Ellery Channing refused to follow the path which was opened to him and three months after entering Harvard in 1834, he left the college. Channing stayed on in the Boston area until 1839, when he moved to Illinois and pursued farming. In 1840 he sold his land and took up newspaper work in Cincinnati, where he met Margaret Fuller's sister, Ellen, whom he married in 1841. The Channings returned to Massachusetts in 1842 and the next year they settled in Concord, where Channing became friends with Emerson, Hawthorne, and Thoreau. In October 1840 Emerson had printed a number of Channing's verses in the *Dial*, the Transcendentalists' periodical, under the title "New Poetry," with a favorable introduction of his own, and in 1843 he helped him to publish his first volume of poems. Channing worked briefly for the *New-York Tribune* and in 1846 visited Europe. The next seven years were uneventful as the Channings stayed in Concord, supported mainly by his relatives. In 1853 Ellen, upset at Channing's neglect and

abusive behavior, left home with their four children. They were reconciled in 1855 and the next year another child was born. Channing took employment with the *New Bedford Mercury*. Ellen died in September 1856 and relatives took over the raising of Channing's children, leaving him free to pursue his easy-going life. He stayed in Concord, remaining close to Thoreau until the latter's death in 1862, and thereafter he returned to his poetry. In his later years he was the house guest of F. B. Sanborn, who drew upon Channing's recollections of Emerson and Thoreau for his own writings. As a writer well-thought of by his Concord friends, Channing promised more than he delivered. His prose is dated and often imitative. His poetry, while containing flashes of originality, is more often lacking in technical accomplishment and does not break new ground. As Thoreau put it, Channing was "all genius, no talent." His best poem, "A Poet's Hope," ends with the famous line, "If my bark sinks, 't is to another sea." His biography of Thoreau, while factually inaccurate, is the best extended study by a contemporary. It was in his genuine friendships with Emerson and Thoreau that Channing's life gained

meaning, and his conversations with these men also helped fill and affect their lives.—*Joel Myerson*

Principal Works: *Poems* (Boston: Little & Brown, 1843); *Poems: Second Series* (Boston: James Munroe, 1847); *Conversations in Rome* (Boston: William Crosby, 1847); *The Wanderer* (Boston: James R. Osgood, 1871); *Thoreau: The Poet-Naturalist* (Boston: Roberts Brothers, 1873); *Poems of Sixty-Five Years*, ed. F. B. Sanborn (Philadelphia & Concord: James H. Bentley, 1902); *The Collected Poems of William Ellery Channing the Younger*, ed. Walter Harding (Gainesville: Scholars' Facsimiles & Reprints, 1967).

Principal References: F. B. Sanborn, *Recollections of Seventy Years*, 2 vols. (Boston: Richard G. Badger, 1909); Jacob Blanck, *Bibliography of American Literature* (New Haven: Yale University Press, 1957), 2:129-133; Frederick T. McGill, Jr., *Channing of Concord* (New Brunswick: Rutgers University Press, 1967); Robert N. Hudspeth, *William Ellery Channing* (New York: Twayne, 1973).

WILLIAM HENRY CHANNING (25 May 1810-23 December 1884), Unitarian minister and social reformer, was born into a well-to-do Boston family. His uncle, the Reverend William Ellery Channing, became a strong influence on young William, who went to the Boston Latin School before entering Harvard College in 1825. By his graduation in 1829, he was familiar with many of the people who would become known as Transcendentalists. Channing attended the Harvard Divinity School from 1830 to 1833, then became an itinerant preacher, eventually being ordained and settling at Cincinnati in 1835.

The next year Channing sailed for Europe and on his return, married and took a ministry among New York's poor. But he resigned a year later, went to Boston, and then returned to Cincinnati in 1839. He was editor of the liberal Unitarian journal, the *Western Messenger*, until its collapse in 1841, when he again moved to New England. There he translated Jouffroy's *Introduction to Ethics* (Boston: Hilliard, Gray, 1841) for George Ripley's *Specimens of Foreign Standard Literature* series and contributed to the Transcendentalists' periodical, the *Dial*. Over the next decade and a half Channing was active in every major reform movement as he held posts in Boston, New York, and Rochester. Through his journals, the *Present* (1841-1843) and the *Spirit of the Age* (1848-1850), he supported anti-slavery, peace, temperance, and woman's rights, and he became personally involved in associationism or socialism as practiced in the Brook Farm and North American Phalanx communities. Channing also memorialized two of his friends in *Memoir of William Ellery Channing* (Boston: Crosby & Nichols, 1848) and, with the help of Ralph Waldo Emerson and James Freeman Clarke, *Memoirs of Margaret Fuller Ossoli* (Boston: Phillips, Sampson, 1852). In 1857 he was honored by replacing England's most influential liberal Unitarian preacher, James Martineau, at Liverpool. Channing remained in England for most of his life, dying in London, although he returned to America during the Civil War, serving as a pastor in Washington, D.C., and as chaplain of the United States Senate, and occasionally thereafter to give lectures, including the prestigious Lowell Lectures in Boston in 1869. A life-long reformer and champion of the average man, Channing was commemorated in Emerson's "Ode. Inscribed to W. H. Channing" as "The evil time's sole patriot." REFERENCE: Octavius Brooks Frothingham, *Memoir of William Henry Channing* (Boston: Houghton, Mifflin, 1886).

—*Joel Myerson*

EDNAH DOW (LITTLEHALE) CHENEY (27 June 1824-19 November 1904), reformer and biographer, was born and educated in Boston. She had literary pretensions and made the acquaintance of Emerson, the Alcotts, Theodore Parker, and Margaret Fuller, whose Conversations she attended and who greatly influenced her. In 1853 she married the painter Seth Cheney. After his death in 1856, she devoted herself to various reform movements, including abolitionism and woman's rights. In her later years she lectured on art and the Transcendentalists at the Concord School of Philosophy. She died in Boston. Her *Louisa May Alcott* (Boston: Roberts Brothers, 1888) is still a useful biography. REFERENCE: Cheney, *Reminiscences of Ednah Dow Cheney* (Boston: Lee & Shepard, 1902).

FRANCIS JAMES CHILD (1 February 1825-11 September 1896), philologist and editor, was born in Boston and educated at the Boston Latin School and Harvard College, from which he graduated in 1846. After a brief stint as a tutor at Harvard, Child went to study comparative philology in Germany at the universities of Berlin and Gottingen, receiving an honorary Ph.D. degree from the latter in 1854. He returned to Cambridge and served on the Harvard faculty from 1851 to his death. Child prepared a scholarly edition of Spenser and wrote the first substantive study of Chaucer's language, but he is best known for his *English and Scottish Ballads*, 8 vols. (Boston: Little, Brown, 1857-1858), which he was revising as *English and Scottish Popular Ballads*, 10 vols. (Boston: Houghton, Mifflin, 1883-1898) at the time of his death. REFERENCES: G. L. Kittredge, "Professor Child," *Atlantic Monthly Magazine*, 78 (December 1896): 737-742; Gamaliel Bradford, *As God Made Them* (Boston: Houghton Mifflin, 1929), pp. 205-236.

Ednah D. Cheney.

F. J. Child

LYDIA MARIA CHILD (11 February 1802-20 October 1880), abolitionist and popular author, was born into a large family at Medford, Massachusetts. At twelve her mother died and she was sent to live with her married sister in Maine. She remained there until 1824, when her brother Convers Francis was married, and she then joined his household at Watertown, Massachusetts. He took a personal hand in her education and introduced her into the circle of friends, including Emerson, that came to his house for discussions. She also met and formed lasting friendships with Theodore Parker and Margaret Fuller. In October 1826 she married David Lee Child, an active reformer who became a founding member of the New England Anti-Slavery Society. Soon after moving to the Boston area, Child found herself the mainstay of the family's finances as her husband remained an unemployed reformer with an occasional unsuccessful foray into agriculture. Starting with *Hobomok, A Tale of Early Times* in 1824, Child published five books by the time of her marriage and edited the *Juvenile Miscellany* from 1826. *The Frugal Housewife*, a compendium of household hints, was a great success in 1830 and was followed by *The Mother's Book* and *The Girl's Own Book* in the next year. Stirred to action by her husband's words, she joined the anti-slavery cause and in 1833 published *An Appeal in Favor of That Class of Americans Called Africans*. Some congratulated her for discussing the subject, but generally the public responded by boycotting her works. Other anti-slavery pieces and books dealing with the exploitation of the Indian also earned her more animosity than money. In May 1841 she agreed to move to New York as editor of the *National Anti-Slavery Standard* for the Anti-Slavery Society. When Child settled into her new role, she found herself opposed to William Lloyd Garrison's belief that the anti-slavery movement should not and could not work through normal governmental channels. Garrison's *Liberator* was abhorrent to her and she tried to avoid "inter-abolitionist controversy" by aiming the *Standard* at the uncommitted general public. The friction between her and Garrison's supporters in the Anti-Slavery Society proved too great and she resigned the *Standard's* editorship in May 1843. David, her associate on the paper, took over as editor and Child returned to writing and editing her own books. Her two series of *Letters from New-York* were financial successes and after David too resigned from the *Standard* in 1844, Child continued to support them by her writing. For the rest of her life she published widely on reform causes for herself and on domestic matters for her purse.

L. Maria Child,

The Childs moved to Massachusetts in 1850 and settled permanently at Wayland in 1852. In 1859 Child gained national attention for her concern over John Brown. After David's death in 1874, Child slowed down her writing pace and only contributed essays to books and journals. A prolific writer—she wrote nearly thirty books, edited a dozen more, edited journals, and authored numerous pamphlets—Child's work today is dated by its often cloying sentimentality. Yet she remains an important figure for her devotion to the anti-slavery cause, which dated from its beginning, and because she was one of the few female authors who made their living exclusively from their writing in mid-nineteenth-century America. *—Joel Myerson*

Principal Works: *Hobomok, A Tale of Early Times* (Boston: Cummings, Hilliard, 1824); *The Frugal Housewife* (Boston: Marsh & Capen, 1829); *An Appeal in Favor of That Class of Americans Called Africans* (Boston: Allen & Ticknor, 1833); *Philothea: A Romance* (Boston: Otis, Broaders, 1836); *Letters from New-York* (Boston: Charles S. Francis, 1843);

Letters from New-York. Second Series (Boston: C. S. Francis, 1845); *The Freedman's Book* (Boston: Ticknor & Fields, 1865).

Principal References: *Letters of Lydia Maria Child* (Boston: Houghton, Mifflin, 1883); Jacob Blanck, *Bibliography of American Literature* (New Haven: Yale University Press, 1957), 2:134-156; Helene G. Baer, *The Heart is Like Heaven: The Life of Lydia Maria Child* (Philadelphia: University of Pennsylvania Press, 1964).

JAMES FREEMAN CLARKE (4 April 1810-8 June 1888), Unitarian minister, theological writer, and translator of German literature, was born in Hanover, New Hampshire. He was educated in Boston at the Latin School (1821-1825), Harvard College (1825-1829), and Harvard Divinity School (1829-1832). During his seven years at Harvard he met most of the men and women who were to be involved in the intellectual and religious upheavals of the next two decades, including Ralph Waldo Emerson and Margaret Fuller. Clarke took up the study of German with Fuller, both having been influenced by the "wild-bugle call" of that literature. After his ordination in 1833, Clarke moved to Louisville, Kentucky. There he prospered and in 1836 helped start a liberal Unitarian journal, the *Western Messenger*, which he edited for the next three years, publishing contributions by the Transcendentalists. In 1839 Clarke married and, feeling isolated from the intellectual climate of Boston, returned there in 1841. He assembled a liberal Unitarian congregation and they founded the Church of the Disciples. Over the next two years, Clarke translated de Witte's *Theodore* for George Ripley's *Specimens of Foreign Standard Literature* series, edited the *Christian World*, and contributed to numerous newspapers and journals. When Theodore Parker was condemned by the Unitarians because of his radical views, Clarke defended his right of free speech and was one of the few ministers still willing to exchange pulpits with him. In 1849 the Church of the Disciples, which had previously met in loaned buildings, built a permanent home, the Freeman Place Chapel, and Emerson soon rented it for his lecture series. Clarke became actively involved in the anti-slavery movement but soon his health failed, causing him to close the Church of the Disciples in 1850, after an unsuccessful rest tour of Europe. He spent the next three years recuperating at his wife's home in Meadville, Pennsylvania, and, when his health improved, returned to Boston. The Church of the Disciples was reorganized and Clarke again became active in public affairs. He was elected secretary of the American Unitarian Association in 1859 and edited their *Journal*. When the Civil War broke out, he offered the Brook Farm land, which he had bought in 1855, as a troop training facility. After the war ended, Clarke became a fixture of Boston life: he joined many clubs and societies, became a long-term member of the Board of Overseers of Harvard, and published a book, usually based on his sermons, every eighteen months until his death in Boston. Clarke based his liberalism on a conservative foundation, believing that changes should occur within existing institutions and not by destroying them. He was a conciliatory man, pursuing the middle ground on most issues. His works appeared in all journals, from the literary conservative (*Atlantic Monthly*) to the radical (*Dial*), and from the religious conservative (*Christian Examiner*) to the radical (*Western Messenger*). His religious writings were solid, if unimaginative; his verse was marred by a studied sentimentality.

—*Joel Myerson*

Principal Works: *Theodore, or the Sceptic's Conversion*—translation (Boston: Hilliard, Gray, 1841); with R. W. Emerson and William Henry Channing, *Memoirs of Margaret Fuller Ossoli*, 2 vols. (Boston: Phillips, Sampson, 1852); *Common-Sense in Religion* (Boston: James R. Osgood, 1874); *Exotics: An Attempt to Domesticate Them*—translation (Boston: James R. Osgood, 1875); *Self-Culture* (Boston: James R. Osgood, 1880); *Epochs and Events in Religious History* (Boston: James R. Osgood, 1881); *Anti-Slavery Days* (New York: A. L. Worthington, 1884); *Nineteenth Century Questions* (Boston: Houghton, Mifflin, 1897).

Principal References: *James Freeman Clarke: Autobiography, Diary and Correspondence*, ed. Edward Everett Hale (Boston: Houghton, Mifflin, 1891); John Wesley Thomas, *James Freeman Clarke: Apostle of German Culture to America* (Boston: John W. Luce, 1949); Arthur S. Bolster, Jr., *James Freeman Clarke: Disciple to Advancing Truth* (Boston: Beacon, 1954); *The Letters of James Freeman Clarke to Margaret Fuller*, ed. John Wesley Thomas (Hamburg: Cram, de Gruyter, 1957).

MONCURE DANIEL CONWAY (17 March 1832-15 November 1907) is considered one of the major disciples of Hegelian philosophy in nineteenth-century America, and an interpreter of David Friedrich Strauss and Ferdinand Christian Baur. As a spokesman of "Natural Religion," he was among the leading pre-Darwinian advocates of evolutionary theory as it applied to human origins, race, and intellectual development. During his fifty years as minister, public speaker, author, and editor, he was close to the large events and the leading personalities of his times. Outspoken and somewhat erratic, his life was, in his own words, "A pilgrimage from pro-slavery to anti-slavery enthusiasm, from Methodism to Freethought." He was born in Stafford County, Virginia, attended Fredericksburg Academy, and was graduated from Dickinson College, a Methodist school in Pennsylvania. Upon his return to the South he became a Methodist circuit rider in the Rockville, Maryland, district of Baltimore during which time (1850-1852) he read some of Ralph Waldo Emerson's essays and listened to the debates on slavery and other issues in the Congress. Because of this influence he left Methodism, went to Cambridge, Massachusetts, visited Concord, became acquainted with Nathaniel Hawthorne, Emerson, Henry David Thoreau, absorbed some of Margaret Fuller's lingering influence, and listened to Theodore Parker preach in Boston. These influences took him to Harvard Divinity School and into the Unitarian Ministry in 1856. During a brief ministry in Washington, D.C., where he spoke out against slavery, he came into contact with leading political figures and knew Walt Whitman. Asked by his congregation to leave in 1856, he was invited to be minister of the First Congregational Church in Cincinnati, Ohio, where he was married to Ellen Davis Dana in 1858. Here he found an anti-slavery congregation and a congenial community where he worked closely with Rabbi Stephen Wise, became acquainted with William Dean Howells, and often invited Emerson and Parker as visiting speakers. Conway helped make Cincinnati a cultural center during the pre-Civil War years. In 1860 he became editor of the *Dial*, patterned after the original Transcendental journal. However, the magazine ceased publication after one year. In 1862 Conway left Cincinnati and returned to Boston to edit the *Commonwealth*, an abolitionist journal. In the war years he had frequent meetings with Charles Sumner, Horace Greeley, and other leaders, including President Lincoln. During the dark days of the war, he accepted a call to the Ethical Society of South Place Chapel, London. Here he

Principal Works: *Dial* (1860); *The Golden Hour* (Boston: Ticknor & Fields, 1862); *The Wandering Jew* (New York: Henry Holt, 1881); *Emerson at Home and Abroad* (Boston: James R. Osgood, 1882); *Life of Nathaniel Hawthorne* (London: Walter Scott, 1890); *Life of Thomas Paine* (New York: Putnam's, 1892); *Solomon and Solomonic Literature* (London: Open Court Publishing Co., 1899); *Autobiography, Memories and Experiences*, 2 vols. (Boston: Houghton, Mifflin, 1904).

Principal References: John MacKinnon, *The Life Pilgrimage of Moncure Daniel Conway* (London: Watts, 1914); Mary Elizabeth Burtis, *Moncure Conway* (New Brunswick, N.J.: Rutgers University Press, 1953); Loyd D. Easton, *Hegel's First American Followers: The Ohio Hegelians, John Strallo, Peter Kaufman, Moncure Conway, August Willich* (Athens: Ohio University Press, 1966).

Moncure D. Conway

spent virtually the rest of his career, establishing a friendship with Thomas Carlyle and other leading minds of England and Europe. He also became the official greeter of leading Americans as they began their European tours. He attracted some notoriety in 1863 by suggesting to John Mason, a confederate envoy in England, that if the Confederacy abolished slavery, the abolitionists would cease their support of the Civil War and urge the recognition of the Confederacy by the United States. He received much criticism for this single-handed diplomacy, but the Lincoln government chose to ignore it rather than prosecute him under the Logan Act. Shortly before his death in Paris in 1907, Conway returned to New York to work on his memoirs and biographical sketches of Edmund Randolph and George Washington. He is remembered as an early advocate of free schools in pre-Civil War Virginia. His real contribution to literature, religion, and history was his "rediscovery" of Thomas Paine, his natural religion, his autobiographical accounts of abolitionism, the return of the escaped slave, Anthony Burns, and his vignettes of the American Transcendentalists. —*J. Wade Caruthers*

CHRISTOPHER PEARSE CRANCH (8 March 1813-20 January 1892), known today primarily as a Transcendental poet, was a talented man with little discipline, a dabbler in music, art, and literature, who tried each before he finally became an artist. He was born in Alexandria, Virginia. From Columbian College (now George Washington University) he entered the Harvard Divinity School in 1831 and, after his graduation four years later, became an itinerant preacher in New England. In 1836 Cranch moved to the Ohio Valley, where he contributed to and helped edit the *Western Messenger*, a liberal Unitarian journal associated with the Transcendentalists. Upon his return to Boston in 1839, he furthered his acquaintance with the Transcendentalists, attending Transcendental Club meetings, and, with Ralph Waldo Emerson's assistance, contributed poetry to their journal, the *Dial*. By 1842 he had left the ministry and in October 1843 he married his wealthy cousin, Elizabeth de Windt. Although his *Poems*—which was dedicated to Emerson—was published in 1844, Cranch's interest turned towards painting and he travelled in Europe from 1846 to 1849 to study the masters. After his return to New York, Cranch patterned his work after the Hudson River landscape school. The Cranches journeyed to Europe again in 1853. During the following decade abroad, Cranch painted, wrote children's books, and translated the *Aeneid*. In his later years he continued to write poetry as his interest in painting waned. He died in Cambridge. His best

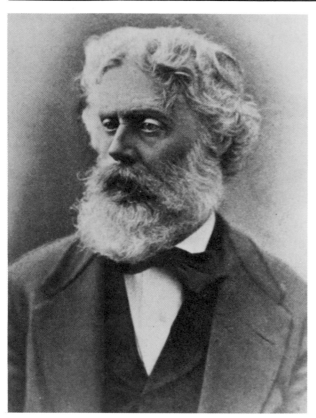

C. P. Cranch

poem, "Correspondences," is an excellent statement of the Transcendentalists' attempt to demonstrate the link between the mind and nature. Cranch was too much of a dilettante to produce works of lasting value and he is best known today for his "New Philosophy Scrapbook," a series of caricatures of Emerson and other Transcendentalists, the most famous of which is a long-legged, barefoot, dinner-coated transparent eyeball (based on the passage in Emerson's *Nature*, "I become a transparent eyeball"). Although drawn mostly in the 1830s, they were not published until 1951. Henry James's description of Cranch best sums up his life: "Christopher Pearse Cranch, painter, poet, musician, mild and melancholy humourist, produced pictures that the American traveller sometimes acquired and left verses that the American compiler sometimes includes." —*Joel Myerson*

Principal Works: *Poems* (Philadelphia: Carey & Hart, 1844); *The Last of the Huggermuggers, a Giant Story*—juvenile (Boston: Phillips, Sampson, 1856); *Kobboltozo: A Sequel to The Last of the Huggermuggers*—juvenile (Boston: Phillips, Sampson, 1857); *The Aeneid of Virgil*—translation (Boston: James R. Osgood, 1872); *Satan: A Libretto* (Boston:

Roberts Brothers, 1874); *The Bird and the Bell, with Other Poems* (Boston: James R. Osgood, 1875); *Ariel and Calaban with Other Poems* (Boston: Houghton, Mifflin, 1887).

Principal References: Leonora Cranch Scott, *The Life and Letters of Christopher Pearse Cranch* (Boston: Houghton Mifflin, 1917); F. DeWolfe Miller, "Christopher Pearse Cranch: New England Transcendentalist," Ph.D. dissertation, University of Virginia, 1942 (contains a comprehensive bibliography of writings by and about Cranch, as well as selections from letters and journals); Miller, *Christopher Pearse Cranch and His Caricatures of New England Transcendentalism* (Cambridge: Harvard University Press, 1951); Jacob Blanck, *Bibliography of American Literature* (New Haven: Yale University Press, 1957), 2:320-328; Marilyn Ruth Nicoson, "The Inworld and the Outworld in the Poetry of Christopher Pearse Cranch," Ph.D. dissertation, University of Pittsburgh, 1974.

GEORGE WILLIAM CURTIS (24 February 1824-31 August 1892), critic and social commentator, was born at Providence, Rhode Island. After failing the entrance examination for Brown University in 1838, Curtis worked in a New York importing house but soon tired of it. What he really wanted to try was literature. Curtis looked towards the Brook Farm community as holding out the best hope for his future; there he planned both to earn a living and to pursue his literary interests. He and his brother Burrill arrived at Brook Farm in May 1842. Although he was able to write, publishing poems in the Transcendentalists' periodical, the *Dial*, and in the Brook Farm's *Harbinger*, Curtis tired of life at the community. Put off by "a selfish and an unheroic aspect" he saw in the Brook Farmers' lives, Curtis left for New York in 1843. The next year he joined Burrill to live in Concord, where he formed a fast friendship with Ralph Waldo Emerson and met Henry David Thoreau. Curtis stayed in Concord, except for the winter of 1845, until 1846, when he sailed for Europe. Over the next four years Curtis travelled on the continent and in Egypt, briefly sending travel letters to the *Harbinger*. Upon his return to New York in 1850, Curtis took employment with the *New-York Tribune* and began writing up his travels in book form. In 1851 and 1852 he published three books based on his wanderings and all were well-received. Curtis helped found

Putnam's Monthly (1853-1857) and served as an editor. For Putnam's he accepted a number of contributions by Herman Melville and Thoreau. The latter proved bothersome and their relationship was strained when Curtis deleted passages from Thoreau's "A Yankee in Canada" because of their "defiant pantheism" without consulting the author first. Curtis also contributed regularly to such major journals as *Harper's Weekly* and *Harper's Monthly*, began a very successful lecture career, and published *Potiphar Papers*, a satirical sketch of New York society. In 1854 he began contributing the "Editor's Easy Chair" column to *Harper's Monthly*, a column he wrote until 1892. Although he married the socially prominent Anna Shaw in 1856, Curtis continued to be an outspoken supporter of unpopular issues, such as woman's suffrage and anti-slavery. Curtis was by now well-established and spent his remaining years commenting on the literary scene rather than contributing new works to it. For the next thirty years Curtis wrote numerous articles on literature in a number of journals and became active in Republic Party politics, campaigning extensively for civil service reform. His social and literary efforts were recognized by an honorary Master of Arts degree from the University

of Rochester in 1852, an honorary Doctor of Laws degree from Madison University in 1864, an appointment as vice-chancellor (1886) and chancellor (1890) of the University of the State of New York, and the publication of his collected works in 1856 and 1863. When he died on Staten Island, New York, there was a brief flurry of interest in his writings, but from the next decade on he was studied more by historians than by literary critics. As the dates of Curtis's collected works indicate, most of his original writing was done early in his life. His travel books are marked by a florid style and sentimentality, yet contain well-conceived individual scenes; his satirical writings, though dated by topical references, still ring true in their portrayal of human foibles. Curtis's literary studies, of which there are many because of the monthly columns he wrote in *Harper's* for over thirty years, are correct and conventional, reflecting very much the opinions of his contemporaries and not breaking new grounds or establishing original critical standards.
—*Joel Myerson*

Principal Works: *Nile Notes of a Howadji* (New York: Harpers, 1851); *The Howadji in Syria* (New York: Harpers, 1852); *Lotus-Eating, A Summer Book* (New York: Harpers, 1852); *Potiphar Papers* (New York: G.P. Putnam, 1853); *Prue and I* (New York: Dix Edwards, 1856); *Trumps* (New York: Harpers, 1861); *Orations and Addresses*, ed. Charles Eliot Norton (New York: Harpers, 1894).

Principal References: Edward Cary, *George William Curtis* (Boston: Houghton, Mifflin, 1894); *Early Letters from George Wm. Curtis to John S. Dwight, Brook Farm and Concord*, ed. George Willis Cooke (New York: Harpers, 1898); Gordon Milne, *George William Curtis & the Genteel Tradition* (Bloomington: Indiana University Press, 1956); Jacob Blanck, *Bibliography of American Literature* (New Haven: Yale University Press, 1957), 2:367-393.

Caroline H Dall

CAROLINE WELLS (HEALEY) DALL (22 June 1822-17 December 1912), woman's rights advocate, was born in Boston and received a fine education from her wealthy father, who wanted her trained to be the intellectual equal of the men around her. In 1841 she attended one of Margaret Fuller's Conversations, later reporting on it in *Margaret and Her Friends* (Boston: Roberts Brothers, 1895). She admired Fuller's independence and consciously modeled herself after the older woman. Her father went bankrupt in 1842 and she taught for a living. Her marriage in 1843 to Charles Dall proved an unhappy one and she turned her energies to writing. *Essays and Sketches* (Boston: S. G. Simpkins, 1849) was the first in nearly a dozen works, many written to promote the rights of women. *Transcendentalism in New England* (Boston: Roberts Brothers, 1897) is an idiosyncratic document that overestimates Fuller's importance in that movement. She died in Washington, D.C. REFERENCES: Dall, *"Along-side"* (Boston: Thomas Todd, 1900); Barbara Welter, "The Merchant's Daughter: A Tale from Life," *New England Quarterly*, 42 (March 1969): 3-22.

RICHARD HENRY DANA, JR. (1 August 1815-6 January 1882), author and lawyer, was the son of Richard Henry Dana, Sr., a minor poet and founder of the *North American Review*. Dana received his elementary education at various schools in the Boston area, including one taught by Emerson, and entered Harvard College in 1831. After a six months' rustication, from March to September 1832, Dana returned to Harvard briefly, but a bout with the measles caused eye problems which eventually forced him to leave college. Faced with having to get an education by means other than reading or study, Dana signed aboard the brig *Pilgrim* as a common sailor. Subsequently, he sailed for California in August 1834. For the next two years Dana lived the life of boredom, drudgery, and adventure which is detailed in *Two Years Before the Mast*. Dana returned to Boston in September 1836 and reentered Harvard, graduating in 1837 after a total of only twelve months' residence. Following graduation, he entered Harvard Law School, and was admitted to the bar in 1840. From this point in his life, until his death in 1882, Dana experienced a few minor triumphs and many severe disappointments. He took up unpopular causes in court and became a spokesman for the Free Soil Party, which led to his being ostracized by the polite society of Boston. However, Dana's practice grew steadily in the 1850s, to the point where he had to abandon most of his writing and lecturing. Exhaustion forced him to take two whirlwind vacations to England and France in 1856, and to Cuba in 1859, and an extended voyage around the world from 1859 to 1860. In 1863 Dana was asked to edit *Henry Wheaton's Elements of International Law* by Wheaton's widow, who was unhappy about William Beach Lawrence's edition of 1855. When Dana's volume was published in 1866, Lawrence sued Dana for plagiarism and for thirteen years Dana fought to clear his name, finally winning the verdict he desired in 1879. Another setback occurred in 1868, when Dana unsuccessfully opposed the notorious Franklin Benjamin Butler for a seat in the House of Representatives. When he was nominated by President Grant to be ambassador to England in 1876, Dana's lifelong goal of political or diplomatic honor seemed within reach. But Lawrence, Butler, and other enemies of Dana converged on the Senate Foreign Relations Committee hearings on his nomination. Ultimately the committee refused Dana the post because, as Senator Cameron, chairman of the committee, said, Dana was "One of those damn literary fellers." Frustrated by his inability to gain a post of public distinction, Dana sailed for Europe in 1878. He settled in France

Rich H. Dana Jr

for nearly four years and travelled to Rome in 1882, where he died after contracting pneumonia during an open carriage ride.

Dana's literary reputation rests solely upon *Two Years Before the Mast*, a hurriedly written narrative, full of egregious stylistic errors. But rhetorical problems do not detract from the central interests of the story, an initiation narrative in diary form which follows Dana from boyhood to manhood and also seeks to introduce the reader to the truth about life at sea and in California in the 1830s. The success of the realistic approach Dana used in *Two Years Before the Mast* is attested to by the public interest the book sparked in the daily life of common seamen and the Spanish colony of California. In subject matter and theme, *Two Years Before the Mast* is an important forerunner of the early novels of Herman Melville, and its balanced structure, which grows organically from the facts of Dana's voyage, prefigures the structure used by Henry David Thoreau, one of Dana's Harvard classmates, in *Walden*. *The Seaman's Friend*, which was also prompted by Dana's experiences aboard

ship, was intended by Dana to be a handbook for the common sailor, including descriptions of ship construction and a glossary of nautical terms, a section describing duties aboard ship, and a practical guide to maritime law. As such, *The Seaman's Friend* is a detailed glimpse of nineteenth-century sailing life for the reader of today. *To Cuba and Back: A Vacation Voyage* is as uneven as one might expect from a rapidly written narrative of Dana's twelve-day trip to Cuba in 1859, but his insights into Cuban life and culture are surprisingly thorough, considering the brevity of his stay. In his later life Dana considered *Two Years Before the Mast* a book for boys written by a boy. He intended his reputation to rest on his legal writing. To that end, Dana planned to write his masterpiece on international law during his final visit to Europe, but that study and other projected works were left incomplete at his death. —*Robert E. Burkholder*

Principal Works: *Two Years Before the Mast: A Personal Narrative of Life at Sea* (New York: Harpers, 1840); *The Seaman's Friend; Containing a Treatise on Practical Seamanship, with Plates; a Dictionary of Sea Terms; Customs and Usages on the Merchant Service; Laws Relating to the Practical Duties of Master and Mariners* (Boston: Little, Brown & Loring, 1841); *To Cuba and Back: A Vacation Voyage* (Boston: Ticknor & Fields, 1859); *Henry Wheaton's Elements of International Law*, ed. Dana (Boston: Little, Brown, 1866); *The Journal of Richard Henry Dana, Jr.*, ed. Robert F. Lucid, 3 vols. (Cambridge: Harvard University Press, 1968).

Principal References: Charles Francis Adams, *Richard Henry Dana: A Biography*, 2 vols. (Boston: Houghton, Mifflin, 1890); James David Hart, "Richard Henry Dana, Jr.," Ph.D. dissertation, Harvard University, 1936; Robert Francis Lucid, "The Composition, Reception, Reputation, and Influence of *Two Years Before the Mast*," Ph.D. dissertation, University of Chicago, 1958; Samuel Shapiro, *Richard Henry Dana, Jr.: 1815-1882* (East Lansing: Michigan State University Press, 1961); Robert L. Gale, *Richard Henry Dana* (New York: Twayne, 1969).

Emily Dickinson

Ruth Miller
State University of New York at Stony Brook

BIRTH: Amherst, Massachusetts, 10 December 1830.

UNMARRIED

DEATH: Amherst, Massachusetts, 15 May 1886.

MAJOR WORKS: *The Poems of Emily Dickinson*, ed. Thomas H. Johnson, 3 vols.—includes "variant readings critically compared with all known manuscripts" (Cambridge: Harvard University Press, 1955). Only seven poems were published in her lifetime. Dickinson's poems were untitled and are usually referred to by the numbers assigned them in Johnson's edition.

Life and Career:

To be a poet was the sole ambition of Emily Dickinson. She achieved what she called her immortality by total commitment to the task, allowing nothing to deter her or intervene. Contrary to the myth that she would not deign to publish her verse, she made herculean efforts to reach out to a world that was not ready for the poems she offered; her manner and form were fifty years ahead of her time. The lines from James Russell Lowell's poem, "The First Snowfall," are typical of popular taste in Dickinson's time; compare them with ones immediately following by Dickinson on the same subject:

> The snow had begun in the gloaming,
>   And busily all the night
> Had been heaping field and highway
>   With a silence deep and white.
>
> Every pine and fir and hemlock
>   Wore ermine too dear for an earl,
> And the poorest twig on the elm-tree
>   Was ridged inch deep with pearl.
>
> From sheds new-roofed with Carrara
>   Came Chanticleer's muffled crow,
> The stiff rails were softened to swan's down,
>   And still fluttered down the snow.
>
> I stood and watched by the window
>   The noiseless work of the sky,
> And the sudden flurried of snow-birds,
>   Like brown leaves whirling by.

and

311

> It sifts from Leaden Sieves—
> It powders all the Wood.
> It fills with Alabaster Wool
> The Wrinkles of the Road—
>
> It makes an Even Face
> Of Mountain, and of Plain—
> Unbroken Forehead from the East
> Unto the East again—
>
> It reaches to the Fence—
> It wraps it Rail by Rail
> Till it is lost in Fleeces—
> It deals Celestial Vail
>
> To Stump, and Stack—and Stem—
> A Summer's empty Room—
> Acres of Joints, where Harvests were,
> Recordless, but for them—
>
> It Ruffles Wrists of Posts
> As Ankles of a Queen—
> Then stills its Artisans—like Ghosts—
> Denying they have been—

To be understood and appreciated, Emily Dickinson had to wait until a major shift in sensibility and expectation occurred in the decade surrounding World War I, when Imagism, a new school of poetry—precise, stripped of all extraneous verbiage, indifferent to traditional form and content, reaching always for the radical and original image, and wholly unsentimental—had established itself, preparing the way for modern American poetry. Amy Lowell's "Night Clouds," an example of the Imagist school, shows a style far more compatible with Dickinson's verse:

> The white mares of the moon rush along the sky
> Beating their golden hoofs upon the glass
>   heavens;
> The white mares of the moon are all standing
>   on their hind legs

Pawing at the green porcelain doors of the
    remote heavens.
Fly, mares!
Strain, your utmost,
Scatter the milky dust of stars,
Or the tiger sun will leap upon you and destroy
    you
With one lick of his vermillion tongue.

Portrait of Dickinson as a child.

Edgar Allan Poe failed in his day; his poems, too, had first to ignite the imagination of the French poet, Charles Baudelaire, who opened the way to Symbolism and modern poetry on the continent, before this country came to read and appreciate Poe. Walt Whitman, too, had a similar fate, although he was of tougher mold, and had the early support of Ralph Waldo Emerson; despite all, Whitman was not accepted, or if read—behind closed doors—not appreciated until our own time. Literary history in America is full of examples of its major writers— Poe, Herman Melville, Nathaniel Hawthorne, Henry David Thoreau, Whitman, Dickinson, perhaps even Henry James—failing in their day, with even a brief success dwindling away; some were driven into isolation and defeat, to be discovered half a century later and given first place. It has been up to modern writers to choose their influences and ours have chosen the isolatos of a former time. Looked at in this way, Emily Dickinson's story is typical of the artist in America: a loner, original in style; a bard, without honor in her own country, until her "letter to the world" reached later generations.

Because the biography of Emily Dickinson is so closely bound up with the meaning and substance of her poetry, a narrative of the events of her life illuminates not only her character and personality, but her poems. Bearing in mind her tendency to self-dramatization and hyperbole, we must read the letters and poems with caution, aware that while she strives to tell the truth, she always tells it "slant." However, there are facts we can be certain of, although much remains mysterious. We know she suffered a traumatic experience between the years of 1858 and 1862, but *what* that was, and whether it took the form of a single event or a cumulative series, leading to a sense of loss or failure or rejection, we cannot prove. We know she withdrew into her father's house and for the last seventeen years of her life did not venture beyond the bounds of the "Homestead" with its conservatory and spacious grounds, but *why*, whether out of bitterness, pride, fear, personality maladjustment, or sickness of soul, we are unable, finally, to say. We know she dressed in white but cannot identify the precise meaning of the symbolic color; it may have meant the robe of the martyr, the garment of the virgin, or the mantle of the poet, or all three. She hid from visitors, refused to enter her brother's house, "a hedge away," for fifteen years, until the sudden illness of her beloved nephew brought her sadly to that bedside, but what caused the rupture is conjecture; we do not know if it was a quarrel or a betrayal, whether it was their choice or hers. We know she wrote over 1,500 poems because we have her manuscripts. We know she copied and recopied 863 of them until they seemed to her perfect, and tied them together into forty-three separate collections called "fascicles," which she placed into her bureau drawer for posterity to find; we know she put aside another 240 poems, not yet finished, with variant words entered on the manuscripts, to await her final decisions as to word choice and sequence. We know she left approximately 400 poems in various stages of incompletion, on scraps of paper, on the backs of grocery lists, bills, programs, flyers, and used envelopes. But why she discarded some and slaved over others, and what principle lay behind her making of the fascicles, we cannot determine. She wrote no essays, and guided only by what she tells us in the many poems she wrote on the creative act, and the cryptic references in her letters, we can only surmise her theory of poetry. There are about 200 poems for which no manuscript has yet been found; whether Dickinson indeed wrote them, or whether they were imitations of the poet's style and substance by other people during the time when her poems, published after her death, began to enjoy a huge success, with family quarrels generating new discoveries of poems, altered, bowdlerized, regularized, "improved," is still open to question.

This is the person Richard Sewall predicts will rank with Whitman as one of two major American poets. She is the poet whose influence on modern American poetry has been documented by Amy Lowell, who once planned to write a biography of Dickinson but immersed herself in the new Imagist movement instead. She is the poet about whom the following have written praise: Genevieve Taggard, Marianne Moore, Conrad Aiken, Winfield Townley Scott, John Crowe Ransom, Richard Wilbur, Louise Bogan, Archibald MacLeish, J. V. Cunningham, Galway Kinnel, William Meredith, Philip Larkin, and Ted Hughes. Her poems have been translated into Polish, Hebrew, Japanese, French, and German, to name a few; and studies of her art have occupied scholars in Italy, Germany, Sweden, Japan, and India.

What little is known of her life may be summarized briefly. Emily was born into a household that stood at the center of culture and social activity of Amherst. Her grandfather was the founder of Amherst College; her father, and later her brother, served as the treasurer of that institution for a span of fifty-nine years. Her father, Edward, was a practicing lawyer and well-known, influential public figure. He was the moderator of the Town Meeting for sixteen years, brought the railroad and telegraph to Amherst, was elected as a representative to the General Court of Massachusetts, served as state senator in 1842-1843, and went to the United States Congress as representative from the Tenth District in Massachusetts in 1854-1855. Edward was admitted to practice law before the Supreme Court, and was pressed to run as a candidate for Lieutenant Governor of Massachusetts in 1869, an offer he declined. In 1873 he was elected to serve on the General Court of Massachusetts, and while there, died suddenly, alone in his hotel room.

Emily's mother was a simple woman, wholly dedicated to her home and family, cheerfully undertaking her domestic duties. After her husband's death she had a stroke and lingered on until 1882, an invalid under the constant care of her daughters. Emily's brother Austin was less respected than his father. Although he, too, practiced law, he was more interested in art and theater, little concerned with politics, but dedicated to the community and the college, though he chafed under the limitations imposed on him by the small town. When he married Susan Gilbert, daughter of a tavern keeper in Amherst, Emily was thrilled to have her dear friend as a sister-in-law. The newlyweds wished to

go to Chicago to start a new life, but Mr. Dickinson prevailed on them to stay, building a house next door to the Homestead, and made Austin a partner in his law firm. The marriage soured early and there was always an atmosphere of tension and emotional instability in "The Evergreens." Susan was a social climber and thought of herself as the hostess of Amherst. To her house came Wendell Phillips and Emerson, Samuel Bowles, the editor of the *Springfield Republican*, Judge Otis P. Lord of Salem, Dr. Josiah Holland, the founder and editor of *Scribner's Magazine*. Bowles and Holland became life-long friends of Emily; near the end of her life she was contemplating marriage with Judge Lord.

T. W. Higginson's "Letter to a Young Contributor" in the Atlantic Monthly *(April 1862).*

Lavinia, Emily's younger sister, was not a profound companion but a forthright, active person with a sharp tongue, amiable enough, and practical—even a gadabout compared to Emily. As Austin and Emily succumbed to psychological distress, Lavinia seemed to grow stronger and thrive despite her own disappointment at not being able to find a young man who would marry her. She, too, remained a spinster, and it was Lavinia who was utterly fanatical about having Emily's poems published after her death.

A few good-hearted girls, children of college faculty members, or of people well established in the town, were Emily's friends, joining with her in the usual round of parties, visits, excursions, going to the same school, and later, sustaining long correspondences. There is little comparable here to the famous friendships that existed between Emerson and Thoreau, Melville and Hawthorne, William Dean Howells and Mark Twain, or Howells and James. But her friends saved her letters, and supplied recollections of a loving but demure, shy, and self-demeaning young woman. From her "secret sharing" we begin to find traces of alienation; at first a merely wistful sense of deprivation, carrying hints of a growing discomfort about the religious conversions that were going on about her, gradually darkening into a concern with death and longings for a fulfillment that was denied to her.

The Dickinson house.

Her friendships with the young men of the town were conventional transient affairs—the students or young instructors or law clerks paid court for a time and moved on. There was no fulfilling love affair. She stayed close to home, reading, working in her garden, doing chores, and writing her poetry. There is evidence that the young law student, Ben Newton, encouraged her to become a poet. He died in 1853, which enables us to come close to an early dating of the budding career. The 1850s began as a time of diversions, innocent and ordinary; they conclude with a withdrawn and isolated poet living in growing solitude. The decade started with conventional friendships and ended with the traumatic relationship with Samuel Bowles, whom she first met in 1858.

Emily had long made it a practice to send a poem to friends and relatives, tucked inside a letter,

hoping it would clarify a point she could not adequately express in prose. Fifty-one poems have been found among the papers of Samuel Bowles and there is no way to tell how many more he received, how many were lost. Her letters to him show an undying hope that he would print one in his newspaper, but he refused. She brooded deeply over his indifference to her verse, noting he easily admitted to the literary columns the sentimental prattle of young lady poets Emily knew she transcended in every way. It never occurred to her that that was precisely why he could not print her verse; he himself did not fully understand her poems, and was far more interested in politics, in good food and strong drink, in glamorous women. Here is an example from the kind of poem Bowles enjoyed, "A Tender Lay" in the 2 July 1857 *Springfield Republican*:

> Be gentle to the new laid egg,
>   For eggs are brilliant things;
> They cannot fly until they're hatched,
>   And have a pair of wings:

Here is what Dickinson could do with the image of the hatched egg:

956

> What shall I do when the Summer troubles—
> What, when the Rose is ripe—
> What when the Eggs fly off in Music
> From the Maple Keep?

It is unpleasant to realize the degree to which Emily Dickinson suffered at the rejection of Bowles, but she was a vulnerable woman, albeit an invulnerable poet. Asking for advice, never taking it, asking for assessment, never believing it, she wrote many wistful, pleading, wry, ironic, sorrowful letters with poems to match. They show a changing relationship from supplication to challenge to suffering and despair. She talked of her fear of death, her doubts of salvation, at the same time confessing her great longings to be recognized as a poet, revealing her absolute conviction that she had a supreme gift.

162

> My River runs to thee—
> Blue Sea! Wilt welcome me?
> My River waits reply—
> Oh Sea—look graciously—
> I'll fetch thee Brooks

From spotted nooks—
Say—Sea—Take *Me*!

But her lyrics looked like nothing Bowles had ever seen; her laments did not rhyme; her tribulations were unmetrical; her figures of speech too original. What else could Bowles do with a poem such as the following except to tuck it away among his papers where it was found in 1893.

792

Through the strait pass of suffering—
The Martyrs—even—trod.
Their feet—upon Temptation—
Their faces—upon God—

A stately—shriven—Company—
Convulsion—playing round—
Harmless—as streaks of Meteor—
Upon a Planet's Bond—

Their faith—the everlasting troth—
Their Expectation—fair—
The Needle—to the North Degree—
Wades—so—thro' polar Air!

On 7 July 1860, an article appeared in the *Springfield Republican* which Emily construed as a public rebuke and a rejection of all her hopes. Bowles calls attention to "the literature of misery," saying that the writers are "chiefly women. . . lonely and unhappy, whose suffering is seldom healthful." He advises them to wait until the storm is passed: "write not from the fullness of a present sorrow." Their poems reveal "a countenance we would gladly brighten, but not by exposing it to the gaze of a worthless world." It became at last apparent to Emily Dickinson there was no more to be hoped for from this quarter.

In the *Atlantic Monthly* for April 1862, she read "Letter to a Young Contributor," written by Thomas Wentworth Higginson, the literary editor, and well-known essayist. The article contained advice to poets, suggesting what they should write about, how they should train themselves, what proper style should be, and so on. At once, Dickinson sent four poems to ask his opinion of her work: "Are you too deeply occupied to say if my Verse is alive?" Higginson was gallant enough to write a reply but advised her not to publish. A correspondence ensued, twenty-two poems coming to the new mentor in the first year, and 102 others during her lifetime. She pretends to be unschooled,

Front of the Dickinson house, showing Emily's room at the upper left.

pretends she is a novice, humble, a willing pupil, and elevates Higginson to the role of preceptor. At no point does he seem ever to have altered his first assessment of her "effusions," as he called them. He was gentle in his counsel that she study the craft, but inflexible, refusing always to sponsor a single one of her poems.

It was about this time that Emily Dickinson withdrew from the world, into a Paradise of her own making, where she occupied herself with the writing of poems to prove to herself again and again that her mentors were wrong.

789

On a Columnar Self—
How ample to rely
In Tumult—or Extremity—
How good the Certainty

That Lever cannot pry—
And Wedge cannot divide
Conviction—That Granitic Base—
Though None be on our Side—

Suffice Us—for a Crowd—
Ourself—and Rectitude—
And that Assembly—not far off
From furthest Spirit—God—

She withdrew into the confines of her house and garden to fulfill her self-appointed mission, working on her poetry—endlessly revising, rewriting, sharpening her observations, and refining the verses. Inside the small room which held a few pieces of furniture—an iron bed, a small writing table, a painted chair, and a bureau in which she stored her finished work—she allowed her imagination to drift through her window, to wander on vast meadows, climb slopes and mountain peaks, sail on turbulent seas, and soar beyond the skies into the heavens. Her bees flew about, her birds took flight, her horses traversed eternities of space, bearing her spirit to the right hand of God. She never ceased to hope one day her cage door would open, her prison door unlock, her coffin lid rise. When she became convinced that the judgment of the world was final, she began to write poems to herself about herself, peering into her soul, traversing a distance between her heart, and her soul, and God. To this period we may trace the poems that pass from self-pity to poise, poems that celebrate the strength of the self, the impregnability of her spirit, the mounting exaltation of the soul, all this coupled with an absolute conviction of the ultimate vindication of her poetry.

530

You cannot put a Fire out
A Thing that can ignite
Can go, itself, without a Fan—
Upon the slowest Night—

You cannot fold a Flood—
Or put it in a Drawer—
Because the Winds would find it out—
And tell your Cedar Floor—

Her themes grew more profound, feeding on the visions she had of truths that went far beyond what she had been taught during her brief schooling at Amherst Academy between 1841 and 1847 and the curtailed year at Mount Holyoke in 1848. Her poems talk of affliction and gradual healing and ultimate patience; they render the solitary self as a conscious choice; they contemplate the problem of knowing, the experience of death, Jesus or God, the nature of Heaven and Immortality; her poems reflect on nature and regeneration. Using devices such as ellipse, epigram, personification, simile, allusion, expanding and contracting metaphors, symbolism, allegory, inventing fresh modes of syntax, adapting conventional patterns of prosody to her new use, she created a style that transformed her thoughts into diabolically elusive and exquisite verse, which later generations would cherish, as she predicted.

883

The Poets light but Lamps—
Themselves—go out—
The Wicks they stimulate—
If vital Light

Inhere as do the Suns—
Each Age a Lens
Disseminating their
Circumference—

The career of Emily Dickinson was without further event. Higginson visited once and found the experience too draining to repeat. She refused medical care when she began to have fainting spells toward the end of her life, saying the doctor might look in on her from the doorway of her bedroom, but that was all. She died of Bright's disease on 15 May 1886. Higginson came to her funeral, and it was to him that Lavinia turned, with her young friend, Mrs. Mabel Loomis Todd, to ask for his help in the projected publication of Emily's poems.

The publishing history of the poems is complex and warrants a detailed account for there is nothing quite like it in the annals of American literature. In her lifetime, Emily Dickinson saw no more than seven poems published, without signature, five in the *Springfield Republican*, one printed by her cousin in an issue of his short-lived journal, and the last slipped into a volume of poetry that was part of the *No Name* series, placed there by Helen Hunt Jackson, and generally ascribed to Emerson. Four years after Dickinson's death, Mrs. Todd and Higginson brought out a first volume of *Poems* that had to be reprinted twice in two months and ran into eleven editions within two years. A second volume was rushed into print in 1891 to take advantage of public acclaim and the editing was geared to please public taste. With Mrs. Todd selecting and revising, Higginson organizing, titling, and advising, because some critics had said that Dickinson was inept, unskilled in the craft, the poems were altered to appear more conventional; words were changed to refine the "harsh exterior," to give her lines a "grace of smoothness," which Howells had implied she lacked, in an otherwise highly laudatory review. And the fascicles had long since been broken apart and the poems chosen according to the familiar themes of love, death, nature, friendship, with many of Dickinson's own rejects included, while those in the fascicles were ignored. *Poems, Second Series* went into five editions by 1893.

Back view of the Dickinson house.

In October 1891, Higginson wrote an article for the *Atlantic Monthly* featuring the letters he had received from Dickinson during the years they had corresponded. He, himself, says it was a deliberate attempt to engage the attention of the potential reader with hints of a love-tragedy, and he made public his impressions of Dickinson as quaint and extravagant, an enigmatic, mysterious, child-like wraith who appeared to be enveloped in a "fiery mist." So successful was this ploy that Mrs. Todd immediately turned her full attention to the task of preparing a collection of Dickinson's letters. Had she not done so, close to the time when there were living friends and relatives to respond to her call, all might have been lost, for it was the custom in New England to burn letters at the death of a loved one, unless there were explicit instructions to the contrary. All Dickinson's papers, except for the poems, were burned by her sister Lavinia.

The *Letters of Emily Dickinson* was stimulating and tantalizing, the editor herself removing what might invade "the sanctities" of privacy. Except for Howells, who, consistent to the last, always said the significance of the poet lay in the unique quality of the verse, no critic seemed interested in the poetry at this point. Mrs. Todd's devotion to her task was assuredly part of her long romantic liaison with Austin Dickinson, Emily's brother.

Soon after her arrival in Amherst in 1881, with her husband and infant daughter, Mrs. Todd met the Dickinsons, except for Emily, and after a flurry of friendship with Susan, it became clear to all that Susan's nineteen-year-old son, Ned, and her husband were both smitten. Ned was sent packing but the father was not. By 1883 the affair became a permanent factor in the life of all the Dickinsons, with Mabel, twenty-seven years younger than Austin, meeting her lover regularly in the Homestead. And Emily, well aware of the intrigue, loving her brother enough, and disliking her sister-in-law enough, to accept the circumstances. At Emily's death, it was natural to turn to Mrs. Todd, who was already well acquainted with the poems, and solicit her help in the editing. She was paid nothing, Lavinia receiving all the money from the publications. Austin did stipulate that a meadow which he owned, adjacent to the Todd property, be given to Mrs. Todd. In 1895, in the midst of the preparation of a third volume of poems, Austin died, and Lavinia agreed to make the transfer, but wished to wait until the new volume, *Poems, Third Series* (1896), was in print.

Recreation of Emily Dickinson's room.

How it was that Lavinia became an ally of Susan is not known, but instead of honoring Austin's will, Lavinia brought suit against Mrs. Todd to prevent the exchange of property. The great scandal of the lawsuit, which Lavinia won, caused Mrs. Todd to end all further association with the poems. She closed the lid of the box containing hundreds of manuscripts, and it was not reopened for nearly forty years. No one knew of her holdings.

The field was left to Susan's daughter. Within the year Lavinia was dead, Susan in sole possession of what she believed to be all of the Dickinson

Samuel Bowles.

necessary and at last possible to bring all the poems together into a definitive edition based on the original manuscripts. The problems besetting Thomas Johnson, the editor of this massive undertaking, are suggested by the fact that Mrs. Bingham, who lived until 1968, would consent to the microfilming of her manuscripts only in the Library of Congress under the trustworthy eyes of Jay Leyda. Working scientifically, using a microscope to match pin-holes and watermarks on the writing paper, a team of scholars restored the fascicles; astute analysis of Dickinson's handwriting by Theodora Ward was the means for establishing approximate dates for the writing of each poem. Since there were no titles, a location number in the *Variorium* was assigned to each poem and fragment. There was commentary to describe the letter in which a poem appeared; all formerly published versions and Dickinson's variants were included.

Dickinson in 1848.

papers, and her daughter, Mrs. Martha Bianchi, worked tirelessly to bring new poems before the public. *The Single Hound* (1914) contained only poems sent to Susan Dickinson during the period when Emily sent copies of her work to "the other house." Mrs. Bianchi steadily refused to use any of the Todd-Higginson versions, and the public was startled to read different versions of familiar verses. Partisans of Dickinson were baffled; dissenting critics were delighted. There was even greater confusion when Mrs. Bianchi collected the poems that had been published in the three series of *Poems*, but in different versions, and combined these with her new discoveries in *The Complete Poems of Emily Dickinson*. More new poems appeared as *Further Poems of Emily Dickinson Withheld From Publication by Her Sister Lavinia* and *Unpublished Poems of Emily Dickinson* (1935). All that had hitherto been published were combined into a complete edition, *The Poems of Emily Dickinson* (1937).

After Mabel Todd's death in 1932, Mrs. Millicent Todd Bingham, her daughter, took up the battle on behalf of her mother. The box was at last opened, and she was free to publish the manuscripts that had lain hidden for almost forty years. In 1945, *Bolts of Melody: New Poems of Emily Dickinson* presented 668 poems to an astonished world. It was

Three years later the same patient and careful scholarship produced a definitive edition of all the extant letters. It was a triumph of Richard Sewall's diplomacy and persistence that he persuaded Mrs. Bingham to release her mother's diaries and letters, so that he could at last write a biography of the poet that resolves much of the mystery surrounding the poems. Sewall believes there are further poems and more letters that will turn up one day, and perhaps the whole process of discovery will begin again. Meanwhile we have an extraordinary canon of poems.

We know now it was at a very early age that Dickinson became fascinated with the art of poetry and began to practice her craft by rewriting poems she saw printed week by week, in newspapers, magazines, and popular anthologies, an activity she was to continue all her life. She was always stimulated to revise 'what she read, to pit her skill against that which had won a public stamp of approval. Anyone with patience can find hundreds of examples, not of borrowings or imitations, but of revisions of verses, found in sources ranging from the *Hampshire and Franklin Express*, a village paper, to the *Springfield Republican* and the *Atlantic Monthly*, to collections of popular verse in her father's library; she pored over Thomas Bridgman's *Inscriptions on the Grave Stones in the Grave Yards of Northhampton, and of other towns in the Valley of Connecticut* and gradually widened her choices to include the major poets of England and America. She responded, in poetry, to passages in prose works such as *Reveries of a Bachelor* by Ik Marvell (Donald Grant Mitchell) and Longfellow's *Kavanagh*. Below is an example of the process:

Literature is attar of roses, one distilled drop from a million blossoms.
(Higginson, "Letter to a Young Contributor")

675

Essential Oils—are wrung—
The Attar from the Rose
Be not expressed by Suns—alone—
It is the gift of Screws—

Or, reading a story or news report that interested her, she might write a poem as if she were a character to whom the event had occurred. "We don't cry—Tim and I" (196) may very well refer to Tiny Tim in Dickens's *A Christmas Carol*. Many of her most provocative lyrics may not have been personal at all, but poems assuming diverse personae in the manner of Robert Browning's dramatic monologues, which she admired and studied.

Nothing was banal or trivial to the poet; the poorest verse by Bayard Taylor caught her attention, as did lines from the *Book of Revelation*. She revised Francis Quarles or Mrs. Frances H. Cook. And this is true of the subject matter and form of her poems as well. Anything transient, particular, or small, enlivens her imagination and leads to an intuition of a profound truth—regeneration, immortality. Ephemeral phenomena catch her fancy: something she hears, as the song of a bird, the rustle of leaves, the hum of a cricket; or something she sees, a sunbeam, a worm, an emerging crocus, a train, a gravestone, snowflakes, as well as a sunset or a ravishing dawn. Beginning with an observation, a poem moves toward a discovery about the meaning of experience, not logically, but by an act of intuition. The reader must be ready to make the leap from one reality to another, from what is on the page to what the poem means. Thus, in the following poem, Dickinson is talking of the miraculous relationship between time and regeneration, not merely of leaves and trees.

6

Frequently the woods are pink—
Frequently are brown.
Frequently the hills undress
Behind my native town.
Oft a head is crested
I was oft to see—
And as oft a cranny
Where it used to be—
And the Earth—they tell me—
On its Axis turned!
Wonderful Rotation!
By but *twelve* performed!

Dickinson knows that if the only road to knowledge is through sense perception, the mortal person is limited, because senses operate only on corporeal reality. But she wishes to know what lies beyond, to know God and Heaven and what awaits us in the life after death. How does she resolve this dilemma? By relying on intuition, by having faith that the emblem of the unknown world is the literal world: what happens here is a reliable sign of what happens there. Not surety, but intuition must content the spirit.

Her faith was often shaken, and doubts tormented her, but she joined no church for doctrine and dogma could not convince the soul. Only direct experience leads to spiritual experience. And like experience itself, always unstable, her feelings changed, shifting from terror to complacence, from anger to joy. Her poems are as varied in feeling as they are in metaphor. The same subject is treated with ironic detachment, indignation, melancholy,

Safe in their Alabas-
ter Chambers -
Untouched by Morning -
And untouched by Noon -
Sleep the meek mem-
bers of the Resurrection -
Rafter of Satin - and
Roof of Stone -

Grand go the Years
In the Crescent - above
them -
Worlds scoop their Arcs -
And Firmaments - row -
Diadems - drop -
And Doges - Surrender -
Soundless as Dots;
On a Disc of Snow.

E. Dickinson

Drawing of Dickinson (1893).

revelation, as well as a beloved person, an editor of a magazine, a neighbor's concern.

There is a striking pattern to the manner in which such poems render the experience of loss. Just as an observation on the known leads to an intuition about the unknown (the unknowable) so deprivation in the real world will be alleviated in a world beyond, either in time (the future) or in place (heaven). If flight, there will be return; the hungry will be fed; a longed for gift will eventually arrive; a separation will lead to ultimate reunion; a loss will be replenished; absence itself guarantees encounter; sunset signifies dawn; snow means spring; decay and disintegration lead to redemption; if there is solitude and isolation on earth, there are promenades in Heaven.

Conventional rhyme schemes or familiar stanza patterns could not serve poems that were documents of revelation. Dickinson's originality did not trouble her but became instead a sign that the poem was true, and therefore good. Nor was she troubled by questions of consistency. A bird in one case may simply be a bird; another time it is the symbol of the song of the poet, singing of heaven; the bird is the ignored poet, or an emblem of the regenerative force

or despair. The image of herself, too, changes from poem to poem. She is a diminutive being in Nature, a bird—a sparrow—or a flower—the humble daisy. But when Dickinson refers to her poems, they are gems—diamonds, rubies, topaz, pearl, amethyst, beryl—set in diadems or crowns. Many of the funeral poems and the poems of captivity are metaphoric renderings of her living death, although she knew she had walked into her room (cage, prison, coffin) and closed the door. There are as many poems praising her isolation, celebrating her exile, proclaiming the superior quality of the life she has chosen. She is a fearful child; she is a mortal subject to decay; she is a martyr suffering as Christ did; she is a bard whose mission it is to proclaim the truth. What eludes her grasp may be variously a crumb, a leaf; a ducat, a certain kind of light, a sound, a in Nature. But the most important emblem for her was her poetry. Just as she must rely on faith that her soul comes from God, so must she believe that her poetic power was God-like and God-given. As her soul was immortal, so must she have faith that the product of her soul, her poems, would achieve lasting fame. Perhaps terrestrial immortality meant more to Dickinson than spiritual immortality; we can only say that her poems testify to both.

945

This is a Blossom of the Brain—
A small—italic Seed
Lodged by Design or Happening
The Spirit fructified—

Shy as the Wind of his Chambers
Swift as a Freshet's Tongue
So of the Flower of the Soul
Its process is unknown.

When it is found, a few rejoice
The Wise convey it Home
Carefully cherishing the spot
If other Flower become.

When it is lost, that Day shall be
The Funeral of God,
Upon his Breast, a closing Soul
The Flower of our Lord.

Other Writings:

Poems, ed. Mabel Loomis Todd and T. W. Higginson (Boston: Roberts Brothers, 1890); *Poems, Second Series*, ed. T. W. Higginson and Mabel Loomis Todd (Boston: Roberts Brothers, 1891); *Poems, Third Series*, ed. Mabel Loomis Todd (Boston: Roberts Brothers, 1896); *The Single Hound*, ed. Martha Dickinson Bianchi (Boston: Little, Brown, 1914); *Further Poems of Emily Dickinson Withheld from Publication by Her Sister Lavinia*, ed. Martha Dickinson Bianchi and Alfred Leete Hampson (Boston: Little, Brown, 1929); *Unpublished Poems of Emily Dickinson*, ed. Martha Dickinson Bianchi and Alfred Leete Hampson (Boston: Little, Brown, 1935); *Bolts of Melody*, ed. Mabel Loomis Todd and Millicent Todd Bingham (New York: Harpers, 1945).

Bibliographies:

Jacob Blanck, *Bibliography of American Literature*, (New Haven: Yale University Press, 1957), 2:446-454; Sheila T. Clendenning, *Emily Dickinson: A Bibliography, 1850-1966* (Kent: Kent State University Press, 1968); Willis J. Buckingham, *Emily Dickinson: An Annotated Bibliography* (Bloomington: Indiana University Press, 1970).

Concordances:

A Concordance to the Poems of Emily Dickinson, ed. S. P. Rosenbaum (Ithaca: Cornell University Press, 1964).

Biographies:

Early biographers depended on hearsay, fragmentary recollections, incomplete letters, bowdlerized poems, and their own imagination to reconstruct the hidden life of the poet. Later biographers, with access to accurate poems and unexpurgated letters, continued to speculate according to their own predilections. Martha Dickinson Bianchi, *The Life and Letters of Emily Dickinson* (Boston: Houghton Mifflin, 1924), seemed authoritative because it was a niece's testimony, and contained the first full narrative of the sentimental attachment of Dickinson for the Reverend Charles Wadsworth. By now most scholars have come to see the tale as fabrication, although many are reluctant to give up the idea of a romantic love affair. Genevieve Taggard, *The Life and Mind of Emily Dickinson* (New York: Alfred A. Knopf, 1930), believed that the secret attachment was to Leonard Humphrey, principal at Amherst Academy during Emily Dickinson's first year (1847) and then transferred to George Gould, editor of the Amherst College monthly. Josephine Pollitt, *Emily Dickinson: The Human Background of Her Poetry* (New York: Harpers, 1930), names Helen Hunt Jackson's second husband, Lieutenant Hunt, as the lost love. Rebecca Patterson, *The Riddle of Emily Dickinson* (Boston: Houghton Mifflin, 1951), guesses an unfulfilled love affair with Kate Anthon drove Dickinson into a psychic prison. Millicent Todd Bingham, *Emily Dickinson: A Relevation* (New York: Harpers, 1954), contains a series of letters conjecturally dated in the late 1870s and early 1880s between Judge Otis P. Lord and Dickinson, and suggests their mutual love might have resulted in marriage had not Judge Lord died suddenly in 1884. *Emily Dickinson's Home: Letters of Edward*

Dickinson and His Family with Documents and Comment (New York: Harpers, 1955), her next volume, shifts attention to the poet's relationship with members of her family, a shift that took hold and persists to the present time. Thomas H. Johnson, *Emily Dickinson: An Interpretive Biography* (Cambridge: Harvard University Press, 1955), joins all of these threads together, dispelling some myths, confirming others. More facts were presented, documentary fashion, in Jay Leyda, *The Years and Hours of Emily Dickinson*, 2 vols. (New Haven: Yale University Press, 1960). The mysterious hiatus in the poet's life continues to attract psycho-biographers. Clark Griffith, *The Long Shadow: Emily Dickinson's Tragic Poetry* (Princeton: Princeton University Press, 1964), argues the cause was sexual fright and a neurotic attachment to the poet's austere and repressive father; John Cody, *After Great Pain: The Inner Life of Emily Dickinson* (Cambridge: Harvard University Press, 1971), claims the pain originated in an unfulfilled attachment to an indifferent and rejecting mother, made doubly unbearable by a scornful sister-in-law, Susan. The definitive biography, with access to the diaries and journals of Mabel Loomis Todd, not before available, is Richard B. Sewall, *The Life of Emily Dickinson*, 2 vols. (New York: Farrar, Straus & Giroux, 1974). Sifting through every conceivable source that may throw light on the life of the poet, it renders all prior work obsolete and speculative.

Letters:

Letters of Emily Dickinson, ed. Mabel Loomis Todd, 2 vols. (Boston: Roberts Brothers, 1894); *Emily Dickinson's Letters to Dr. and Mrs. Josiah Gilbert Holland*, ed. Theodora Van Wagenen Ward (Cambridge: Harvard University Press, 1951); *The Letters of Emily Dickinson*, ed. Thomas H. Johnson and Theodora Ward, 3 vols.—supersedes previous editions (Cambridge: Harvard University Press, 1958); *The Lyman Letters; New Light on Emily Dickinson and Her Family*, ed. Richard B. Sewall—contains the correspondence with Joseph Bardwell Lyman, a one-time suitor of Lavinia (Amherst: University of Massachusetts Press, 1965).

Criticism:

George Frisbie Whicher, *This Was a Poet: A Critical Biography of Emily Dickinson* (New York: Scribners, 1938); Richard Chase, *Emily Dickinson* (New York: William Sloan, 1951); Charles Anderson, *Emily Dickinson's Poetry: Stairway of Surprise*

(New York: Holt, Rinehart & Winston, 1960); Jack L. Capps, *Emily Dickinson's Reading: 1836-1886* (Cambridge: Harvard University Press, 1966); Ralph W. Franklin, *The Editing of Emily Dickinson: A Reconsideration* (Madison: University of Wisconsin Press, 1967); Mary C. De Jong, "Structure in the Poetry of Emerson, Emily Dickinson, and Frost," Ph.D. dissertation, University of Michigan, 1968; Brita Lindberg-Seyerstad, *The Voice of the Poet: Aspects of Style in the Poetry of Emily Dickinson* (Cambridge: Harvard University Press, 1968); Ruth Miller, *The Poetry of Emily Dickinson* (Middletown, Ct.: Wesleyan University Press, 1968); Barton L. St. Armand, "In the American Manner: An Inquiry into the Aesthetics of Emily Dickinson and Edgar Allan Poe," Ph.D. dissertation, Brown University, 1968; Dolores Dyer Lucas, *Emily Dickinson and Riddle* (DeKalb: Northern Illinois University Press, 1969); Joanne [Diehl] Feit, " 'Another Way to See,' Dickinson and Her English Romantic Precursors," Ph.D. dissertation, Yale University, 1974; Inder Nath Kher, *The Landscape of Absence: Emily Dickinson's Poetry* (New Haven: Yale University Press, 1974); Jean McClure Mudge, *Emily Dickinson and the Image of Home* (Amherst: University of Massachusetts Press, 1975); Robert Weisbuch, *Emily Dickinson's Poetry* (Chicago: University of Chicago Press, 1975).

Papers:

The "quarrel between the houses" led to the deposit of letters and literary manuscripts in two separate libraries. The manuscripts that led to the Bianchi publications are now in the Houghton Library of Harvard University. Mabel Loomis Todd, having kept all that was in her possession at the time she ceased her task of editing the poems, left these manuscripts to her daughter who gave them to the Frost Library at Amherst College. There are relevant materials in the Margaret Jane Pershing Collection of Emily Dickinson at Princeton University, the Galatea Collection at the Boston Public Library, the Jones Library at Amherst, and the Todd-Bingham Archive at Yale University.

E. Marshall, *Dorothea Dix: Forgotten Samaritan* (Chapel Hill: University of North Carolina Press, 1937).

Dorothea Lynde Dix.

Frederick Douglass [signature]

DOROTHEA LYNDE DIX (4 April 1802-18 July 1887), reformer and miscellaneous writer, left an unhappy home environment in Hampden, Maine, when she was ten to live with her grandparents in Boston. In 1821 she opened a school and over the next thirteen years taught, wrote devotional works reflecting her firm Unitarian convictions, and authored *Conversations on Common Things* (Boston: Munroe & Francis, 1824), a widely used science textbook. Ill health forced her to close the school and she spent the next few years travelling and recuperating. The turning point in Dix's career came in 1841, when she began teaching at the East Cambridge House of Corrections. Shocked by the cruel and primitive conditions she saw there, Dix devoted the rest of her life to the reform of prisons and mental institutions. She became active politically and her *Memorial to the Legislature of Massachusetts* (Boston: Munroe & Francis, 1843) and *Remarks on Prisons and Prison Discipline* (Boston: Munroe & Francis, 1845), written at Horace Mann's suggestion, were influential in bringing about changes in mental health care and penal reform. She died in Trenton, New Jersey. **REFERENCE:** Helen

FREDERICK DOUGLASS (1817?-20 February 1895), reformer and journalist, was born to a black slave in Tuckahoe, Maryland. Upon his escape from slavery in 1838, he adopted the last name of Douglass. He married a free black woman and settled in New Bedford, Massachusetts. Douglass so impressed the Massachusetts Anti-Slavery Society when he spoke before them in 1841 that they hired him, and during the next four years he toured the country, speaking out against slavery. His *The Narrative of the Life of Frederick Douglass: An American Slave* (Boston: American Anti-Slavery Office, 1845) is a frank and intelligent discussion of slavery by one who knew its restrictions firsthand. He soon aligned himself with the conservative abolitionists. From 1847 to 1860 he edited the *North Star* (later called *Frederick Douglass' Paper*) and continued his lecturing. In later years he published two more autobiographical works: *My Bondage and My Freedom* (New York: Miller, Orton & Mulligan, 1855) and *Life and Times of Frederick Douglass* (Hartford, Ct.: Park Publishing Co., 1881). He died in Washington, D.C. REFERENCE: Arna Bontemps, *Free at Last: The Life of Frederick Douglass* (New York: Dodd, Mead, 1971).

JOHN SULLIVAN DWIGHT (13 May 1813-5 September 1893), editor and music critic, was from his birth in Boston given a gentleman's education; from the Latin School he entered Harvard. After his graduation in 1832, he briefly considered a musical career, but in 1834 he entered the Harvard Divinity School. Soon Dwight met most of those who would become known as Transcendentalists. He graduated in 1836 and two years later edited *Selected Minor Poems. . . of Goethe and Schiller* (Boston: Hilliard, Gray) for George Ripley's *Specimens of Foreign*

Standard Literature series. Dwight was ordained in 1840 and installed at Northampton, Massachusetts. Unhappy in the ministry, Dwight joined the Brook Farm community in 1841. There he became active in associationist or socialist reforms, writing *A Lecture on Association, In Its Connection with Education* (Boston: Benjamin H. Greene, 1844), and in 1845 became a major contributor to the community's periodical, the *Harbinger*. But in 1847, Brook Farm failed, and Dwight returned to Boston, where he was an editor of the *Harbinger* until its collapse in 1849. He contributed to the daily papers until 1851, when he became music editor of both *Sartain's Magazine* and the Boston *Commonwealth*. In that year Dwight also married. The next year Dwight started his own publication, *Dwight's Journal of Music*, which soon had 1,000 subscribers. A European trip in 1860-1861 was marred by the death of his wife at home soon after his departure. Dwight remained active in the Boston musical scene but in 1881 he closed down his journal which had become too sectarian to remain financially successful. He died in Boston. Dwight is remembered more for being, in the pages of his journal, an historian of American music than as a pioneering critic. His aim was to interpret music "through the medium of a poet's mind," and this view did not compare well with the professional music criticism of the late nineteenth century. REFERENCES: George Willis Cooke, *John Sullivan Dwight: Brook Farmer, Editor, and Critic of Music* (Boston: Small, Maynard, 1898); Walter L. Fertig, "John Sullivan Dwight: Transcendentalist and Literary Amateur of Music," Ph.D. dissertation, University of Maryland, 1952. —*Joel Myerson*

Ralph Waldo Emerson

Lawrence Buell
Oberlin College

BIRTH: Boston, Massachusetts, 25 May 1803.

MARRIAGE: Ellen Tucker (1811-1831), 1829; Lydia ("Lidian") Jackson (1802-1892), 1835. Four children: Waldo (1836-1842), Ellen (1839-1909), Edith (1841-1929), Edward (1844-1930).

DEATH: Concord, Massachusetts, 27 April 1882.

MAJOR WORKS: *Nature* (Boston: James Munroe, 1836); *An Oration, Delivered Before the Phi Beta Kappa Society, at Cambridge* ("The American Scholar") (Boston: James Munroe, 1837); *An Address Delivered Before the Senior Class in Divinity College, Cambridge* (Boston: James Munroe, 1838); *Essays* (Boston: James Munroe, 1841); *Essays: Second Series* (Boston: James Munroe, 1844); *Poems* (Boston: James Munroe, 1847); *Representative Men* (Boston: Phillips, Sampson, 1850); *English Traits* (Boston: Phillips, Sampson, 1856); *The Conduct of Life* (Boston: Ticknor & Fields, 1860); *May-Day and Other Pieces* (Boston: Ticknor & Fields, 1867); *Society and Solitude* (Boston: Fields, Osgood, 1870).

Life and Career:

Emerson is perhaps the single most influential figure in American literary history. More than any other author of his day, he was responsible for shaping the literary style and vision of the American Romantic period, the era when the United States first developed a distinctively national literature worthy of comparison to that of the mother country. Henry David Thoreau, Herman Melville, Walt Whitman, and Emily Dickinson were all deeply indebted to Emerson and helped to transmit his legacy. As the leading expositor of New England Transcendentalism, Emerson also had a decisive impact upon the course of American philosophy and religion. Any serious discussion of such "American" traits as individualism, optimism, pietism, glorification of nature and wilderness, egalitarianism, utopianism, and literary experimentalism must take account of Emerson's pronouncements on these subjects. Because he was an eclectic and unsystematic thinker, Emerson has often been criticized as a superficial popularizer. But his historical significance is undeniable, and the vitality of his best work still has a way of making his detractors look pedantic by comparison.

Ellen Tucker Emerson.

For the first thirty years of his life, Emerson did nothing to distinguish himself from respectable mediocrity. His educational and vocational choices were quite predictable for the son of a Harvard-educated Boston minister of a liberal Congregationalist (later Unitarian) parish. Although his father's death in 1811 left the family in straitened circumstances, young Emerson duly attended Boston Latin School, Harvard College (A.B., 1821), and (after several years of reluctant school teaching) Harvard Divinity School. His undergraduate record was lackluster (he was thirtieth in a class of fifty-nine), and his career as a theology student was still more uneven: his course of study was irregular and constantly interrupted by sickness. But Emerson's character, connections, and preaching abilities were attractive enough to gain him, in 1829, the post of assistant to his former divinity instructor, Henry Ware, Jr., at Boston's Second Church (Unitarian). Emerson's almost immediate promotion to head pastor and his marriage to Ellen Louisa Tucker, a well-to-do merchant's daughter, seemed to complete a relatively easy transition into an establishment position which many New England youths would have envied.

Privately, however, Emerson was unsatisfied. He was too shy and sensitive to be comfortable in a clergyman's role, and he was plagued by doubts about the validity of Christian doctrine and the institutional church. These doubts had originally been raised by the Unitarians themselves, who sought to reform Congregationalism by liberating it from the rigors of Calvinism. Now Emerson and a number of his contemporaries, inspired by such reformers as the Reverend William Ellery Channing, had become discontent with Unitarianism itself. In particular, Emerson questioned his mentors' insistence on the supernatural basis of religion, on the necessity of accepting the miracles of Jesus as the decisive proof of the authenticity of his mission. Emerson wished to think of religion as based not on tradition but upon religious experience, upon man's capacity for inspiration. Yet the possibility of this seemed to be cut off by the Unitarians' acceptance of the psychological empiricism of John Locke, who argued that human knowledge derives only from the

perceptions of the senses. During the late 1820s, however, Emerson increasingly found support in such diverse sources as Platonism, Swedenborgianism, and European Romanticism, especially the writings of Samuel Taylor Coleridge. When Emerson at last matured intellectually in the mid-1830s, he adopted Coleridge's (innacurate) version of Immanuel Kant's distinction between the two mental faculties of "Understanding" (the power of empirical reasoning which works as Locke described) and "Reason" (a higher and intuitive power of comprehending intellectual and spiritual truth) as the basis of his own philosophy of mind.

Emerson's study.

Emerson might not have advanced past the stage of vague speculation and discontent had it not been for some reversals in his external life. In 1831 his wife died of the tuberculosis which had threatened her since before their marriage. Emerson, a devoted and loving husband, was plunged into deep grief, succeeded by a state of spiritual excitement in which he reached the most significant "discovery" of his inner life: the conviction that God dwells within the individual soul and that the individual is, in this sense, identical with God. This insight is the basis of Emerson's concept of self-reliance. His domestic ties cut, his spiritual independence increasing, Emerson soon found himself at odds with his church for refusing to administer the Lord's Supper on grounds of conscience. Since his parishioners would not excuse him from the ceremony, Emerson resigned in 1832, apparently to their sorrow, perhaps to his own relief, and unquestionably to the dismay of the Unitarian clergy, some of whom later viewed this event as the symbolic end of Unitarianism as a unified force.

Emerson then undertook a solitary ten-month journey to Europe to recover his bearings and his

Emerson's grave in Concord.

health. Never robust until his forties, Emerson suffered especially at times of emotional stress. In Europe, he was often lonely and depressed, but he also had some lastingly significant experiences. First and foremost, he met a number of his literary idols, such as William Wordsworth, Coleridge, and especially Thomas Carlyle, with whom he maintained a lifelong though somewhat troubled friendship. This was the first step toward a broadening of intellectual relationships beyond Boston and vicinity which eventually made Emerson the most cosmopolitan of the major American romantics. Also, in Paris, at the Jardin des Plants, Emerson was struck with a vision of the mystical correspondence between man and the forms of nature, an idea he had met with in his reading but never experienced with such immediacy. This inspired his first important poems and prose works, and much of his writing thereafter.

Upon his return to America, Emerson continued to preach intermittently on a substitute basis but turned increasingly to a new forum: the lyceum. The lyceum movement, which began in the 1820s and spread during the nineteenth century throughout all parts of America where New Englanders had settled, was a spontaneous proliferation of community-based organizations which sponsored programs of visiting lecturers and performers, including many ex-ministers. The lyceum was, in effect, a stage in the secularization of New England culture, whereby edification and entertainment were mixed in a way that recalled the traditional sermon but broke from it in tone and subject matter. For Emerson, undergoing the same kind of transition himself, the lyceum proved an ideal forum for advancing the literary career he had always secretly wanted without, as yet, having found a way of attaining it outside the ministry. His love of eloquence had been his main reason for choosing the ministry over other professions; he was better as a speaker than as a reasoner; his powers of organization were limited, but he had a gift for the keen aperçu, the apt illustration, the sally of wit, the sudden transition, the provocative aside. His previous (and settled) habits as a student, desultory and eclectic rather than intensive and methodical, now seemed professional assets; and his distrust of orthodox formulations was more a source of excitement than an affront to his audiences. Above all, Emerson's commitment to the "moral imagination" spoke to many who, like him, were increasingly in search of a viable faith as the unprecedented pace of social change made traditional religion seem ever more remote.

Emerson started his lyceum career almost immediately upon his return from Europe, with four lectures on natural history (1833-1834). Thereafter, for the rest of his active career, he customarily gave an annual course of six to twelve lectures in Boston and elsewhere, extending his travels until, by 1850, his itinerary took him as far west as Missouri and Iowa. Topics of lecture series included "English Literature," "The Philosophy of History," "Human Life," and "The Present Age." Most of Emerson's published works were reworkings of earlier lectures. Emerson's platform style, conservative by lyceum standards, struck some listeners as too subdued and cerebral; but in general he was well received, particularly by serious-minded, well-educated, aesthetically sensitive young adults. For most of his career, lecturing was his main source of income.

Lecturing, preaching, and a legacy from his wife's estate gave Emerson a precarious financial stability by 1834. In that year he moved permanently from a Boston suburb to his ancestral village of Concord, and in 1835 he married one of his admirers, Lydia Jackson of Plymouth. Unlike his first marriage, this was a union of kindred intellects rather than a love match. Her growing conservatism and his lack of passion eventually caused some friction between them, but the marriage was on the whole successful.

Emerson was now coming into closer contact with the other aspiring and original liberal thinkers of the day, such as Margaret Fuller, Amos Bronson

Alcott, and Thoreau, all of whom had begun to look to Emerson for intellectual leadership. These and others formed a growing circle of acquaintances and visitors which Emerson gathered around him in Concord to bring intellectual stimulation into his sheltered country retreat. In 1836 Emerson also helped to organize what later became known as the Transcendental Club, which met irregularly over the next four years to discuss topics chiefly of a religious nature. The group at first consisted entirely of liberal Unitarian ministers, with the exception of Alcott. Later, moderates and other laymen—and women—were invited, and at one time or another every major figure associated with the Transcendentalist movement attended. Eventually disputes over such matters as the nature of intuitive knowledge and the mission of the church broke the group apart.

This outcome illustrates the difficulty of defining precisely what Transcendentalism was. The movement had no official program, no membership list, no rigid organization; and the participants often quarreled. Emerson once defined Transcendentalism simply as "Idealism as it appears in 1842." Perhaps the movement is best summarized as the aggregate efforts of a group of liberal Unitarians to define and to apply the concept of self-reliance in at least five areas: theology, epistemology, art, the theory of nature, and social reform. No one figure attempted to do this comprehensively, however, and individual Transcendentalists (including Emerson himself) varied in their estimates of the extent to which human nature is truly God-like.

The day after the Transcendental Club's first meeting, Emerson's first significant publication appeared: *Nature*, an anonymously-published ninety-five-page mixture of treatise, lyricism, and manifesto. This slim volume is the most memorable American statement of the Romantic idea of nature as a substitute for Revelation. We need not, Emerson argues, take our knowledge from tradition alone. Through nature we can "enjoy an original relation to the universe." Emerson attempts to show how nature serves and fulfills man on every level of existence. Characteristically, he organizes his topics in terms of ascending order of importance and levels of abstraction. He begins with an informal account of how nature has spoken to him, then enumerates four primary "uses" of nature: as a material resource, a standard of beauty, a network of visible symbols from which we make language and metaphor, and as a discipline for both the Understanding and the Reason. After this, Emerson moves from the subject of nature's uses to the abstruser question of epistemology. He entertains the notion that our minds simply create the world we see, only to reject it in favor of the belief that nature is really man's spiritual counterpart, a parallel creation of the same omnipresent spirit.

This idea of a spiritual correspondence between man and nature, derived from many sources from Plato through Emanuel Swedenborg and Coleridge, actually underlies all of *Nature* and constitutes the second most important principle in Emerson's thought, next to self-reliance. Correspondential vision is the key to Emerson's aesthetic. He described himself very accurately as "a poet in the sense of a perceiver & dear lover of the harmonies that are in the soul & in matter, & specially of the correspondences between these & those." Both in his literary style and in his critical theory, Emerson attached great importance to the symbolic image. The "argument" of *Nature* is much less important than its poetic celebration of nature's spiritual significance. Stylistically, the book marks a shift from the comparative lucidity and orderliness of Emerson's earlier prose to the discontinuous, highly metaphorical quality of his mature essays.

For an unconventional book by an anonymous author, *Nature* was reviewed attentively, receiving the extremes of praise and blame according to the reviewer's orthodoxy and commitment to systematic reasoning. *Nature* was not a publishing sensation, but Emerson was rightly pleased by the sale of 500 copies within a month. It impressed his American sympathizers, and, due largely to Carlyle's efforts, it established a small following for him in Britain as well.

During the years 1836-1844 Emerson was at the peak of his literary abilities and produced his most original work. In addition to *Nature*, he published *Essays* (1841) and *Essays: Second Series* (1844), served as one of the editors and major contributors to the Transcendentalist periodical, the *Dial* (1840-1844), and delivered some of his finest public addresses. His Harvard Phi Beta Kappa Society oration on "The American Scholar" (1837) enlivened the rather trite subject of the need for American literary independence with characteristically Emersonian appeals to study nature and cultivate self-trust. "Books," he insists, "are for the scholar's idle times," when his inspiration is temporarily darkened. The 500 printed copies of the address sold out within a month. One of its auditors, Oliver Wendell Holmes, characterized it as America's "intellectual Declaration of Independence," and thanks to Emerson's later fame, the description has endured. Later readers have rightly detected in the portrayal of the scholar an idealized self-image of the author.

In 1838 Harvard's handful of graduating divinity students invited Emerson to deliver "the customary discourse, on occasion of their entering upon the active Christian ministry." Emerson responded with the most controversial, subversive, and electrifying speech of his career. In the presence of Unitarianism's leading dignitaries, Emerson argued that a living religion is not based on forms or doctrines but upon the experience of inspiration. Christianity has superstitiously exaggerated the uniqueness of the man Jesus and his miracles, thereby obscuring the fact that inspiration is as accessible to us as it was to him. Thus the young minister's duty, as "a newborn bard of the Holy Ghost," is to "cast behind [him] all conformity, and acquaint men at first hand with Deity." Here and elsewhere Emerson identifies prophet and poet: religious inspiration expresses itself poetically; poetic inspiration is inherently religious. Like many other writers in the Romanticist tradition, Emerson saw art as a branch of religion—and vice versa.

The Divinity School Address aroused a fierce debate between moderate Unitarianism and its radical Transcendental wing over the relative importance of external vs. internal evidence (e.g. miracles vs. inspiration) in authenticating religion. Emerson, who instinctively shrank from public controversy, stayed aloof, retracting nothing, but

disconcerted by the attacks upon him. The event was a watershed in his life. He soon ceased preaching altogether and virtually severed his ties with the institutional church until old age. Furthermore, the experience increased his natural reluctance to participate in reform movements of any sort. For the next dozen years, apart from a few pronouncements against slavery, Emerson disappointed his activist friends by his lukewarm, often satirical attitude toward organized attempts to social change. His amused tolerance for the Utopian experiments, Brook Farm and Fruitlands, exemplifies his position.

The Emerson house.

Since the mid-1830s, Transcendentalists had discussed the desirability of a magazine dedicated to the new thought. The eventual result was the *Dial*, appropriately subtitled "A Magazine for Literature, Philosophy, and Religion." Edited first by Margaret Fuller and then by Emerson, it lasted for sixteen numbers between 1840 and 1844. To it Emerson contributed numerous poems and prose pieces, the best of which he later published in book form. Though enthusiastic at the outset, Emerson was disappointed by the actual thinness of the content. Nevertheless the *Dial* proved to be one of the most significant in a series of lifelong attempts by Emerson to gain a public hearing for promising literary unknowns whom we now value much more highly than the public did then. Beginning with his first American edition of *Sartor Resartus* in 1836, Emerson edited or promoted works by Carlyle, Alcott, Thoreau, Whitman, Jones Very, Ellery Channing, and numerous others. Emerson's encouragement could be a mixed blessing, because it tended to follow the pattern of initial encomium giving way to far more critical second thoughts. Ellery Channing, for instance, was first spoiled by Emerson, then made to feel inadequate. But in the long run, Emerson's patronage of fellow-writers was beneficial to them and vital to the development of American literature.

In 1841, Emerson published his most ambitious book to date, the first series of *Essays*, containing twelve pieces on moral, religious, and intellectual concepts arranged in groups of two, each pair surveying common or analogous subjects from contrasting or complementary angles (e.g. "Love" and "Friendship," "Prudence" and "Heroism"). Among other significant items, *Essays* contains Emerson's fullest statements on "Self-Reliance" and "The Over-Soul" or divine principle. "Self-Reliance" is perhaps the most important of all Emerson's essays. In the slashing manner of the Divinity School Address, Emerson here attacks the importance we normally attach to consistency and conformity. Sooner or later, Emerson argues, we must fall back upon our own intuitions of what is right and what we are; otherwise we commit moral suicide. The justification for this individualism is that in turning inward, we find, if we seek rightly, a divinity within us, "the aboriginal Self, on which a universal reliance may be grounded." Should men dare to commit themselves to this Self, the result would be a transformation of society. At times the essay, like much of Emerson's writing, seems naive and grandiose. This impression changes when we understand that the gospel of self-reliance was in the first instance a message Emerson preached to himself, as an antidote to what he felt was his own chronic and deplorable lack of self-distrust. His private journals show this conclusively.

The structure of *Essays*, like that of *Nature*, is typical of Emerson. His two favorite organizing principles are an ascending order of topics and a dialectic of opposites or complements. These approaches, in turn, roughly correspond to Emerson's two favorite models of natural order: nature as a scale of being or evolutionary progression and nature as a bipolar unity of opposites. The longest of the individual *Essays* are less than half the length of *Nature* and considerably less formal in structure. As such they set the pattern for all of Emerson's significant later prose works. Essentially they reflect a three-stage process of composition. Emerson gathered the raw materials for his writings from the entries in his journals, a multi-volume series of manuscripts extending over a fifty-year period, in themselves one of the most remarkable literary monuments in American history. The journal material was cut, pasted, and assembled into lectures, which in turn were later revised, distilled, and supplemented with additional journal gleanings to make the final essay. This laborious procedure of condensation and piecework made for a finished product more notable for its dazzling passages than for well-crafted literary wholes. Alcott claimed that one could read Emerson backwards just as well as forwards. The best essays, however, are more intricately crafted than meets the eye, partly because Emerson believed that art should follow the method of nature, and that the method of nature included an element of disguise.

Waldo Emerson.

Critical opinion of *Essays* was even more fiercely divided than the reviews of *Nature*, and on the same grounds. The polarization, in part, reflected Emerson's growing fame, as did his sales. The first American edition of 1,500 sold out; and for the first time (and continuously thereafter) Emerson was simultaneously published in England, with Carlyle's assistance. The English edition of 750 sold well enough to encourage a pirated version in 1843. A second, revised American edition was published in 1847.

Essays: Second Series (1844), a collection of nine pieces, marks a gradual but distinct shift in Emerson's thought. Emerson here qualifies his optimistic assertions about man's capacity to transform himself. "Experience" stresses the torpidity of our normal state of consciousness and our liability to self-delusion. "Nature," in contrast to Emerson's first book, stresses nature's elusiveness rather than man's power to fathom her. In several essays, individuality is seen as a positive threat to true self-reliance by keeping one from moving from the particular to the universal. On the other hand, the volume's lead essay, "The Poet," is Emerson's most fulsome tribute to the creative imagination. Emerson defines the poet in quasi-religious terms as the articulator of the meaning of the universe and presents a revised version of the theory, first published in *Nature*, that poetry is a reflection of the emblematic quality of nature itself. Whereas in *Nature* Emerson had suggested a schematic view of nature as a fixed allegorical system, here he regards nature, more characteristically, as in a state of perpetual flow, in which any one object or image can be seen as having innumerable meanings. Here and elsewhere in this volume we see Emerson moving from an old-fashioned myth of nature as static hierarchy to a proto-evolutionary conception of nature as a process of development from lower to higher forms. Both models, however, coexist in peaceful contradiction throughout Emerson's work.

Despite its exuberance, "The Poet" only confirms Emerson's conservative drift. It celebrates the power of a special being whom the rest of the volume shows to be far above the common lot. "I look in vain for the poet whom I describe," Emerson confesses. The shift in Emerson's view of universal order also reflects a new humility on his part: he now regards mankind less as nature's rightful master and more as her product, subject to the same instability and flux. From this point until the end of his life, Emerson's Transcendentalism becomes more muted, his appraisal of humanity more skeptical, his attitude toward social institutions more positive, his sympathy for antisocial gestures more grudging, his sense of irony more keen, his evaluations of all issues more balanced and temperate. Emerson never abandoned his earlier positions, but he qualified them considerably. He continued to believe that "The one thing in the world of value is the active soul"; but he resigned himself to the fact that the soul's normal state is inactivity. Whether this shift represents a surrender of his original idealism or an awakening to common sense depends largely upon the values of the interpreter.

Essays: Second Series, published in an edition of 2,000, sold well enough to justify a second edition by 1850. Although one reviewer found it of "less interest" than its predecessor, the volume was in general better received, partly because it seemed less overtly critical of established religion, partly because readers were getting more accustomed to Emerson's oracular style. American Unitarianism's leading periodical, the *Christian Examiner*, hostile to Emerson since the Divinity School Address, allowed his friend Frederic Henry Hedge to give the book a favorable notice. Thereafter the *Examiner* was solidly pro-Emerson, tempering its praise with expressions of chagrin at his paganism which became increasingly more pro forma as time went on.

Lidian Emerson.

The conservative drift in Emerson's thought has sometimes been explained in terms of a personal catastrophe: the death of his first and favorite child, Waldo, of scarlatina in 1842 at the age of five. Emerson was devastated both by the loss of a part of himself and by the realization that his grief itself could not last; and he rationalized his despair, in his elegy "Threnody," by acquiescing in the myth of a purposive world-spirit which might be trusted as benign even when it seemed destructive. This note of stoical optimism becomes progressively more emphatic in Emerson's later work. Yet the changes in Emerson's inner life are probably less attributable to any particular event than to such general factors as aging and success. By the end of the 1840s, Emerson had become a New England institution, internationally famous, tolerated even by many of those whose interests he criticized. New editions of all his major books and speeches were called for between 1847 and 1850. In 1847-1848 he took a highly successful lecture tour through Great Britain, meeting many dignitaries and virtually all the important Victorian literary figures. Upon his return, he seemed to have become a more gregarious, even convivial person. He played an active part, for example, in the organization of a Concord and a Boston social circle, both of which he enjoyed for the rest of his life. These changes of style and tone inspired mixed reactions among Emerson's Transcendentalist friends: Alcott was bemused, Thoreau was dismayed. Emerson, in turn, began to take a more disparaging view of Thoreau's defiance of convention and aloofness from respectable society.

Since his school days, Emerson had written poetry. At Harvard, he was class poet (after six others had declined the office), and in 1834 he delivered the annual poem before Harvard's Phi Beta Kappa Society. Since the early 1830s, Emerson had been composing at intervals poems of real if uneven merit. In 1847 many of these were collected in *Poems*, printed in an edition of 1,500. Of all Emerson's literary efforts to date, this was perhaps the hardest for his admirers to accept, since critical opinion, then as now, regarded Emerson as an awkward versifier whose best poetry is in his prose. The poet himself did not help matters by putting his most cryptic and unrhythmic composition, "The Sphinx," at the head of the volume. But though the *North American Review* dismissed Emerson's "professed poetry" as "the most prosaic and unintelligible stuff that it has ever been our fortune to encounter," a number of reviews recognized the subtlety and originality of Emerson's best passages. Within a year the sales had reached 850 and Emerson had made a modest profit.

Emerson's most distinctive quality as a poet is his gift for terse, often elliptical, gnomic expression which interweaves symbolic images and provocative statement. Though overly addicted to clockwork tetrameter, Emerson is at least intermittently capable of handling conventional forms with grace. More important, Emerson dares to experiment with irregularities in rhythm, rhyme, and line length in order to capture the "artful thunder" of the ancient bards. Taken together with the less impressive *May-Day and Other Pieces* (1867), *Poems* shows American literature's first steps away from conventional prosody in the direction of the American

Emerson in 1854.

experimentalist tradition fully realized in Whitman and Dickinson. Just as Whitman's free verse reflects Emerson's prose rhythms, so Dickinson may have been influenced by Emerson's poetry.

Emerson's next work, *Representative Men* (1850), consists of essays on the "Uses of Great Men" and six individual figures: Plato, Swedenborg, Montaigne, Shakespeare, Napoleon, and Goethe. Each is treated not simply as an individual but as exemplary of a vocational and mental type. The choices of Montaigne and Napoleon suggest Emerson's growing respect for skeptics and for men of action. Another sign of the former is his tendency to evaluate each figure severely in light of the highest ideal. Even heroes finally seem narrow; no one is a complete human being. On the one hand, Emerson's preoccupation with individual greatness, a lifelong fascination for him, betrays a moral elitism which links him with the Brahmin inheritance he resisted in the 1830s, but was now in the process of accommodating himself to. On the other hand, Emerson's refusal to be completely swept up by his heroes gives his book a more egalitarian, democratic emphasis than Carlyle's writings on the same subject.

Reviewers were, by and large, more cordial to *Representative Men* than to Emerson's previous books. For the first time, the *North American Review* grudgingly conceded that "Mr. Emerson is a great writer," though not the "Phoebus Apollo" that his "idolaters" consider him. Even New England's Baptist review found the book "a little less objectionable" than its predecessors. On the other hand, it began to be suggested that Emerson was past his peak: In some respects, this was confirmed by his next two books, in which Emerson appears more in the role of reporter-compiler than as an original thinker. In 1852 he helped to edit the *Memoirs of Margaret Fuller Ossoli*, a valuable sourcebook on Transcendentalism which, however, reads in places more like an attempt to explain away the editors' deep and complicated reactions to Fuller than like a fully sympathetic account of her life and work. *English Traits* (1856) is the literary result of Emerson's British visit. Like *Representative Men*, it had solidified through years of successful presentation on the lecture circuit.

A topical analysis of the nature and achievements of British society punctuated by a few chapters of personal anecdote, *English Traits* is the most straightforward and readable of Emerson's major works. It was also the fastest seller. It ran through an initial printing of 3,000 copies within a month, and a new printing of 2,000 sold quickly also. Reviews were generally favorable; one went so far as to declare that Emerson's position in American literature was now permanently settled and all further controversy superfluous. Yet *English Traits* also aroused criticism on both sides of the Atlantic, part of which was the ironic result of the book's principal virtue: Emerson attempted a balanced appraisal at a time when both British and American readers still preferred partisanship. In general, Emerson's overview of the English is, in fact, a restatement of a characteristic Emersonian dichotomy. England, he says, is "the best of actual nations," in the sense that its traditions are the most distinguished and its cultural development the most advanced from a materialistic standpoint. But the English "mind is in a state of arrested development"; it lacks vision, flexibility, spiritual awareness. These qualities belong to the New World. Thus England is to America as Understanding is to Reason, as Matter is to Spirit. It is significant, however, that the middle-aged Emerson pays sincere tribute to the virtues with which he does credit the English. He

The Rowse portrait of Emerson (1857).

now is prepared to respect goods and institutions not simply as emblems of spiritual power but as a genuine stage in their development.

The social consciousness of Emerson's major works of the 1850s reflects a new departure in his personal life, and in that of the nation as a whole. Like many other liberal New Englanders, Emerson was outraged by the Compromise of 1850, which resulted in the strengthening of the Fugitive Slave Law. Emerson's immediate reaction was an unprecedented journal diatribe against Daniel Webster and political chicanery; the long-range result was that Emerson became between 1850-1865 an active spokesman for abolitionism and the Union cause. He publicly announced his intention to defy the new law (and he did); he defended John Brown; he made patriotic speeches throughout the Civil War. Part of his motivation was humanitarian sympathy for the slave; an even more important impetus, as for many of his associates, was the desire to keep New England free from any taint of complicity with the slave power. His activities sometimes required considerable personal courage, as when abolitionist rallies were confronted by hostile mobs.

Despite this furor, Emerson continued his customary round of lecturing, producing two more volumes of essays on selected aspects of manners and morals: *Conduct of Life* (1860) and *Society and Solitude* (1870). The first is perhaps the most intricately organized of all Emerson's miscellaneous essay collections. It would appear that Emerson tried to arrange the nine essays in an ascending order of abstractness from the material to the cultural to the intellectual, and that the nine chapters are further divided into triads, each of which consists of a pair of contrasting essays (e.g. "Fate" and "Power," "Behavior" and "Culture") whose considerations are synthesized in the third piece. This scheme is not perfectly executed, but Emerson nearly brings it off. Stylistically, the volume is not as impressive: Emerson was less able to synthesize and compress journal and lecture material than in his earlier work.

Emerson in 1859.

The most original essays in *Conduct of Life* are the first and the last, "Fate" and "Illusions." The first comes as close as Emerson ever did to responding to the common charge that he ignores the problem of evil. Emerson here defines "the book of Nature" as "the book of Fate," cataloguing numerous instances of nature's cruelty and destructiveness. Whereas in 1836 nature was seen as possibility, now it is seen as limitation, almost as the antagonist to spirit. At the end, Emerson tried to

conclude optimistically with the vision of a "Beautiful Necessity" underlying the apparently amoral process, and the possibility of spirit overcoming fate; but the individual life is seen as essentially a minor element in a cosmic process. The same sense of human littleness is expressed in a different way in "Illusions," where the universe is pictured as a visible illusion, the true meaning of which can be sensed only in brief glimpses of the hidden gods. This notion is similar to the theme of "Experience," but the tone is different—not so much anguished as wryly detached, as if in imitation of the phenomenon it describes.

Altogether *Conduct of Life* has a greater boldness of speculation than Emerson's books of the 1850s, and it seems to have stirred its readers more deeply. Carlyle considered it Emerson's best book. The *Christian Examiner* found it a distinct advance over the first essays "in firmness and facility of handling." Conservative critics were prompted to new attacks on Emerson's infidelity, partly because of an irreverent essay on "Worship." After *Conduct of Life*, however, the quality of Emerson's writing sharply declined. *Society and Solitude* is chatty and diffuse, relying heavily on lectures written much earlier. Most of his subsequent publications were put together only with the aid of his literary executor, James Elliot Cabot, and his daughter Ellen, who became his lecturing assistant and travelling companion. By the mid-1860s, Emerson's memory began to fail. The honor of being asked to lecture at Harvard on his philosophy in 1869-1870 turned into a grievous frustration as he struggled to organize his thoughts. The burning of his house in 1872 caused a severe emotional shock which pushed Emerson irretrievably into senescence, though well-wishers cheered him by arranging for him and Ellen to go to Europe and Egypt while the house was being restored. During the 1870s, Emerson continued to write and to lecture occasionally, but his effective life was over. He died peacefully in his eightieth year.

Emerson's personality was something of an enigma during his lifetime and still remains so today. Apart from his first wife and his brother Charles (d. 1836), he had few real intimates. Most of his friends saw only a part of him. His manner was gracious and considerate, an engaging mixture of incisiveness and self-deprecation. His conversation was often brilliant, and he enjoyed companionship, but he valued solitude as much or more. Though anxious to encourage others, particularly young people in whom he saw promise, Emerson preferred to keep such relationships on a level of impersonal cordiality. He avoided contention as much as he avoided personal entanglements. Though very ambitious in his literary aims and in his quest for wisdom, he never forgot his lack of precocity (two of his younger brothers were far better students than he) and he always tended to credit his achievements to a higher power and to believe that he was a lesser man than he was thought to be, or ought to be. Though a very serious-minded person, a preacher even after he left the ministry, Emerson also had a keen wit and sense of the ridiculous which the casual reader often misses. The life of the mind for him included a sense of intellectual play. Some considered Emerson's charming aloof coyness delightful; others considered it impenetrable. Most, however, agreed that he was a remarkable person. Perhaps the most striking sign of his was his resistance of the temptation to mold his admirers in his own image. He once congratulated himself on having no disciples. When those whom he had influenced reacted against him, as Thoreau and Whitman did, Emerson remained, for a sage, surprisingly composed. Both his reaction and theirs illustrate the practical value of Emersonian self-reliance.

Emerson's posthumous reputation might be said to have passed through three phases. Until about World War I, Emerson was widely revered as a thinker and sage. Though he was also criticized in some quarters for irreverence, muddle-headedness, and superficiality, seminal thinkers in various disciplines were deeply influenced by him. Through his impact on William James and John Dewey, Emerson helped to shape the development of Pragmatism, America's most distinctive contribution to the history of philosophy. Through his impact on Theodore Parker and other minister-reformers, Emerson helped prepare the way for the Social Gospel movement. Creative writers from Walt Whitman to Robert Frost paid homage to Emerson, as did artists in several other fields, like the composer Charles Ives. Most important, Emerson was looked to by many as the expositor of a secularized faith which combined individualism, optimism, and democracy in a way which could serve as a guide to life for those who no longer believed in traditional religion.

Between the world wars, criticism of Emerson increased. His prestige as an American prophet made some such reaction inevitable. He was now charged not only with such familiar defects as vagueness and superficiality but also with having lent encouragement to some of the worst tendencies in American culture, such as naivete, capitalism, and moralism. Emerson might speak to youth, said

the historian James T. Adams, but not to mature adults. Emerson's critics tended to regard him at best as an early stage in America's intellectual growth from adolescence toward maturity, at worst as "a fraud and a sentimentalist."

Emerson in 1873.

Since the latter attack by Yvor Winters in 1938, however, Emerson has been more sympathetically reappraised. Recent commentators have tended to emphasize his historical significance, his affinities with modern intellectual trends like symbolic philosophy and existentialism, and his achievement as a writer. The apparent murkiness of his essays has been explained as the expression of a conscious aesthetic within the tradition of the Romantic movement and the major Victorian prose writers. The world's foremost historian of literary criticism, Rene Wellek, has called Emerson "the outstanding representative of romantic symbolism in the English-speaking world." The amount of attention now being given to Emerson as a literary figure he himself would have regarded as disproportionate. Like most of the great Romanticists, he looked upon craftsmanship as ancillary to the writer's larger purpose as visionary prophet and law-giver to his age. Emerson would have been amused, to say the least, by scholarly editions of his writings, and by laborious critiques of his style which display no

Emerson in old age.

sense of urgency about his underlying message. Yet to read Emerson as a poet is, finally, to take him at his word.

Other Writings:

Nature; Addresses, and Lectures (Boston: James Munroe, 1849); *Memoirs of Margaret Fuller Ossoli,* ed. with James Freeman Clarke and William Henry Channing, 2 vols. (Boston: Phillips, Sampson, 1852); *Parnassus,* ed. Emerson—anthology of poetry (Boston: James R. Osgood, 1875). The following were prepared partly or entirely by James Elliot Cabot and/or Edward Waldo Emerson: *Letters and Social Aims* (Boston: James R. Osgood, 1876); *Lectures and Biographical Sketches* (Boston: Houghton, Mifflin, 1884); *Miscellanies* (Boston: Houghton, Mifflin, 1884); and *The Natural History of Intellect* (Boston: Houghton, Mifflin, 1893). The standard or "Centenary Edition" of Emerson, including all works mentioned above and in the headnote to this article except for *Parnassus* and the Ossoli *Memoirs,* is *The Complete Works,* ed. Edward Waldo Emerson, 12 vols. (Boston: Houghton, Mifflin, 1903-1904). This edition will be superseded

by a scholarly edition now being published by Harvard University Press; one volume has appeared so far: *Nature, Addresses, and Lectures,* ed. Alfred R. Ferguson and Robert E. Spiller (1971). Also: *Uncollected Writings,* ed. Charles C. Bigelow (New York: Lamb, 1912); *Young Emerson Speaks,* ed. Arthur C. McGiffert—a collection of early sermons (Boston: Houghton Mifflin, 1938); Carl F. Strauch, "Emerson's Phi Beta Kappa Poem," *New England Quarterly,* 23 (March 1950): 65-90; and *The Early Lectures of Ralph Waldo Emerson,* ed. Stephen E. Whicher, Robert E. Spiller, and Wallace E. Williams, 3 vols. (Cambridge: Harvard University Press, 1959-1972).

Bibliographies:

George Willis Cooke, *A Bibliography of Ralph Waldo Emerson* (Boston: Houghton, Mifflin, 1908); Frederic Ives Carpenter, *Emerson Handbook* (New York: Hendricks House, 1953); Jacob Blanck, *The Bibliography of American Literature* (New Haven: Yale University Press, 1959), 3:16-70; William Charvat, *Emerson's American Lecture Engagements* (New York: New York Public Library, 1961); Jackson R. Bryer and Robert A. Rees, *A Checklist of Emerson Criticism 1951-1961* (Hartford, Ct.: Transcendental Books, 1964); Walter Harding, *Emerson's Library* (Charlottesville: University Press of Virginia, 1967); Floyd Stovall, "Ralph Waldo Emerson," in *Eight American Authors,* ed. James Woodress, rev. ed. (New York: Norton, 1971), pp. 37-83.

Biographies:

Moncure Daniel Conway, *Emerson at Home and Abroad* (Boston: James R. Osgood, 1882); James Elliot Cabot, *A Memoir of Ralph Waldo Emerson,* 2 vols. (Boston: Houghton, Mifflin, 1889); Denton.J. Snider, *A Biography of Ralph Waldo Emerson* (St. Louis: William Harvey Miner, 1921); Townsend Scudder, *The Lonely Wayfaring Man: Emerson and Some Englishmen* (New York: Oxford University Press, 1936); Ralph L. Rusk, *The Life of Ralph Waldo Emerson* (New York: Scribners, 1949); Henry F. Pommer, *Emerson's First Marriage* (Carbondale: Southern Illinois University Press, 1967).

Letters and Journals:

A Correspondence Between John Sterling and Ralph Waldo Emerson, ed. Edward W. Emerson (Boston: Houghton, Mifflin, 1897); *Letters from Ralph Waldo Emerson to a Friend* [Samuel Gray

Ward], ed. Charles Eliot Norton (Boston: Houghton, Mifflin, 1899); *Correspondence Between Ralph Waldo Emerson and Herman Grimm*, ed. Frederick William Holls (Boston: Houghton, Mifflin, 1903); *The Journals of Ralph Waldo Emerson*, ed. Edward Waldo Emerson and Waldo Emerson Forbes, 10 vols. (Boston: Houghton Mifflin, 1909-1914); *Records of a Lifelong Friendship 1807-1882* [Emerson-W. H. Furness], ed. H. H. Furness (Boston: Houghton Mifflin, 1910); *Emerson-Clough Letters,* ed. Howard F. Lowry and Ralph Leslie Rusk (Cleveland: Rowfant Club, 1934); *The Letters of Ralph Waldo Emerson*, ed. Ralph L. Rusk, 6 vols. (New York: Columbia University Press, 1939); *The Journals and Miscellaneous Notebooks of Ralph Waldo Emerson*, ed. William H. Gilman *et al.*, 13 vols. to date—will supersede *Journals* (1909-1914) (Cambridge: Harvard University Press, 1960-); *The Correspondence of Emerson and Carlyle*, ed. Joseph Slater (New York: Columbia University Press, 1964); *One First Love: The Letters of Ellen Louisa Tucker to Ralph Waldo Emerson*, ed. Edith W. Gregg (Cambridge: Harvard University Press, 1962).

Criticism:

The Genius and Character of Emerson, ed. F. B. Sanborn (Boston: James R. Osgood, 1885); Oscar W. Firkins, *Ralph Waldo Emerson* (Boston: Houghton Mifflin, 1915); F. O. Matthiessen, *American Renaissance: Art and Expression in the Age of Emerson and Whitman* (New York: Oxford University Press, 1941); *The Transcendentalists: An Anthology*, ed. Perry Miller—contains much perceptive commentary (Cambridge: Harvard Univer-

sity Press, 1950); Vivian Hopkins, *Spires of Form: A Study of Emerson's Aesthetic Theory* (Cambridge: Harvard˙ University Press, 1951); Sherman Paul, *Emerson's Angle of Vision* (Cambridge: Harvard University Press, 1952); Stephen E. Whicher, *Freedom and Fate: An Inner Life of Ralph Waldo Emerson*—the best study of Emerson's thought (Philadelphia: University of Pennsylvania Press, 1953); Charles Feidelson, Jr., *Symbolism and American Literature* (Chicago: University of Chicago Press, 1961); Jonathan Bishop, *Emerson on the Soul* (Cambridge: Harvard University Press, 1964); Joel Porte, *Emerson and Thoreau: Transcendentalists in Conflict* (Middletown, Ct.: Wesleyan University Press, 1966); *Emerson Among His Contemporaries*, ed. Kenneth Walter Cameron—nineteenth-century estimates (Hartford, Ct.: Transcendental Books, 1967); Lawrence Buell, *Literary Transcendentalism* (Ithaca: Cornell University Press, 1973); Edward Wagenknecht, *Ralph Waldo Emerson: Portrait of a Balanced Soul*—an introductory overview (New York: Oxford University Press, 1974); Sacvan Bercovich, *The Puritan Origins of the American Self* —Emerson as heir of the Puritans (New Haven: Yale University Press, 1975); Hyatt Waggoner, *Emerson as Poet* (Princeton: Princeton University Press, 1975).

Papers:

The majority of Emerson's papers, including letters, journals, and literary manuscripts, are deposited in the Ralph Waldo Emerson Memorial Association collection at the Houghton Library at Harvard University.

EDWARD EVERETT (11 April 1794-15 January 1865) was a noted nineteenth-century educator and clergyman, and was one of the New England Brahmins whose credentials were not unlike those of George Bancroft, Edward Everett Hale, and others. The Everett name had been established firmly in New England since 1642, when Richard Everett settled at Dedham, Massachusetts. His descendant, Oliver Everett, father of Edward, graduated in 1779 from Harvard College and became minister of the New South Church in Boston. Poor health required that he move to Dorchester, where he was prominent in the Federalist Party and served as a Judge of the Court of Common Pleas. Edward Everett was born in Dorchester on 11 April 1794, one of eight children.

Edward Everett.

In 1807 Edward graduated from the Phillips Exeter Academy in New Hampshire. His delivery of the Valedictory Latin Address was the first sign of the recognition of his talents as an orator. In 1807 Everett entered Harvard College, and in 1814 received the degree of M.A. in divinity. While at Harvard, Everett received added acclaim for his abilities as an orator. He also showed promise of his later outstanding career as a writer by organizing and editing the *Harvard Lyceum*. In 1813 Everett accepted an invitation to become minister of the

fashionable Brattle Street Church (Unitarian) in Boston, and was installed in February 1814 at the age of nineteen. After a year's service, Everett accepted a chair at Harvard, and journeyed to Europe in 1815 for additional study. After being awarded a Ph.D. at Gottingen in 1817, the first such degree given to an American, he joined the Harvard faculty and soon became editor of the *North American Review*. Soon Everett's abilities as an orator led him to politics, and he served Massachusetts in the United States Congress from 1825 to 1835. Gradually Everett's political fortunes increased, due in part to his abilities as a speaker and writer. After serving four terms as governor of Massachusetts during the 1830s, he was appointed minister to the Court of St. James, and in 1852 was appointed secretary of state. His position as a moderate New England Whig produced both his election to the Senate in 1853 and his nomination in 1860 as Vice-President on the ticket of the Constitutional Union Party. A strong advocate of the Union cause during the Civil War, Everett is perhaps known best for his 1863 oration which preceded that of President Abraham Lincoln at the dedication of the national cemetery at Gettysburg. He died of pneumonia in Boston in 1865. His works were collected as *Orations and Speeches on Various Occasions*, 4 vols. (Boston: Little & Brown, 1850-1868). REFERENCES: Paul Revere Frothingham, *Edward Everett: Orator and Statesman* (Boston: Houghton Mifflin, 1925); Orie William Long, *Literary Pioneers: Early American Explorers of European Culture* (Cambridge: Harvard University Press, 1935). —*Thomas L. Connelly*

CORNELIUS CONWAY FELTON (6 November 1807-26 February 1862), classical scholar, was born in Newbury, Massachusetts. He graduated from Harvard College in 1827. Lacking funds to pursue an independent career, he continued teaching at Harvard, going from a tutor in Latin to Elliot Professor of Greek Literature in 1834, and finally was named president of the school in 1860. His long service ended with his death, in Chester, Pennsylvania, of continued ill health, two years later. Felton is known mainly for his *Greece: Ancient and Modern* (Boston: Ticknor & Fields, 1867), a posthumous collection of his Lowell Institute lectures designed for a general audience. REFERENCE: George S. Hilliard, "Memoir of Cornelius Conway Felton," *Proceedings of the Massachusetts Historical Society*, 10 (1867-1869): 352-368.

JAMES THOMAS FIELDS (31 December 1817-24 April 1881), poet, editor, and publisher, was born the son of a ship's captain at Portsmouth, New Hampshire. His father died when he was two and he and his younger brother George were raised by their mother. From an early age, Fields read widely and received as good an education as possible. But a lack of money prevented his attending college, and in 1831 he went to work in Boston at Carter and Hendee's Bookstore (later called the Old Corner Bookstore). Fields soon became an active participant in the literary and social life of Boston: he regularly attended the Reverend William Ellery Channing's church; his rooms became a place for socials attended by such people as Edwin Percy Whipple and Longfellow; and he joined the Boston Mercantile Library Association. His poetic aspirations were also fulfilled when his verses were printed in the *Portsmouth Journal, Knickerbocker Magazine, The Token, New Hampshire Book*, Rufus W. Griswold's *Poets and Poetry of America*, and Whittier's anti-slavery annual, *The North Star*. In 1831 the bookstore had been taken over by the publishing firm of Allen and Ticknor, with William D. Ticknor soon emerging as sole proprietor. By 1840 Fields was taking an active role in both the bookstore and Ticknor's publishing firm, and his successful ventures publishing English authors, including Alfred Lord Tennyson, whom he introduced to American audiences, made the firm much money. Ticknor recognized Fields's business and publishing acumen and in 1843 made him a junior partner. Fields capped his success with a trip to Europe in 1847, but was deeply grieved when his mother died soon after his return. In 1849 public recognition of Fields's ability came when Ticknor changed the firm's imprint to "Ticknor, Reed, and Fields." More successes followed in 1849, when Fields's *Poems* was published and he joined the short-lived Town and Country Club organized by Bronson Alcott. The next year he married Eliza Willard but she died of tuberculosis after a year. Fields left his mourning for another European trip, returning in 1852 after arranging for William Thackeray to make an American lecture visit. In 1854, Fields's professional and private lives peaked: he became a full partner in the firm, now called "Ticknor and Fields," and he married Annie Adams, buying a house at the foot of fashionable Beacon Hill, which became the center of the best-known literary salon in America. During the 1850s, Fields continued to bring major authors into his firm's fold and in 1858 he received a much-cherished honorary Master of Arts degree from Harvard University. The

The Old Corner Bookstore.

next decade was also a period of great activity for Fields. In 1860 the firm took over the *Atlantic Monthly Magazine*, edited by James Russell Lowell. When Lowell resigned in 1861, Fields himself became editor, a post he held for five years before turning it over to William Dean Howells. When Ticknor died in 1864 while on a walking tour with Hawthorne, Fields became senior partner and moved the firm's location to Tremont Street, at the corner of the Boston Commons. Also in that year the firm took over the prestigious *North American Review* and Fields was admitted to the most famous conversational group in New England, the Saturday Club. Following a dispute with Ticknor's son, Fields in 1868 bought him out and changed the firm's name to "Fields, Osgood, and Company." However, a long business life had tired Fields and, after an 1869-1870 trip to Europe, he retired from publishing and the firm became "James R. Osgood and Company." Fields now embarked on a career as a successful lecturer, talking on his wide reading and his many literary friendships. At his death in Boston in 1881, he left his wife an estate of $150,000. Fields's own literary achievement is small; his biographer calls his poetry full of "humor, nostalgia for the countryside, and sweetly sentimental vignettes of death and children." His most popular work was *Yesterdays with Authors*, a volume recollecting his friendships with some of the most famous writers of the day. It was as a publisher that Fields excelled. His firm eventually became the authorized American publisher of Matthew Arnold, Robert Browning, Thomas De Quincey, Charles Dickens, Emerson, Hawthorne, Holmes, Julia Ward Howe, Leigh Hunt, Longfellow, Harriet Beecher Stowe, Thoreau, and Whittier. His relations with authors were always very friendly, personal, and, above all, honest. In the early days, when American publishers reprinted English authors without paying royalties, a legal practice in the absence of an international copyright agreement, Fields always paid for the privilege of reprinting. Although later errors in judgment and the impersonality of the rapidly growing firm sometimes contributed to mis-understandings, such as one with Hawthorne's widow, Ticknor retained a high place in the estimation of his authors. —*Joel Myerson*

Principal Works: *Poems* (Boston: William D. Ticknor, 1849); *Yesterdays with Authors* (Boston: James R. Osgood, 1872); *Ballads and Other Poems* (Boston: Houghton, Mifflin, 1881).

Principal References: Annie Fields, *James T. Fields* (Boston: Houghton, Mifflin, 1881); James C. Austin, *Fields of the ATLANTIC MONTHLY* (San Marino, Cal.: Henry E. Huntington Library, 1953); Jacob Blanck, *Bibliography of American Literature* (New Haven: Yale University Press, 1959), 3:142-158; W. S. Tryon, *Parnassus Corner: A Life of James T. Fields* (Boston: Houghton Mifflin, 1963).

ELIZA LEE (CABOT) FOLLEN (15 August 1787-26 January 1860), reformer and juvenile author, used her Boston background to obtain a good education and to become a major participant in the city's literary and religious life. In 1828 she married a German refugee, Charles Follen, who soon became the first German professor at Harvard College. When Follen's appointment was not renewed—possibly because of the anti-slavery activities of him and his wife—he tried preaching, but anti-abolitionists caused his removal. Follen died in 1840 in a steamboat fire. Mrs. Follen settled with her son at West Roxbury, Massachusetts, and wrote for a living. After *The Works of Charles Follen, with a Memoir of His Life*, 5 vols. (Boston: Hilliard, Gray, 1841-1842), she devoted herself to juvenile literature. Earlier she had edited the *Christian Teachers' Manual* (1828-1830) and had published a number of instructional works; now she returned to this field, editing the *Child's Friend* (1843-1850) and producing numerous volumes of stories. In her later years she used her pen in the anti-slavery cause, writing a number of tracts, the most famous being *A Letter to Mothers in the Free States* (New York: American Anti-Slavery Society, 1855). She died in Brookline, near Boston. REFERENCE: Elizabeth Bancroft Schlesinger, "Two Early Harvard Wives: Eliza Farrar and Eliza Follen," *New England Quarterly*, 38 (June 1965): 141-167.

Convers Francis.

CONVERS FRANCIS (9 November 1795-7 April 1863), Unitarian minister, biographer, and historian, was born in West Cambridge, Massachusetts. He graduated from Harvard College in 1815, continued as a divinity student, and was ordained in 1819 at Watertown. Francis took time from his pastoral duties to contribute to religious periodicals and to write *An Historical Sketch of Watertown* (Cambridge: E. W. Metcalf, 1830) and a *Life of John Eliot* (Boston: Hilliard, Gray, 1836), the apostle to the Indians. His house at Watertown was frequented by his friends, including his sister, Lydia Maria Child, Emerson, and Theodore Parker, whom Francis tutored prior to his entering the Harvard Divinity School. In 1836 Francis became a member of the Transcendental Club and, as the eldest member, its moderator. Francis left Watertown in 1842 to become Parkman Professor of Pulpit Eloquence at Harvard, a post he held until his death. Francis never approached the social radicalism of Parker or the intellectual radicalism of Emerson because he was more interested in working from within existing institutions than attacking them, in crusaderlike fashion, from without. REFERENCES: John Weiss, *Discourse Occasioned by the Death of Convers Francis* (Cambridge: privately printed, 1863); William Newell, "Memoir of the Rev. Convers Francis," *Proceedings of the Massachusetts Historical Society*, 8 (March 1865): 233-253.

OCTAVIUS BROOKS FROTHINGHAM (26 November 1822-27 November 1895) was a religious and literary figure who reached his audience through the pulpit, press, published sermons, and biographies of leading figures. Most scholars today know him only as the author of *Transcendentalism in New England*. As the leader of a group of religious radicals, he was the foremost advocate of anti-Christian Unitarianism and the first president of the Free Religious Association (1867-1878). He was probably the most intellectual and eloquent spokesman of his generation for interpreting German Biblical criticism and the Religion of Humanity. Born in Boston of a Unitarian family, he grew up in the Brahmin atmosphere of genteel ideas and affluence. His father, Nathaniel Langdon Frothingham, was minister of the influential First Church of Boston. His maternal grandfather was the wealthy Peter Chardon Brooks, and Henry Adams was his first cousin. His childhood and youth included the Boston Latin School and a home atmosphere where Ralph Waldo Emerson often came for dinner. Daniel Webster passed his door to be admired by young Frothingham, who later recalled him as "a great locomotive pulling the train of civilization." Frothingham went to Harvard College where he was graduated in 1843. From there he went to Harvard Divinity School, graduated in 1847, and took his first ministry in Salem, Massachusetts (1847-1854). His marriage to Caroline Curtis, daughter of a well-to-do Boston merchant, in 1847, reinforced his social position. His second pulpit was in Jersey City, New Jersey, where he gained prominence as a radical theologian and outspoken critic of slavery. Soon he attracted the attention of Henry Bellows of All Souls Church in New York City who was instrumental in Frothingham's move to that city in 1859. There he established the Third Congregational Society and his main career began. As Theodore Parker had done before him, Frothingham led his congregation out of the Unitarian denomination and set up his Independent Liberal Church. He attracted intellectual and public figures such as Horace Greeley, editor of the New-

York Tribune; F. A. P. Barnard, president of Columbia University; Calvert Vaux, architect; Edmund C. Stedman, writer; George Haven Putnam, publisher; and George Ripley, formerly of Brook Farm. His weekly "discourses" also drew a wide audience of actors, "come outers," and nonconformists—a "church for the un-churched," he called it. From this vantage point he became the leader of the radical Unitarians and Reformed Jews of his generation. In 1867 he helped form the Free Religious Association, whose announced purpose was to view Christianity as a denomination soon to disappear, and to usher in an era of The Religion of Humanity. He wrote for the *Index*, the unofficial journal for the Free Religious Association, and dominated the annual meetings of the group in various cities from 1867 until his retirement in 1879. After two years abroad, the rest of his life was spent in Boston and his summer home in Beverly, Massachusetts, as a writer of history, biography, and social commentary. Throughout his career he was an awesome figure, loved by a few, feared by some, and respected by all. In many ways he went beyond

the radicalism of Emerson and Parker. Though not as original, he elaborated and expanded upon their ideas, and certainly his sermons and writings were as profound as theirs and better organized. He was the leader of the second-generation Transcendentalists.
—*J. Wade Caruthers*

Principal Works: *Story of the Patriarchs* (Boston: Walter Chase, 1864); *Religion and Humanity* (New York: D. G. Francis, 1873); *Life of Theodore Parker* (Boston: James R. Osgood, 1874); *Transcendentalism in New England* (New York: Putnam's, 1876);

Gerrit Smith (New York: Putnam's, 1876); *George Ripley* (Boston: Houghton, Mifflin, 1882); *Boston Unitarianism 1820-1850* (New York: Putnam's, 1890); *Recollections and Impressions 1827-1891* (New York: Putnam's, 1891).

Principal References: Edmund Clarence Stedman, *Octavius Frothingham and the New Faith* (New York: Putnam's, 1876); J. Wade Caruthers, *Octavius Brooks Frothingham, Gentle Radical* (University: University of Alabama Press, 1977).

Sarah Margaret Fuller, Marchesa D'Ossoli

Joel Myerson
University of South Carolina

BIRTH: Cambridgeport, Massachusetts, near Boston, 23 May 1810.

MARRIAGE: Giovanni Ossoli, in Italy, late 1849. One child, Angelo (1848-1850).

DEATH: At sea, off Fire Island, New York, 19 July 1850.

MAJOR WORKS: *Summer on the Lakes, in 1843* (Boston: Little & Brown, 1844); *Woman in the Nineteenth Century* (New York: Greeley & McElrath, 1845); *Papers on Literature and Art* (New York: Wiley & Putnam, 1846).

Life and Career:

Fuller's permanence lies in that most intangible quality, herself. Realizing that her position in life would have been different and much higher had she been a man, Fuller from youth concentrated on cultivating her mental powers and competing with men on purely intellectual terms. The pattern of her life—from prodigy to author to revolutionary—is not only intrinsically interesting, but also influenced the lives of those who knew her. Horace Greeley, Nathaniel Hawthorne, Henry David Thoreau, and especially Ralph Waldo Emerson, whose usually defensive reserves she tried to break

down, were all affected by her during important phases of their lives. Fuller's personality and what happened when she came in conflict with the restraints of the time are of interest to all students of the history of women in America. Her influence on her contemporaries, especially on Emerson in such works of his as "Friendship," is an equally rewarding area of study.

Margaret Fuller's life was anything but typical of that lead by an early nineteenth-century American woman. At her birth, her father was disappointed that his first child was a girl. He had wanted a boy to train for and to prepare to follow his own manner of intellectual life. Nevertheless, he soon began to assign his daughter the same intellectual tasks young men of a comparable age would have undertaken and, as a result, Margaret was raised to take full advantage of an excellent education. By age fifteen her schedule included reading literary and philosophical works in four languages during a day that lasted from five in the morning until eleven at night. The only break in this scholarly routine was the few hours reserved for walking, singing, and playing the piano. She was an omnivorous reader, and her interest in German literature brought her to the attention of the new religious and philosophical dissenters, the Transcendentalists. Her family moved to Cambridge in the early 1830s and she soon

Margaret Fuller in New York.

met most of the people who would become involved with the Transcendental Club and the *Dial*. Already well on her way to that "predetermination to *eat* this big universe as her oyster or her egg," which Thomas Carlyle later noticed in her, Fuller, who was bothered by her own physical shortcomings (including nearsightedness, complexion problems, and obesity), set for herself the task of cultivating her intellectual powers, hoping that showing her attainments in that area would make men consider her their equal. She nearly succeeded in her plan, but at a cost; many felt she had sacrificed the traditional concept of femininity, and Fuller's own ego sometimes showed to others "the presence of a rather mountainous ME."

The death of her father in October 1835 changed the course of her action. Plans for a European trip were cancelled, and Fuller took up teaching to support herself and her family. A brief stint at Bronson Alcott's progressive Temple School in Boston proved informative but unremunerative, and in June 1837 she went to Providence, Rhode Island, where she took a post at the new Greene Street School at the then-generous salary of $1,000 a year.

At Providence, Fuller continued to develop her literary powers. Beginning in 1835, she had been an occasional contributor of poems and reviews of foreign literature to the *Western Messenger*, a liberal Unitarian journal in the Ohio valley edited by her friend, James Freeman Clarke. When George Ripley began his *Specimens of Foreign Standard Literature* series in 1838, Fuller proposed to write a life of Goethe for it. Indeed, one reason for her taking the job at Providence had been that it allowed her time for scholarly pursuits. Her continuing study of German literature bore results; when John S. Dwight solicited aid from his friends for his edition of *Select Minor Poems, Translated from the German of Goethe and Schiller* in Ripley's series, Fuller contributed two translations.

Manuscript page of "Lines Written in Her Brother's Journal."

Teaching school for Fuller was a means and not an end. She keenly felt her separation from Boston and only in her correspondence with the Transcendentalists did she feel close to the center of activity. She began to believe she had not yet really accomplished anything, not yet left her mark on the world, and that her time to do so was rapidly running out. Accordingly, she left Providence in December 1838 for Boston, where she supported herself by giving private language lessons while working on her biography of Goethe.

Fuller had first given classes in German, Italian, and French literature in 1836 and her purposes this time were the same: to enable her students, "with ease and pleasure, to appropriate some part of the treasures of thought, which are contained in the classical works of foreign living languages." The biography of Goethe soon proved a greater task than she had anticipated, and the only product of her labors was a translation of Eckermann's *Conversations with Goethe in the Last Years of His Life*, which was published in May 1839 as the fourth volume in Ripley's *Specimens* series.

Margaret Fuller's cottage at Brook Farm.

Living in Boston again placed Fuller at the center of things and she quickly resumed her close association with the Transcendentalists. In October 1839, with Emerson's support, she volunteered to be editor of their periodical, the *Dial*. Fuller officially assumed her editorial duties in January 1840 and for two years presided over an eclectic journal of literature, philosophy, and religion, in which "all kinds of people" had "freedom to say their say, for better, for worse." But the reviewers, choosing the *Dial* as a convenient scapegoat for all the unpopular aspects of Transcendentalism, abused the new journal, and the public, unable to grasp or digest the varied articles, declined to buy the *Dial*. In March 1842, hampered by ill health and upset that none of her promised salary had been paid, Fuller resigned. The experience was valuable for Fuller, though, in teaching her to write review articles and in providing her with a ready outlet for her literary productions.

While editing the *Dial*, Fuller had supported herself by holding "Conversations" on various topics, including Greek mythology. She believed women had been educated solely for display and not to think, and she wished to rectify this mistake. By March 1841 the course had become so popular—even

though it was one of the most expensive series in Boston—that men were admitted. She also continued her study of German literature, and in 1842 she translated part of Bettina's correspondence with Gunderode for the press of Elizabeth Peabody. It was easy for Fuller to identify with Gunderode who, in Fuller's words, threw himself "into the river because the world is all too narrow." The book was published in March, just as Fuller left the cares of editing the *Dial* behind her.

During the spring and summer of 1842, Fuller travelled a great deal, stopping in Concord for the month of September as Emerson's houseguest. That November, she began her fourth annual series of winter "Conversations" in Boston and used the proceeds to embark the following May on a tour through the mid-west. She returned to Boston in September, started another round of "Conversations," contributed some reviews to the *Dial,* and worked at writing up the record of her travels in book form. After the "Conversations" ended in April 1844, she concentrated on her book—which she researched at the usually all-male sanctuary of the Harvard University Library—and on 4 June her account of her summer travels was published as *Summer on the Lakes, in 1843*.

Fuller's first book was typical of all her writings: its best parts were superb and made the weaker sections seem even more so. The value of *Summer on the Lakes* lies not in its factual matter, for Fuller had aimed at giving her "poetic impression of the country at large," but in its commentary on the people and their manners. She immediately sympathized with the plight of the Indian and wondered why he had not murdered the white man outright after the latter's territorial imperative was made manifest. Throughout her trip she was amazed at the beauty of the country, a beauty often overlooked by the local residents, as she remarked of a boat captain who "presented a striking instance how men, for the sake of getting a living, forget to live." Fuller saw that the desire of some to imitate European and Eastern standards would cause a basic conflict: "If the little girls grow up strong, resolute, able to exert their faculties, their mothers mourn over their want of fashionable delicacy." To prevent this, parents sent their children to schools, the result of which was "most likely to make them useless and unhappy at home." The artistic success of the book was hampered, though, by an unconscionable padding, as Fuller included large excerpts from and summaries of her reading—one extending over thirty-five pages—so that less than half the book actually dealt with the subject matter promised by its title. Most reviewers complimented Fuller's power of observation and the book was well-received. Sales were, however, disappointing: although nearly 700 copies were printed, 400 had to be sold off as remainders.

Summer on the Lakes was important for Fuller's career: it not only hurried recognition of her as a literary figure, but also brought her to the attention of Horace Greeley, editor of the *New-York Tribune*. He invited her to become the literary critic of his newspaper and offered to publish her next book, which would be an expansion and revision of her "The Great Lawsuit. Man *versus* Men. Woman *versus* Women" from the July 1843 *Dial*. Fuller accepted both offers, finishing the book in November, and began boarding with the Greeley family the next month. Her first review for the *Tribune*—one of Emerson's *Essays*—appeared on 7 December 1844 and *Woman in the Nineteenth Century* was published in early February 1845.

Engraved title page, 1845.

Woman in the Nineteenth Century is Fuller's most important work and is a major document in the history of American feminism. The book is striking, sometimes pedantic, but more often impassioned and direct in its arguments. Fuller especially attacked the hypocrisy of men, an hypocrisy that allowed them to campaign to free the black man while simultaneously legislating restrictions on women; an hypocrisy that complained of woman's physical and emotional unsuitability for positions of high responsibility in public life, yet that saw nothing inconsistent with allowing her the "killing

labors" of the seamstress or the field hand, or assigning to her the role of raising children. She also felt that man had "educated woman more as a servant than a daughter," and as woman became less equal, man had lost respect for her. Fuller wanted a time when there would be equality, when woman could live for "God's sake" and not sink into "weakness and poverty" through idolatry, with "imperfect man her god." Nearly all the reviewers praised Fuller herself and expressed agreement with the need to discuss the questions which she had raised, but they disagreed with her solutions. Fuller had decried the traditional stereotyped roles for men and women, saying that individuals should express themselves and not be merely what others think they should be because of their sex. Clearly, the reviewers felt, Fuller did not understand that woman's position as wife and mother was the highest role she could aspire to; in fact, it was so high that to grant her equality would be a demotion. To support Fuller, therefore, was to endanger woman's natural superiority and to remove her from the pedestal upon which she had been placed. The book sold well: all 1,500 copies went and a pirated edition appeared in England.

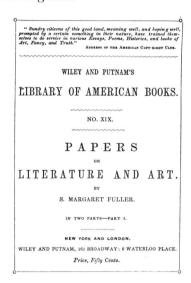

Front wrapper, 1846.

Seeing *Woman in the Nineteenth Century* through the press had exhausted Fuller, but its reception was gratifying. Fuller was also pleased with the opportunities which life in New York was opening to her. She took in its cultural attractions and interested herself in various reform movements. However, her tenure as the *Tribune*'s literary critic took its toll. She continued to be plagued by headaches (the result of her nearsightedness), an infirmity made worse by the pressure to meet deadlines. Greeley wanted someone who could write copy on demand, and he grew impatient when Fuller instead waited for the mood to strike her. Fuller's energies were also drained by an unsuccessful romance with James Nathan which left her feeling used and hurt. Still, she managed to write nearly 250 reviews and occasional essays for the *Tribune* over the next year and a half. By the summer of 1846 she had saved enough money to plan a trip to Europe and in August she sailed for England, shortly before her next book was published in New York.

Papers on Literature and Art, published in September 1846, contained critical reviews on English, American, and continental literature and art. Fuller's comments on American authors were uncannily accurate in an age that saw in Henry Wadsworth Longfellow the best that American poetry could offer: William Cullen Bryant's "range is not great, nor his genius fertile"; James Russell Lowell, "to the grief of some friends, and the disgust of more," was found "absolutely wanting in the true spirit and tone of poesy"; Longfellow was "a man of cultivated taste, delicate though not deep feeling, and some, though not much, poetic force." Emerson, to Fuller, took "the highest rank" among her contemporaries. The reception of *Papers on Literature and Art* was generally good: Fuller was praised for her candor, though some reviewers complained of "a tendency to philosophise beyond her powers." The book evidently sold well and a second printing was released in 1848.

It had been over ten years since Fuller had been forced to cancel her European trip when her father died, a postponement which doubtless made her journey at this time even more appreciated. She landed in England, met the literary giants of the time, including Carlyle and Wordsworth, and in November she sailed for the continent, settling in Paris, where she stayed until the following February. The American public was kept aware of her during this time; as one of the *Tribune*'s foreign correspondents, she contributed some three dozen travel letters to that paper. In April she took up residence at Rome and in the summer of 1847 made an extended tour through northern Italy, a trip reported on to the *Tribune*'s readers. What she did not report, even to her private correspondents, was that she had met and been captivated by an Italian count, Giovanni Ossoli, eleven years her junior.

Rome, as seen by Fuller when she returned in October, was in a state of turmoil. The Roman Revolution was in full swing and she was caught up by it: "I am deeply interested in this public drama, and wish to see it played out. Methinks I have *my part* therein, either as actor or historian." It was under these conditions that Fuller accepted Ossoli as her lover. Since it was already known that Ossoli supported the republicans, his marriage to this foreigner—and a non-Catholic at that—would have ended in his being disowned by his aristocratic family. As a result, though the affair was soon physically consummated, the marriage itself was delayed for nearly a year.

Romanticized version of Fuller's death.

Fuller spent a miserable winter, bothered by headaches and the interminable rains, and in July she moved to Rieti, near Rome, to await the birth of her child. On 5 September 1848 a boy, named Angelo, was born. Fuller spent the winter at Rieti, visiting Rome and Ossoli, a sergeant in the Civic Guard, only for short periods of time. In April 1849 she came to Rome, leaving her child behind with a wet nurse, and served well on hospital duty during the tumultuous and decisive months that followed. But Rome fell in July and the hopes of the Revolution with it. Both Ossoli, discredited by his support of the losing side, and Fuller, as a foreigner sympathetic with the rebels, were declared *personae non gratae* and were forced to leave. They returned to Rieti where they found Angelo ill, and, after nursing him back to health, journeyed to Florence in November.

Police pressures continued at Florence and combined with a diminishing amount of funds and Fuller's homesickness to force another move. The Ossolis planned to return to the United States, where she could arrange for the publication of her account of the Roman Revolution, then in manuscript. They sailed in May, despite her premonitions that the voyage would be ill-fated. It certainly began that way: the captain died of smallpox off Gibraltar, and Angelo was almost lost to the same disease during the crossing. On 18 July land was sighted but, as the ship approached, a storm rose, causing the inexperienced acting captain to run the vessel aground off shore, near Fire Island, New York, where it remained fast. The storm subsided and attempts were made to swim to the nearby beach. Fuller would not be separated from her husband and, though she encouraged others to make for shore, she resolutely resigned herself to death. The next day, after the storm resumed, she gave Angelo to a sailor in a last rescue effort; but she and Ossoli stayed aboard and, as the ship was finally pulled apart under the pounding of the sea, they drowned. The body of Angelo was washed ashore but the Ossolis—and her Roman manuscript—were never found.

Early studies of Fuller examined the woman, not the writer. The *Memoirs* of 1852 portrayed Fuller as an egotistical, intellectually aloof person, a picture that T. W. Higginson tried to balance in his 1884 biography. In this reaction to her life by contemporaries and later writers, one can trace the history of woman's position in America: as woman's role became less confining, the less "traditional" aspects of Fuller's life—her individualism, her aggressive intellectuality, her liaison with Ossoli—became more acceptable. Most recent studies have centered on her feminist positions, her interest in continental—and especially German—literatures, and her critical writings. Fuller wanted all women to be considered as individuals and not as types, and she put these ideas into action during her "Conversations" for women in Boston from 1839 to 1844, and in print with *Woman in the Nineteenth Century*, the first important feminist book by an American woman. This desire for equality extended to her criticism and she attempted to set standards by which writers were judged by their adherence to definite critical principles and not by the whim of a particular critic or time. Her views were radical for her day. But her activities had little effect: *Woman in the Nineteenth Century* produced no change in the position of her contemporaries, her promotion of foreign literature had little immediate influence, and no one adopted her critical standards.

Other Writings:

Conversations with Goethe in the Last Years of His Life—translation (Boston: Hilliard, Gray, 1839); *Gunderode*—translation (Boston: Elizabeth Peabody, 1842). The following were collected and edited posthumously by her brother, Arthur B. Fuller: *Woman in the Nineteenth Century, and Kindred Papers* (Boston: John P. Jewett, 1855); *At Home and Abroad* (Boston: Crosby, Nichols, 1856); *Life Without and Life Within* (Boston: Brown, Taggard & Chase, 1860); and *Art, Literature, and the Drama* (Boston: Brown, Taggard, & Chase, 1860). Collected editions of the previous four titles and the *Memoirs* in six volumes were published in 1860 (Boston: Brown, Taggard & Chase), 1869 (New York: Tribune Association), and 1874 (Boston: Roberts Brothers). Caroline Dall, *Margaret and Her Friends* (Boston: Roberts Brothers, 1895), reports a series of Conversations in 1841. Also: *Margaret Fuller: American Romantic*, ed. Perry Miller (Garden City, N.Y.: Doubleday, 1965; reprinted, Ithaca, N.Y.: Cornell University Press, 1970); *The Woman and the Myth: Margaret Fuller's Life and Writings*, ed. Bell Gale Chevigny (Old Westbury, N.Y.: Feminist Press, 1976); and *Margaret Fuller: Essays on American Life and Letters*, ed. Joel Myerson (New Haven: College and University Press, 1977).

Bibliographies:

Joel Myerson, *Margaret Fuller: A Descriptive Primary Bibliography* (Pittsburgh: University of Pittsburgh Press, forthcoming); Myerson, *Margaret Fuller: An Annotated Secondary Bibliography* (New York: Burt Franklin, 1977).

Biographies:

Ralph Waldo Emerson, William Henry Channing, and James Freeman Clarke, *Memoirs of Margaret Fuller Ossoli*, 2 vols.—includes selections from letters and journals (Boston: Phillips, Sampson, 1852); Thomas Wentworth Higginson, *Margaret Fuller Ossoli*—includes selections from letters (Boston: Houghton, Mifflin, 1884); Mason Wade, *Margaret Fuller: Whetstone of Genius* (New York: Viking, 1940); Madeleine B. Stern, *The Life of*

Margaret Fuller (New York: Dutton, 1942); Arthur W. Brown, *Margaret Fuller* (New York: Twayne, 1964); Joseph Jay Deiss, *The Roman Years of Margaret Fuller* (New York: Crowell, 1969).

Letters and Journals:

Love-Letters of Margaret Fuller 1845-1846 (New York: Appleton, 1903); *The Letters of Ralph Waldo Emerson*, ed. Ralph L. Rusk, 6 vols. (New York: Columbia University Press, 1939); Leona Rostenberg, "Margaret Fuller's Roman Diary," *Journal of Modern History*, 12 (June 1940): 209-220; Joel Myerson, "Margaret Fuller's 1842 Journal: At Concord with the Emersons," *Harvard Library Bulletin*, 21 (July 1973): 320-340.

Criticism:

Helen Neill McMaster, "Margaret Fuller as a Literary Critic," *University of Buffalo Studies*, 7 (December 1928): 35-100; Wilma R. Ebbitt, "Margaret Fuller's Ideas on Criticism," *Boston Public Library Quarterly*, 3 (July 1951): 171-187; Stanley M. Vogel, *German Literary Influences on the American Transcendentalists* (New Haven: Yale University Press, 1955); Francis Edward Kearns, "Margaret Fuller's Social Criticism," Ph.D. dissertation, University of North Carolina, 1960; Russell E. Durning, *Margaret Fuller, Citizen of the World. An Intermediary Between European and American Literatures* (Heidelberg: Carl Winter, 1969); Lawrence Buell, *Literary Transcendentalism: Style and Vision in the American Renaissance* (Ithaca, N.Y.: Cornell University Press, 1973); Marie Mitchell Olesen Urbanski, "Margaret Fuller's *Woman in the Nineteenth Century*," Ph.D. dissertation, University of Kentucky, 1973.

Papers:

The Fuller Family Papers are at the Houghton Library of Harvard University. Material used by Higginson in his biography is at the Boston Public Library.

WILLIAM HENRY FURNESS (20 April 1802-30 January 1896), Unitarian religious writer, was born in Boston and educated at the Boston Latin School, where he befriended Emerson. He graduated from Harvard College in 1820 and from the Divinity School in 1823. In 1825 he was ordained and installed as minister of the Unitarian Church in Philadelphia, a post he held until his death. Furness's most important work is his *Remarks on the Four Gospels* (Philadelphia: Carey, Lea & Blanchard, 1836). Contrary to the established Unitarian view that the miracles of the New Testament were performed as God's way of convincing man of the truth of Christianity, Furness argued that man has an intuitive perception of religious truths which requires no such confirmation, thus making Christianity depend upon the teachings of Christ rather than His supposed deeds. His book, published in the same year as Emerson's *Nature*, was an important influence on the Transcendentalists, applying as it did transcendental philosophy to Biblical criticism. Furness was also interested in the life of Christ and published the results of his studies in *Jesus and His Biographers*

(Philadelphia: Carey, Lea & Blanchard, 1838) and three subsequent works. In the area of social reform, Furness actively supported the anti-slavery cause. He also edited numerous Unitarian hymnbooks and was an early translator of German literature in America. His friendship with Emerson lasted until the latter's death; their correspondence is printed in *Records of a Lifelong Friendship* (Boston: Houghton Mifflin, 1910). REFERENCE: "William Henry Furness," in *Heralds of a Liberal Faith*, ed. Samuel A. Eliot (Boston: American Unitarian Association, 1910), 3:133-138. —*Joel Myerson*

William Lloyd Garrison

WILLIAM LLOYD GARRISON (10 December 1805-24 May 1879) is remembered as the foremost journalist of the anti-slavery cause, but he was intimately involved with the whole spectrum of humanitarian reform in the early nineteenth century, including the crusades for peace, for temperance, and for woman's rights, as well as abolition. He was born in Newburyport, Massachusetts, to parents recently arrived from Nova Scotia. After his father deserted the family in 1808, William Lloyd's childhood became a series of difficult adjustments. He served a partial apprenticeship as a shoemaker, ran away from another as cabinetmaker, and finally found his niche as a printer's apprentice in 1818. His youthful associations were solidly Baptist and Federalist; their rigidity imposed itself on Garrison's mind.

During his years as a printer's apprentice, Garrison, like Benjamin Franklin before him, honed his writing skills by composing essays for the paper, first anonymously and later in his own name. After completing his training he edited the *Newburyport Free Press* for six months, then did job printing for a time before taking over the *National Philanthropist* at Boston. He expanded the scope of this temperance paper to cover other reforms and imparted to it a militant tone. His crisp style attracted attention and brought him an invitation to edit the *Journal of the Times* at Bennington, Vermont.

Before leaving Boston, Garrison met the Quaker abolitionist Benjamin Lundy and was converted to the anti-slavery cause. He used the *Journal of the Times*, which he edited from October 1828 to April 1829, to attack both slavery and Andrew Jackson, and after Jackson's election Garrison moved to Baltimore to join Lundy in editing his peripatetic *Genius of Universal Emancipation*.

On his way to Baltimore Garrison stopped in Boston to deliver a ringing address in Park Street Church calling on all Christians to mount a crusade against slavery. He had already moved beyond Lundy's views, which favored gradual abolition and colonization of the slaves abroad, to a conviction in favor of immediate emancipation. Garrison was not long with the *Genius* before he was jailed for libelling a Newburyport slave ship owner. Released after forty-nine days by a contribution from the New York philanthropist Arthur Tappan, Garrison settled in Boston and began the *Liberator* in January 1831. The peroration of his opening editorial is his most famous utterance: "I am in earnest. I will not equivocate. I will not excuse. I will not retreat a

Wm. Lloyd Garrison

single inch. AND I *WILL* BE HEARD."

Garrison was as good as his word. For the next thirty-five years, in speeches and in the columns of the *Liberator*, he poured fiery invective on the heads of slaveholders and all those willing to compromise with slavery. His tirades made such an impression on the South that it came to be believed there that all Northerners, or at least all abolitionists, thought like Garrison. Yet in the North he was mobbed and threatened as well. His zeal led to the founding of the American Anti-Slavery Society in 1833, but also contributed to its breakup in 1840 because Garrison insisted that all reforms were one, that pacifism and woman's rights could not be shuffled aside in favor of the abolition crusade alone. Garrison almost single-handedly destroyed the American Colonization Society by persuading English abolitionists to shun it. But he wielded less and less influence in organized anti-slavery in America as those who had been won to the cause by his eloquence turned to political action, while Garrison, holding to the perfectionist creed, denounced the Constitution in the words of Jeremiah as "a covenant with death and an agreement with hell." From 1843 the *Liberator* carried on its masthead the motto, "No Union With Slaveholders," and Garrison maintained his secession position until, as he said, "death and hell" themselves seceded, when he took up the cause of the Union and backed Lincoln. With the Emancipation Proclamation and the Thirteenth Amendment he believed his work was ended, and he concluded the *Liberator* in December 1865. He remained a reformer but his later approach was more mellow than his earlier uncompromising stands, and he ended as a supporter of the "conservative" American Woman Suffrage Association in opposition to its "radical" rival. He died in New York City.

Garrison's later reputation has varied with the climate of opinion on race in America, but his preeminence as the spokesman of radical perfectionism has never been questioned. To the often windy rhetoric of mid-century reform he brought a prose which cut like a flaming sword through pompous periods and pious attitudes. Many disliked what Garrison said, but he said it so well that no one found it possible to ignore him. —*Linda Maloney*

Principal Works: *Liberator* (Boston, 1831-1865); *Thoughts on African Colonization* (Boston: Garrison & Knapp, 1832); *Selections from the Writings and Speeches of William Lloyd Garrison* (Boston: R. F. Walcutt, 1852); *Documents of Upheaval*, ed. Truman Nelson (New York: Hill & Wang, 1966); *The Letters of William Lloyd Garrison*, ed. Walter Merrill & Louis Ruchames, 4 vols. to date (Cambridge: Harvard University Press, 1971-).

Principal References: Wendell Phillips Garrison and Francis Jackson Garrison, *William Lloyd Garrison: the Story of His Life told by His Children*, 4 vols. (New York: Houghton, Mifflin, 1885-1889); Russel B. Nye, *William Lloyd Garrison and the Humanitarian Reformers* (Boston: Little, Brown, 1955); David A. Williams, "William Lloyd Garrison, the Historians, and the Abolition Movement," *Essex Institute Historical Collections* 98 (April 1962): 84-99; Walter M. Merrill, *Against Wind and Tide: A Biography of William Lloyd Garrison* (Cambridge: Harvard University Press, 1963); John L. Thomas, *The Liberator: William Lloyd Garrison* (Boston: Little, Brown, 1963), with an extensive bibliography of manuscript and printed sources; Aileen S. Kraditor, *Means and Ends in American Abolitionism: Garrison and His Critics on Strategy and Tactics* (New York: Random House, 1968).

SAMUEL GRISWOLD GOODRICH (19 August 1793-9 May 1860), author and publisher of juvenile literature, is known today for his series of Peter Parley books. Born at Ridgefield, Connecticut, Goodrich finished his formal education at age twelve and began clerking in 1808. Three years later he moved to Hartford and served briefly in the War of 1812. In 1816 he entered the publishing world by reprinting Walter Scott's *Family Bible* and in 1820 published John Trumbull's epic *M'Fingal*. He married in 1818 but his wife died four years later. During 1823-1824 he travelled in Europe. In England he met Hannah More, author of moralistic and didactic tales of instruction, and decided that his calling would be to write similar works, but for children. His first venture, *The Tales of Peter Parley About America* (Boston: Carter, Hendee, 1827), was an immediate success and launched Goodrich's career. Over the next thirty years Goodrich produced dozens of Peter Parley tales, which sold nearly 12,000,000 copies by the end of the century. Wanting to be closer to Boston, a leading publishing center, Goodrich, who had remarried in 1826, moved to Jamaica Plain in 1833. There he continued to write and publish his juvenile works and took an interest in politics, serving in the state legislature (1837-1838) and as United States Consul to Paris (1851-1853). In 1858 he returned to Connecticut but died there of a heart ailment soon afterwards. Goodrich's prolific career—he claimed to have written over 100 books and to have supervised the writing of another fifty—was based on crudely-illustrated, moralistic tales and textbooks for children. In addition to the Peter Parley tales, there were school textbooks such as readers, geographies (the first of which sold 2,000,000 copies), and histories (which at one time sold 50,000 copies annually), as well as magazines, *Parley's Magazine* (1833-1834) and *Robert Merry's Museum* (1841-1854). For adults, Goodrich published his own verse, *The Outcast and Other Poems* (Boston: Russell, Shattuck, & Williams, 1836), and edited *The Token* (1827-1842), an annual giftbook, which published some of the best authors of the day. Goodrich's writings reflected his shrill bias for things American, his lack of understanding of other cultures, his moralistic concerns, and often warned against the evils of slavery. By making a single narrator, Peter Parley ("an old silverhaired gentleman with a gouty foot and a wooden cane"), run through all his works, Goodrich achieved a continuity that appealed to children even more than his juvenile heroes, such as Dick Boldhero and Gilbert Go-Ahead, did. He helped Hawthorne in the early stages of his career, paying him for numerous contributions to *The Token* and for writing *Peter Parley's Universal History* (1845), and helped him to publish *Twice-Told Tales* (1837). REFERENCES: Samuel G. Goodrich, *Recollections of a Lifetime*, 2 vols. (New York & Auburn: Miller, Orton & Mulligan, 1856); Daniel Roselle, *Samuel Griswold Goodrich, Creator of Peter Parley* (Albany: State University of New York Press, 1968). —*Joel Myerson*

ASA GRAY (18 November 1810-30 January 1888), botanist, was born and raised in Sauquoit, New York. Although he graduated from Fairfield Medical School in 1831 with a M.D. degree, he never practiced medicine. He taught high school briefly, spending his summers on botanical field trips. On one of these he met the pioneer American botanist, John Torrey, whom he later collaborated with in writing *Flora of North America* (New York: Wiley & Putnam, 1838-1843). Gray's skill was quickly recognized and he was appointed curator of the New York Lyceum of Natural History in 1836, professor of botany at the University of Michigan in 1838 (though he resigned before ever visiting the school), and, finally, Fisher Professor of Natural History at Harvard College. In the latter post, which he held until his death, in Cambridge, he achieved his greatest fame and recognition as America's foremost botanist. Gray served as president of the American Academy of Arts and Sciences and the American Association for the Advancement of Science, contributed regularly to the *American Journal of Science* and the *Nation*, and authored numerous books, including his pioneering *Manual of the Botany of the Northern United States* (Boston: James Munroe, 1848). He is important as the chief

supporter of Charles Darwin in America.
REFERENCES: Jane Loring Gray, *Letters of Asa Gray*, 2 vols. (Boston: Houghton, Mifflin, 1893); A. Hunter Dupree, *Asa Gray* (Cambridge: Harvard University Press, 1959).

HORATIO GREENOUGH (6 September 1805-18 December 1852) was the first American to become a professional sculptor. The son of a wealthy Boston merchant, Greenough was reared in a cultural atmosphere. At Harvard College he pursued the normal course of classical studies, but his real interest was sculpting. He was certainly encouraged in this interest by Washington Allston, whom Greenough met in 1823 and often acknowledged as his spiritual father and aesthetic mentor. In 1825, when his class graduated, Greenough's diploma had to be sent to him because he was aboard a ship bound for Rome to study with Albert Bertel Thorswalden; subsequently spending most of the rest of his life in Europe with only infrequent trips to the United States. A friendship with James Fenimore Cooper resulted in a commission from the United States

Congress in 1832 for Greenough's most dubiously famous work: a colossal, seminude statue of George Washington modelled after Phidius's Zeus. A second oversized work, *The Rescue*, realistically depicting a mother and child being saved from an Indian attacker, was completed in 1851 and placed on a buttress of the Capitol portico. Greenough also produced a series of portrait busts and a number of idealistic pieces in bas-relief. Greenough's functional theories about art, as revealed in his periodical writings and his one book, *The Travels, Observations, and Experiences of a Yankee Stonecutter*, published under the pseudonym "Horace Bender," are his single most important legacy. He died in Somerville, Massachusetts. In his essays Greenough presented a democratic aesthetic which offered an alternative to the turgid European aesthetics he deplored, and proposed a theory to serve as the basis for a completely American art. This theory was the "organic" or "functional" theory which held that works which develop organically from the forces within a democratic society and in which function dictates form, like the sailing ship or the assembly line, are truly beautiful. Emerson enthusiastically accepted Greenough's organic aesthetic because he saw it as an expression of his own beliefs about art by a man much better equipped to discuss aesthetic principles. Thoreau, apparently in reaction to Emerson's enthusiasm, developed a strong dislike for Greenough. Ironically, Greenough's theory was brought to its most dramatic fulfillment in the architectural style of Louis Sullivan, who claimed that his principle of "form is function" was suggested by Whitman's *Leaves of Grass*.

—*Robert E. Burkholder*

Principal Works: *The Travels, Observations, and Experiences of a Yankee Stonecutter* (New York: Putnam's, 1852); *Form and Function: Remarks on Art by Horatio Greenough*, ed. Harold Small (Berkeley: University of California Press, 1947).

Principal References: *A Memorial of Horatio Greenough: Consisting of a Memoir, Selections from His Writings and Tributes to His Genius*, ed. Henry T. Tuckerman (New York: Putnam's, 1853); *Letters of Horatio Greenough to His Brother, Henry Greenough*, ed. Frances Boott Greenough (Boston: Ticknor, 1887); Charles R. Metzger, *Emerson and Greenough: Transcendental Pioneers of an American Esthetic* (Berkeley: University of California Press, 1954); *The Letters of Horatio Greenough*, ed. Nathalia Wright (Madison: University of Wisconsin Press, 1972).

EDWARD EVERETT HALE (3 April 1822-10 June 1909), Unitarian minister, essayist, and novelist, was representative of the changing society of the Boston Brahmins in the early nineteenth century. He possessed some of the typical advantages of the Brahmin group. His father, Nathan Hale, was a nephew of the famed Revolutionary War martyr, and editor and owner of the *Boston Daily Advertiser*. Young Hale's mother, Sarah Preston Everett, was a sister of prominent Unitarian clergyman and statesman Edward Everett, whose ministry at the Brattle Street Church had produced strong connections with such notables as Henry Clay. Edward Everett Hale also benefited from a typical Brahmin education. After preparatory work at the Boston Latin School, he entered Harvard College at the age of thirteen, and graduated second in the class of 1839, with membership in Phi Beta Kappa. Though he intended to pursue a career in the ministry, Hale spurned theological training, and occupied his time temporarily as an instructor at the Boston Latin School and writing essays for such journals as the *Boston Miscellany of Literature and Fashion*. Then in 1842 he preached a trial sermon before the Boston Association of Unitarian Ministers, was licensed to preach to that body, and in 1846 was appointed minister of the Church of the Unity in Worcester, Massachusetts. In 1856 he accepted a position as pastor of the South Congregational Church in Boston, when its minister, Frederic Huntington, left to serve as a professor at Harvard. Hale served as minister of the South Church until his resignation in 1899. The intermittent years produced literary activity typical of the liberal New England theologian and essayist. Although best known for his short story "The Man Without a Country," first published in the *Atlantic Monthly* in 1863, Hale penned three volumes of autobiography and wrote several fictional pieces. In 1903 he was appointed chaplain of the United States Senate, and died in Boston in 1909. REFERENCES: Edward Everett Hale, *Memoirs of a Hundred Years*, 2 vols. (New York: Macmillan, 1902); Jean Holloway, *Edward Everett Hale: A Biography* (Austin: University of Texas Press, 1956). —*Thomas L. Connelly*

SARAH JOSEPHA (BUELL) HALE (24 October 1788-30 April 1879), editor, poet, and novelist, was born in Newport, New Hampshire. She was well-educated in the classics by her family and her desire to learn continued after her marriage in 1813 to a lawyer, David Hale, as they studied together in the evenings. After the death of her husband in 1822, Hale turned to writing to support herself and her five children. In 1828, after publishing a volume of verse and a novel, *Northwood* (Boston: Bowles & Dearborn, 1827), she accepted the editorship of the *Ladies' Magazine* and moved to Boston. Her work attracted the attention of a competitor, Louis Godey, and in 1836 he offered to buy her magazine (since 1834 called the *American Ladies' Magazine*) and merge it with his own *Lady's Book*. The first number of the new *Lady's Book*, with Hale as editor, appeared in January 1837, and in 1840 its title was changed to *Godey's Lady's Book*. Hale, who moved permanently to Philadelphia in 1841, continued to edit the magazine until 1877. As an editor, Hale was outstanding: through the use of color illustrations of the latest fashions and original contributions by nearly all the famous American authors of the day, she raised the circulation of the magazine to 150,000 at its peak. Although Hale devoted much space to discussing "woman's role," she was too much rooted in the eighteenth century to deny the traditional distinction between the sexes: man was physically stronger and the breadwinner, while woman, weaker in strength but spiritually superior, provided moral guidance and uplifting. She often criticized those female reformers who left the home for the "man's world" by lecturing in public for woman's rights. Yet she did complain about woman's intellectual inferiority with man, which she considered the result of poor training rather than an inherent quality, and she championed greater educational opportunities for women. Her most famous publication is *Woman's Record: or Sketches of All Distinguished Women, from the Creation to A.D. 1854* (New York: Harpers, 1855), one of the first biographical dictionaries devoted exclusively to women. Godey's editorial policy of noncontroversy limited Hale's reform activities but she was an important advocate of many public campaigns, including raising funds for the Bunker Hill Monument and for making Mount Vernon a national shrine, and declaring Thanksgiving a national holiday. In later years she proved a tireless author of her own instructional works and editor of writings by others, producing nearly fifty volumes by her death. Her views of woman's role and "woman's sphere" are summed up in *Manners; or, Happy Homes and Good Society All the Year Round* (Boston: J. E. Tilton, 1868). REFERENCES: Ruth E. Finley, *The Lady of Godey's* (Philadelphia: J. B. Lippincott, 1941); Isabelle Webb Entriken, *Sarah Josepha Hale and "Godey's Lady's Book"* (Philadelphia: Lancaster Press, 1946).

—*Joel Myerson*

Nathaniel Hawthorne

Arlin Turner
Duke University

BIRTH: Salem, Massachusetts, 4 July 1804.

MARRIAGE: Sophia Amelia Peabody (1811-1871), 9 July 1842. Children: Una (1844-1877), Julian (1846-1934), Rose (1852-1926).

DEATH: Plymouth, New Hampshire, 19 May 1864.

MAJOR WORKS: *Fanshawe, A Tale* (Boston: Marsh & Capen, 1828); *Twice-Told Tales* (Boston: American Stationers Co., 1837); *Mosses from an Old Manse*, 2 vols. (New York: Wiley & Putnam, 1846); *The Scarlet Letter* (Boston: Ticknor, Reed & Fields, 1850); *The House of the Seven Gables* (Boston: Ticknor, Reed & Fields, 1851); *The Snow-Image, and Other Twice-Told Tales* (Boston: Ticknor, Reed & Fields, 1852); *The Blithedale Romance* (Boston: Ticknor, Reed & Fields, 1852); *The Marble Faun: or, The Romance of Monte Beni*, 2 vols. (Boston: Ticknor & Fields, 1860); *Our Old Home: A Series of English Sketches* (Boston: Ticknor & Fields, 1863).

Life and Career:

In sketches, tales, and romances published in the second third of the nineteenth century, Hawthorne chose mainly American materials, drawing especially on the history of colonial New England and his native Salem in the time of his early American ancestors. Heir to the Puritan tradition and alert to the transcendental thought prominent in his region and time, he subjected both to his skeptical, questioning scrutiny in the moral and psychological probing that is characteristic of his fictional works. Considering guilt—actual or imagined, revealed or concealed—to be a universal human experience, he traced out in his characters the types and the effects of guilt. The seriousness of his literary purpose, his independence of mind, and his intellectual and artistic integrity were recognized by Herman Melville and others of his contemporaries. He placed a number of characters and scenes among the most memorable in world literature; he was master of a prose style that is individual, simple and direct, and yet richly varied. In the habit of seeing meanings in everything, he thought in symbols and wrote in symbols which often are so commonplace and natural as to escape notice. Melville in his own time and Henry James and William Faulkner later are among the authors who have been influenced by

Portrait of Hawthorne painted by Charles Osgood in 1840.

Hawthorne, particularly by his symbolic method and his attention to the dark elements in human experience. Through both direct statement and example, he helped define for his age the literary sketch, the tale, and long fiction which fuses romance and psychological realism.

Nathaniel Hawthorne was born in Salem, Massachusetts, where his paternal ancestors had been prominent since the founding generation. (In England and America the family name had been spelled both with and without *w*; the novelist first spelled it with *w* about 1827.) When he began writing fiction, he was drawn into a search for material in the careers of his early ancestors and in the history of colonial New England. The first American ancestor, William Hathorne (1606?-1681), who pronounced sentence on early Quakers, is reflected in the tale "The Gentle Boy." The role of his son, John (1641-1717), as a magistrate during the witch trials of 1692 contributed to a number of Hawthorne's works which include the lore of witchcraft, the idea of a hereditary curse, and the effect of one generation on another. Hawthorne's grandfather, Daniel Hathorne, a sea captain who sailed as a privateersman during the Revolution, was the hero of an encounter narrated in a ballad, "Bold Hathorne."

IN TESTIMONY WHEREOF, I have hereunto subscribed my name, and affixed the Seal of my Office, at the Port of Liverpool, this *16*

Day of *May* . 185*7* ———

Nath' Hawthorne

Consular document.

Hawthorne's birthplace in Salem.

The maternal antecedents of the novelist, the Mannings, were yeomen who came over nearly as early as the Hathornes and developed a line of self-reliant citizens in the new land. Hawthorne grew up in the Manning household from the age of four, when his father, Nathaniel Hathorne (1775-1808), a ship captain, died in Surinam. Realizing early that he had special gifts, the Mannings furnished the private schooling needed, sent him to Bowdoin College (1821-1825), and supported him through a dozen years of literary apprenticeship.

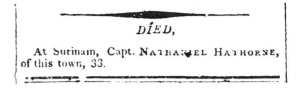

DÍED,

At Surinam, Capt. NATHANIEL HATHORNE, of this town, 33.

Newspaper obituary notice, 1808.

Before entering college, Hawthorne had spent some months on the undeveloped land owned by the Mannings at Raymond, Maine, where he roamed in the forests on the shores of Lake Sebago and where, he said afterward, he got his habit of solitude. He also had published, by hand lettering for family circulation, a newspaper, "The Spectator," in which he evidenced, besides uncommon care and patience, an aptness in composition and a turn of mind that would appear prominently in his later writings. At college his best records were in composition and languages. He graduated in the middle of his class, having spent much of his time, it seems, in the reading of literary authors not included in the curriculum. Among his college mates, several were to remain his close friends: Horatio Bridge, who was his most intimate friend for the rest of his life; Franklin Pierce, whose biography he wrote for the presidential campaign of 1852; Jonathan Cilley, who was killed in a duel soon after being elected to Congress, and for whom he wrote a memorial sketch in 1838; and Henry Wadsworth Longfellow, with whom he had a mutually satisfying personal and literary friendship.

While still at college, Hawthorne began writing tales or a romance or both. In 1828, he published at his own expense a romance, *Fanshawe*. At about the same time a collection, to be entitled "Tales of My Native Land," was accepted for publication by a Salem printer, Ferdinand Andrews, but it was withdrawn before publication and at least some of the tales were burned. Another collection, "Provincial Tales," also failed of publication.

Fanshawe is a story of concealed identity, abduction, flight, and pursuit, reflecting the author's reading in Sir Walter Scott and the Gothic romances. It is set at a college identifiable in many details as Bowdoin College. Some of the characters have touches of individuality and portions of the scene have convincing reality, indicating a reliance on observation to modify the conventions of the romance of adventure being followed. The plot is well conceived and well managed; but in many chapters the book reads like a scenario rather than a fleshed-out work of fiction.

Bowdoin College in 1821.

With the firmness of decision that was a lifelong characteristic of his, Hawthorne withdrew *Fanshawe* and destroyed as many copies as possible, including those in the hands of friends and relatives; and he did not include it afterward among his acknowledged works. The titles and the subject matter Hawthorne's sister Elizabeth remembered from her reading of the "Tales of My Native Land" in manuscript indicate that those tales were, like *Fanshawe*, narratives of adventure and mystery. One of the tales believed to have escaped the fire, "Alice Doane's Appeal," has an author read to his listeners on Gallows Hill, where the witches were hanged in 1692, a tale of mistaken identity, abduction, murder, and supposed incest. As published, the action of this inner story appears only in a few scenes and summaries of others, leaving the focus on the author's response and that of his listeners to the story of wizardry and horror at the scene of the witch hangings. In reviewing a book by William Gilmore Simms in 1846, Hawthorne remarked that it was "time to break up and fling away" the model by which historical novels had been written by Simms and Sir Walter Scott. His own action in destroying *Fanshawe* and the "Seven Tales" signaled a turn toward the new type of fiction he had concluded was required.

The first story Hawthorne published, "The Hollow of the Three Hills" (1830), is of the new type. A short, compact narrative presenting but one scene, it yet embodies many of the materials and the qualities of style, method, and outlook that have come to be recognized as Hawthornesque. It is a tale of guilt, or rather, a tale of the effects of guilt on a

FANSHAWE,

A TALE.

" Wilt thou go on with me ?"—SOUTHEY.

BOSTON :
MARSH & CAPEN, 362 WASHINGTON STREET.
PRESS OF PUTNAM AND HUNT.
1828.

young woman for whom a witch calls up sounds, not sights, reminding her of the sorrow and suffering she has caused parents, husband, and child. Details of the scene are spare, each item bearing symbolic meaning that is the more effective for being so natural as almost to conceal itself. Little is said literally or exactly, but through indefiniteness and suggestion the reader is induced to supply in his own imagination the conclusions, the meanings, the significances that the author has brought to his attention but has not propounded.

This tale was published in the *Salem Gazette*, as were several other tales and sketches (probably without pay). In the early 1830s Hawthorne prepared the manuscript for a two-volume collection to be entitled "The Story-Teller." It contained pieces he had attempted earlier to publish as "Provincial Tales," some of them probably held over from the "Seven Tales of My Native Land." They were enclosed within the narrative framework of the Story-Teller's travels over New England and westward to Detroit, reciting his stories from the platform. Hawthorne had begun by 1830 or earlier travelling in the summer to accumulate materials for

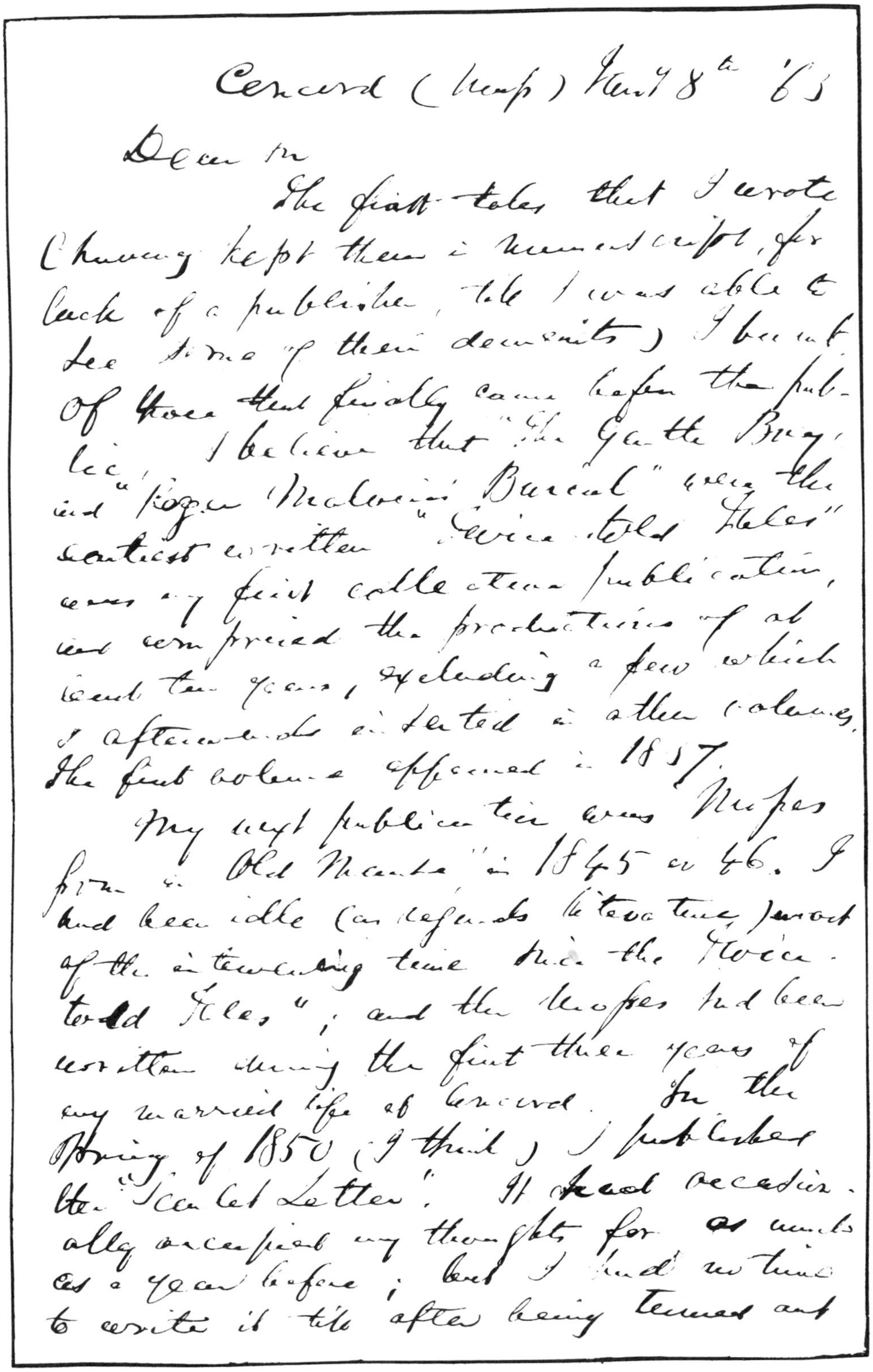

Concord (Mass.) Jan.y 8th '63

Dear Sir

The first tales that I wrote (having kept them in manuscript, for lack of a publisher, till I was able to see some of their demerits) I burnt. Of those that finally came before the public, I believe that "The Gentle Boy," and "Roger Malvin's Burial" were the earliest written. "Twice-told Tales" was my first collection publication, and comprised the productions of at least ten years, excluding a few which I afterwards inserted in other volumes. The first volume appeared in 1837.

My next publication was "Mosses from an Old Manse" in 1845 or 46. I had been idle (as regards literature) most of the intervening time since the "Twice-told Tales"; and the Mosses had been written during the first three years of my married life at Concord. In the Spring of 1850 (I think) I published the "Scarlet Letter". It had occasionally occupied my thoughts for as much as a year before; but I had no time to write it till after being turned out

Hawthorne to Samuel M. Cleaveland, 8 January 1863.

EDITORIAL NOTICE.

Owing to circumstances unforeseen when we assumed the charge of this periodical, (in March last,) the present Number will probably terminate our connection with it. The brevity of our continuance in the Chair Editorial will excuse us from any lengthened ceremony in resigning it. In truth, there is very little to be said on the occasion. We have endeavoured to fill our pages with a pleasant variety of wholesome matter. The reader must judge how far the attempt has been successful. It is proper to remark that we have not had full controul over the contents of the Magazine; inasmuch as the embellishments have chiefly been selected by the executive officers of the Boston Bewick Company, or by the engravers themselves; and our humble duty has consisted merely in preparing the literary illustrations. In some few cases, perhaps, the interests of the work might have been promoted by allowing the Editor the privilege of a veto, at least, on all engravings which were to be presented to the Public under his auspices, and for which his taste and judgment would inevitably be held responsible. In general, however, the embellishments have done no discredit either to the artists or their employers. Any causes, which may hitherto have impeded the prosperity of the concern, will probably be done away in future, and the Magazine be rendered worthier of the public favour, both as regards Literature and Art.

Hawthorne's notice terminating his editing of the American Magazine *(August 1836).*

literary use. He had set out in the summer of 1832 to make observations he could use in the frame narrative of the Story-Teller's travels. At least as early as 1835, he had kept a notebook in which he set down ideas for stories and recorded material from his observation and his reading. A number of the ideas were developed later in tales and sketches, and many descriptive and narrative passages were moved, with only slight changes, from the notebooks to fictional works. Failing to find a publisher for the Story-Teller manuscript, Hawthorne permitted it to be broken up and the stories and sketches to be published separately, sometimes with portions of the travel narrative included. Some of the contents appeared in *The Token*, an annual in which Samuel G. Goodrich had first published work by Hawthorne in 1831; Park Benjamin published portions of the manuscript, first in the *New-England Magazine* and later in the *American Monthly Magazine*.

Upon leaving college, Hawthorne returned to what he called his "chamber under the eaves" in the Manning house on Herbert Street in Salem, where he lived for a dozen years in some degree of seclusion, which he probably exaggerated in writing about it afterward. Modest funds that came from the Mannings made it possible for him to pass this extended literary apprenticeship in musing, dreaming, and thinking, he said, and in reading, writing, and burning much of what he wrote. The character Oberon, whose name Hawthorne had used in signing letters to Horatio Bridge, appears in the story "The Devil in Manuscript" and in the sections of the "Story-Teller" framework published as "Fragments from the Journal of a Solitary Man." Oberon is a fusion of what Hawthorne was and what he liked to pretend he was: a young author of high ambitions and a devotion to literature, who found no favor with the public and in a mood of ironic protest burned his manuscripts. Hawthorne spoke often in later years about the manuscripts he had burned, but it has to be noted that he destroyed and disowned them, as with *Fanshawe*, not simply because the public was indifferent, but because he had come to think the works unworthy.

THE TOKEN

AND

ATLANTIC SOUVENIR

A

CHRISTMAS AND NEW YEAR'S PRESENT

EDITED BY S. G. GOODRICH.

BOSTON.
PUBLISHED BY CHARLES BOWEN.
MDCCCXXXVII.

At the end of his seclusion under the eaves, Hawthorne went to Boston as the editor, from March to August 1836, of the *American Magazine of Useful and Entertaining Knowledge,* for which, with aid from his sister Elizabeth, he wrote or excerpted from other publications the entire contents of each number. Leaving the position because his salary was not paid and he did not have full control over the contents, he wrote, again with Elizabeth's help, *Peter Parley's Universal History* (1837) for a series published by Goodrich. In 1837, Goodrich arranged for the publication of *Twice-Told Tales,* with Horatio Bridge silently guaranteeing the publisher against loss. This volume contained tales and sketches, all previously published and some of them the best Hawthorne ever wrote.

TWICE-TOLD TALES.

BY

NATHANIEL HAWTHORNE.

BOSTON:
AMERICAN STATIONERS CO.
JOHN B. RUSSELL.
1837.

"The Gray Champion" was chosen to open the book, probably because it had several lines of appeal to readers: the patriotic tone, the recalling of the struggle for national independence, the mystery of the champion's identity, and the assurance that he will return at future times of danger. Other tales drawing heavily on early New England history include "The Maypole of Merry Mount," which shows the early Puritan colonists in conflict with the Anglicans under Thomas Morton. In Hawthorne's questioning mind, the Merry Mounters merit his and the reader's sympathy, as their bright, carefree existence is destroyed by the company of grim Puritans under John Endicott, but he makes it clear that the Puritans are capable of founding a nation and the Merry Mounters are not. Even the sternest Puritan of them all, Endicott, is softened by the love he sees in the Lord and the Lady of the May, who in turn join the Puritan colony without a regretful glance backward. Here, as is normal with Hawthorne, the moral tones first appear as opposing light and dark, but later are fused into gray. In "The Gentle Boy," sympathy flows to the Quakers, as the weak and oppressed in their struggle against the Puritans, particularly in the person of the boy, who has been orphaned in the hanging of his father by the colonial government. The tale is less a study of theological, social, or governmental issues than an exploration of human nature and character. The Quaker episode in Massachusetts history furnished Hawthorne suitable and impressive situations into which to place his characters for study, as did witchcraft in others of his works, and alchemy in still others. His habit was to open questions rather than to close them, to ask whether there might be more than one side, to portray character and action against tentative and evolving, rather than absolute, criteria. The Puritans and the Quakers of "The Gentle Boy" are both fanatics.

Several sketches in *Twice-Told Tales* record the author's observations about his native town, presented in the whimsy, the irony, and the fusion of the literal and the imaginative that were congenial to his mind: "Sunday at Home," "Little Annie's Ramble," "A Rill from the Town Pump," and "Sights from a Steeple." Several tales explore themes that would appear again and again in his later works: in "The Minister's Black Veil," the universality of sin and the isolation it produces; in "The Great Carbuncle," the varieties of motivation among seekers after an ideal; in "The Prophetic Pictures," the powers and the responsibilities of the artist; in "The Hollow of the Three Hills," the effects of guilt on both guilty and victim; in "Fancy's Show Box," the concept of sin in the heart. "The Wedding Knell" has a funeral knell ironically but appropriately sounded at the marriage of an aged

Sophia Hawthorne's drawing for The Gentle Boy *(1842).*

couple, the bride twice married already and the groom an unworldly man who has remained faithful to their early engagement. "Dr. Heidegger's Experiment" is a farcical experiment of three white-bearded men and a withered woman who have drunk the water of the fountain of youth. Two of the tales are clearly from the repertoire of the Story-Teller: "The Vision of the Fountain," a slight tale of youthful sentiment supposedly read to an audience of young women, and "Mr. Higginbotham's Catastrophe," an extravagant narrative of coincidence with implications as to the nature of rumor.

After Hawthorne had left the editorship of the *American Magazine of Useful and Entertaining Knowledge,* college-mates of his attempted to place him in another editorship or as historian on an expedition to the South Seas. Late in 1837, he became acquainted with Elizabeth, Mary, and Sophia

Peabody, who had been neighbors in his childhood and now, living in Salem after an absence of several years, pursued an acquaintance with him and his sisters. Elizabeth Peabody wrote an essay-review of *Twice-Told Tales* for the *New-Yorker* of March 1838—the longest review yet published—in which she declared that Hawthorne had more clearly the marks of a genius than any other writer of fiction in his time. With her usual readiness to champion good causes, she urged the historian George Bancroft, at the time collector of customs at Boston, to assist Hawthorne to a political appointment. Bancroft named him a measurer in the Boston custom house, where he served two years, beginning in January 1839.

At about the same time, Hawthorne became engaged to Sophia Peabody, after it had been assumed by many, perhaps including both Sophia

Sophia Peabody Hawthorne.

and Elizabeth, that his greater interest was in Elizabeth. Accepting at face value the report another young woman of Salem, Mary Croninshield Silsbee, gave him on Louis O'Sullivan's conduct toward her, he was ready in February 1838 to challenge O'Sullivan to a duel on her account; but explanations were made and he and O'Sullivan became generous friends. O'Sullivan had solicited contributions from him when he founded the *Democratic Review* and had begun publishing Hawthorne with the number for October 1837.

Hawthorne was a commendable officer of the customs, and he was pleased to learn that he could hold his own among men of practical affairs; but he discovered that he could not write fiction under the circumstances, in fact could not even write in his notebook. Through the Peabody sisters, he was drawn into the edges of "the Newness" and found that his own thought corresponded at many points with the Transcendentalism being propounded in the Transcendental Club, in the *Dial*, in the "Conversations" being conducted by Margaret Fuller and others, and in the social gatherings in

which he found himself occasionally, in spite of a reluctance to be drawn out of his solitude. When the Brook Farm community was organized under the leadership of George Ripley, he joined the "band of dreamers" and, on 12 April 1841, arrived at the West Roxbury farm, nine miles from Boston. The belief underlying the communal experiment at Brook Farm was that, by the sharing of labor and the fruits of labor, members of the community would be able to make a living and still have time left over in which to practice the arts. Expecting to make a home for his fiancee there, Hawthorne invested $1,000 in the venture and later advanced $500 toward the construction of a house. He was elected an officer in the community. In spite of his normal skepticism of reform efforts and his inclination to act alone, he had faith enough in his fellowmen, he said, and confidence enough in this endeavor, to commit himself and his savings—though such prominent idealists and Transcendentalists as Ralph Waldo Emerson, Henry David Thoreau, and Margaret Fuller held back. Finding again that he lacked the time he required for the thinking, musing, and dreaming he must have to write fiction, he withdrew from full membership in August to become a boarder, and at the end of October left the community. He did not regain any of the money he had invested.

Feeling some assurance of an income from his pen, particularly from contributions to the *Democratic Review*, he was married to Sophia Peabody on 9 July 1842. The letters he had written her during the three and a half years of their engagement, later published with others of his letters to her, reveal his imaginative and idealistic and also thoroughly human qualities. He rented the Old Manse at Concord and began three years of idyllic existence in what he and his bride often called a new Eden. Although he had Emerson and other Transcendentalists as neighbors, and although he had in common with them an emphasis on spirit and a habit of seeing and speaking in symbols, he held back from their enthusiasms and their extremes. In "The Old Manse," an autobiographical sketch introducing *Mosses from an Old Manse*, a collection of his writings at Concord, he stated that the "mountain atmosphere" of Emerson's thought, "in the brains of some people, wrought a singular giddiness," and in another sketch, "The Hall of Fantasy," he said that "sometimes, the truth assumes a mystic unreality and shadowyness" in Emerson's grasp. Hawthorne's inclinations, influenced perhaps by an intellectual affinity with his Puritan ancestors and by observations of his fellow beings, were not to follow

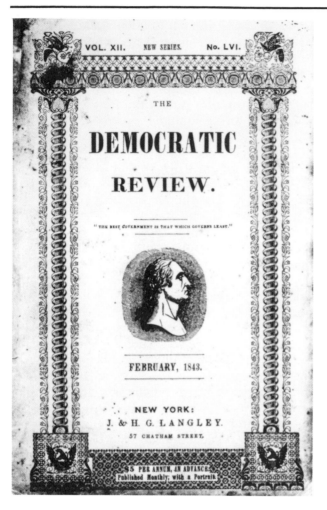

Front wrapper for the Democratic Review *containing "The New Adam and Eve."*

Emerson in denying the existence of evil, and not to conclude, as Herman Melville felt he must, that the existence of evil would argue for the rejection of the creator of the universe. In Hawthorne's pragmatic view, man is a creature of limitations, who nevertheless possesses the ability to choose among possibilities, and is subject to an iron necessity of cause and effect, an inevitability of consequences. A universe would not make sense to him in which the chain of necessity might be broken by either chance or divine whim. Thoreau was more welcome company to Hawthorne than Emerson, Amos Bronson Alcott, Ellery Channing, Margaret Fuller, or any of his other neighbors at Concord, perhaps in part because each could respect the other's silences. He and Thoreau were often together, rowing or skating on the Concord River or walking on the neighboring paths. He left enough comment in his sketches, notebooks, and letters to suggest that, while recognizing the quirks in Thoreau's nature, he

appreciated the qualities of his mind and character more justly than did anyone else in his time.

The Old Manse in Concord.

Although Hawthorne did not have interferences to literary work at the Old Manse such as he had experienced in the Boston custom house and at Brook Farm, many of the tales he wrote there seem not to have evolved in the musing and dreaming that produced his early tales, but to have been planned as variants on a predetermined pattern. There may be a partial explanation in his hopes to support his family by his pen and hence the compulsion under which he finished stories and sent them to O'Sullivan for the *Democratic Review.* Following a miscarriage in February 1843, his wife had her first child, Una, on 3 March 1844. Several of the tales and sketches of these years display items of curious interest, individually or taken together ("A Virtuoso's Collection," "P's Correspondence," "The Intelligence Office"); others assemble persons ("A Select Party," "The Hall of Fantasy"); still others catalogue series of manifestations of an idea ("The Procession of Life," "The New Adam and Eve," "The Christmas Banquet," "Earth's Holocaust," "Egotism; or, The Bosom Serpent"). "The Celestial Railroad" is an adaptation of *The Pilgrim's Progress* for satirizing current theological and philosophical shortcuts to heaven. Three of the tales written at the Old Manse rank with the best of the earlier ones; they include the probing into the complexities of human character and human motives that characterizes Hawthorne's best work, the same speculation and balancing of possibilities. "The Birthmark" presents the inevitable tragic consequences of a noble but unnatural and misguided devotion to perfection. "Rappaccini's Daughter" employs a luxuriant setting to present the legends of poisons and antidotes, the lore of man's attempts to modify nature for his own purposes, the complex interrelations of parental affection, conjugal love, isolation, generosity, tolerance, jealousy, rivalry. In "The Artist of the Beautiful," Hawthorne returns to the nature of artistic creation, the rewards of the artist, and the artist in society. These three tales draw on the traditions of alchemy and science to explore man's purposes in the realms of plants, animals, and human beings. They concern themselves with the miscarriage or the misunderstanding of noble intentions, the narrow line separating good from evil in the results of human actions. In these three stories, the author allows full play of his creative imagination on moral and psychological questions.

It had been Hawthorne's assumption that he could supplement his income by some kind of literary drudgery, as editor or as writer of school books, or that he could have another political appointment. When the owner of the Old Manse wanted it for his own use, Hawthorne moved to Salem in October 1845. He had begun preparing a collection of the tales and sketches written at Concord, along with others of earlier date not included in the original *Twice-Told Tales* or in the second volume added in the new edition of 1842. *Mosses from an Old Manse* was published in two volumes in June 1846. The introductory essay, "The Old Manse," is descriptive and autobiographical, as is another essay, "Buds and Bird Voices," and taken together they furnish the tone and many details of existence at the Manse. "The Old Manse" was written after the move to Salem and was intended as a summary assessment of this special episode in the author's life and of his associates at Concord.

The Custom-House in Salem.

In April 1846, Hawthorne was installed as surveyor of the port of Salem. For several years he had kept alive his candidacy for an appointment such as the Salem postmastership. Late in 1845 his friends renewed their efforts, for his funds were so depleted that he had to borrow from Horatio Bridge to pay for the move to Salem and had no choice but to move into spare rooms in the Manning house on Herbert Street. His supporters spoke mainly about his literary achievement, but in the official letter of appointment, George Bancroft referred to his memorial essay on Jonathan Cilley, a Democratic Congressman. His pay as surveyor was to have been $1,200 a year, but it was probably no more than $900, because the fees collected at the port were decreasing as the shipping decreased. Mrs. Hawthorne applied her artistic talents in the decoration of lamp shades and screens as a means of augmenting the family income.

Hawthorne's Custom-House Stencil.

After the Whigs had won the national election and local party members had demanded that the appointees of the previous Democratic administration be replaced by Whigs, Hawthorne received notice on 8 June 1849 that he was removed from the custom house. Disappointed that fellow townsmen of his, including friends of long standing, were the ones who sought his removal, and that no significant defense was offered locally, and faced with the necessity to earn support for his family (his second child, Julian, had been born in 1846), he at first hoped to be reinstated. Editors of Democratic newspapers and friends of both parties protested at his removal, arguing that his appointment had not been political. After a time Hawthorne became reconciled, but hardly forgiving of those who had made false charges against him, such as Charles W. Upham, a Salem minister turned politician. It may be, as some believed at the time, that Hawthorne had Upham in mind when he drew the character Judge

Buds and Bird-Voices.
By Nathaniel Hawthorne,

Manuscript of "Buds and Bird Voices."

Various bindings for Twice-Told Tales.

Contents pages for The Token *(1837) with Hawthorne's
contributions marked.*

The House of the Seven Gables in Salem.

Pyncheon in *The House of the Seven Gables*.

Although Hawthorne had declared it his intention not to write any more short pieces for the magazines, he had begun during his years in the Salem custom house planning and perhaps writing tales for a new collection. After being turned out of office, he took up his literary pen again and proceeded with one of the tales intended for the new collection that interested him particularly, the story of a young woman in Boston condemned to wear the letter "A" on her bosom. He accepted the suggestion of James T. Fields that this story be published separately, although he feared that the other stories intended to accompany it would be needed to relieve its gloom. He was able to write *The Scarlet Letter* rapidly, he noted afterward; once he had got his pitch, he "could then go on interminably." His pitch was determined in part by his removal from the

Salem custom house, the death of his mother, on 31 July 1849, and his observations of his two children as they played patient and doctor during her final illness. He wrote an introductory essay, "The Custom House," to summarize his ties to his native town through heritage and affection, to defend himself against those who brought about his removal from the custom house, and to narrate his presumed discovery of a scarlet letter and an accompanying manuscript left by a predecessor, Surveyor Pue. One purpose of the introductory essay was to lighten the tone of the book, but a more important purpose was the same as for "The Old Manse," to report and evaluate a closed episode in his life, giving it a clear shape and meaning that would enable him to dismiss it from his mind, or at least to put it in perspective with the preceding generations of his ancestors who had mixed their dust with the dust of Salem. He remarked afterward that his readers probably liked "The Custom House" more than *The Scarlet Letter*, having in mind the treatment of the controversy over his removal from office; but he realized that here, as in "The Old Manse," he was at his best in the whimsical interplay of the literal and the fanciful, the ironic view of himself in the circumstances described. In autobiographical narratives, he intermixed fanciful elements, such as might appear in his fiction, and thus was better able to see and to present the essential truth of the matter in hand. "The Custom House" is important, moreover, for its definition—the earliest of the four he wrote in commenting on his four romances—of the romance, such as he conceived *The Scarlet Letter* to be, as distinct from the novel. So long as the writer of a romance, he said, holds to psychological truth, he may employ "a neutral ground" between fiction and reality, "a sort of poetic or fairy precinct" where actualities will not be so necessary as in a novel.

THE

SCARLET LETTER,

A ROMANCE.

BY

NATHANIEL HAWTHORNE.

BOSTON:
TICKNOR, REED, AND FIELDS.
M DCCC L.

In *The Scarlet Letter*, Hawthorne turned back to the age of his first American ancestor for a historical background against which to display a tragic drama of guilt—revealed and concealed, real and imagined—and its effects on those touched by the guilt. It is a short narrative, dramatic in its presentation through memorable scenes, particularly the three scaffold scenes symmetrically arranged at the beginning, the middle, and the end of the plot. The substance of the book is moral, religious, theological; the characters confront questions endemic to the Puritan community at Boston in the middle of the seventeenth century. This substance is not at issue; it is given and is accepted by the author and by his characters. What is at issue includes primarily the psychological effects produced in the characters by the background and the situation as given. Few works in all literatures equal *The Scarlet Letter* in intensity, compression, and effective use of images and symbols.

Hawthorne published, in 1851, his final collection of short pieces, *The Snow-Image and Other Twice-Told Tales*, which contains two of his best stories, along with others left over from previous collections. "Main Street" traces the history of Salem through a dioramic record of its Main Street, later Essex Street, accenting the elements Hawthorne found most useful in his fiction. "Ethan Brand," first intended to be a part of a longer work and published as "A Chapter from an Abortive Romance," presents the age-old concept of an unpardonable sin through a lime-burner who returns from a world-wide search with the realization that the unpardonable sin is in his own heart. For scene and character it drew heavily on notebook observations Hawthorne had recorded during a visit in the summer of 1838 to North Adams in western Massachusetts. In 1851, a new edition of the *Twice-Told Tales* was issued, with a dedicatory letter that is one of the author's most perceptive essays in self-criticism.

Hawthorne said in "The Custom House" that he would be henceforth "a citizen of somewhere else," and would bring up his children elsewhere. In April 1850, he took his family to Boston and in July settled at Lenox, in the Berkshires of western Massachusetts, where he had as a neighbor Herman Melville, living at Pittsfield. Melville published one of the major pieces of Hawthorne criticism ("Hawthorne and His Mosses") and apparently was influenced by his acquaintance with Hawthorne and his works to modify his plan for *Moby-Dick* in midcourse of composition. Hawthorne wrote *The House of the Seven Gables* and the first of two works adapting classical myths for children, *A Wonder-Book for Girls and Boys*. The second, *Tanglewood Tales*, appeared in 1853. A decade earlier Hawthorne had published three children's books, later collected under the title *Grandfather's Chair* (1841), recounting episodes from American history, and afterward *Biographical Stories for Children* (1842). Since he published "Little Annie's Ramble" in 1835, he had felt that he had talents in writing for children and might turn to such writing to earn a living.

The House of the Seven Gables is set in the Salem of the author's time and includes scenes and some characters such as he might have found on the streets he knew. The dominant theme of the romance, the weight of the past on subsequent generations, leads into a background of wizardry and hereditary evil, such as is suggested by the seven-gabled house, with its secret stairway, secret compartment, dim legends, and accretions of wrong from a distant past, manifested in the dwarfed chickens and the poisoned well. Again Hawthorne drew upon the history of his region and his family, including the legend of the lost deed to extensive lands and the working out of an inherited curse pronounced originally by one accused of witchcraft. Hepzibah Pyncheon in her shop, the scene of Jaffrey Pyncheon's death, and the flight of Hepzibah and Clifford Pyncheon from the old house are scenes that remain in the reader's mind. The marriage of the young couple, Phoebe and Holgrave, provides the only happy conclusion in Hawthorne's four romances, uniting as it does the two families long separated by an accusation of witchcraft and the consequent curse, "God will give him blood to drink!"

Hawthorne said he thought *The House of the Seven Gables* a better work than *The Scarlet Letter* and more characteristic of his mind. His reference was particularly to his success in pouring "some setting sunshine" over the work. He had revised the last chapters for that purpose, after finding that the story "darkens damnably toward the close." The wish that God had given him the power to write a cheerful book and his assertion that the devil got into his ink well echo throughout his self-criticism, particularly in comments on his four romances. Reviewers he respected, such as E. P. Whipple, pointed to the shadows in his fiction as a shortcoming, and he would assume that Transcendentalists among his associates would endorse that opinion. Yet there is no evidence that he seriously undertook to adjust his writing to accommodate such criticism.

The Hawthornes moved from Lenox in November 1851. The four seasons in the Berkshires had been a welcome experience, but Hawthorne objected to the remoteness and, as always, longed to be near the sea. He was now thankful that he had been turned out of office, and had no thought of returning to Salem. He took his family temporarily to West Newton, near Boston, and in the following May moved to Concord to occupy the house formerly owned by Bronson Alcott, which he bought and named the Wayside.

THE

BLITHEDALE ROMANCE.

BY

NATHANIEL HAWTHORNE.

BOSTON:
TICKNOR, REED, AND FIELDS.
M DCCC LII.

While at West Newton, Hawthorne wrote *The Blithedale Romance*, drawing heavily on his residence at Brook Farm for the underlying theme and the broad outline of the plot, for the buildings and the terrain, and for some of the characters and incidents. While acknowledging in his preface that he had the Brook Farm community in mind, he declared that fact to be only incidental, adding that his characters might have put in their appearance at Brook Farm but did not, and that it was not his purpose to comment on the community or the theory underlying its existence. Contemporaries of his readily identified some of his minor characters with residents of the community, and his Blithedale undeniably provides comment on the community of which Hawthorne was a member.

The story of *The Blithedale Romance* is told by Miles Coverdale, a poet who is far more than the conventional internal narrator. He in many ways represents the author, and is in fact the main character. The other characters and the action are seen through his eyes, and he is himself revealed by the way in which they appear to him. An observer of life, rather than a full participant, he is something of the coldly disinterested Paul Pry whom Hawthorne half-seriously feared he might become. Coverdale, like Hawthorne at Brook Farm, joined the communal experiment hopeful that it would succeed, that it would prove brotherhood and mutual support toward worthy goals to be feasible. But in Hollingsworth, Hawthorne drew the kind of character he feared any reformer might become, if his zeal and self-assurance were strong enough to destroy his balance, even his humanity. Hollingsworth's monomania in pursuit of what begins as a worthy humanitarian purpose, the rehabilitation of criminals, brings death to Zenobia and a somber prospect for Priscilla and himself. Coverdale's futility throughout and his loss of Priscilla, whom he loves, to Hollingsworth are traceable to his own coldness, his refusal to accept a cause. Thus he stands finally, in his unintended self-portrait, the antithesis of Hollingsworth, equally thwarted.

When Franklin Pierce was nominated the Democratic Party candidate for the presidency in 1852, Hawthorne volunteered to write his campaign biography. After the election he was appointed consul at Liverpool, sailed on 6 July 1853, and served from 1 September until 1 October 1857. He saw the consulship as a means of laying away savings for the future, and providing European travel, including a year in Italy. It served both purposes, and gave him an especially satisfying acquaintance with the English and English life. He was a faithful and efficient foreign service officer, not simply looking after routine affairs, but forwarding useful information that came to his attention and offering suggestions for improving the regulations and procedures. He urged action by the President, the Department of State, and the Congress to redeem the merchant marine, particularly through better

discipline and better administration of justice. He won no support and intended to write something on the matter after he left the office, but did not.

As consul Hawthorne wrote nothing except his full notebook records, but he began thinking toward a romance that would deal with an American's return to claim an English inheritance. He was no more willing in England than in America to take the initiative, and consequently met very few English authors of any note; but he had several pleasant friendships among lesser authors who sought him out or whom he met by chance.

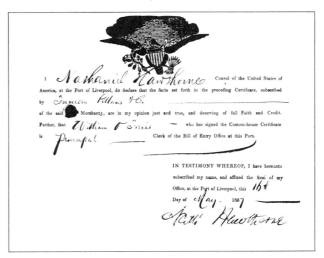

Consular document signed by Hawthorne.

Residing in Rome from January to May 1858, in Florence from June to October, and in Rome again from October until May 1859, Hawthorne continued the study of painting, sculpture, architecture, and other art forms that he had begun in England. He was associated with Robert and Elizabeth Barrett Browning, among other literary figures, and with a number of artists living in Italy, especially William Wetmore Story, Hiram Powers, and Maria Louisa Lander, who made a bust of him, and other American artists.

By July 1858, in Florence, Hawthorne had laid aside the English romance he had worked on during the spring and began sketching an Italian romance, for which he had been storing materials in his mind and in his notebook. He had frequented the museums and galleries, the studios of his friends, and the historical scenes in Rome and Florence; he had talked with his friends about artistic theories and techniques, nudity in art, tinted statues, the old masters. He had observed Americans in the presence of an ancient and foreign culture, and had been especially interested in such young American women as Harriet Hosmer and Maria Lander, who like his character Hilda in *The Marble Faun*, lived independently and safely, it seemed, in defiance of European standards of conduct. He had completed the plot sketch before returning to Rome in October and had completed a draft before leaving Italy in May 1859. His daughter Una had the Roman fever and was close to death in November 1858, and again the next spring. Contrary to his usual practice of laying his pen aside when his musing and dreaming were disturbed, he wrote all but a few days through the months of Una's desperate illness. He himself suffered from colds and lamented the bad weather in Italy more than ever before, even more than in Liverpool.

In the preface to *The Marble Faun*, Hawthorne took up again the definition of romance that he had begun in "The Custom House" and had continued in later prefaces. Taken together, these introductory statements describe the type of fiction he wrote, the romance in contrast to the novel. He had said of *The Blithedale Romance* that he had used the communal society and the circumstances of existence he knew at Brook Farm to "establish a theatre, a little removed from the highway of ordinary travel, where the creatures of his brain may play their phantasmagorical antics, without exposing them to too close a comparison with the actual events of real lives." Finding no such theater in current America, he had moved back in *The Scarlet Letter* to the seventeenth century; he had created the old house and grounds and the legendary past in *The House of the Seven Gables*; in *The Marble Faun* he would employ the Italian scene, with the richness of art, character, and episode that the centuries had piled up, layer on layer. He had declared again and again that he would prefer to write realistic fiction; he had said that in the day-to-day activities of the Salem custom house there was a better book than the one he had written, *The Scarlet Letter*; he even said that he preferred Anthony Trollope's novels, and that if he encountered books like his own written by another author, he would not be able to read them. In his romances after *The Scarlet Letter* he did introduce more realistic detail; but vagueness and fantasy remained dominant, and he made only the meagerest attempts to write cheerful books or to let the sunshine of day into his stories of guilt and suffering.

The Marble Faun re-enacts the fall of man from innocence to knowledge, hence to the maturity of full humanity and, as a consequence, to the possibility of guilt and suffering. Attracted to the idea embodied in the Faun of Praxiteles, Hawthorne

The "Fawn of Praxiteles" used in The Marble Faun.

drew the character Donatello and inducted him, in the company of the mysterious Miriam, into humanity—the transformation being observed by a New England couple, Hilda and Kenyon, who attempt to fathom its meaning from their separate stations on the scale between innocence and understanding. The romance is so rich in descriptions of the art galleries and the historical sites that it has been called a guidebook to Rome and Florence. The character Hilda was a model for the innocent young American women introduced by Henry James and William Dean Howells into their fictional studies of Americans in the old world.

Hawthorne stayed in England a year in order to complete *The Marble Faun* and secure a British copyright. He arrived in Boston on 28 June 1860, after an absence of seven years, and settled again at the Wayside in Concord. He had thought of his English notebooks as a storehouse of publishable material, except for the frankness of his comment on England and the English. From October 1862 to the next August, he contributed to the *Atlantic Monthly*, now edited by James T. Fields, ten essays based on his English notebooks, and with the addition of one unpublished essay, "Consular Experiences," and one in print earlier, he published the collection under the title *Our Old Home* (1853). The work showed a fondness for the home of his ancestors and a genuine feeling that it was his own old home; it shows him at the same time a patriotic American. He approved President Pierce's stand against British encroachments on American rights during the Crimean War, and he was firm in condemning the English class system and the failure to relieve the poverty he encountered at every turn. He was critical of his own country especially for its political antagonisms and for its failure to achieve such a national unity as the English had. He remarked that he was more severe on his own countrymen than on the English, and he was both disappointed and saddened by the protests against the book advanced by English reviewers and English friends of his.

Hawthorne was so distressed at the opening of the Civil War that he could think of little else. In the spring of 1862, he went to Washington at the

Brady photograph of Hawthorne taken in 1862-1863.

invitation of Horatio Bridge and used the occasion to learn all he could about the struggle that he thought would leave the Union broken. In an essay for the July *Atlantic Monthly,* "Chiefly about War Matters," he reported on his visit of three weeks in and near Washington. He had supported Daniel Webster's defense of the Union a decade earlier, and in the campaign biography had found it easy to explain Pierce's opposition to the abolitionists' position because he held the same views. Once the war had begun, he thought it must be fought through to victory, but he would then let the Confederate States go their way. He concluded "Chiefly about War Matters" with the acknowledgement that part of the Union might be lopped off. He could not join the "Peace Democrats," nor could he agree with Pierce in 1863 that war should be stopped and negotiations commenced anew on the slavery question. He nevertheless dedicated *Our Old Home* to Pierce, against the urging of his publishers, friends, and relatives. Pierce, his friend of more than forty years, had appointed him to the post which made the writing of the book possible. He was dedicating the book to the friend, not the politician, he said, and it would have been "a piece of paltroonry" to cancel the dedication in order to sell more copies or to meet the objections of his neighbors.

To

FRANKLIN PIERCE,

AS A SLIGHT MEMORIAL OF A COLLEGE FRIENDSHIP, PROLONGED
THROUGH MANHOOD, AND RETAINING ALL ITS VITALITY
IN OUR AUTUMNAL YEARS,

This Volume is Inscribed

By NATHANIEL HAWTHORNE.

Dedication, Our Old Home *(1863).*

Late in the year 1862 Hawthorne's health was failing noticeably. It was said that he had never recovered from his fear and sorrow when his daughter Una was near death of Roman fever; it was also said that his vitality had been sapped by his sorrow over the war and his estrangement from relatives and friends over issues related to the war. He refused to consult a physician, but put some faith in the seaside vacations he took in the late summer of 1862 and 1863, and spoke of travel and possibly residence abroad. Fearful that his savings and the royalties from his published works would be inadequate, he struggled in vain to finish another romance. He had begun developing while in Italy the idea of an American's claim to an English inheritance, together with the emblematic bloody footstep he had described in his English notebook. The result was the short manuscript fragment, "The Ancestral Footstep." Expanding the same idea by beginning the action in America produced a book-length but unfinished manuscript, *Dr. Grimshawe's Secret*. The idea of an elixir of life, long floating about in his mind, had occupied his attention also, resulting in two long fragments, published as *Septimius Felton*. Three fragmentary chapters of *The Dolliver Romance* were the final efforts of his pen.

The Wayside in Concord.

On a journey undertaken for his health, Hawthorne set out from Boston on 28 March 1864 with his publisher friend, William D. Ticknor. In Philadelphia, on 9 April, Ticknor died, and Hawthorne returned home severely shaken. He went to Boston on 11 May, was examined informally by Oliver Wendell Holmes, and the next day went with Franklin Pierce to his home in Concord, New Hampshire. The two departed on 16 May, intending to drive by carriage, as their whims might dictate, through the mountainous region to the north. At Plymouth, New Hampshire, Hawthorne died in his sleep in the early morning hours of 19 May. He was buried on 23 May in Sleepy Hollow Cemetery, Concord, Massachusetts.

The brief reviews of *Fanshawe* characterized it as a satisfactory romance conforming to an established pattern. Comments on anything Hawthorne published afterward were likely to note the distinctive qualities of his work, his individual prose style, and the special turn of his mind. So it was when his contributions to *The Token* in the early 1830s were singled out for praise by Park Benjamin in American magazines and Henry Chorley in the London *Athenaeum*. Chorley remained a steady

Left to right: James T. Fields, Hawthorne, and William D. Ticknor.

voice of support in England whenever a new work of Hawthorne's appeared. The 1837 *Twice-Told Tales* drew more attention than normally would have been given to a collection of tales being reprinted. Among others, Henry Wadsworth Longfellow wrote a genial and favorable estimate, and Elizabeth Peabody, a longer and more detailed review in which she declared the author indubitably a genius. The 1842 edition elicited a thoughtful, balanced review by Evert Duyckinck, and it gave occasion for Edgar Allan Poe to write a perceptive, laudatory review, in which he also set down the rules by which short stories would be written and judged during the following century. Herman Melville's review of the *Mosses from an Old Manse* brought Hawthorne's work again under serious literary scrutiny, in which it was declared worth mentioning along with Shakespeare's work, and the reviewer ranged afield

Hawthorne's grave in Concord.

into an argument for a national literature and a plea for recognition of native authors.

Following Poe and Melville, reviewers were prepared to take any work of Hawthorne's seriously, and often to pass from the book being reviewed into an assessment of his total work. Two aspects of *The Scarlet Letter* drew special comment: the personal and political elements in "The Custom House" and the moral question some reviewers saw in the introduction of Hester as a character and the failure to provide for her the punishment normally to be expected. Those who did not wish to plead the cause of Salem against the author, as a rule, found "The Custom House" a delightful sketch; and even those who attacked the romance on moral or theological grounds, as did Orestes Brownson, were ready to grant Hawthorne's power and artistry. *The House of the Seven Gables* was reviewed by a number of prominent authors: James Russell Lowell, Rufus Wilmot Griswold, Henry T. Tuckerman, and E. P. Whipple. They tended to turn their reviews into inclusive essays and left no doubt that they were evaluating an author of the first order. Whipple stressed a judgment that had been a commonplace in reviews of Hawthorne, that he was an original genius and founded "a new principality of his own."

The Blithedale Romance drew similarly general and favorable comment, though a number of the reviewers took time to question the relation of the book and its characters to the author's residence at Brook Farm. Hawthorne had come to value Whipple's criticism above that of others. He had taken advice from Whipple's reviews on the question of gloom and sunshine in his works; for example, Whipple had noted that in *The House of the Seven*

Gables the author had experienced "a slight fitfulness toward the conclusion" and had lost something of "the integrity of the original conception"—as if Whipple had known that Hawthorne had altered his plan as he neared the conclusion. Whipple was aware that in *The Blithedale Romance* Coverdale is a character in the plot and in his narration interprets the other characters; he remarks that at times he, as reader, disagrees with Coverdale's "interpretation of an act or expression of the persons he is observing." In reviewing *The Marble Faun*, Whipple wrote another essay on Hawthorne's total work. He objected to the vagueness of the conclusion, but without the outrage of many reviewers, especially in England. In this instance the author acceded to the protests, reluctantly, and added a postscript, but still revealed less than was wanted, he said, by those who did not know how to read a romance.

The fragments published after Hawthorne's death, the notebooks, and the biographical accounts by members of his family served mainly to fill out the record of his career and to document his devotion and his integrity as literary author. Critical works about the same time, such as the book by Henry James, the magazine article by Anthony Trollope, essays by W. D. Howells and others, tended to reveal more about each critic and his views than about Hawthorne, but they tended to take for granted Hawthorne's literary mastery. The influence Hawthorne exerted on James and Howells and many after them is testimony to the great worth they have found in him. Since the study of American literature entered colleges and universities about 1930, Hawthorne has been the subject of wide academic attention. He has maintained his ground as few of our authors have done through variations in literary taste, critical theory, and approach to literary study.

Other Writings:

Peter Parley's Universal History, on the Basis of Geography, 2 vols. (Boston: American Stationers' Co., 1837); *Grandfather's Chair: A History for Youth* (Boston: E. P. Peabody, 1841); *Famous Old People: Being the Second Epoch of Grandfather's Chair* (Boston: E. P. Peabody, 1841); *Liberty Tree: With the Last Words of Grandfather's Chair* (Boston: E. P. Peabody, 1841); *Biographical Stories for Children* (Boston: Tappan & Dennet, 1842); *Journal of an African Cruiser*, ed. Hawthorne (New York: Wiley & Putnam, 1845); *A Wonder-Book for Girls and Boys* (Boston: Ticknor, Reed & Fields, 1852); *Life of Franklin Pierce* (Boston: Ticknor, Reed & Fields,

1852); *Tanglewood Tales, for Girls and Boys; Being a Second Wonder-Book* (Boston: Ticknor, Reed & Fields, 1853); *Septimius Felton; or, The Elixir of Life*, ed. Una Hawthorne and Robert Browning (Boston: James R. Osgood, 1872); *The Dolliver Romance and Other Pieces* (Boston: James R. Osgood, 1876); *Dr. Grimshawe's Secret*, ed. Julian Hawthorne (Boston: James R. Osgood, 1883), now superseded by that edited by Edward H. Davidson (Cambridge: Harvard University Press, 1954); Elizabeth L. Chandler, "Hawthorne's *Spectator*," *New England Quarterly*, 4 (April 1931): 289-330; *Hawthorne as Editor: Selections from His Writings in the American Magazine of Useful and Entertaining Knowledge*, ed. Arlin Turner (University: Louisiana State University Press, 1941); *Nathaniel Hawthorne Poems*, ed. Richard E. Peck (Charlottesville: Bibliographical Society of the University of Virginia, 1967). The standard edition is *The Centenary Edition of the Works of Nathaniel Hawthorne*, ed. William Charvat *et al.*, 11 vols. to date (Columbus: Ohio State University Press, 1962-).

Bibliographies:

Nina E. Browne, *A Bibliography of Nathaniel Hawthorne* (Boston: Houghton, Mifflin, 1905); Wallace Hugh Cathcart, *Bibliography of the Works of Nathaniel Hawthorne* (Cleveland: Rowfant Club, 1905); Jacob Blanck, *Bibliography of American Literature* (New Haven: Yale University Press, 1963), 4:1-36; Beatrice Ricks, Joseph D. Adams, Jack O. Hazlerig, *Nathaniel Hawthorne: A Reference Bibliography, 1900-1971, with Selected Nineteenth-Century Materials* (Boston: G. K. Hall, 1972); C. E. Frazer Clark, Jr., *Nathaniel Hawthorne: A Descriptive Bibliography* (Pittsburgh: University of Pittsburgh Press, forthcoming).

Biographies:

James T. Fields, *Yesterdays with Authors* (Boston: James R. Osgood, 1872); George Parsons Lathrop, *A Study of Hawthorne* (Boston: James R. Osgood, 1876); Julian Hawthorne, *Nathaniel Hawthorne and His Wife*, 2 vols. (Boston: James R. Osgood, 1884); Horatio Bridge, *Personal Recollections of Nathaniel Hawthorne* (New York: Harpers, 1893); Rose Hawthorne Lathrop, *Memories of Hawthorne* (Boston: Houghton, Mifflin, 1897); George E. Woodberry, *Nathaniel Hawthorne* (Boston: Houghton, Mifflin, 1902); Julian Hawthorne, *Hawthorne and His Circle* (New York: Harpers, 1903); Lloyd Morris, *The Rebellious Puritan* (New York:

Harcourt, Brace, 1927); Herbert Gorham, *Hawthorne: A Study in Solitude* (New York: George H. Doran, 1927); Robert Cantwell, *Nathaniel Hawthorne: The American Years* (New York: Rinehart, 1948); Randall Stewart, *Nathaniel Hawthorne: A Biography* (New Haven: Yale University Press, 1948); Vernon Loggins, *The Hawthornes: The Story of Seven Generations of an American Family* (New York: Columbia University Press, 1951); Edward Charles Wagenknecht, *Nathaniel Hawthorne: Man and Writer* (New York: Oxford University Press, 1961); Hubert H. Hoeltje, *Inward Sky: The Heart and Mind of Nathaniel Hawthorne* (Durham: Duke University Press, 1962).

Letters and Journals:

Love Letters of Nathaniel Hawthorne, 2 vols. (Chicago: Society of the Dofobs, 1907); *Letters of Hawthorne to William D. Ticknor*, 2 vols. (Newark, N.J.: Carteret Book Club, 1910); Randall Stewart, "Hawthorne and Politics: Unpublished Letters to William B. Pike," *New England Quarterly*, 5 (April 1932): 237-263; James C. Austin, *Fields of the Atlantic: Letters to an Editor, 1861-1870* (San Marino, Cal.: Huntington Library, 1953); *Passages from the American Note-Books of Nathaniel Hawthorne*, ed. Sophia Hawthorne, 2 vols. (Boston: Ticknor & Fields, 1868), now superseded by *The American Notebooks*, ed. Claude M. Simpson (Columbus: Ohio State University Press, 1972); *Passages from the English Note-Books of Nathaniel Hawthorne*, ed. Sophia Hawthorne, 2 vols. (Boston: Fields, Osgood, 1870), now superseded by *The English Notebooks*, ed. Randall Stewart (New York: Modern Language Association, 1941); *Passages from the French and Italian Note-Books of Nathaniel Hawthorne*, ed. Una Hawthorne, 2 vols. (Boston: James R. Osgood, 1872), superseded by Norman Holmes Pearson, "The French and Italian Notebooks," Ph.D. dissertation, Yale University, 1941; *Hawthorne's First Diary*, ed. Samuel T. Pickard—authenticity uncertain (Boston: Houghton, Mifflin, 1897).

Criticism:

Henry James, *Hawthorne* (New York: Harpers, 1879); L. Dhaleine, *N. Hawthorne: Sa vie et son oeuvre* (Paris: Hachette, 1905); Newton Arvin, *Hawthorne* (Boston: Little, Brown, 1929); Bertha Faust, *Hawthorne's Contemporaneous Reputation: A Study in Literary Opinion in America and England, 1828-1864*, Ph.D. dissertation, University of Pennsylvania, 1939; F. O. Matthiessen, *American Renaissance: Art and Expression in the Age of Emerson and Whitman* (New York: Oxford University Press, 1941); Lawrence Sargent Hall, *Hawthorne: Critic of Society* (New Haven: Yale University Press, 1944); Edward H. Davidson, *Hawthorne's Last Phase* (New Haven: Yale University Press, 1949); Mark Van Doren, *Nathaniel Hawthorne* (New York: William Sloane, 1949); Richard Harter Fogle, *Hawthorne's Fiction: The Light and the Dark* (Norman: University of Oklahoma Press, 1952); William Bysshe Stein, *Hawthorne's Faust: A Study of the Devil Archetype* (Gainesville: University of Florida Press, 1953); Rudolph Von Abele, *The Death of the Artist: A Study of Hawthorne's Disintegration* (The Hague: Martinus Nijhof, 1955); Hyatt H. Waggoner, *Hawthorne: A Critical Study* (Cambridge: Harvard University Press, 1955); Roy R. Male, *Hawthorne's Tragic Vision* (Austin: University of Texas Press, 1957); Harry Levin, *The Power of Blackness: Hawthorne, Poe, and Melville* (New York: Alfred A. Knopf, 1958); Arlin Turner, *Nathaniel Hawthorne: An Introduction and Interpretation* (New York: Barnes & Noble, 1961); Millicent Bell, *Hawthorne's View of the Artist* (Albany: State University of New York Press, 1962); Jean Normand, *Nathaniel Hawthorne: An Approach to an Analysis of Artistic Creation* (Cleveland, Ohio: Case Western Reserve University Press, 1969; Paris edition in 1964); *Hawthorne Centenary Essays*, ed. Roy Harvey Pearce (Columbus: Ohio State University Press, 1964); Terence Martin, *Nathaniel Hawthorne* (New York: Twayne, 1965); Frederick C. Crews, *The Sins of the Fathers: Hawthorne's Psychological Themes* (New York: Oxford University Press, 1966); Marjorie J. Elder, *Nathaniel Hawthorne: Transcendental Symbolist* (Athens: Ohio University Press, 1969); Richard Harter Fogle, *Hawthorne's Imagery: The "Proper Light and Shadow" in the Major Romances* (Norman: University of Oklahoma Press, 1969); Hugo McPherson, *Hawthorne as Myth-Maker: A Study in Imagination* (Toronto: University of Toronto Press, 1969); Michael Davitt Bell, *Hawthorne and the Historical Romance of New England* (Princeton: Princeton University Press, 1971); Neal F. Doubleday, *Hawthorne's Early Tales: A Critical Study* (Durham: Duke University Press, 1972); Nina Baym, *The Shape of Hawthorne's Career* (Ithaca: Cornell University Press, 1976).

Papers:

The major collections of Hawthorne's papers are at the Berg Collection of the New York Public Library, Boston Public Library, Bowdoin College Library, Essex Institute, Henry E. Huntington Library, and Pierpont Morgan Library. See also Kenneth Walter Cameron, "Inventory of Hawthorne Manuscripts, Part One," *Emerson Society Quarterly*, No. 29 (1 Quarter 1962): 5-20.

ISAAC THOMAS HECKER (18 December 1819-22 December 1888), priest, author, and editor, was born and grew up in New York City, the son of German immigrants. The most important event for the ultimate direction of Hecker's life occurred in 1841 when he met Orestes A. Brownson. It was Brownson who suggested in January 1843 that Hecker join the Brook Farm community. Dissatisfaction with the spiritual life at Brook Farm led Hecker to Bronson Alcott's Fruitlands for a brief stay, and finally to return to New York in August 1843. Once again through the influence of Brownson, Hecker decided to convert to Catholicism and attempted also to convert Thoreau and George William Curtis. He was baptized in August 1844 and travelled to Europe to study for the priesthood. In 1849 Hecker was ordained in the Redemptorist order. He was dismissed from that order in 1857 through a misunderstanding with his superior concerning permission to travel, and the next year was returned to the United States to found his own order, The Missionary Priests of St. Paul the Apostle (the Paulist Fathers). Hecker spent the rest of his life proselytizing for the Catholic Church in America,

and attempting to further his own ideas about the essentially democratic nature of Catholicism. He died in New York City. Hecker's two books mirror his desire to make Catholicism a logical alternative for American Protestants: *Questions of the Soul* (New York: Appleton, 1852) is in part an autobiography which seeks to answer the questions raised by Hecker's own life, but is largely a definition of man's nature and an argument for Catholicism as the only religion which can fulfill man's spiritual needs; *Aspirations of Nature* (New York: J. B. Kirker, 1857) presents Catholicism as the religious instrument through which man can best direct his reason and will. Hecker's championing of the Catholic press in America resulted in his founding the *Catholic World* in 1865 and the *Young Catholic* in 1870, as well as his organization of the Catholic Publication Society in 1866.

REFERENCES: Walter Elliot, *The Life of Father Hecker* (New York: Columbus Press, 1891); Vincent F. Holden, *The Early Years of Isaac Thomas Hecker* (Washington, D.C.: Catholic University of America Press, 1939); Holden, *The Yankee Paul: Isaac Thomas Hecker* (Milwaukee: Bruce Publishing, 1958). —*Robert E. Burkholder*

FREDERIC HENRY HEDGE (12 December 1805-21 August 1890), Unitarian minister, theological writer, and translator of German literature, was born in Cambridge, Massachusetts. Levi Hedge, a professor at Harvard University, gave his talented son the best education available. Tutored by the brilliant young George Bancroft, who accompanied him to Germany where Hedge attended school from 1818 to 1822, he was granted junior standing when he entered Harvard. Although he considered poetry and medicine as possible careers, Hedge followed his father's wishes and entered the Harvard Divinity School in 1825. After his graduation in 1829, he was ordained pastor at West Cambridge, where he married a girl from his congregation in 1830. His love for Germany and his location kept Hedge from becoming a quiet parish preacher who rarely left home. As one of the few people who at that time had actually studied in Germany, his conversation was much in demand. Following the publication of his important and favorable article on Coleridge and German philosophy in the March 1833 *Christian Examiner*, he was firmly established in his position as a popular member of any conversational group. In February 1835 Hedge proposed a new journal

"devoted to a spiritual philosophy," to be conducted by such men as himself and his former classmates, Ralph Waldo Emerson and George Ripley. But in May 1835 Hedge left Cambridge to become the minister to a Unitarian society at Bangor, Maine, and the publishing project collapsed. Hedge did not allow his new position to isolate him from his old friends and in 1836, with Emerson's help, he organized "for the free discussion of theological and moral subjects" what would become known as the Transcendental Club. When in 1840 the Transcendentalists began a journal, the *Dial*, Hedge was approached for aid by its editor, his old friend, Margaret Fuller. But Hedge declined to contribute because he was worried about being identified in the public's mind with Bronson Alcott and Emerson, whose ideas he now disagreed with. Hedge believed in the futility of public debates over reform,

preferring instead for the social organization to develop naturally from internal pressures, and he wished, partly to pacify his conservative congregation, to keep out of the limelight. He remained in Bangor, contributing to journals and becoming recognized as an expert on German literature, until 1850, when he moved on to Providence, Rhode Island. In 1856 he settled in Brookline, Massachusetts, and supplemented his ministerial salary with a part-time appointment as professor of ecclesiastical history at Harvard, a post he held until 1878. These were busy years for Hedge: he edited the influential *Christian Examiner* from 1857 to 1861 and was president of the American Unitarian Association from 1859 to 1862. Appointed Professor of German at Harvard in 1872, Hedge left his pastorate and moved to Cambridge. In 1881 he retired from Harvard, but remained in Cambridge and quietly published his sermons and writings on German literature until his death there. Hedge, although an early supporter of reform, soon became a believer in "enlightened Conservatism," opposing the Transcendentalists' dislike of existing institutions, distrust of the past, intense reliance on individual intuition, and nonacceptance of the miracles of the New Testament. His major contribution was in supporting the study of German literature, from the 1848 *Prose Writers of Germany*, containing biographical and critical sketches and translations of twenty-eight authors, to the 1886 *Hours with German Classics*, a collection of his Harvard lectures. A broad, appreciative critic of literature, Hedge was the most prolific translator of German literature in America besides Charles Timothy Brooks. Highly regarded in his day, later critics have sometimes complained that his translations give more of the spirit than the technical form of the original. Hedge's theological and literary efforts were rewarded by Harvard with honorary degrees: Doctor of Divinity in 1852 and Doctor of Laws in 1886. —*Joel Myerson*

Principal Works: *Conservatism and Reform* (Boston: Little & Brown, 1843); *Prose Writers of Germany* (Philadelphia: Carey & Hart, 1848); *Reason in Religion* (Boston: Walker, Fuller, 1865); *Ways of the Spirit* (Boston: Roberts Brothers, 1877); *Atheism in Philosophy* (Boston: Roberts Brothers, 1884); *Hours with German Classics* (Boston: Roberts Brothers, 1886); *Martin Luther and Other Essays* (Boston: Roberts Brothers, 1888); *Sermons* (Boston: Roberts Brothers, 1891).

Frederic Henry Hedge

Principal References: Martha Ilona Tuomi, "Dr. Frederic Henry Hedge: His Life and Works to the End of His Bangor Pastorate," M.A. thesis, University of Maine, 1935; O. W. Long, *Frederic Henry Hedge: A Cosmopolitan Scholar* (Portland, Maine: Southworth-Anthoensen Press, 1940); Roland Vale Wells, *Three Christian Transcendentalists* (New York: Columbia University Press, 1943); Joel Myerson, "Frederic Henry Hedge and the Failure of Transcendentalism," *Harvard Library Bulletin*, 23 (October 1975): 396-410.

T W. Higginson

THOMAS WENTWORTH HIGGINSON (22 December 1822-9 May 1911), known through most of his mature life as "Colonel Higginson" because of his Civil War service with black troops, is to be remembered as a man of letters, author, speaker, radical religionist, and advocate of equality for women. He was born, raised, and died in Cambridge. Higginson was married twice, first to his cousin, Mary Channing, and upon her death, to Mary Thacher, who survived him. His father, Stephen Higginson, after having gone bankrupt, was Bursar of Harvard College when Thomas Wentworth attended. During his years at Harvard, where he was graduated in 1841, he had the reputation of being a dilettante, reading literature, poetry, or whatever struck his fancy. He was given to roaming the fields outside of Cambridge or dreaming under a tree on the banks of the Charles River, but after teaching and maturing a year or so, he entered the Divinity School and was graduated in 1847. This was a vintage period which produced the leaders of a religious revolt against the mild Unitarianism of the age. At Divinity Hall Higginson met Samuel Johnson, Samuel Longfellow, and Octavius Brooks Frothingham. Together they listened to the sermons of Theodore Parker, frowned on by the Harvard authorities, and formed some of their radical views of religion. Higginson was called to be pastor of Newburyport Unitarian Church in 1847, but after three years he was asked to leave because of his anti-slavery sermons. In 1852 he settled in Worcester, Massachusetts, and established the Free Church, a congregation of radicals with loose Unitarian connections, modeled after Parker's Twenty-Eighth Congregational Society in Boston. This became the first Free Church of his generation of Unitarian ministers and, doubtless, pointed the way for Johnson, Longfellow, and Frothingham. During Higginson's Worcester years he became involved in the anti-slavery dispute, was wounded by a police saber during the Anthony Burns affair in 1854, helped raise money and equipment for the anti-slavery side in the Kansas struggle, and was on the scene writing firsthand reports for publication in the *Atlantic Monthly*. When the Civil War broke out, he volunteered as Captain in the 51st Massachusetts Regiment, and later as a Colonel led the 1st South Carolina Volunteers (33rd colored U. S. Troops), the first freedmen mustered into the Federal service in the Civil War. In small diversionary campaigns, his troops captured and held Jacksonville, Florida, and invaded and held an area in Tide Water, South Carolina. Confederate artillery disabled him near Willow Bluff and he resigned from the Army in 1864. After his military career, he moved to Newport, Rhode Island, where he free-lanced as a writer and speaker until 1878. The rest of his life was spent in Cambridge, Massachusetts, where he continued his life as writer, speaker, and mentor of aspiring intellectuals. After the Civil War, he enlarged his already-wide reputation by his work in the Free Religious Association for which he often spoke, wrote for the *Index*, the Free Religious Association journal, and later served as president following Frothingham and Felix Adler. In 1880-1881 he served in the Massachusetts legislature and on the State Board of Education. He is remembered as one of Emily Dickinson's mentors and an early advocate of black equality and woman's rights. His memory lives on as a man of genial spirit and humor, humane, broad-visioned, if not profound, but able to understand his age and speak to it.

—*J. Wade Caruthers*

Principal Works: *Does Slavery Christianize the Negro?* (New York: Anti-Slavery Society, 1855); *Malbone: An Old Newport Romance* (Boston: Fields, Osgood, 1869); *The Sympathy of Religions* (Boston: Reprinted from the *Radical*, 1870); *Army Life in a Black Regiment* (Boston: Fields, Osgood, 1876); *Common Sense About Women* (Boston: Lee & Shepard, 1882); *Margaret Fuller Ossoli* (Boston: Houghton, Mifflin, 1884); Emily Dickinson, *Poems*, ed. with Mabel Loomis Todd (Boston: Roberts Brothers, 1891); *Cheerful Yesterdays* (Boston: Houghton, Mifflin, 1898); *Women and the Alphabet* (Boston: Houghton, Mifflin, 1900); *Henry Wadsworth Longfellow* (Boston: Houghton, Mifflin, 1902); *John Greenleaf Whittier* (New York: Macmillan, 1902); *Part of a Man's Life* (Boston: Houghton, Mifflin, 1905).

Principal References: *Old Cambridge* (New York: Macmillan, 1899); Mary Thacher Higginson, *Thomas Wentworth Higginson: The Story of His Life* (Boston: Houghton, Mifflin, 1914); *Letters and Journals of Thomas Wentworth Higginson*, ed. Mary Thacher Higginson (Boston: Houghton, Mifflin, 1921); Jacob Blanck, *Bibliography of American Literature* (New Haven: Yale University Press, 1963), 4:139-184; Anna M. Wells, *Dear Preceptor: Life and Times of Thomas Wentworth Higginson* (Boston: Houghton Mifflin, 1963); Howard N. Meyer, *Colonel of the Black Regiment* (New York: W. W. Norton, 1967); Tilden Edelstein, *Strange Enthusiasm: A Life of Thomas Wentworth Higginson* (New Haven: Yale University Press, 1968).

RICHARD HILDRETH (28 June 1807-11 July 1865), historian, novelist, and political writer, was born at Deerfield, Massachusetts. He graduated from Harvard College in 1826 and was admitted to the bar in 1830. His law practice was put aside, though, as Hildreth became interested in literature, and he co-edited the Boston *Daily Atlas* while regularly contributing miscellaneous articles to the major journals of the day. During a two-year stay in Florida for his health, Hildreth wrote *The Slave: or, Memoirs of Archy Moore*, 2 vols. (Boston: John H. Eastburn, 1836), one of the first American anti-slavery novels. After his return to Boston, Hildreth's ill health continued, and in 1840 he began a four-year stay in British Guiana, where he edited two anti-slavery papers. Hildreth's major work, *History of the United States*, 6 vols. (New York: Harpers, 1849-1852), is well-documented, though its stodgy style put off readers. His books on banking and politics reflect Hildreth's generally positive, utilitarian philosophy of life. In 1861 President Lincoln appointed Hildreth United States Consul to Trieste, Italy, but he resigned in 1864 because of poor health and died in Florence the following year.
REFERENCES: Arthur M. Schlesinger, Jr., "The

Problem of Richard Hildreth," *New England Quarterly*, 13 (June 1940): 223-245; Martha M. Pingel, *An American Utilitarian: Richard Hildreth as a Philosopher* (New York: Columbia University Press, 1948).

Oliver Wendell Holmes

Barry Menikoff
University of Hawaii

BIRTH: Cambridge, Massachusetts, 29 August 1809.

MARRIAGE: Amelia Lee Jackson, 15 June 1840. Children: Oliver Wendell Holmes, Jr. (1841-1935); Amelia Jackson Holmes (1843- ?); Edward Jackson Holmes (1846-1884).

DEATH: Boston, 10 October 1894.

MAJOR WORKS: *The Autocrat of the Breakfast-Table* (Boston: Phillips, Sampson, 1858); *The Professor at the Breakfast-Table* (Boston: Ticknor & Fields, 1860); *Currents and Counter-Currents in Medical Science* (Boston: Ticknor & Fields, 1861); *Elsie Venner: A Romance of Destiny*, 2 vols. (Boston: Ticknor & Fields, 1861); *Songs in Many Keys* (Boston: Ticknor & Fields, 1862); *Mechanism in Thought and Morals* (Boston: James R. Osgood, 1871); *The Poet at the Breakfast-Table* (Boston: James R. Osgood, 1872).

Holmes's house in Boston.

Life and Career:

For nearly a quarter of a century, from the publication in 1858 of *The Autocrat of the Breakfast-Table* until his resignation from the Harvard Medical School in 1882, Dr. Oliver Wendell Holmes dominated the intellectual life of Boston and Cambridge. Unlike his friend Nathaniel Hawthorne, who brought a symbolic dimension to the art of prose fiction, or Ralph Waldo Emerson, who transformed the consciousness of his audience through the essay, Holmes left no distinctive mark on any single literary form. Yet at one time his influence as an essayist rivaled that of Emerson, his novels were compared favorably with Hawthorne's, and he was unofficially regarded as the poet laureate of Boston. What was it about Holmes's work that gave it such enormous popularity and unmistakable prestige? For one thing, Holmes never divorced himself from his writing. Whether he adopted the mask of the Autocrat or the Professor or the Poet, as he did in the breakfast-table series, his subject was always the same: "A Boswell, writing out himself!" The memory of his early exposure to Calvinism (Abiel Holmes, his father, was minister of the First Church in Cambridge) never left him: "When it came to the threats of future punishment as described in the sermons of the more hardened theologians, my instincts were shocked and disgusted beyond endurance." And it provided him with his one great subject. Holmes anatomized religious orthodoxy (doctrines of predestination, the depravity of human

Thy sacred leaves, fair Freedom's flower,
Shall ever float on dome and tower,
To all their heavenly colors true
In blackening frost or crimson dew,
And God love us as we love thee,
Thrice holy Flower of Liberty!
Then hail the banner of the free,
The starry Flower of Liberty!

Oliver Wendell Holmes

nature, the inherited guilt of all men) with a scientific scalpel. His purpose was not so much to expose the cruelty of Calvinism as the falsity of its notions. Sin, a term the religionists were so fond of, in Holmes's view had to be extirpated from the language or redefined. It was not an emblem of moral evil but rather the condition of an ill or suffering human body. Holmes regarded behavioral disorders (he was particularly interested in the problems of criminals) as a function of genetic weaknesses and/or impoverished and abusive environments. He recognized significant, often severe, limitations on the freedom of the will in all men. And he believed these limitations absolved them, in differing degrees, of legal responsibility for behavior over which they had no control. But Holmes acknowledged no restrictions whatever on men's political freedom. Indeed, he championed free inquiry and free speech because he was convinced it would lead to the discovery of truth ("chiefest among the virtues") and the advancement of knowledge—which in Holmes's mind was equivalent to the advancement of science. Thus his satiric yet reasoned attacks on Johnathan Edwards, the intellectual figurehead of Calvinism, and on the practitioners (and practice) of homeopathic medicine, were motivated by his belief that they impeded the pursuit of truth and retarded mankind's progress toward a lovelier and healthier world. When Holmes knew the truth, as he certainly did after marshalling the evidence on the contagiousness of puerperal fever, he was unsparing of those physicians who adamantly refused to accept his argument—an argument which earned him professional esteem during his lifetime and a place in the history of medicine forever.

Oliver Wendell Holmes, the son of a "gentle scholar" who preached a hard religion, was educated first at Phillips Academy (a citadel of orthodox religious thought) and after at Harvard College. It was at Harvard that Holmes developed his gift for verse and also established the contacts with his classmates that he was to maintain throughout his long life. He read law for a year following his graduation before he turned to the study of medicine under the tutorship of Dr. James Jackson. His explanation for the change (in a letter of March 1831) was simple: "I know I might have made an indifferent lawyer,—I think I may make a tolerable physician,—I did not like the one, and I do like the other." Holmes's great opportunity came when he left for France in order to pursue his studies at the Ecole de Medicine. The professors in Paris— Lisfranc, Velpeau, Andral, and Ricord—were among the best in the world. And one, Pierre Charles Alexandre Louis, exercised a major influence on Holmes's life. Following Louis around the wards at La Pitie, Holmes learned the techniques of modern clinical medicine—to study and diagnose disease through the close and careful observation of facts. The significance of Holmes's career in Paris as a medical student scarcely can be overstated. It provided an intense motivation for his life's work.

Holmes in his study (1888).

107

While literary history is replete with examples of writers who were physicians—Rabelais, Sir Thomas Browne, Oliver Goldsmith, Somerset Maugham, William Carlos Williams—few expended as much energy in the practice and profession of medicine as Holmes did. Indeed it has often been argued that medicine was Holmes's vocation and literature his avocation. His commemorative tablet at King's Chapel, Boston, reads "Teacher of Anatomy, Essayist, and Poet"—in that order.

Holmes returned to America from Europe in late 1835, quickly wrote an essay on *Acute Pericarditis* in order to satisfy a requirement for the Harvard Medical School, and was granted the M.D. degree in February 1836. His first volume of verse was published in the same year. *Poems* consisted mainly of pieces which had been printed earlier in small magazines, and included "Old Ironsides," the lyric that first appeared in a Boston newspaper and saved the frigate *Constitution* from being dismantled. One editor said of *Poems*: "It was. . . high time that Holmes should collect his verses into a volume bearing his name on the title-page, for they were being copied with increasing frequency into gift-annuals and other contemporary collections of poems, very often without his name attached." In 1836 and 1837 Holmes won three Boylston prizes—an unprecedented feat—for medical essays on direct exploration in medical practice, on neuralgia, and on intermittent fever (malaria) in New England. The publication in 1838 of the *Boylston Prize Dissertations For the Years 1836 and 1837* undoubtedly led to his appointment in 1839 as Professor of Anatomy and Physiology at Dartmouth Medical College. He relinquished the post after two terms, however, married Amelia Jackson on 15 June 1840, and settled in Boston to practice medicine. He was an active public lecturer during the 1840s and he used the lecture platform as a forum for exposing the quackeries of the day—the most notable being homeopathy and its "kindred delusions." On 13 February 1843 he delivered before the Boston Society for Medical Improvement his essay on "The Contagiousness of Puerperal Fever." Thus Holmes had already achieved eminence in medical circles when Harvard Medical School in 1847 offered him the Parkman Professorship of Anatomy and Physiology. He held this chair (the Physiology half was dropped in 1870) for the next thirty-five years.

From about 1830 to 1860 the diversity of Holmes's pursuits was perhaps the salient feature of his career. He was a student, a researcher, a lecturer, a physician, a teacher, and, not least, an occasional poet. He was acknowledged in a circle that included

Caricature of Holmes by "Spy" in Vanity Fair.

James Russell Lowell, Emerson, John Lothrop Motley, and Henry Wadsworth Longfellow as a wit and a brilliant conversationalist. Thus when a new publication was proposed for Boston, and Lowell agreed to serve as editor, it was inevitable that Holmes would be asked for a contribution. Not only did Holmes provide the name for the magazine—

Part of Holmes's library.

Atlantic Monthly—but he was the primary agent for its literary and commercial success. The opening number in November 1857 contained the first installment of *The Autocrat of the Breakfast-Table*. Holmes now had a rostrum for doing what those who knew him privately admitted he did best—talk. Conversation in his view was a fine art whose purpose was educational rather than decorative. It was a means of expressing the thoughts and secrets and fears that lay hidden within the self. It was important, too, because—perhaps anticipating Shaw's *Pygmalion*—it was expressive of an individual's background and character. The essay form gave Holmes the widest possible latitude for informing the public and improving their well-being. He adopted the device in *The Autocrat* of a Boston boarding-house whose various residents meet daily at the dining table. The Autocrat, one of the boarders, guides and directs the conversation. The device enabled Holmes to fill his twelve serial numbers with his ideas on the limitations of the will, on art, on youth and age, on love. Above all it gave him a forum for expressing his conviction that all men—and women, for he fought unsuccessfully for their admission to Harvard Medical School—should extend their capacities and live as fully as possible.

The combination of prose and verse (Holmes ended each chapter with a poem), the device of a *raconteur*, the creation of a set of characters with distinctive personalities that were developed in the course of the narrative, the adoption of a colloquial and familiar style—all these features ensured the success of *The Autocrat of the Breakfast-Table*. Holmes was compared with the major essayists from Montaigne through Charles Lamb. He capitalized on his success with the publication of *The Professor at the Breakfast-Table*. The pattern was the same but there were thematic differences. Holmes dealt with

religion more openly than before (of course, "The Deacon's Masterpiece" had appeared in *The Autocrat*, but it was not until 1900 that anyone publicly discussed the poem as an allegorical satire on Calvinism). The conflict between religion and science—the one representative of rigidity and orthodoxy, the other the agent of knowledge and truth—discussions of individualism, of political freedom, of democracy, of the new world versus the old—all these issues were dwelt upon in the second volume. One of Holmes's masterful achievements in *The Professor* was the creation of Little Boston, a character whose broken frame could not stifle his patriotic spirit. Although he is not the figure who declared that "Boston State-House is the hub of the solar system" (that was said in *The Autocrat*), his sentiments are aligned with that speaker. The delicate relationship between Boston and Iris, and his death at the end of the book, were handled with simplicity and poignancy.

Holmes exhibited an extraordinary burst of creative energy in the 1860s and early 1870s. *The Professor at the Breakfast-Table* appeared in book form in 1860; *Currents and Counter-Currents in*

Holmes as a young man.

Medical Science, a collection of his best medical essays, was published the following year; *Elsie Venner*, his major novel, came out in 1861; *Songs in Many Keys*, the first significant edition of his poems in thirteen years, including the best of the verses from *The Autocrat* and *The Professor*, was printed in 1862; and in 1867 he brought out a second novel, *The Guardian Angel*. During this period he continued to produce occasional poems and prose pieces with astonishing regularity.

Holmes in his twenties.

The edition of *Currents and Counter-Currents*, dedicated to Dr. James Jackson, included the essay on puerperal fever. This piece serves as an excellent illustration of Holmes's work as a medical researcher. He was not an experimental scientist and he made no original contribution to the field of anatomy, his specialty. But he possessed a splendid gift for collecting material from disparate sources—from practicing physicians, from ancient and modern medical studies—and systematically organizing the evidence in order to draw an inescapable conclusion. Thus the assertion that puerperal fever "is so far contagious as to be frequently carried from patient to patient by physicians and nurses" was demonstrated rationally rather than experimentally. The achievement was

remarkable for its time because the idea of contagion was dimly understood—Holmes wrote before Pasteur established the bacteriological basis for disease. If "The Contagiousness of Puerperal Fever" presented a practical consideration of a specific medical problem, then "Currents and Counter-Currents in Medical Science" offered a theoretical discourse on the philosophy of medicine. Holmes speculated on the role of nature versus art in medical practice, on the use and/or abuse of drugs in treatment, and on the relationship between medicine and society. As a result of Dr. Jacob Bigelow's *Discourse on Self-Limited Diseases*, published in 1835, he was inclined to favor nature over art and to allow diseases to run their course without unnecessary intervention. He was also opposed to the widespread practice of administering drugs to patients—especially since in his day the physicians dispensed the drugs at the same time that they prescribed them. "Currents and Counter-Currents in Medical Science" evinces the lean and forceful style of Holmes's medical writings; it is unquestionably one of his finest essays.

Although *Elsie Venner* seemed odd to an unprepared public—one reviewer considered Elsie a case for the "morbid pathologist" rather than the novelist—Holmes believed it to be nothing more than the continuation of a major theme. He transformed the story of a young girl whose mother had been bitten by a snake during pregnancy and who therefore inherited ophidian characteristics (powers of fascination and repulsion) into an allegory of original sin and moral responsibility. The snake symbolized the "evil principle" and Elsie served as an emblem for the snake. To condemn her for her behavior, for which she was not responsible, was tantamount to condemning her for her inheritance. Holmes in *Elsie Venner*—like Hawthorne in *The House of the Seven Gables* and Thomas Hardy in the later *Tess of the D'Urbervilles*—explored the matter of family histories within the context of the relatively new field of genetics. The imagery of breeding dominates the book. Why did some families thrive? Why do others decline? Why did "The Brahmin Caste of New England" prosper? Holmes sought answers to these questions in Francis Galton's genetic theories and in contemporary physiological psychology.

During the 1870s Holmes produced two essays that summarized his positions on determinism, freedom, and responsibility. "Mechanism in Thought and Morals" was delivered as a lecture in June 1870 before the Phi Beta Kappa Society of Harvard University. Holmes began with a description of thought as a

The consequence of Holmes's work was to replace the determinism of Calvinistic theology with the mechanism of contemporary psychology. Since his writing served the needs of the weak and the handicapped, he saw no irony in substituting a scientific for a religious fatalism. At least the one proferred pity and charity to the victims of life, while the other held out nothing but the prospect of hell. For the majority of men who were not dysfunctional Holmes allowed a measure of freedom. This freedom had no basis in logic or reason—any more than Holmes's belief in God—but he perceived it to be an undeniable fact of life. And Holmes trusted facts more than logic. Furthermore, he had no fear of the future, no fear that science might disprove the existence of any freedom. For people believed they were free—and the power of that belief was sufficient to keep most men decent and responsible.

With the publication in 1872 of *The Poet at the Breakfast-Table* Holmes brought to a close his trilogy. By now the form was well known to all readers. The guide for this final volume was the Poet. Two of the principal characters were the Young Astronomer and the Master. The Poet was drawn toward scientific analysis; the Astronomer possessed a passion for poetry; and the Master had a gift for talking authoritatively on virtually any philosophical subject. Although each one is a distinct dramatic figure in the narrative, taken together they symbolize Holmes's career as professor/scientist, essayist/philosopher, and poet/artist. The volume treated familiar topics: the unconscious, creativity, the value of love, freedom of discussion, the limitation of the will, and the progress of mankind. And there was the same blend of poetry and prose. This time, however, the poetic sections (which were the reveries of the Astronomer) were linked throughout the narrative. As a single long poem, *Wind-Clouds and Star-Drifts* constituted the most ambitious poetic effort of Holmes's career. The style of *The Poet* was witty and ironic, as in the earlier books, but there was an added elegiac note, perhaps a function of the childhood reminiscences, perhaps a consequence of the dispersion of the boarders at the end of the book. Oliver Wendell Holmes was sixty-three years old when he finished this last volume of his major literary work.

Holmes resigned from Harvard Medical School in 1882—ending an official connection with the University that dated back fifty-seven years to his first entrance as a student. But he maintained his active literary career. *Medical Essays* and *Pages from an Old Volume of Life* were published in 1883. A critical biography of Emerson and a third

Holmes in mid-life.

mechanical function of the brain. We control our thinking no more than we control our breathing. Additionally our thoughts are activated or propelled by our unconscious—an idea that was current in Holmes's time and which he used to underpin his argument that our thinking is mechanical and automatic. Yet the condition of the moral world according to Holmes is that every act depends upon choice, upon a personal and individual act of the will. How do we reconcile the mechanistic nature of our being with the freedom of the will that is a prerequisite for a moral order? Holmes turned to this issue in "Crime and Automatism," a review of a study by a French criminologist which he wrote for the *Atlantic Monthly* in April 1875. He believed that the will was not free. In the case of criminals it was frequently governed by organic conditions, such as insanity, and environmental conditions, such as child abuse. And individuals who suffered these conditions could not be held legally or morally accountable for their behavior. Holmes asserted that criminals were damaged physically and emotionally. His position augmented a general shift in society's attitude toward criminals and the insane from a moral model (that they were evil) to a medical model (that they were diseased and needed treatment).

"medicated" novel, *A Mortal Antipathy*, appeared two years later. He toured England in 1886, recounting his adventures in *Our Hundred Days in Europe*. Four years later he attempted to revive the format of the breakfast-table books in *Over the Teacups*. In 1891 Houghton, Mifflin produced the handsome Riverside edition of *The Writings of Oliver Wendell Holmes*, for which the author supplied a set of new prefaces. By this time Holmes had indeed become "the last leaf" of his own poem (composed more than sixty years earlier). As he wrote to his publishers in the final year of his life: "I am one of the very last of the leaves that still cling to the bough of life that budded in the spring of the nineteenth century." He died at his home in Boston in 1894.

Unquestionably the breakfast-table books were regarded as Holmes's major contribution to literature. From the beginning they were admired for their wit and humor, their shrewd observations on life, and their ingenious criticism of art, literature, and philosophy. The originality of the prose and the inventiveness of the created characters were successful artistic features of the trilogy—although *The Autocrat* was the volume universally applauded. These books further encouraged critics to comment on aspects of Holmes's personality: his independent intellectual attitude, his aversion to any restraint on free thought, and his speculative and scientific habit of mind. Furthermore, critics admired Holmes's sympathy for people less privileged than himself—for widows and old men living alone in boarding houses, for young women forced to survive with few financial resources. Yet his sympathy (or geniality) was often considered a limitation, depriving his work of genuine passion. In much the same way his versatility (in prose and verse and science) imparted to his work, in one critic's judgment, "the spirit of a *dilettante*."

By the early part of the twentieth century, the criticism of Oliver Wendell Holmes had established common themes. If he no longer enjoyed the popular audience that his works had commanded during his lifetime, he nevertheless appeared regularly in literary histories. He was admired for his liberal spirit; for his sanity and common sense and practical philosophy; for his rationalism and anti-Calvinism; and, above all, for his "unbroken perfection of style" in the breakfast-table books. Indeed, Brander Matthews, writing in the *Cambridge History of American Literature*, praised Holmes for his talk and for the civilizing influence he exerted on his time. But a number of negative evaluations of Holmes's work were published in the 1920s. He was

Holmes as an old man.

seen as a social conservative who failed to appreciate the economic and social changes of his own time. One critic chided him for his reticence about sex. And he was dismissed as a minor figure in New England's literary history.

During the 1930s there was an effort at revaluating Holmes's place in American literature. Critics turned their attention away from the breakfast-table books to his novels and prose essays. His conversation was seen as a functional element in his work. As Van Wyck Brooks said, "Emotions that can shape themselves in language open the gate . . . into the great community of human affections." The determinism that shocked his contemporaries was now viewed as a foreshadowing of the ideas of writers such as Freud and Theodore Dreiser. His concern with the question of human responsibility as it related to an aberrant or disordered mind was regarded as a fundamentally modern theme. Critics also turned to Holmes's medical essays (they rediscovered that he was at the forefront of medical thought in his own day) and integrated them into the canon of his literary publications. Science, art, and philosophy are interwoven in the work of Oliver Wendell Holmes.

Other Writings:

The Guardian Angel (Boston: Ticknor & Fields, 1867); *John Lothrop Motley* (Boston: Houghton, Osgood, 1879); *Medical Essays* (Boston: Houghton, Mifflin, 1883); *Pages from an Old Volume of Life* (Boston: Houghton, Mifflin, 1883); *Ralph Waldo Emerson* (Boston: Houghton, Mifflin, 1885); *A Mortal Antipathy* (Boston: Houghton, Mifflin, 1885); *Our Hundred Days in Europe* (Boston: Houghton, Mifflin, 1887); *Over the Teacups* (Boston: Houghton, Mifflin, 1891); *The Writings of Oliver Wendell Holmes*, 13 vols. (Boston: Houghton, Mifflin, 1891). Also: *The Poetical Works of Oliver Wendell Holmes*, ed. Eleanor M. Tilton (Boston: Houghton Mifflin, 1975).

Bibliographies:

Thomas Franklin Currier and Eleanor M. Tilton, *A Bibliography of Oliver Wendell Holmes* (New York: New York University Press, 1953); Barry Menikoff, "Oliver Wendell Holmes," in *Fifteen American Authors Before 1900*, ed. Robert A. Rees and Earl N. Harbert (Madison: University of Wisconsin Press, 1971), pp. 207-228.

Biographies:

John T. Morse, Jr., *Life and Letters of Oliver Wendell Holmes*, 2 vols. (Boston: Houghton, Mifflin, 1896); M. A. DeWolfe Howe, *Holmes of the Breakfast-Table* (New York: Oxford University Press, 1939); Eleanor M. Tilton, *Amiable Autocrat: A Biography of Dr. Oliver Wendell Holmes* (New York: Henry Schuman, 1947); Miriam Rossiter Small, *Oliver Wendell Holmes* (New York: Twayne, 1962).

Letters:

John T. Morse, Jr., *Life and Letters of Oliver Wendell Holmes*.

Criticism:

S. I. Hayakawa and Howard Mumford Jones, *Oliver Wendell Holmes: Representative Selections* (New York: American Book Company, 1939).

Papers:

The major Holmes Collection is in the Houghton Library at Harvard University. Additional repositories are: Library of Congress, Francis A. Countway Library of Medicine in Boston, Harvard University Archives, and Henry E. Huntington Library.

JULIA WARD HOWE (27 May 1819-17 October 1910), reformer and author of "The Battle Hymn of the Republic," was born in New York City to a comfortable banking family and was educated privately. In 1843 she married Samuel Gridley Howe, her senior by some twenty years, and head of the Perkins Institution for the Blind in Boston. Maternal duties were coupled with marital problems, and the witty, scholarly Mrs. Howe sought self-expression and release from personal tension in verse and plays. Her first work, *Passion-Flowers* (1854), was published anonymously, to be followed by *Words for the Hour* and *A Trip to Cuba*. It was not until December 1861, when she wrote "The Battle Hymn of the Republic," that she captured the public imagination. Various versions of its composition exist. According to one, Mrs. Howe, having watched a review of the Army of the Potomac, returned to Washington with a party of Bostonians who sang "John Brown's Body"; the next morning she penciled the stanzas in her room at Willard's Hotel. According to another version, Mrs. Howe was inspired while visiting a camp near the capital with the party of Governor John A. Andrew of Massachusetts, and scribbled the lines in a tent. James Freeman Clarke is said to have urged her to write suitable words to the chant. With a title phrased by James T. Fields, "The Battle Hymn of the Republic" was first published in his *Atlantic Monthly* (February 1862), and the author was paid $4. Almost immediately the poem achieved tremendous popularity, except perhaps among the soldiers themselves. Its Biblical cadences echoed sonorously; its lines stirred a nation at war; its organ tones swept the North. With a single poem, Julia Ward Howe was on her way to becoming a legend in her time. The periodical press carried her imitative verses and idealistic articles. The *Galaxy* paid her $10 to $20 a poem. For *Is Polite Society Polite?* she received a 10% royalty until costs were earned and then 15%. She was a vice-president of the Association of American Authors and the first woman elected (1908) to the American Academy of Arts and Letters. She died in Middletown, Rhode Island. As late as 1921, George S. Hellman could describe her as "the most notable woman of letters born and bred in the metropolis of America." Such a statement appears without foundation today. It is more accurate to regard her as the "Dearest Old Lady in America." As she aged she allied herself with universal reforms: woman suffrage and the woman's club movement, peace and prison reform. The diminutive Mrs. Howe, who resembled Queen Victoria, was ubiquitous on the lecture and convention platform, peering over silver-

rimmed spectacles and urging in a crisp Boston accent her lofty reforms. "The Battle Hymn of the Republic" was sung or recited at most of her appearances. Though she continued to write essays and studies of social manners for half a century, the moment of genius that had produced "The Battle Hymn" never recurred. It was fittingly sung at Boston's Symphony Hall for her memorial service, and it is still sung today. —*Madeleine B. Stern*

Principal Works: *Passion-Flowers* (Boston: Ticknor, Reed & Fields, 1854); *Words for the Hour* (Boston: Ticknor & Fields, 1857); *A Trip to Cuba* (Boston: Ticknor & Fields, 1860); *Later Lyrics* (Boston: J. E. Tilton, 1866); *From the Oak to the Olive. A Plain Record of a Pleasant Journey* (Boston: Lee & Shepard, 1868); *Memoir of Dr. Samuel Gridley Howe* (Boston: Albert J. Wright, 1876); *Modern Society* (Boston: Roberts Brothers, 1881); *Margaret Fuller (Marchesa Ossoli)* (Boston: Roberts Brothers, 1883); *Is Polite Society Polite? and Other Essays* (Boston & New York: Lamson, Wolffe, 1895); *From Sunset Ridge Poems Old and New* (Boston: Houghton, Mifflin, 1898); *Reminiscences 1819-1899* (Boston: Houghton, Mifflin, 1899).

Principal References: Laura E. Richards and Maud Howe Elliott, *Julia Ward Howe 1819-1910*, 2 vols. (Boston: Houghton Mifflin, 1915); Louise Hall Tharp, *Three Saints and a Sinner: Julia Ward Howe, Louisa, Annie and Sam Ward* (Boston: Little, Brown, 1956).

SAMUEL JOHNSON (10 October 1822-19 February 1882), Transcendentalist minister and Orientalist, was born in Salem, Massachusetts. A graduate of Harvard Divinity School, Johnson refused ordination and instead accepted an invitation to minister to a Unitarian society in Lynn, Massachusetts, on the condition that it sever all ties to the Unitarian body and reorganize as an independent group. His connection with the Lynn Free Church lasted from 1853 until his retirement in 1870. During his tenure, he preached abolitionism, temperance, woman's rights, labor rights, and universal religion. The latter topic was of particular importance to Johnson, who viewed the various religions of the world as evolving toward a single or universal religion.

Johnson elaborated his theory in sermons and speeches throughout New England and finally brought it to focus in *Oriental Religions and Their Relation to Universal Religion*, three large volumes on *India* (Boston: James R. Osgood, 1872), *China* (Boston: James R. Osgood, 1877), and *Persia* (Boston: Houghton, Mifflin, 1885). Although soon outdated because of rapid advances in Western knowledge of the cultures and sacred literature of Asia, the importance of the works lies in their synthesizing approach. They are a natural extension of the Transcendentalist quest for communion between East and West first articulated by Ralph Waldo Emerson and Henry David Thoreau, and an important link with such later investigators as Paul Carus, Alan Watts, and the hundreds of lesser-known figures currently exploring ways in which the religions of the East may speak to the spiritual condition of the West. He died in Andover, Massachusetts. REFERENCES: *Lectures, Essays, and Sermons, With a Memoir by Samuel Longfellow* (Boston: Houghton, Mifflin, 1883); Carl T. Jackson, "The Orient in Post-Bellum American Thought: Three Pioneer Popularizers," *American Quarterly*, 12 (Spring 1970): 68-72; Roger C. Mueller, "Samuel Johnson (1822-1882): Universal Religion in the Nineteenth Century," *The Aryan Path*, 43 (April 1972): 164-168; Jackson, "Oriental Ideas in American Thought," *Dictionary of the History of Ideas*, ed. Philip P. Wiener (New York: Scribners, 1973), 3:427-439.

—Roger C. Mueller

Sylvester Judd

Brockway, "Sylvester Judd: Novelist of Transcendentalism," *New England Quarterly*, 13 (December 1940): 654-657; Jacob Blanck, *Bibliography of American Literature* (New Haven: Yale University Press, 1969), 5: 224-227.

Charles Lane.

[signature: Sylvester Judd]

SYLVESTER JUDD (23 July 1813-26 January 1853), novelist and reformer, was born in Westhampton, Massachusetts, and educated at Yale University, graduating in 1836. Soon afterwards he converted to Unitarianism and attended the Harvard Divinity School, receiving his degree in 1840. He settled permanently in Augusta, Maine, and in 1841 was married. Judd was a lifelong reformer, promoting church reform, woman's rights, and temperance. His best-known work is *Margaret: A Tale of the Real and Ideal* (Boston: Jordan & Wiley, 1845), which combines an accurate portrayal of life in early New England with, through the influence of Unitarianism and Emerson, a picture of an idealistic utopia. Many critics have called it the only Transcendental novel. Judd's long poem, *Philo: An Evangeliad* (Boston: Phillips, Sampson, 1850), also espouses religious and social reform. REFERENCES: Arethusa Hall, *Life and Character of the Rev. Sylvester Judd* (Boston: Crosby, Nichols, 1854); Hall, *Memorabilia: From the Journals of Sylvester Judd* (Northampton, Mass.: Metcalf, 1882); Philip Judd

CHARLES LANE (31 March 1800-5 January 1870), English Transcendentalist and social reformer, greatly aided Bronson Alcott in establishing his Fruitlands community at Harvard, Massachusetts, in 1843. Alcott met Lane while in England in 1842 and brought him back with him to America. Lane provided the capital for Alcott's utopian venture and when it failed in 1844, he lived with the Shakers. In 1846 Lane returned to England for good. His most important work is his favorable "A. Bronson Alcott's Works" (*Dial*, 3 [April 1843]: 417-453).
REFERENCES: Roger William Cummins, "The Second Eden: Charles Lane and American Transcendentalism," Ph.D. dissertation, University of Minnesota, 1967; Robert Howard Walker, "Charles Lane and the Fruitlands Utopia," Ph.D. dissertation, University of Texas, 1967.

Henry Wadsworth Longfellow

Steven Allaback
University of California at Santa Barbara

BIRTH: Portland, Maine, 27 February 1807.

MARRIAGES: Mary Storer Potter (1812-1835), in Portland, Maine, 14 September 1831. Frances Appleton (1817-1861), in Boston, 13 July 1843. Six children: Charles (1844-1893), Ernest (1845-1921), Fanny (1847-1848), Alice (1850-1928), Edith (1853-1915), Anne (1855-1934).

DEATH: Cambridge, Massachusetts, 24 March 1882.

MAJOR WORKS: *Voices of the Night* (Cambridge: John Owen, 1839); *Ballads and Other Poems* (Cambridge: John Owen, 1842); *The Belfry of Bruges and Other Poems* (Cambridge: John Owen, 1846); *Evangeline, A Tale of Acadie* (Boston: William D. Ticknor, 1847); *The Seaside and the Fireside* (Boston: Ticknor, Reed & Fields, 1850); *The Song of Hiawatha* (Boston: Ticknor & Fields, 1855); *The Courtship of Miles Standish and Other Poems* (Boston: Ticknor & Fields, 1858); *Tales of a Wayside Inn* (Boston: Ticknor & Fields, 1863).

Life and Career:

During his lifetime and for some years after his death, Henry Wadsworth Longfellow was by far the most popular and widely read American poet in the world. Although his reputation today is greatly diminished, a portion of his work is still respected by critics, is enjoyed by ordinary readers, and stands as a permanent addition to literature and folklore. Longfellow wrote prolifically for nearly a half century and was very much a man of his time. To students of history his work is a valuable repository of the moral and spiritual ideals of Victorian America. A remarkably well-educated and well-travelled man, Longfellow was also an important scholar and educator. He was a college professor, a translator, a writer of textbooks, a compiler of anthologies. Because he and his wife were famous for their hospitality and good natures, his home in Cambridge became a gathering place for prominent people of many different occupations—writers, politicians, musicians, businessmen, teachers. Their influence upon one another, under the benign auspices of Longfellow, is incalculable.

Stephen Longfellow, the poet's father, was a successful Portland lawyer and politician, a member of the Eighteenth Congress of the United States, and trustee of Bowdoin College in Brunswick, Maine, where Henry went in 1822, at the age of fifteen, after a full and happy childhood. Henry's mother, Zilpah Wadsworth Longfellow, was highly intelligent, devoutly religious, a lover of books and culture, and encouraged her son to pursue his literary ambitions. While still a student at Bowdoin, Longfellow published poems and essays in such places as the *American Monthly Magazine* and the *United States Literary Gazette*. He began to "aspire after future eminence in literature," as he wrote his father during his senior year, "my whole soul burns most ardently for it." "Nothing delights me more," he realized, "than reading and writing. . . ."

Upon graduation in 1825 (he was fourth in a class of thirty-eight), he read law in his father's office for a few months and then embarked for Europe, partly to satisfy what he called his "voracious appetite for knowledge" and partly to prepare himself for the newly established chair of modern languages at Bowdoin to which he would soon be appointed. For the next three years he studied and travelled in France, Germany, Spain, and Italy, trying to master the languages, meeting new people and establishing friendships, immersing himself in as many exotic settings as he could. His European experiences would subsequently be the inspiration for much of his work, including his first substantial literary effort, *Outre-Mer; A Pilgrimage Beyond the Sea* (New York: Harpers, 1835), a series of sketches and observations in imitation of Washington Irving.

From 1829 to 1835 Longfellow was at Bowdoin College where he made himself into an admired teacher and one of the most promising young scholars of his day. Although he occasionally wrote poetry during these years, most of his time was spent preparing textbooks and translations for use in his own classes. Several essays on literary subjects, including "The Defense of Poetry" in 1832, appeared in the *North American Review* and helped to make his name known outside Brunswick. In late 1834, he was offered the position of Smith Professor of Modern Languages at Harvard to succeed George Ticknor. He was also given the opportunity to spend a year in Europe so that he could achieve, according to the letter of nomination, "a more perfect attainment of the German. . . ." Weary of the insulated life in the small college town, still eager to make his mark on a wider world, he called himself "a very lucky fellow" and joyfully accepted the new job.

In the spring of 1835, accompanied by his pregnant wife, Mary, and two of her friends, Longfellow set out on his second trip to Europe. But in November of that year, in Rotterdam, his young wife died of complications following a miscarriage. This unexpected event caused him more sustained anguish than he had ever known and helped to turn him into a dedicated poet and away from an exclusively scholarly career. In Longfellow's highly autobiographical *Hypérion; A Romance* (New York: S. Colman, 1839), the hero, Paul Flemming, after the death of his wife, wanders distractedly over Europe. The world "seemed to him less beautiful, and life became earnest." *Hyperion* has some interest as an account of contemporary Europe as seen from an American viewpoint.

Craigie-Longfellow house in Cambridge.

In the fall of 1836 Longfellow took up residence in Cambridge, Massachusetts, where he would live for the rest of his life. For the next few years he devoted himself to his onerous teaching duties, to a long and frustrating courtship, to cultivating convivial friendships with such men as Charles Sumner and Cornelius Felton, and to his writing. His work appeared regularly in newspapers and magazines in New York and Philadelphia and poems like "A Psalm of Life" and "The Wreck of the Hesperus" were already famous by the time they were collected into *Voices of the Night* (1839) and *Ballads and Other Poems* (1841).

With these two volumes, however, Longfellow's popularity soared even higher. *Voices of the Night* went through six editions in two years and such lines as "Tell me not, in mournful number, / Life is but

an empty dream!" became to thousands of readers more familiar than any lines yet written by an American. Longfellow dealt with important subjects clearly and forthrightly while adopting a frankly didactic and inspirational tone. He believed that poetry should be "an instrument for improving the condition of society, and advancing the great purpose of human happiness." Poetry could be, and often had been, debased and perverted, but its proper function was to exalt, to purify, to stir the human spirit. Longfellow admired Wordsworth because "the republican simplicity of his poetry" was "in unison with our moral and political doctrines." In *Voices of the Night*, as in the majority of his shorter poems for the next forty years, the emphasis is on simple truths: "Learn to labor and to wait"; "Know how sublime a thing it is / To suffer and be strong"; "Faith shineth as a morning star, / Our ghostly fears are dead."

Although an interest in foreign languages and literatures would always be a hallmark of Longfellow's work, in *Ballads and Other Poems* are several poems, including "The Village Blacksmith," written solely on American themes, the discovery and development of which became one of his enthusiasms. In 1840 he had told a friend that the national ballad "is a virgin soil here in New England; and there are good materials. Besides I have a great notion of working upon *people's feelings*," a notion which he retained throughout his career.

In "The Village Blacksmith" is the stanza:

> Toiling,—rejoicing,—sorrowing,
> Onward through life he goes;
> Each morning sees some task begin,
> Each evening sees it close;
> Something attempted, something done,
> Has earned a night's repose.

As in so many of his poems, the metrical regularity here and the careful rhyme help to reinforce Longfellow's basic assumptions that life is meaningful, has its regular cycles and distinct rhythms, and that "toiling" and "sorrowing" should always be kept in clear perspective. In "The Rainy Day" are these couplets:

> Be still, sad heart! and cease repining;
> Behind the clouds is the sun still shining;
> Thy fate is the common fate of all,
> Into each life some rain must fall. . .

Bracing and confident, this is the voice of a man who is embarrassed by strident complainers and by overly

> There in the twilight cold and gray,
> Lifeless but beautiful he lay,
> And from the sky serene and far
> A voice fell like a falling star
>
> Excelsior!
>
> *Henry W. Longfellow.*

complicated explanations of man's fate. Longfellow always believed that if a poet "wishes the world to listen and be edified, he will do well to choose a language that is generally understood."

Despite the success of his first two volumes of poetry, in 1842 Longfellow was in ill health, profoundly depressed, and very lonely, and so he took a leave of absence from Harvard and went again to Europe, this time to take the water-cure at Marienberg. During the year he finished *Poems on Slavery* (Cambridge: John Owen, 1842), an undistinguished but sincere collection which Longfellow himself called "mild" and which told of the evils of slavery and warned of the possible conflagration to come. He also formed lasting friendships with Charles Dickens and Ferdinand Freiligrath, the German poet.

The physical and emotional distress which prompted Longfellow's third trip to Europe had been caused principally by his failure, after nearly seven years of courtship, to win the hand of Frances Appleton, the beautiful and accomplished daughter of a wealthy Boston merchant. But a few months after his return to the United States, Fanny changed her mind, and Longfellow's life was instantly transformed. "My whole soul," he said in May 1843, "is filled with peace and serenity . . . all that so agitated me, and sent me swinging and ill-poised through the void and empty space, all this is ended." For a wedding present, Nathan Appleton gave his daughter and new son-in-law the already famous Craigie House. The next eighteen years, until Fanny's death in 1861, were the happiest and most productive of Longfellow's career.

The Belfry of Bruges and Other Poems (1845) continued to increase his fame and to demonstrate his remarkable metrical facility and the great range of his subjects—from "The Arsenal at Springfield" to "Rain in Summer" to "Nuremberg" to the fine sonnet "Mezzo Cammin."

Evangeline, A Tale of Acadie (1847), his first long narrative poem, daringly written in hexameters, went through six printings in nine weeks and remained one of Longfellow's best-known works throughout the century. Set during the French and Indian War at the time when the English expelled about 6,000 French Acadians from Nova Scotia, it tells the story of Evangeline Bellefontaine's separation from her bridegroom, Gabriel Lajeuness. After spending her life wandering over the United States in search of him, she finally encounters Gabriel, old and dying in an almshouse, in Philadelphia, where she had become a Sister of Mercy. Although the main characters themselves are a trifle insipid, Longfellow exploits the ancient themes of separation, exile, search, and constancy, and his careful attention to details of the landscape—rivers, prairies, forests, mountain ranges—makes the poem a distinctively American narrative.

The Seaside and the Fireside (1850) sold more than 30,000 copies in the next five years. It contains such gentle poems as "The Fire of Driftwood" and "The Secret of the Sea," the beginning of which reveals one of Longfellow's favorite subjects and most characteristic moods:

> Ah! what pleasant visions haunt me
>   As I gaze upon the sea!
> All the old romantic legends,
>   All my dreams, come back to me.

During the 1840s and into the 1850s Longfellow frequently complained in his journal and to his closest friends about his pressing college obligations, his increasingly large numbers of visitors and distractions, and his ever-widening correspondence, yet he continued to work hard. In addition to poetry, he wrote a novel, *Kavanagh* (Boston: Ticknor, Reed & Fields, 1849), a verse drama, *The Golden Legend* (Boston: Ticknor, Reed & Fields, 1851), and he edited three anthologies, including the enormously influential *Poets and Poetry of Europe* (Philadelphia: Carey & Hart, 1845), a compendium of Longfellow's own scholarship and the most complete volume of its type to appear in America up to then. During these years he also fathered six children, watched over the affairs of his parents and his brothers, lived a busy social life, and shrewdly managed his financial arrangements with various publishers. Primarily because he had been able to change almost single-handedly the reading public's attitude towards poets and poetry, Longfellow also became the first American poet to make substantial sums from his work.

In 1854, after years of talking about it, Longfellow finally resigned from Harvard. Along with George Ticknor before him, he had succeeded in establishing the field of modern languages and literatures in this country, and his value as a one man force against American academic provincialism has perhaps never been fully appreciated. Shortly after

Longfellow at age forty-four.

he delivered his final college lecture, Longfellow set to work on *The Song of Hiawatha* (1855), the epic about the son of the west wind. Hiawatha is raised among the Ojibwas, attains supernatural powers, has many adventures, including his separation from and return to his people, marries the beautiful Dacotah, Minnehaha, and becomes a benevolent and wise ruler. Eventually famine, fever, and the encroaching whites force him to leave, but he tells his people to heed the new religion brought by the missionaries. As early as 1823 Longfellow had told his father that the Indians "are a race possessing magnanimity, generosity, benevolence, and pure religion without hypocrisy" and who "have been most barbarously maltreated by the whites." Twenty years later in *Hiawatha* Longfellow intended to "weave together their beautiful traditions into a whole." It sold 50,000 copies within a year and a half. Even though shortly after publication a loud controversy developed over its indebtedness to the Finnish epic, *Kalevala*, *Hiawatha* became Longfellow's most popular work.

In the middle 1850s Longfellow's productivity fell off by comparison to earlier years, a fact which he lamented from time to time ("I lead the life of any respectable gentleman," he said in 1857, "whose time is frittered away with the nothings of every-day existence"), but he nevertheless continued to write whenever he could. Not long after his fiftieth birthday he calculated that his books had sold more than 300,000 copies. In 1858, after several false starts, Longfellow finally concluded his third long poem of American life, *The Courtship of Miles Standish,* which he called "an idyll of old Colony times." It tells how Captain Standish asks his friend John Alden to woo the maid Priscilla on his behalf and then loses her to him. On the day of John and Priscilla's wedding, however, all three are reconciled and vow to continue their friendship forever. As the happy bride and groom cross a brook to their new house,

> Like a picture it seemed of the primitive,
>   pastoral ages,
> Fresh with the youth of the world, and
>   recalling Rebecca and Isaac,
> Old and yet ever new, and simple and
>   beautiful always,
> Love immortal and young in the endless
>   succession of lovers.

In July 1861, tragedy struck Longfellow for the second time. While sealing packets of her daughters' hair with wax, Fanny Longfellow's dress suddenly caught on fire. She ran to her husband and he tried to smother the flames with a small rug, but she was badly burned and died the next day. The Longfellows' marriage had been monumentally successful, their relationship the envy of everyone who knew them, and Fanny's death was a bitter blow to Henry. A muted sense of loss pervades much of his later work, but probably the most moving testimony of his grief is "The Cross of Snow," written eighteen years after the event.

In 1863 Longfellow published the first part of *Tales of a Wayside Inn,* a collection of tales and interludes in the manner of *The Canterbury Tales,* and among the more variegated, delightful, and underrated of his works. Gathered at a New England inn are a number of people—including a student, a musician, and a landlord—each of whom tell a tale, the most famous of which, told by the landlord, is "Paul Revere's Ride." It is a stirring example of a kind of American folk chant which Longfellow could often do so well: "Listen, my children, and you shall hear / Of the midnight ride of Paul Revere...." Further segments of *Tales of a Wayside Inn* were published in 1872 and 1873.

From the conclusion of the Civil War to the end

Longfellow at age forty-seven.

of his life Longfellow experienced an outpouring of worldwide veneration and respect that few writers— few people—have ever known. With his long hair and white beard (which he had grown to conceal the scars from burns received while trying to save Fanny) he was an impressive looking figure, and because he was kind, friendly, and accessible, the public adored Longfellow the man as enthusiastically as it read his poetry. His trip to Europe in 1868 turned into a triumphant tour. Oxford and Cambridge granted him degrees, he was received by the Queen and the Archbishop of Canterbury, he visited Charles Dickens, Alfred Tennyson, William Gladstone, and on the continent he was acclaimed by Victor Hugo and became the center of attention wherever he travelled. In parts of the United States during the 1870s, school children celebrated his birthday as if it were a national holiday. He was continually being visited at the Craigie House by distinguished foreign visitors—Anthony Trollope, Wilkie Collins, the Duke of Argyll—as well as by hundreds of beginning authors and readers of his work. By the time of his death in 1882 he was, as one biographer has called him, the "grand old man of American letters."

In his later years, in addition to guiding his children to maturity, Longfellow completed several large projects including his translation of *The Divine Comedy*, 3 vols. (Boston: Ticknor & Fields, 1865-1867), a labor of love he had worked on since his Harvard days. His lifelong interest in Christianity culminated in the epic, *Christus: A Mystery* (Boston: James R. Osgood, 1872). He was editor-in-chief of a huge, thirty-one volume anthology, *Poems of Places* (Boston: James R. Osgood, 1877-1878; Boston: Houghton, Osgood, 1878-1879). But with the exception of an occasional medium length piece like "Keramos" and "Morituri Salutamus," written for the fiftieth reunion of his Bowdoin College class, his finest achievements were in the short lyric. A stately poem like "The Tide Rises, the Tide Falls," written three years before his death, is a good example of Longfellow's view of life as a somewhat sad but purposeful journey which is being taken in conjunction with certain orderly natural processes. It begins:

> The tide rises, the tide falls,
> The twilight darkens, the curlew calls,
> Along the sea-sands damp and brown
> The traveller hastens toward the town,
>   And the tide rises, the tide falls.

In Longfellow's later poetry there are a number of cheerless and somber moments, as in "Autumn Within":

> It is autumn; not without,
>   But within me is the cold.
> Youth and spring are all about;
>   It is I that have grown old.

And there are a number of ambivalent attitudes expressed toward God and Heaven, such as these lines from "Moonlight":

> We see but what we have the gift
>   Of seeing; what we bring we find.

He refers frequently to the "vast Unknown" and often notes (with approval) how much is beyond man's knowledge: "There are great truths that pitch their shining tents / Outside our walls. . . ."

But the majority of poems written in his final years are expressions of faith and hope: that "death is a beginning, not an end," that there is a balancing-out in life (the "lowest ebb is the turn of the tide"), and that we are faced less often with blank stone walls than with possibilities. The last lines he wrote, from "The Bells of San Blas," are, appropriately, these:

> Out of the shadows of night

> The world rolls into light;
> It is daybreak everywhere.

Shortly after *Voices of the Night* was published in 1839 Hawthorne wrote Longfellow that "Nothing equal to some of them was ever written in this world,—this western world, I mean; and it would not hurt my conscience much to include the other hemisphere." The *North American Review* proclaimed that "they are among the most remarkable poetical compositions which have ever appeared in the United States." In 1851 John Ruskin said that Longfellow's poems have more influence than "all Byron's works put together" and appeal to "the strongest minds of the day." In 1869 the *Illustrated London News* said that there "is no English poet now living who has so many readers in England as Longfellow. His writings are, indeed, known to the million; they find a place on shelf or table in the humblest artisan's house, where Tennyson and Browning have not yet come." In 1876, by his own calculation, Longfellow had had twenty-two different publishers in England alone. Although there were always a few dissenting voices—Margaret Fuller and Edgar Allan Poe, to name two—Longfellow's reputation among both the public and literary critics remained uniformly high until long after his death.

By the end of the century, however, the new science and technology, the rise of realism and naturalism, westward expansion, industrialization, immigration, all began to make the quiet verities of Longfellow seem old-fashioned if not obsolete to most of the younger critics. But the ordinary reader continued to enjoy him. The British publishing house of Routledge sold more than 716,000 copies of his poems by 1900; Frederick Warne & Co. sold 411,000 between 1865 and 1900; and they were only two of many firms which sold his works. Longfellow remained a favorite in America until World War I.

Between the two wars Longfellow's reputation steadily declined among all readers. He began to be commonly regarded as an easy poet, a children's poet, a naive and sentimental man, something of an embarrassment. Some of his most famous poems had become shopworn, the object of parody and contempt, perhaps the object of too much memorization in the public schools. In 1915 Van Wyck Brooks said that Longfellow "is to poetry what the barrel-organ is to music," and in the early thirties Ludwig Lewisohn asked the now infamous question, "Who, except wretched school children, now reads Longfellow?" In Brooks and Warrens'

Longfellow in mid-life.

1962 and 1964 came biographies by Newton Arvin and Cecil B. Williams; and several studies since have seen Longfellow as a folk poet or a parlor poet or a people's poet. Today, most readers would probably agree with Howard Nemerov that many Longfellow poems have "an interest other than historical, scholarly, or biographical—an interest truly poetical, and undiminished by time." The consensus among critics is that much of his work is bad, best forgotten, but there is a considerable portion that is quite good.

Longfellow in old age.

Understanding Poetry (1938), a harbinger of the New Criticism, as important in its day as Longfellow's *Poets and Poetry of Europe* was in its own, the single Longfellow poem included is virtually laughed at.

In 1837, in his review of Hawthorne's *Twice-Told Tales*, Longfellow had claimed that "the true poet is a friendly man" who looks upon all things "in the spirit of love." To him all things have "a life, an end and aim," and all things "are beautiful and holy." The poetic mind feels "a universal sympathy with Nature, both in the material world and in the soul of man." It is not surprising that in the fragmented and violent twentieth century most readers of poetry become distrustful, even resentful, of this sort of voice.

In 1955 Edward Wagenknecht published *Long-fellow: A Full-Length Portrait*, and a reassessment of Longfellow began. In 1959 came Howard Nemerov's balanced and appreciative *Longfellow* in the widely distributed Laurel Poetry Series (Dell); in

As Newton Arvin puts it, the "author of *Hiawatha*, or *Tales of a Wayside Inn*, of *Michael Angelo* was a lesser but not a little writer, a minor poet but not a poetaster." For Longfellow a poem was often a deliberate idealization and simplification of idea and feeling, a sweet-sounding distillation of common truth. He has left at least thirty to fifty short, unpretentious lyrics, in addition to a few longer pieces, that are likely to have readers far into the future.

Other Writings:

Coplas de Don Jorge Manrique—translation (Boston:

Allen & Ticknor, 1833); *The Spanish Student, A Play in Three Acts* (Cambridge: John Owen, 1843); *The Waif*—anthology (Cambridge: John Owen, 1844); *The Estray*—anthology (Boston: William D. Ticknor, 1846); *Drift Wood, A Collection of Essays* (Boston: Ticknor & Fields, 1857); *Flower-de-Luce* (Boston: Ticknor & Fields, 1867); *The New England Tragedies* (Boston: Ticknor & Fields, 1868); *The Divine Tragedy* (Boston: James R. Osgood, 1871); *Three Books of Song* (Boston: James R. Osgood, 1872); *Aftermath* (Boston: James R. Osgood, 1873); *The Hanging of the Crane* (Boston: James R. Osgood, 1874); *The Masque of Pandora and Other Poems* (Boston: James R. Osgood, 1875); *Keramos and Other Poems* (Boston: Houghton, Osgood, 1878); *Ultima Thule* (Boston: Houghton, Mifflin, 1880); *In the Harbor* (Boston: Houghton, Mifflin, 1882); *Michael Angelo* (Boston: Houghton, Mifflin, 1884). Also: *Complete Works*, ed. by Horace E. Scudder, Riverside Edition, 11 vols. (Boston: Houghton, Mifflin, 1886); reprinted in Standard Library Edition, with *Life* by Samuel Longfellow, 14 vols. (Boston: Houghton, Mifflin, 1891); reprinted in Craigie Edition, 11 vols. (Boston: Houghton, Mifflin, 1904).

Bibliographies:

Luther S. Livingston, *A Bibliography of the First Editions in Book Form of the Writings of Henry Wadsworth Longfellow* (New York: privately printed, 1908); H. W. L. Dana, "Henry Wadsworth Longfellow," in Vol. II of the *Cambridge History of American Literature* (New York: Putnam's, 1917); Jacob Blanck, *Bibliography of American Literature* (New Haven: Yale University Press, 1969), 5:468-640.

Biographies:

William Sloane Kennedy, *Henry W. Longfellow: Biography, Anecdote, Letters, Criticism* (Cambridge: Moses King, 1882); George L. Austin, *Henry Wadsworth Longfellow; His Life, His Works, His Friendships* (Boston: Lee & Shepard, 1883); Samuel Longfellow, *Life of Henry Wadsworth Longfellow*, 2 vols. (Boston: Ticknor, 1886), and *Final Memorials of Henry Wadsworth Longfellow* (Boston: Ticknor, 1887); Ernest Wadsworth Longfellow, *Random Memories* (Boston: Houghton Mifflin, 1922); Herbert Gorman, *A Victorian American, Henry Wadsworth Longfellow* (New York: Doran, 1926); Lawrance Thompson, *Young Longfellow, 1807-1843* (New York: Macmillan, 1938); Edward

Wagenknecht, *Longfellow: A Full-Length Portrait* (New York: Longmans, Green, 1955); Newton Arvin, *Longfellow: His Life and Work* (Boston: Little, Brown, 1962); Cecil B. Williams, *Henry Wadsworth Longfellow* (New York: Twayne, 1964).

Letters:

The Letters of Henry Wadsworth Longfellow, ed. Andrew Hilen, 4 vols. to date (Cambridge: Harvard University Press, 1967-).

Criticism:

E. C. Stedman, *Poets of America* (Boston: Houghton, Mifflin, 1885); Charles E. Norton, *Henry Wadsworth Longfellow* (Boston: Houghton, Mifflin, 1907); Oliphant Smeaton, *Longfellow & His Poetry* (London: G. Harrap, 1919); Iris Whitman, *Longfellow and Spain* (New York: Instituto de las Espanas en los Estados Unidos, 1927); James T. Hatfield, *New Light on Longfellow* (Boston: Houghton, Mifflin, 1933); John Van Schaick Jr., *The Characters in "Tales of a Wayside Inn"* (Boston: Universalist Publishing House, 1939); Carl L. Johnson, *Professor Longfellow of Harvard* (Eugene: University of Oregon Press, 1944); Andrew Hilen, *Longfellow and Scandinavia* (New Haven: Yale University Press, 1947); George Arms, *The Fields Were Green* (Stanford: Stanford University Press, 1948); Edward Wagenknecht, *The Unknown Longfellow* (Boston: Boston University Press, 1954); Howard Nemerov, "Introduction" to *Longfellow* (New York: Dell, 1959); Edward L. Hirsh, *Henry Wadsworth Longfellow* (Minneapolis: University of Minnesota Press, 1964); *Longfellow Reconsidered: A Symposium*, ed. J. Chesley Mathews (Hartford, Ct.: Transcendental Books, 1973).

Papers:

The bulk of The Longfellow Papers are at the Houghton Library of Harvard University.

SAMUEL LONGFELLOW (18 June 1819-3 October 1892), Unitarian clergyman, hymn writer, and essayist, is best known as the biographer of his oldest brother, Henry Wadsworth Longfellow. He was born in Portland, Maine, attended the Portland Academy, and in 1835 entered Harvard College. Upon graduation in 1838, he taught school and tutored for a time, and in 1842 entered the Harvard Divinity School, where he became deeply interested in Transcendentalism and liberal theology in general. In 1848 he was ordained Unitarian minister at Fall River, Massachusetts, and in 1853 he assumed the pastorate at the Second Unitarian Church in Brooklyn, New York. Here he first introduced the vesper service to the Unitarian Church, emphasized the solving of social problems, and wrote a series of hymns. After 1860 he travelled, held various temporary pastorates, and devoted his time to writing. In 1886 he published the two-volume *Life of Henry Wadsworth Longfellow* (Boston: Ticknor), and in 1887, *Final Memorials of Henry Wadsworth Longfellow* (Boston: Ticknor). He died in Portland. In 1854, with Thomas Wentworth Higginson, he had published *Thalatta: A Book for the Seaside*

(Boston: Ticknor, Reed & Fields), in 1860, *A Book of Hymns and Tunes* (New York: Gray), and in 1864, with Samuel Johnson, *Hymns of the Spirit* (Boston: James R. Osgood). His hymns are fervid, very beautiful, and nondenominational, and a few are still being sung today. He was known as a pure Theist who was somewhat radical even for a Unitarian. An incident in Henry W. Longfellow's novel, *Kavanagh* (1849), is based on the consequences of Samuel Longfellow's opposition from the pulpit to the Mexican War. REFERENCES: A. P. Putnam, *Singers and Songs of the Liberal Faith* (Boston: Roberts Brothers, 1875); O. F. Adams, "Samuel Longfellow," *New England Magazine* (October 1894): 205-213; Joseph May, *Samuel Longfellow: Memoirs and Letters* (Boston: Houghton, Mifflin, 1894). —*Steven Allaback*

James Russell Lowell

Thomas Wortham
University of California, Los Angeles

BIRTH: Cambridge, Massachusetts, 22 February 1819.

MARRIAGES: Maria White (1821-1853), in Watertown, Massachusetts, 26 December 1844; four children: Blanche (1845-1847), Mabel (1847-1898), Rose (1849-1850), Walter (1850-1852); Frances Dunlap (1823-1885), in Portland, Maine, 16 September 1857; no children.

DEATH: Cambridge, Massachusetts, 12 August 1891.

MAJOR WORKS: *A Fable for Critics* (New York: Putnam's, 1848); *The Biglow Papers* (Cambridge: Nichols, 1848); *The Vision of Sir Launfal* (Cambridge: Nichols, 1848); *The Biglow Papers, Second Series* (Boston: Ticknor & Fields, 1867); *The Cathedral* (Boston: Fields, Osgood, 1870); *Among My Books* (Boston: Fields, Osgood, 1870); *My Study Windows* (Boston: James R. Osgood, 1871); *Among My Books, Second Series* (Boston: James R. Osgood, 1876).

Life and Career:

Lowell's achievements are impressive from many points of view. Though his lyrical verse was overrated in his own time, his merits as a critic, a satirist, an essayist, an educator, a diplomat, a journalist, and a letter writer continue to be acknowledged by discriminating and knowledgeable critics. The most versatile of the New Englanders at mid-century, Lowell, both in his life and his work, is a vital force in the history of American literature and thought during the nineteenth century. Hailed by such dissimilar groups as pacifists and New Humanists, Lowell's final importance has been hard to measure but impossible to ignore. His range and penetration in literary criticism were unequalled in nineteenth-century America. He did more than anyone before Mark Twain in elevating the vernacular to a medium of serious artistic expression, and *The Biglow Papers* ranks among the first of political satires in American literature. His public odes expressed a mind and an outlook that drew the praise of Henry Adams, William James, and William Dean Howells. His personal charm made Lowell both an effective diplomat during the period of America's emergence

as a world power and one of his country's finest letter writers.

Although familiar with the life and literature of the great world, Lowell remained, from first to last, a native of Cambridge in Massachusetts. The New England legacy he inherited there was rich by American standards, and it accounts significantly for the vast difference which separates Lowell from his exact contemporaries, Herman Melville and Walt Whitman. Ministers, judges, business and political leaders were his ancestry, and being a Lowell was both a privilege and a responsibility. Lowell's task in his creative life was in working out solutions to the problem not only of self, but also of place and name.

Educated in Cambridge and Boston, Lowell graduated from Harvard College in 1838. Two years later he was awarded the bachelor of laws degree by Harvard's Law School, but his energies were already dedicated to the profession of letters, and he soon

126

abandoned a legal career. He wanted to be a poet.

Throughout his life Lowell attempted to master a poetic voice, but his efforts were largely unsuccessful, especially in the lyrical mode. The deficiencies which characterized his work in his first volume, *A Year's Life* (1841), are never entirely absent from his more mature performances: technical infelicities and irregularities, didacticism, obscurity, and excessive literosity. Emerson's complaint that Lowell in one of his poems had had to pump too hard describes well the forced quality in most of his poetry. Lowell was probably as much aware of his limitations as were his critics, and he frequently expressed to friends his misgivings. His reference to the volume of poems, *Under the Willows* (1869), as "Under the Billows or dredgings from the Atlantic" is not only a masterful pun (many of the poems had first appeared in the *Atlantic Monthly*) but very close to the truth.

Lowell at age thirty-one.

But as a public poet—either in his Pindaric odes or in his satiric verse—Lowell has no equal in American literature. Drawn into the anti-slavery movement in the early 1840s, Lowell wrote during that decade scores of articles and poems in defense of abolition and other reform causes. His shrewdness

and wit found their natural expression in satire, and while his times greatly praised such poems as "The Present Crisis" (1845) and "On the Capture of Fugitive Slaves near Washington" (1845), it has been *The Biglow Papers* (1848) that has endured. The book purports to be the collected verses of Hosea Biglow, a Yankee farmer who is vehemently opposed to the Mexican War, and the prose commentaries of the Reverend Homer Wilbur, the quintessence of what Oliver Wendell Holmes would later call the Brahmin caste of New England. Both for its satirical portraiture and its sustained irony, *The Biglow Papers* ranks among the masterpieces of American literature.

Maria White Lowell.

Though Lowell never abandoned the cause of reform, he did withdraw from active participation, especially after the death of his first wife in 1853. In 1855 he succeeded Henry Wadsworth Longfellow as professor of modern languages at Harvard, and during the next two decades Lowell produced his finest critical work. While his literary criticism lacks the theoretical or philosophical bent which characterizes the work of his European contemporaries, Matthew Arnold and Hippolyte Taine, it confronts the literary text with unusual success, perhaps because Lowell's approach was largely free of prior purpose. His best essays—"Dryden" (1868), "Shakespeare Once More" (1868), "Chaucer" (1870),

> " Then comes Poe with his raven like Barnaby Rudge,
> Three fifths of him genius & two fifths sheer fudge,
> Who talks like a book of iambs & pentameters,
> In a way to make people of commonsense damn metres,
> Who has written some things quite the best of their kind,
> But the heart in 'em 's wholly squeezed out by the mind,
> Who — but heyday! what's this? Messieurs Mathews & Poe
> You must n't fling mudballs at Longfellow so,
> Does it make a man worse that his character's such
> As to make his friends love him (as you think) too much?
> Why, there is not a bard at this moment alive
> More willing than he that his fellows should thrive;
> While you are abusing him thus, even now
> He would help either one of you out of a slough.
> You may say that he's smooth & all that till you're hoarse
> But remember that elegance also is force;
> After polishing granite as much as you will,
> The heart keeps its tough old persistency still,

Manuscript page from A Fable for Critics *describing*
Edgar Allan Poe.

"Dante" (1872), "Spenser" (1875), and "Gray" (1886)—are distinguished by their common sense, their vigor of expression, their extensive knowledge, their certainty of taste, and a humorous outlook that will not be overawed by the work of man. While Lowell wrote only occasional pieces on American literature, his editorship of the *Atlantic Monthly* (founded in 1857) during its formative years contributed much to the growing realities of an American literature. Though Lowell was not sympathetic to the romantic "egotism" of Thoreau (when Lowell deleted without permission a sentence in one of Thoreau's essays that was printed in the *Atlantic*, Thoreau, in a frenzied outburst, withdrew his support from the new venture) or the poetic experimentations of Whitman, few other writers of significance at the time failed to find their place in the magazine.

Following the Civil War, Lowell lived increasingly in the public eye. In "The Cathedral" (1870), "Agassiz" (1874), and the famed "Commemoration Ode" (1865), there spoke nobly and effectively an American mind that should be considered with Whitman of *Democratic Vistas* and "Respondez!" and, a little later, Henry Adams of *Mont-Saint-Michel and Chartres* and *The Education*. It was altogether natural in the pattern of nineteenth-century American life that Lowell should spend his last years as a representative of his government and culture abroad, first as United States minister to the Spanish court (1877-1880), and afterwards to the Court of St. James in England (1880-1885). Even after his official duties ended, Lowell continued to spend much of his time abroad, either in London or at Whitby in rural Yorkshire, whose simplicity reminded him of the lost American world of his youth. It was during these "diplomatic" years that Lowell made his two finest utterances on the role of the individual in the life of the community, a role he had learned by experience and success: "Democracy" (1884) and "The Place of the Independent in Politics" (1888). This was the Lowell that Henry James knew and recalled in his memorial of Lowell: "He was strong without narrowness; he was wise without bitterness and bright without folly. That appears for the most part the clearest ideal of those who handle the English form, and he was altogether in the straight tradition. This tradition will surely not forfeit its great part in the world so long as we continue occasionally to know it by what is so solid in performance and so stainless in character."

Lowell in 1844.

Lowell in his library.

Lowell's reputation at the time of his death in 1891 was, to use William C. Brownell's term, a superstition. His fame as a man of letters was international, but he was not in any respect a popular writer. Except for a few school-room pieces like "The Vision of Sir Launfal," Lowell's poetry was considered too difficult by most readers; his literary essays, though they enjoyed a larger audience than such do today, nevertheless appealed to a relatively small class of readers; and his early reform writings meant little to a people notorious for their lack of an historical consciousness. His political addresses were widely reported in the press, often quoted at great length in leading newspapers, but compared to such figures as Carl Schurz or even E. L. Godkin, Lowell can hardly be said to have been a popular political writer. It is safe to say that during the last decade of the nineteenth century, readers read more about Lowell than by him.

Increasingly since, readers have read little in either category. Lowell's reputation was so much a matter of received opinion that the attack on it made during the early decades of the twentieth century met with little resistance. Unlike Longfellow and John

Greenleaf Whittier, Lowell has had few advocates, and since World War II, only a handful of significant items have been published about him and his work.

Lowell's decline in the literary market place is both an index to changing literary tastes and values, and the result of critical conflicts and misfortunes. His merits as a writer were not those valued by the New Critics, though, ironically, it was in Lowell that academic criticism had its first significant manifestation in America. His biography has been another battleground for the continuing war between the North and the South, with Horace E. Scudder, Ferris Greenslet, and others praising him largely in terms of New England culture, and Richmond Croom Beatty and Leon Howard damning him on the same grounds. More recently, Martin Duberman, first attracted to Lowell because of Lowell's abolitionist activities, afterwards was disenchanted by Lowell's moderation and eventual suspicion of organized reform movements. While those associated with New Humanism such as Norman Foerster and Harry Hayden Clark rightly viewed Lowell as a precursor to their intellectual outlook, their opponents attacked Lowell, labelling

Elmwood, Lowell's house in Cambridge.

Lowell in old age.

him "Victorian," "genteel," "conservative," and "academic," the same terms they applied to the New Humanists. Finally, the cosmopolitan point of view which characterized Lowell's later life and much of his best work found few admirers during the "national period" of American literary criticism of the 1930s and the 1940s, though Walter Blair, Jennette Tandy, and H. L. Mencken pointed out that Lowell in *The Biglow Papers* contributed greatly to "native" American literature.

The critical silence of the present time should not be taken as an indication that Lowell has been or will be forgotten. Very appropriately did Robert E. Rees conclude his useful survey of writings about Lowell: "No one as richly versatile and influential as Lowell will forever remain unattractive or unrewarding to scholars."

Other Writings:

Class Poem (Cambridge: Metcalf, Torry & Ballou, 1838); *A Year's Life* (Boston: Little & Brown, 1841); *Poems* (Cambridge: Owen, 1844); *Conversations on Some of the Old Poets* (Cambridge: Owen, 1845); *Poems: Second Series* (Cambridge: Nichols, 1848); *Poems* (Boston: Ticknor, Reed & Fields, 1849); *Fireside Travels* (Boston: Ticknor & Fields, 1864); *Ode Recited at the Commemoration of the Living and Dead Soldiers of Harvard University* (Cambridge: privately printed, 1865); *Under the Willows and Other Poems* (Boston: Fields, Osgood, 1869); *Three Memorial Poems* (Boston: James R. Osgood, 1877); *Democracy and Other Addresses* (Boston: Houghton, Mifflin, 1887); *Heartsease and Rue* (Boston: Houghton, Mifflin, 1888); and *Political Essays* (Boston: Houghton, Mifflin, 1888). The standard collected edition is *The Writings of James Russell Lowell*, Riverside Edition, 10 vols. (Boston:

Houghton, Mifflin, 1890). The following were collected and edited posthumously: *Last Literary Essays and Addresses*, ed. Charles Eliot Norton (Boston: Houghton, Mifflin, 1892); *Last Poems*, ed. Charles Eliot Norton (Boston: Houghton, Mifflin, 1895); *Lectures on English Poets*, ed. S. A. Jones (Cleveland: The Rowfant Club, 1897); *Impressions of Spain*, ed. Joseph B. Gilder (Boston: Houghton, Mifflin, 1899); *Early Prose Writings*, ed. Edward Everett Hale (London: Lane, 1902); *The Anti-Slavery Papers*, ed. William Belmont Parker (Boston: Houghton, Mifflin, 1902); *The Function of the Poet, and Other Essays*, ed. Albert Mordell (Boston: Houghton Mifflin, 1920); *Uncollected Poems*, ed. Thelma M. Smith (Philadelphia: University of Pennsylvania Press, 1950). Also: *James Russell Lowell: Representative Selections*, ed. Harry Hayden Clark and Norman Foerster (New York: American Book Company, 1947), and *The Biglow Papers [First Series]: A Critical Edition*, ed. Thomas Wortham (DeKalb: Northern Illinois University Press, 1977).

Bibliographies:

George Willis Cooke, *A Bibliography of James Russell Lowell* (Boston: Houghton Mifflin, 1906); Luther S. Livingston, *A Bibliography of the First Editions in Book Form of the Writings of James Russell Lowell* (New York: privately printed, 1914); Jacob Blanck, *Bibliography of American Literature* (New Haven: Yale University Press, 1973), 6:21-105; Robert A. Rees, "James Russell Lowell," in *Fifteen American Authors before 1900*, ed. Rees and Earl N. Harbert (Madison: University of Wisconsin Press, 1971).

Biographies:

Horace E. Scudder, *James Russell Lowell: A Biography*, 2 vols. (Boston: Houghton, Mifflin, 1901); Ferris Greenslet, *James Russell Lowell: His Life and Work* (Boston: Houghton, Mifflin, 1905); Richmond Croom Beatty, *James Russell Lowell* (Nashville, Tenn.: Vanderbilt University Press, 1942); Leon Howard, *Victorian Knight-Errant: A Study of the Early Literary Career of James Russell Lowell* (Berkeley and Los Angeles: University of California Press, 1952); Martin Duberman, *James Russell Lowell* (Boston: Houghton Mifflin, 1966).

Letters and Journals:

Letters of James Russell Lowell, ed. Charles Eliot Norton, 3 vols. (Boston: Houghton, Mifflin, 1904); *New Letters of James Russell Lowell*, ed. M. A. DeWolfe Howe (New York: Harpers, 1932); *The Scholar-Friends: Letters of Francis James Child and James Russell Lowell*, ed. M. A. DeWolfe Howe and G. W. Cottrell, Jr. (Cambridge: Harvard University Press, 1952); James C. Austin, *Fields of the Atlantic Monthly: Letters to an Editor, 1861-1870* (San Marino, Cal.: Huntington Library, 1953); James L. Woodress, Jr., "The Lowell-Howells Friendship: Some Unpublished Letters," *New England Quarterly*, 26 (December 1953): 523-528; Philip Graham, "Some Lowell Letters," *Texas Studies in Literature and Language*, 3 (Winter 1962): 557-582; *Browning to His American Friends: Letters Between the Brownings, the Storys and James Russell Lowell, 1841-1890*, ed. Gertrude Reese Hudson (London: James & Bowes, 1965); *Transatlantic Dialogue*, ed. Paul F. Mattheisen and Michael Millgate (Austin: University of Texas Press, 1965). There is no edition of Lowell's journals.

Criticism:

Henry James, *Essays in London and Elsewhere* (New York: Harpers, 1893); William Dean Howells, *Literary Friends and Acquaintance* (New York: Harpers, 1900); William C. Brownell, *American Prose Masters* (New York: Scribners, 1909); Joseph J. Reilly, *James Russell Lowell as a Critic* (New York: Putnam's, 1915); Norman Foerster, *American Criticism: A Study in Literary Theory from Poe to the Present* (Boston: Houghton Mifflin, 1928); Harry Hayden Clark, "Lowell—Humanitarian, Nationalist, or Humanist?" *Studies in Philology*, 27 (July 1930): 411-441; George Arms, *The Fields Were Green* (Stanford, Cal.: Stanford University Press, 1953).

Papers:

The James Russell Lowell Papers are at the Houghton Library at Harvard University. The Berg Collection at the New York Public Library also has a major collection.

HORACE MANN (4 May 1796-2 August 1859), prolific writer and persuasive spokesman for educational reform, is known today as the father of the American public school system. He grew up in a hard-working farm family in Franklin, Massachusetts. A small legacy from his father enabled Mann to attend Brown University. He entered as a sophomore, was graduated at the head of his class in 1819, and interrupted his study of law to return to Brown as a tutor.

Mann began to practice law in Dedham, Massachusetts, in 1823, and within a few years became the local representative to the state legislature. After the death of Charlotte Messer, to whom he had been married for less than two years, Mann moved to Boston in 1833. Elected to the state senate in 1834 as a Whig, he served as president in 1836 and 1837. During his decade in the state legislature, Mann was active in many humanitarian reforms, including the establishment of the first state mental hospital, temperance, religious liberty, and revision of the debtor laws.

When Mann accepted the office of secretary of the newly created Massachusetts Board of Education in 1837, he explained, "I have abandoned jurisprudence and betaken myself to the larger sphere of mind and morals." For the next twelve years he devoted himself wholeheartedly to the cause of education. A zealous convert, he preached the gospel of common school reform in pursuing his specified duties to collect and diffuse information on education and the common schools. Mann prepared abstracts of local school returns and published some of his lectures at the request of the Board, but his most influential writings were his twelve *Annual Reports*, which were frequently reprinted as well as reported and discussed in newspapers. He initiated and for ten years edited the *Common School Journal*, wrote many articles on education for other magazines, spoke frequently and eloquently at town meetings, county conventions, and lyceums, and conducted an extensive correspondence, responding to requests for advice and encouraging educators throughout the nation. Mary Peabody, whom Mann married in 1843, aided him in his educational endeavors and later published many of his writings, including letters and excerpts from his journal, as well as his public speeches and reports.

Mann resigned his position with the Board of Education to succeed John Quincy Adams in Congress in 1848, where he became an outspoken abolitionist. In 1852, he accepted an offer to become the first president of Antioch College, writing to a friend that "the moulding of a youthful mind and

manners is the noblest work that man or angels could do." Mann endeavored to implement his educational and religious ideals in the fledgling institution, but soon had to concentrate all his energies on saving the college from financial disaster. In his final address, delivered only a few weeks before he died, he told the Antioch graduates, "Be ashamed to die until you have won some victory for humanity." Mann's greatest victory for humanity was the common or public school.

Horace Mann had incredible faith in education— "the first of all causes" and the preventive, rather than remedial, reform which would end the need for further reforms. *"The common school is the greatest discovery ever made by man,"* he confidently declared, and optimistically believed it would become "the most effective and benignant of all the forces of civilization." More specifically, he envisioned that public schools would end poverty and crime, increase prosperity and productivity, and be "the great equalizer of the conditions of men—the balance wheel of the social machinery." The highflown rhetoric reflected the optimism of his era, but it was, of course, a utopian dream.

However, Mann did effectively use his speeches

and writings to persuade the public and legislature of the need to improve public schools. He wrote extensively on the condition and improvement of schoolhouses, inadequate teacher salaries, the need for more regular attendance, improvement of teacher training, school libraries, teaching methods, physical education, religious and moral education, and the economic and political value of education. Mann's educational ideas were pragmatic, rather than philosophical, and eclectic, derived primarily from Pestalozzi and phrenology. Supremely self-confident and uncompromising, Mann sometimes polarized issues, perceiving opposition as conspiracy and himself as a martyr. This tendency exaggerated conflicts over sectarianism, discipline, and pedagogy, while the resulting publicity engendered increased majority support for the common schools.

When Mann resigned in 1848, the Board noted that he had "thoroughly aroused the people of this Commonwealth to the importance of a Common School education." Mann proudly recounted the achievements of his term which included the doubling of local appropriations for schools, an increase in the proportion of women teachers, and greatly improved preparation of teachers through the organization of the first state normal schools and teacher institutes.

Horace Mann was the leading educator of his generation and the authority most frequently quoted in educational periodicals in the 1840s and 1850s. Indefatigable reformer and idealist, he was an extraordinarily successful evangelist and crusader for education in the formative era of the American public school system. —*Natalie A. Naylor*

Principal Works: Massachusetts Board of Education, *Report, Together with the Report of the Secretary of the Board*, 1st-12th, 12 vols. (Boston: Dutton & Wentworth, 1838-1849; reprinted, Washington, D.C.: National Education Association, 1947-1952); *Lectures on Education* (Boston: Wm. B. Fowle & N. Capen, 1845); *A Few Thoughts for a Young Man* (Boston: Ticknor, Reed & Fields, 1850); *Life and Works of Horace Mann*, ed. Mrs. Mary Mann, 3 vols. (Boston: Walker, Fuller, 1865-1868); *The Republic and the School: Horace Mann on The Education of Free Men*, ed. Lawrence A. Cremin—selections from annual reports (New York: Teachers College, 1957); *Horace Mann on the Crisis in Education*, ed. Louis Filler (Yellow Springs, Ohio: Antioch Press, 1965).

Principal References: Raymond B. Culver, *Horace Mann and Religion in the Massachusetts Public Schools* (New Haven: Yale University Press, 1929); E. I. F. Williams, *Horace Mann, Educational Statesman* (New York: Macmillan, 1937); Louise Hall Tharp, *Until Victory: Horace Mann and Mary Peabody* (Boston: Little, Brown, 1953); Jonathan Messerli, *Horace Mann: A Biography* (New York: Alfred A. Knopf, 1972); Robert B. Downs, *Horace Mann, Champion of Public Schools* (New York: Twayne, 1974).

George Perkins Marsh

George P. Marsh

GEORGE PERKINS MARSH (15 March 1801-23 July 1882), philologist and miscellaneous writer, was born in Woodstock, Vermont. His cousin was James Marsh, the philosopher-president of the University of Vermont. Marsh graduated from Dartmouth College in 1820 with a brilliant record but, after an unhappy year of teaching, returned home to study law. He was admitted to the bar in 1825. From 1835 on, Marsh was active in politics, and from 1861 to his death was minister to Italy. A brilliant, self-taught man, Marsh's interests were eclectic. His many accomplishments include: translating an Icelandic grammar (1838); promoting the domestication of the camel in America; assisting on the Oxford Dictionary; and publishing numerous philological works, such as *Lectures on the History of the English Language* (New York: Scribners, 1860) and *The Origin and History of the English Language* (New York: Scribners, 1862).

REFERENCES: Caroline Crane Marsh, *Life and Letters of George Perkins Marsh* (New York:

Scribners, 1888); David Lowenthal, *George Perkins Marsh* (New York: Columbia University Press, 1958).

JAMES MARSH (19 July 1794-3 July 1842) is best remembered as editor of the first American edition of Samuel Taylor Coleridge's *Aids to Reflection*. This is as it should be, for in the 1830s *Aids* had a momentous impact on that circle of thinkers who were known as Transcendentalists, many of them recording their debt to Marsh (and Coleridge) in their journals and correspondence.

Born in the rugged farmland of eastern Vermont, at Hartford, James was the second son of a large family and was slated to take over his father's farm. But when his older brother, Roswell, refused to carry a leg of mutton to nearby Dartmouth College to help defray his academic expenses, James Marsh went in his place. At Dartmouth, where he distinguished himself as a scholar, Marsh underwent a religious crisis in the spring of his sophomore year which resulted in his earnest conversion to Christianity. It was in Hanover, too, that he met Lucia Wheelock, the granddaughter of Dartmouth's founder and first president, who became his wife in 1824.

Following his graduation from Dartmouth, Marsh attended Andover Theological Seminary (as did several classmates), returning to Hanover for two formative years as Tutor of Latin and Greek. They were crucial years for Marsh's intellectual development because for the first time in his relatively brief academic career, he had the opportunity to read widely in the great literatures of the ancient and modern worlds. When he went back to Andover to complete his ministerial studies, James Marsh was a learned man. His first published essay, "Ancient and Modern Poetry," which appeared in 1822 in the prestigious *North American Review*, was of such high quality that some critics assumed that its anonymous author must have been George Ticknor, the brilliant and well-travelled Harvard professor. Ticknor was flattered; he respected Marsh's erudition and wrote Marsh, whom he had known for some time, that it was as good a piece as the *North American* had ever published. At Andover, Marsh had begun to study German under the controversial Professor Moses Stuart, and by 1822 Marsh completed his translation of Bellerman's *Geography of the Scriptures*, a recondite work which attracted little notice. His later translations shared a

James Marsh.

similar fate—they were directed at a narrow audience and were not well-known outside theological circles. After divinity school, Marsh was faced with the same problem that plagued Ralph Waldo Emerson throughout his own life—what to do. In Marsh's case there were complications: he was well-prepared *intellectually* for the ministry, but he was not a good public speaker; in addition, he had little self-confidence in his ability to shepherd a congregation. As a result, Marsh looked with some reluctance to the profession of teaching. His earlier success as a teacher at Dartmouth (where his students expressed their gratitude in the form of a handsome set of books and an appreciative accompanying letter) encouraged Marsh to accept a position at Hampden-Sydney College, a small Virginia school below Richmond.

Marsh was unhappy and relatively unproductive at the southern college. He had been offered the presidency of the University of Vermont while still in divinity school, a position he wisely refused. But when the offer was renewed in 1826, Marsh was eager and ready to return to his native state. His educational reforms at Vermont, modelled on the ideas of both Coleridge and Ticknor, made the backwoods Burlington college one of the most progressive

institutions in America.

The nine essays on popular education which Marsh wrote for a Congregational paper, the *Vermont Chronicle*, during the first four months of 1829 attracted, naturally, a rather limited audience. But this was not the case with Marsh's other important publication later the same year, *Aids to Reflection*. Printed by his brother-in-law, Chauncey Goodrich, three years after Marsh assumed the presidency of the University of Vermont, *Aids* was a book intended for Christian scholars. It reached a much wider audience than Marsh anticipated, causing considerable turmoil in some of the more conservative seminaries for the simple reason that Coleridge and Marsh proposed a new way of looking at religion, a way to synthesize the philosophical-religious schism which had only widened under the then-prevalent Scottish "Common Sense" philosophy. What led one famous twentieth-century critic of American literature to call *Aids* "the most immediate force behind American Transcendentalism" was the distinction Coleridge made between Reason and Understanding. Elaborating on Coleridge's sometimes difficult wording in his own long "Preliminary Essay," Marsh made *Aids* more accessible and more understandable to its readers.

Marsh's interest in Coleridge shifted in the last decade of his life to other German idealist philosophers, some of whose work had laid the foundations for Coleridge's own thinking. Columbia and Amherst both honored Marsh with honorary doctorates in the early 1830s when Marsh stepped down as president to devote more time to his studies and teaching. He continued to teach philosophy and what we would call psychology at Vermont until his death in 1842. Had he lived in Boston rather than Burlington, he might well have been better known today. But as teacher, college president, and editor of Coleridge, the man one critic called "the Father of American Transcendentalism" made his mark on a generation of thinkers. —*Douglas Greenwood*

Principal Works: "Ancient and Modern Poetry," *North American Review*, 22 (July 1822): 94-131; Coleridge, *Aids to Reflection*, ed. Marsh, with Notes and "Preliminary Essay" (Burlington, Vt.: Chauncey Goodrich, 1829); Coleridge, *The Friend*, ed. Marsh (Burlington, Vt.: Chauncey Goodrich, 1833).

Principal References: Joseph Torrey, *The Remains of the Rev. James Marsh...with a Memoir of his Life* (Boston: Crocker & Brewster, 1843); Ronald Vale Wells, *Three Christian Transcendentalists*, rev. ed. (New York: Octagon Books, 1972); John J. Duffy,

Coleridge's American Disciples: The Selected Correspondence of James Marsh (Amherst: University of Massachusetts Press, 1973); Peter Coulter Carafiol, "James Marsh: Transcendental Puritan," Ph.D. dissertation, Claremont Graduate School, 1974; Douglas Greenwood, "James Marsh and the Transcendental Temper," Ph.D. dissertation, University of North Carolina, 1977.

DONALD GRANT MITCHELL (12 April 1822-15 December 1908), essayist and editor, was born in Norwich, Connecticut, and educated at Yale University, from which he graduated in 1841. Mitchell spent most of his life alternating between farming at his Connecticut homes and travelling abroad: in the mid-1840s he saw England and the continent, in 1848 he was a newspaper correspondent in Paris during the revolution, in 1853 he served as United States Consul to Venice, and in 1854 he lived in Paris. He was married in 1853. Mitchell took great pride in his agricultural skills and most of his dozen books reflect this rural interest. He died at his estate, near New Haven, Connecticut. Today Mitchell is known for *The Lorgnette,* 2 vols. (New York Henry Kernot, 1850), a satirical view of New York society published under the pseudonym of "John Timon"; *Reveries of a Bachelor* (New York: Baker & Scribner, 1850) and *Dream Life* (New York: Charles Scribner, 1851), both published under the pseudonym of "Ik Marvell," sentimental rhapsodies of the simple life that sold in the tens of thousands; and *American Lands and Letters,* 2 vols. (New York: Scribners, 1897-1899), a still interesting history of American literature.

REFERENCES: Waldo H. Dunn, *The Life of Donald G. Mitchell: Ik Marvell* (New York: Scribners, 1922); Jacob Blanck, *Bibliography of American Literature* (New Haven: Yale University Press, 1973), 6:218-243.

JOHN LOTHROP MOTLEY (15 April 1814-29 May 1877), historian, was one of the most prominent figures in the mid-nineteenth century "classic age" of historical writing in the United States. He was born into a mercantile family in Dorchester, Massachusetts. His education began at George Bancroft's Round Hill school, continued at Harvard from 1827 to 1831, and then from 1832 to 1834 in Germany, first at the University of Gottingen and then in Berlin. From childhood he was an omnivorous reader and showed a talent for languages which he put to good use in Germany in the study of Roman and international law and classical history. At Berlin, Motley roomed with Otto von Bismarck, who became his lifelong friend and whom he portrayed, thinly disguised as Otto von Rabenmark, in his novel, *Morton of Morton's Hope,* in 1839.

Motley returned to Boston in 1835 and in 1837 married Mary Benjamin, sister of the writer Park Benjamin. His social and financial position made it unnecessary for him to practice law, and one term in the Massachusetts legislature satisfied his limited political ambitions. The only public career to which he aspired was diplomacy, but a tour to St. Petersburg as secretary of legation in 1841-1842 brought him no satisfaction. His real love was literature, dating from his college days when he had joined Oliver Wendell Holmes and John O. Sargent in editing the *Harvard Register,* an undergraduate magazine. Motley had then written a long essay on "The Genius and Character of Goethe." In the 1830s,

he began writing again; two more articles on Goethe were published in the *New York Review* in 1838 and 1839, and in the latter year *Morton of Morton's Hope* appeared, to no acclaim even from his friends. He wrote a second novel, *Merrymount*, but suppressed its publication until 1849. By that time he had located the real focus for his talents in the writing of history. An essay of 1849, "The Polity of the Puritans," showed that he had found his theme in the story of the triumph of representative institutions and freedom of conscience over the reactionary forces of Popery and tyranny.

Motley's first great book, *The Rise of the Dutch Republic*, was begun in 1846 and was, in effect, rewritten twice before its publication ten years later. He worked on the book for five years in Boston; then, realizing the need for better sources, he took his family to Dresden where he spent two more years. Moving on to The Hague and Brussels, he found so much new archival material that he had to rewrite his manuscript once more. The resulting work was published at his own expense, as neither Motley nor his publishers expected much sale. But 30,000 copies of the three volumes sold in the first year and the book's popularity continued for half a century. It was abridged, revised for young readers, and translated into Dutch, French, German, Swedish, and Russian.

The Rise of the Dutch Republic and its successors, *The History of the United Netherlands* (1861-1868) and *The Life and Death of John of Barneveld* (1874), which carried the narrative up to the outbreak of the Thirty Years' War, orchestrated Motley's idealist theme: there are certain "true principles" in human history, which will triumph despite the actions of individuals, though some great men, like William the Silent, may forward their advance. These "true principles" are the great liberal ideas of freedom and democracy. In Motley's books the villains are the minions of Catholicism; the heroes are the champions of Protestantism. There is, moreover, a dominant racial theme: the Northern, Germanic races have a natural propensity to freedom and representative institutions, while the Southern Europeans are prone to superstition and tyranny. Motley carried this race idea to a ridiculous extreme when he used it to explain the division between the United Provinces, which revolted against Spanish rule, and the Belgians, who remained loyal to Spain. This was Motley's basic weakness: a determination to make the facts fit his presuppositions. But he was an extremely effective writer. He shared his philosophy of history with his great American contemporaries, George Bancroft, William Hickling Prescott, and Francis Parkman. His method has been likened to that of the nineteenth-century historical painters: the production of an effect through the accumulation of overwhelming detail. His aim, well achieved, was to produce in his readers an impression of reality; that is, to make them believe that the historic past as he reproduced it had as much truth as the world they saw about them in the present. As he himself expressed it: "If ten people in the world hate despotism a little more and love civil and religious liberty a little better in consequence of what I have written, I shall be satisfied."

The outbreak of the Civil War brought Motley back to America to seek appointment as Minister at The Hague. He was miffed at being given Vienna instead, but served well there, in spite of his disappointment at finding that he, as a diplomat, could not be admitted to the Austrian archives where he had hoped to begin work on his projected volumes about the Thirty Years' War. He was recalled in 1866 because of a supposed hostility to the Johnson administration. In 1869-1870 he was Minister to England, but again was recalled, probably because of the quarrel between President Grant and Motley's patron, Senator Charles Sumner. Motley remained in England, where his daughters had married, and died there in 1877. —*Linda Maloney*

John Lothrop Motley

Principal Works: *The Rise of the Dutch Republic*, 3 vols. (New York: Harpers, 1856); *History of the United Netherlands*, 4 vols. (New York: Harpers, 1861-1868); *The Life and Death of John of Barneveld*, 2 vols. (New York: Harpers, 1874); *Correspondence*, ed. George William Curtis, 2 vols. (New York: Harpers, 1889);*Writings*, 17 vols. (New York: Harpers, 1900); *John Lothrop Motley, Representative Selections*, ed. Chester Penn Higby and B. T. Schantz (New York: American Book Co., 1939).

Principal References: Oliver W. Holmes, *John Lothrop Motley: a Memoir* (Boston: Houghton, Mifflin, 1898); Sister M. Claire Lynch, O. S. B., *The Diplomatic Mission of John Lothrop Motley to Austria, 1861-1867* (Washington, D.C.: Catholic University of America Press, 1944); Allan Nevins, *The Gateway to History*, rev. ed. (New York: Doubleday Anchor, 1962); Robert Wheaton, "Motley and the Dutch Historians," *New England Quarterly*, 35 (September 1962): 318-336.

JOHN NEAL (25 August 1793-20 June 1876), editor and novelist, left his home in Falmouth, Maine, to become a dry goods merchant in Baltimore. When his business failed in 1815, he read law and was admitted to the bar in 1819. Neal briefly edited the Baltimore *Telegraph* and the *Portico*, and drew on American themes in a series of novels such as *Rachel Dyer: A North American Story* (Portland, Maine: Shirley & Hyde, 1828), a tale of witchcraft in early Salem. In 1823 he went to England, where he contributed a number of reviews of American writers to *Blackwood's Magazine* (later collected as *American Writers*, ed. F. L. Pattee [Durham: Duke University Press, 1937]) and served as Jeremy Bentham's secretary. He returned to America in 1827 and the next year married and settled in Portland, Maine. Neal remained in Portland for the rest of his life, turning out more novels, and editing at various times the *Yankee*, the *New England Galaxy*, and the comic *Brother Jonathan*. A supporter of causes and people, Neal advocated woman's rights and the abolition of capital punishment, and promoted the writings of Edgar Allan Poe, Hawthorne, and Longfellow during the important early stages of their careers. REFERENCES: Neal, *Wandering Recollections of a Somewhat Busy Life* (Boston: Roberts Brothers, 1869); Benjamin Lease, *That Wild Fellow John Neal and the American Literary Revolution* (Chicago: University of Chicago Press, 1972); Jacob Blanck, *Bibliography of American Literature* (New Haven: Yale University Press, 1973), 6:417-434.

138

Charles King Newcomb.

CHARLES KING NEWCOMB (1820-1894), Transcendental author whose "The Two Dolons" in the July 1842 *Dial* (3:112-123) is often used to ridicule the "Transcendental" aspects of the journal, was born at Providence, Rhode Island. Through his mother, a blue-stocking with literary pretensions, he met many contemporary authors, including Margaret Fuller, with whom he formed an unreturned romantic attachment. From 1841 to 1845 Newcomb lived at the Brook Farm community. Ralph Waldo Emerson, who thought highly of him, urged Newcomb to write for the *Dial* and helped edit his "The Two Dolons," which is partly a disguised hymn to Emerson's son, Waldo, who had died in January 1842. But Newcomb never published another piece, returning to Providence in 1845 and, after five years in Philadelphia, sailed for Europe in 1871, where he stayed until his death. Emerson, who drew him as Benedict in the "Worship" chapter of *Conduct of Life*, concluded that while Newcomb had shown "rich possibilities," his "result is zero."
REFERENCE: *The Journals of Charles King Newcomb*, ed. Judith Kennedy Johnson (Providence: Brown University, 1946).

MARY SARGEANT (NEAL) GOVE NICHOLS (10 August 1810-30 May 1884), reformer and popular author, was a self-educated Goffstown, New Hampshire, girl. In 1831 she married Hiram Gove, an unscrupulous man whose domineering attitude made their marriage an unhappy one, ending in divorce after a long separation, in 1847. Mary Gove made a name for herself by being associated with "free love" ideas and by supporting all nature of reforms, including mesmerism, spiritualism, Fourierism, and temperance, but she is best known for her activities on behalf of health reform. She had lectured young women on health throughout the 1830s and in 1842 wrote *Lectures to Ladies in Anatomy and Physiology* (Boston: Saxton & Peirce). In the 1840s she moved to New York City, where she befriended Edgar Allan Poe and became interested in water-cure, a system proposing that water, as applied by various methods and in varying temperatures, could have medicinal value. She also published a number of stories and novels. In 1848 she married a fellow reformer, Thomas Low Nichols, and they published *Nichols' Journal of Health, Water-Cure, and Human Progress*. Her novel, *Mary Lyndon; or the Revelations of a Life* (New York: Stringer & Townsend, 1855), describes her own reform activities and personal life. The Nichols moved to England at the outbreak of the Civil War and remained there until their deaths. REFERENCES: Bertha-Monica Stearns, "Two Forgotten New England Reformers," *New England Quarterly*, 6 (March 1933): 59-84; John B. Blake, "Mary Gove Nichols: Prophetess of Health," *Proceedings of the American Philosophical Society*, 106 (June 1962): 219-234.

ANDREWS NORTON (31 December 1786-18 September 1853), editor and Biblical scholar, was born in Hingham, Massachusetts. He attended Harvard College and studied with the Divinity faculty, graduating in 1809. He taught one year at Bowdoin College before returning to Harvard as a tutor and librarian. In 1819 he was appointed Dexter Professor of Sacred Literature, a post he held until 1830. Norton married into Boston society in 1821 and, with the former Catharine Eliot, moved to "Shady Hill," his house in Cambridge. Their son, Charles Eliot Norton, later became a distinguished scholar. Norton died at Newport, Rhode Island.

Norton's life work was to demonstrate the validity and accuracy of the Bible. His *The Evidences of the Genuineness of the Gospels*, 3 vols. (Boston: J. B. Russell, 1837-1844), analyzed the language and culture of biblical authors to defend the Bible's claim to divine inspiration. This work, his position at the Divinity School, and his editorship of the influential *North American Review*, all helped establish Norton as a major force in American Unitarianism. Therefore, when Emerson's "Divinity School Address" was delivered in 1838, Norton felt called upon to answer its charges that the miracles of the New Testament did not actually happen. His *A Discourse on the Latest Form of Infidelity* (Cambridge: J. Owen, 1839), as well as his newspaper attacks on Emerson and George Ripley, proved an embarrassment, as Norton challenged the qualifications of his critics, both former students of his at Harvard, while ignoring their substantive arguments. Unfortunately, Norton is remembered more for this debate, which made even the conservative Unitarians uncomfortable, than for his other real accomplishments. His *Internal Evidences of the Genuineness of the Gospels* (Boston: Little, Brown, 1855) came after many of his ideas had been passed by; his *Verses* (Boston: privately printed, 1853) are conventionally moralistic and of little note. REFERENCES: Allen R. Clark, "Andrews Norton: A Conservative Unitarian," Harvard University Honors Thesis, 1942; William R. Hutchison, *The Transcendentalist Ministers* (New Haven: Yale University Press, 1959).

—*Joel Myerson*

Charles Eliot Norton.

CHARLES ELIOT NORTON (16 November 1827-21 October 1908), businessman, author, translator, and teacher, was a true Boston Brahmin; born in Cambridge, the son of Andrews Norton, Dexter Professor of Sacred Literature at Harvard College, and Catharine Eliot, he could trace his ancestry in this country back to 1634. After graduation from Harvard in 1846 at the age of nineteen, he became involved in the family import business and travelled extensively. Beginning in 1857, Norton turned to literary endeavors: first contributing to the *Atlantic Monthly*, and later editing the *North American Review* (with James Russell Lowell) from 1864 to 1868, editing broadsides for the New England Loyal Publications Society during the Civil War, and aiding in the founding of the *Nation* in 1865. As a teacher at Harvard from 1873 to 1897 Norton attempted to raise the fine arts from neglect because he believed them to be an expression of the nation's moral aspirations. He died in Cambridge. Although he was concerned from the beginning of his literary career with developing the conditions for American creativity and the freedom of American tastes from European influence, Norton's major literary works were his translation of Dante's *The Divine Comedy*, 3 vols. (Boston: Houghton, Mifflin, 1891-1892) and an edition of *The Poems of John Donne*, 2 vols.

(New York: The Grolier Club, 1895). His *Historical Studies of Church-Building in the Middle Ages* (New York: Harpers, 1880) is important because Norton viewed the Gothic Cathedrals of Europe as products of artistic and religious fervor, thus giving credence to the morally-based theory of art he propounded for America. But despite his contributions to scholarship in the fine arts, Norton's greatest talent was making friends. Many of his friendships, like those with Carlyle and Lowell, bore fruit in the form of publications, particularly *The Correspondence of Thomas Carlyle and Ralph Waldo Emerson, 1834-1872*, 2 vols. (Boston: James R. Osgood, 1883), and *Last Poems of James Russell Lowell* (Boston: Houghton, Mifflin, 1895). A thoroughgoing Emersonian as a young man, Norton later tempered his optimism with a respect for the past and attempted to teach the values of tradition to the rootless and materialistic society of post-Civil War America. REFERENCES: *Letters of Charles Eliot Norton*, ed. Sara Norton and M. A. DeWolfe Howe, 2 vols. (Boston: Houghton, Mifflin, 1913); Kermit Vanderbilt, *Charles Eliot Norton: Apostle of Culture in Democracy* (Cambridge: Harvard University Press, 1959).

—*Robert E. Burkholder*

and a desire to get to the sources of Christianity through the knowledge and use of ancient languages. But Palfrey's greatest fame came with the publication of his *History of New England*, 5 vols. (Boston: Little & Brown, 1858-1890). This work deserves recognition as a major contribution to the fledgling discipline of historiography. Palfrey researched all available primary sources and amply documented those sources in his text, a practice almost unheard of at that time. But the wealth of information contained in the footnotes does not outweigh Palfrey's bias. Although the *History of New England* was lauded for its impartiality when it was first published, Palfrey's opinions are clear. All of the misdeeds of the Puritans, including intolerance, are justified; in cases of disputes between Massachusetts and other colonies Palfrey always sides with Massachusetts; and the Revolution, to Palfrey, is a case of the tyrannical aggression of the English versus the patriotism of the colonies.
REFERENCE: Frank Otto Gatell, *John Gorham Palfrey and the New England Conscience* (Cambridge: Harvard University Press, 1963).

—*Robert E. Burkholder*

JOHN GORHAM PALFREY (2 May 1796-26 April 1881), editor, theologian, Unitarian minister, historian, professor, legislator, and postmaster of Boston, led a rather aimless life, although it was filled with accomplishment. He was born and died in Boston. Palfrey graduated from Harvard College in 1815 in the same class as Jared Sparks. In 1817 he began writing articles for the *North American Review*, which Sparks edited. In 1825 he edited the review while Sparks was in Europe. Later Palfrey bought the magazine and controlled it until 1843. As dean of the theological faculty at Harvard, beginning in 1831, Palfrey was in the center of the controversy over Emerson's "Divinity School Address" and was forced to resign in 1839 because of pressure from both liberal and conservative Unitarians. Palfrey's writings fall into two broad areas of interest: theology and history. His theological work is best represented by *Academical Lectures on the Jewish Scriptures and Antiquities*, 4 vols. (Boston: James Munroe, 1838-1852), which, like his teaching, emphasizes the importance of Biblical interpretation

Theodore Parker

Conrad Wright
Harvard Divinity School

BIRTH: Lexington, Massachusetts, 24 August 1810.

MARRIAGE: Lydia D. Cabot (1813-1880) of Newton, Massachusetts, 20 April 1837. No children.

DEATH: Florence, Italy, 10 May 1860.

MAJOR WORKS: *A Discourse of Matters Pertaining to Religion* (Boston: Little & Brown, 1842); *Critical and Miscellaneous Writings*—includes "A Discourse of the Transient and Permanent in Christianity" (Boston: James Munroe, 1843); *Speeches, Addresses, and Occasional Sermons*, 2 vols.—includes "The True Idea of a Christian Church" (Boston: Crosby & Nichols, 1852); *Theodore Parker's Experience as a Minister* (Boston: Rufus Leighton, 1859).

Parker's library.

Parker was selected by Octavius Brooks Frothingham (in his *Transcendentalism in New England*) to serve as the type figure of "The Preacher" of the movement. He was, to be sure, not the only preacher among the Transcendentalists. But Ralph Waldo Emerson left the ministry, as did George Ripley; Frederic Henry Hedge is remembered chiefly as a scholar; and James Freeman Clarke was a church reformer and builder, whose preaching was ancillary to other things. Parker's lasting image, however, is that of a man on the platform of the Music Hall, where his Twenty-Eighth Congregational Society met, attacking the popular theology of the day or speaking a prophetic word with respect to slavery and other social ills. The sermon, or the lecture as the secular equivalent, was his chosen medium. And so, on his monument in the old Protestant cemetery in Florence, the inscription reads: "The Great American Preacher."

Theodore Parker was born in Lexington, Massachusetts, the youngest child of a farmer and the grandson of the Captain John Parker who commanded the Lexington minutemen on the morning of 19 April 1775. This part of his family tradition meant much to him: his grandfather's muskets hung over his mantelpiece, and in the agitation over the rendition of fugitive slaves in the 1850s he was ready to follow the method of forcible resistance to the denial of liberties. His childhood and youth on the farm accustomed him to physical labor, but also meant that much of his early education was irregular. By extensive and compulsive self-education he compensated for the fact that he was financially unable to enroll at Harvard College. Because of his early closeness to the soil, he always thought of himself as one of the common people, at least in contrast with the cultivated Unitarian clergy who occupied Boston pulpits. He never overcame his sense of being an outsider among them. Often abrasive in manner, yet supersensitive to slights and fancied slights, he took comfort in describing himself as "the best hated man in America."

Parker taught school to earn money, in Watertown, among other places. There he met and became engaged to Lydia Cabot, who taught in the Sunday School of the local church, which he had undertaken to direct. They were not married at that time, for in 1834 he entered the Harvard Divinity School to prepare for the ministry. The school was small and intimate. The faculty consisted of John Gorham Palfrey, responsible for biblical criticism, especially the Old Testament; Henry Ware, Sr., who taught Christian evidences, among other things; and Henry Ware, Jr., professor of preaching and pastoral care. Among the students were future Transcendentalists, like Cyrus A. Bartol, Christopher P. Cranch, and John Sullivan Dwight, as well as future leaders of the Unitarian denomination, such as Henry W. Bellows. Life at the Divinity School allowed Parker time to go beyond the prescribed course of studies and do extensive reading on his own. "I left the Theological School with reluctance," he recalled long afterwards, "conscious of knowing so little of what I must presently teach, and wishing more years for research and thought."

Parker was married to Lydia Cabot in April 1837. Then, on the longest day of that year, he was ordained and settled in West Roxbury, then a rural village a dozen miles from Boston, where the congregation was made up of "farmers, mechanics, and milkmen." From West Roxbury he walked to Cambridge on 15 July 1838 to hear Emerson's Divinity School address, which seemed to him "the noblest, most inspiring strain" he had ever listened to. When dispute broke out over the address, ranging the younger adherents of what they termed the "spiritual philosophy" against the older generation, Parker found his place with the former, with the Transcendentalists.

Parker's grave.

The immediate issue was the question whether Christianity is a revealed religion, attested by the miracles recorded in the gospels. Behind this issue were larger ones. There was the epistemological problem, whether religious truth must be based on sense experience, either of the world about us, or of historic events of which the report has come down to us; or whether the great truths of religion are apprehended as immediate intuitions, a product of the inner consciousness. If religious truth is a product of intuition rather than external evidences, what becomes of the claim of Christianity to present a unique revelation of God to man in the person and teachings of an historic figure, Jesus Christ?

Parker's first involvement in this debate was a tract published in 1840 under the pseudonym of Levi Blodgett. But it was a sermon preached the following year that made him the center of controversy. The occasion was an ordination in South Boston, and the sermon was entitled: "The Transient and Permanent in Christianity." What Parker regarded as permanents are "absolute, pure Morality; absolute, pure Religion; the love of man; the love of God acting without let or hindrance." What he declared to be transient is the form in which these principles of absolute religion have been expressed. Doctrines, rites, creeds, institutions are subject to change; but if we are faithful, "the great truths of morality and religion, the deep sentiment of love to man and love to God, are perceived intuitively, and by instinct, as it were, though our theology be imperfect and miserable."

Parker thus was arguing that the claim of Christianity rests on its correspondence with Absolute Religion, not on the authority of its founder. For evangelical Protestants of the day, and for most Unitarians as well, this was equivalent to undermining the position of Christianity as a divinely inspired religion, a unique revelation of God's will. Parker soon found himself the target of the same kind of criticism that had greeted Emerson's Divinity School address. When he elaborated his position in a series of lectures delivered in Boston in the winter of 1841-1842, a number of the ministers who had previously exchanged with him found it prudent to do so no longer.

The lectures were collected in *A Discourse on Matters Pertaining to Religion* (1842). Reprinted several times, both in this country and in England, it represents Parker's most ambitious attempt to adumbrate a religious philosophy. It asserts a universal religious element in Man, experienced as a sense of dependence, and affirms that the religious consciousness has its proper object, which we term God. It then relates this basic insight to inspiration, to Jesus and Christianity, to the Bible, and to the Church. The book was buttressed with learned citations from sources in many languages, but it was not really a book for scholars only. It did much to encourage religious seekers for whom the Christian tradition as transmitted by the churches seemed and that he had no intention of resigning. His critics would have been much relieved had he withdrawn of his own accord; but there was no disposition to force him out, and no precedent for exclusion. But when, in December 1844, he delivered a Thursday Lecture, praising Jesus as "the greatest person of the ages," but expressing the view that "God has greater men in store," it seemed once again to be a denial of the uniqueness of Christ and the religion taught in his name; and people drew away from him accordingly.

THEODORE PARKER'S

EXPERIENCE AS A MINISTER,

WITH

SOME ACCOUNT OF HIS EARLY LIFE,

AND

EDUCATION FOR THE MINISTRY;

CONTAINED IN A LETTER FROM HIM TO THE MEMBERS OF THE
TWENTY-EIGHTH CONGREGATIONAL SOCIETY OF BOSTON.

BOSTON:
RUFUS LEIGHTON, JR.
1859.

Parker in mid-life.

limiting and intellectually oppressive. Yet Parker himself had not turned away from Christianity, but thought of his views as leading to a purification of it; and in his prayers and devotional writings he embraced Jesus with an almost evangelical warmth. In this respect, he was more conservative than Emerson, whose radical individualism led to indifference to the Church, and for whom the focus of religious emotions was minimally Christian if Christian at all.

The coolness between Parker and many of his fellow ministers—ostracism, he felt it to be—was reinforced by the *Discourse*. In January 1843, some of the members of the Boston Association, to which he belonged, even suggested that, having rejected the miracles of Christ, he properly should not continue as a member of an organization of Christian ministers. He responded that the principle of free inquiry was at stake; that there had never been a doctrinal test for membership in the Association;

A group of gentlemen in Boston met, however, and passed a resolution: "That the Rev. Theodore Parker shall have a chance to be heard in Boston." They rented a hall, and in due course organized the Twenty-Eighth Congregational Society. Parker moved to Boston, though for a year he continued to serve his West Roxbury church also, and took up a new ministry in the bustling city. It was a situation very different from his rural parish. He began to attract large congregations, first at the Melodeon and afterwards at the Boston Music Hall; but many of those who came were listeners and transients, not actively participating members. There was a very

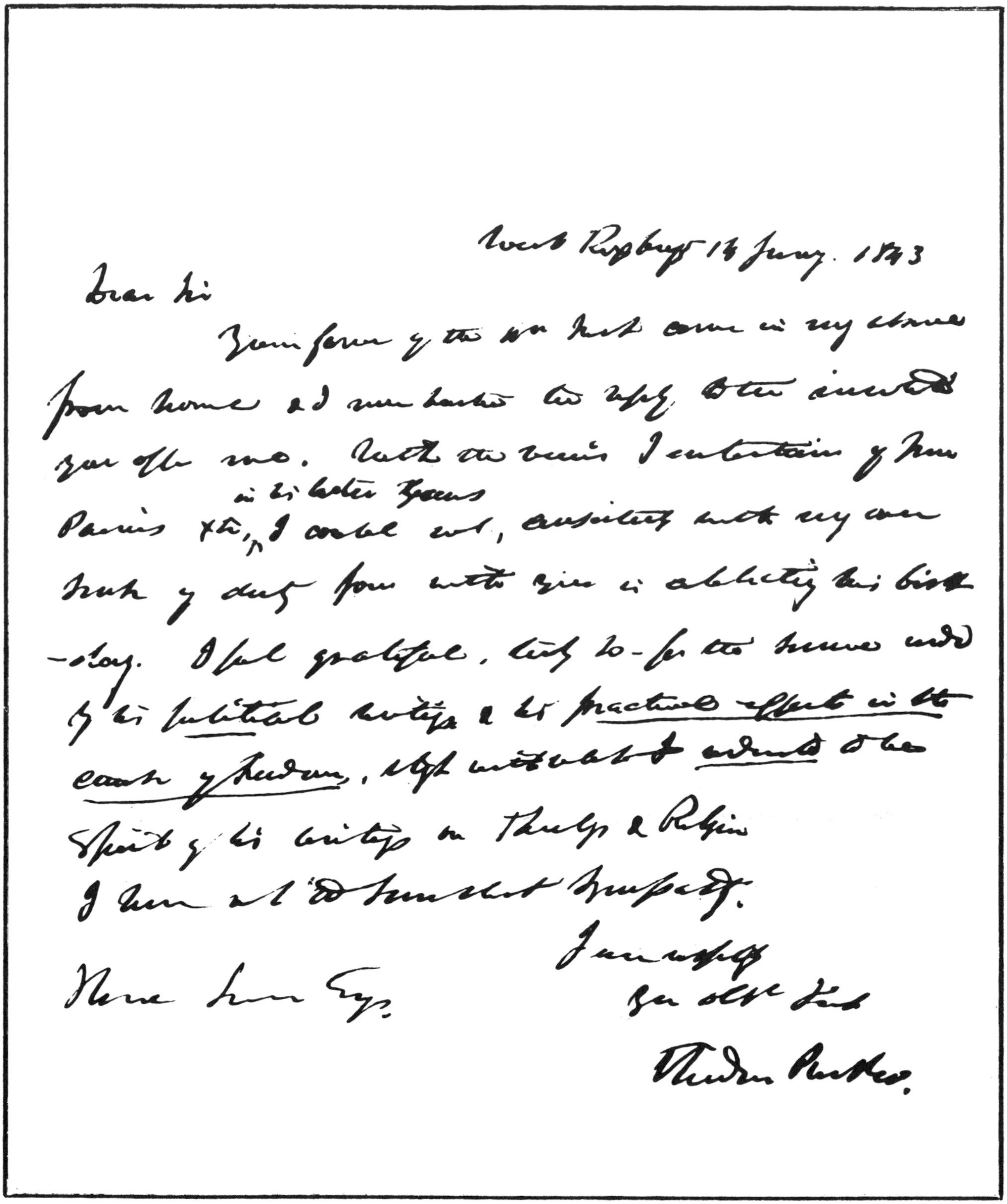

small core group, which constituted the real church within a large shifting congregation. Parker found it hard to maintain the usual parochial activities, apart from Sunday worship, and he came to be more than anything else a public speaker addressing a mass audience.

The Boston Music Hall, where Parker preached.

In his installation sermon in Boston, "The True Idea of a Christian Church," Parker declared that a Christian church should be "a means of reforming the world, of forming it after the pattern of Christian ideas." In Boston he was confronted by the social problems of urban society and was quickly drawn into a variety of movements for social reform. Sabbath reform, capital punishment, crime and prisons, war, the condition of women, industrial society and the wretchedness of the laboring classes—all these and more were subjects for prophetic preaching and public agitation. Parker's sermons on social issues were characteristically crammed with facts and statistics, but they were also suffused with moral fervor.

Of the reform movements of the day, it was antislavery above all that enlisted Parker's active involvement, especially in the 1850s. That decade began with the passage of the Fugitive Slave Act, as part of the Compromise of 1850. The Constitution had specifically provided that persons held to service in one state escaping to another should be returned; but for Parker and other radical abolitionists there was a higher law than the Constitution, and by it slavery was condemned. A matter of moral principle was involved on which Parker would not temporize or yield to prudential or practical considerations.

Among Parker's parishioners were William and Ellen Crafts, fugitives from Georgia. When he learned that they were being sought, he led a

Parker's church in West Roxbury.

"vigilance committee" in intimidating the slave-catchers, and the Crafts were able to escape to England. Other cases involving the rendition of fugitive slaves followed, stirring opinion in Boston to a high pitch. The climax of Parker's involvement was the case of Anthony Burns in 1854. A public meeting at Faneuil Hall was intended to be the rallying point for an organized attempt to overcome the guards at the courthouse and release Burns by force, but the plans miscarried. Parker and six others were indicted for "obstructing, resisting, and opposing the execution of the law." He prepared an elaborate argument and defense, and looked forward to the trial as an opportunity to appeal to public opinion; but the episode ended in anticlimax when the indictment was dismissed on technical grounds.

While much of Parker's published work as minister of the Twenty-Eighth Congregational Society dealt with slavery and other social ills, his preaching and lecturing was not limited to these topics. More purely religious themes concerned him as well, and a collection of *Ten Sermons of Religion* appeared in 1852. The errors of the "popular theology"—election, human depravity, eternal punishment—he regarded as "the most fatal mischiefs in the land," to be rejected in favor of the

CAUTION!!

COLORED PEOPLE

OF BOSTON, ONE & ALL,

You are hereby respectfully CAUTIONED and advised, to avoid conversing with the

Watchmen and Police Officers of Boston,

For since the recent ORDER OF THE MAYOR & ALDERMEN, they are empowered to act as

KIDNAPPERS

AND

Slave Catchers,

And they have already been actually employed in KIDNAPPING, CATCHING, AND KEEPING SLAVES. Therefore, if you value your LIBERTY, and the *Welfare of the Fugitives* among you, *Shun* them in every possible manner, as so many *HOUNDS* on the track of the most unfortunate of your race.

Keep a Sharp Look Out for KIDNAPPERS, and have TOP EYE open.

APRIL 24, 1851.

Poster written by Parker warning fugitive slaves.

infinite perfection of God, and the relative perfection of human nature, capable of progressive development of all its manifold powers. For three years, from 1847 to 1850, he edited the *Massachusetts Quarterly Review*, for which he prepared critical essays on literary and historical subjects, including pieces on the Reverend William Ellery Channing, Emerson, William Hickling Prescott, Thomas Babington Macaulay, and others. He shared the prevalent assumption of the Unitarian clergy of the day that ministers have a responsibility to foster the life of the mind in its several manifestations—humane letters and the sciences, as well as the disciplines of theology. Novels, to be sure, he thought generally frivolous and lacking in moral substance, only to be approved of "just so far as they stimulate the intellect, the conscience, the soul, to healthful action, and set the man to work."

Parker came from a family susceptible to consumption, and he, too, fell victim to the disease. In January 1859 his doctors insisted that he give up his pulpit, seek a warmer climate, and find relief from the exhausting routine of preaching, lecturing, and writing to which he was driven by some inner compulsion. He left Boston, never to return. At Fredericksted in the Virgin Islands he prepared an extended account of his life and ministry, published as *Theodore Parker's Experience as a Minister* (1859). It is a basic document for understanding the intellectual currents that went into the making of New England Transcendentalism, and the social reform movements of the day. It deserves to be read along with Emerson's "Historic Notes on Life and Letters in New England," and Orestes Brownson's *The Convert*.

From the West Indies, the Parkers sailed for Europe. For a time, in the summer of 1859, his health seemed to improve; but a dreary winter in Rome took its toll, and he died in Florence on 10 May 1860.

Parker is read today because his writings tell us much about religious and philosophical issues of his time, his involvement with Transcendentalism, and the interplay of political forces and social reform. His career spanned the New England Renaissance, and he was very much a part of it. He contributed to the *Dial*; his West Roxbury church was scarcely a mile away from Brook Farm; he knew Emerson, Ripley, Thomas Wentworth Higginson, James Freeman Clarke, and other Transcendentalists more or less intimately. The student of the literary culture of New England in the 1840s and 1850s will encounter him at every turn. The historian of the anti-slavery movement will find him to be one of the pivotal figures.

He had his warm admirers and supporters, and equally his critics and detractors. The former thought of him as warm and compassionate, the friend of the friendless and the comfort of those in distress. But those with whom he disagreed saw another side of his character. He was unsparing of his opponents, his moral fervor taking on an especially sharp edge because he was at least partially an outsider criticizing the establishment. Sarcasm and invective were often his weapons, caricature and even repeated misrepresentation of his opponents were sometimes resorted to. His contentious spirit, which even his friends regretted, made him needless enemies.

He won an especially devoted following among younger Unitarian ministers, attracted both by his theological vision and by the forthrightness with which he attacked social problems. His influence on the development of liberal theology may be seen in the organization after the Civil War of the Free Religious Association. This was a movement of free spirits, or "radicals," most of them Unitarian ministers unhappy with tendencies toward denominational consolidation and insistent on perfect freedom to maintain individual religious belief unrestrained by creeds, creedlets, or inherited doctrines. Octavius Brooks Frothingham was for several years the president of the Association, and his religious radicalism had resulted from contacts with Parker in the 1850s. It must be acknowledged, however, that the intuitional epistemology of Parker and the other Transcendentalists was not universally accepted among the free religionists, many of whom, like Francis Ellingwood Abbot, sought a scientific grounding for religious belief. The long-term residue of Parker's theology was not his intuitional epistemology, but his contribution to the development of a relativism that accorded Christianity no special rank among the religions of the world. Parker himself did not go so far; but whether one applauds or condemns the result, Parker's conservative critics were right in suggesting what the outcome would be.

Parker's influence has also continued to the extent that he has served as a role model for younger ministers down to the present who may be inspired by his readiness to proclaim righteousness as he understood it, to condemn evil institutions as he saw them, and to suffer the consequences of obloquy if need be. Thus John Haynes Holmes, life-long pacifist and defender of civil liberties in New York City, the grandson of one of the laymen in Parker's church, hoped to be and was thought of by others as in some measure a reincarnation of Parker.

More recently, in the civil rights movement, the attempt has been made to find precedents and inspiration in the earlier anti-slavery agitation, and so Parker's example has seemed newly relevant. Truman Nelson's *The Sin of the Prophet* (1952), a fictionalized account of the Anthony Burns kidnapping, has Parker as its hero. But Stanley Elkins's *Slavery* (1959), itself a controversial book, criticizes Parker for an excessively individualistic approach to an evil social institution. "Not only did these men fail to analyze slavery itself as an institution," Elkins writes, "but they failed equally to consider and exploit institutional means for subverting it." The debate over Parker's personality and the strategy for reform that it dictated has not ended.

Other Writings:

The Works of Theodore Parker, The Centenary Edition, 15 vols. (Boston: American Unitarian Association, 1907-1916). Includes *Theism, Atheism, and the Popular Theology, Sermons of Religion, Lessons from the World of Matter, The World of Matter and the Spirit of Man, Historic Americans, The American Scholar, Sins and Safeguards of Society, Social Classes in a Republic, The Slave Power, The Rights of Man in America,* and *Autobiography, Poems, and Prayers.*

Bibliographies:

"Bibliography of Theodore Parker's Published Writings, and of Others Having Reference to Him," *Bibliography and Index,* in *Works* (1912), 15:13-50; Herbert E. Hudson, "A Parker Bibliography: 1937-1960," *Proceedings of the Unitarian Historical Society,* 13, Part 1 (1960): 36-38.

Biographies:

John Weiss, *Life and Correspondence of Theodore Parker,* 2 vols. (New York: D. Appleton, 1864); Octavius Brooks Frothingham, *Theodore Parker* (New York: Putnam's, 1874); John White Chadwick, *Theodore Parker: Preacher and Reformer* (Boston: Houghton, Mifflin, 1900); Henry Steele Commager, *Theodore Parker* (Boston: Little, Brown, 1936).

Letters and Journals:

There is no edition of either Parker's letters or journals. Selections are printed in Weiss, *Life and Correspondence of Theodore Parker.*

Criticism:

John E. Dirks, *The Critical Theology of Theodore Parker*—reprints the Levi Blodgett letter (New York: Columbia University Press, 1948); George F. Newbrough, "Reason and Understanding in the Works of Theodore Parker," *South Atlantic Quarterly,* 47 (January 1948): 64-75; H. Shelton Smith, "Was Theodore Parker a Transcendentalist?" *New England Quarterly,* 23 (September 1950): 351-364; William R. Hutchison, *The Transcendentalist Ministers* (New Haven: Yale University Press, 1959); Perry Miller, "Theodore Parker: Apostasy Within Liberalism," *Nature's Nation* (Cambridge: Harvard University Press, 1967), pp. 134-149; John C. Broderick, "Problems of the Literary Executor: The Case of Theodore Parker," *Quarterly Journal of the Library of Congress,* 23 (October 1966): 260-273; Lawrence Buell, *Literary Transcendentalism: Style and Vision in the American Renaissance* (Ithaca: Cornell University Press, 1973); Michael Fellman, "Theodore Parker and the Abolitionist Role in the 1850s," *Journal of American History,* 61 (December 1974): 666-684.

Papers:

Massachusetts Historical Society; Boston Public Library; Andover Harvard Library; Library of Congress.

FRANCIS PARKMAN, JR. (16 September 1823-8 November 1893), was the eldest son of the Reverend Francis Parkman, pastor of the New York Church and a leader in orthodox Unitarianism in Boston. Young Parkman shared the social prominence and affluence which characterized the Boston Brahmins. His ancestor, Elias Parkman, had come to Massachusetts Bay in 1633, and his grandfather, Samuel Parkman, had been one of Boston's wealthiest merchants. Francis Parkman's mother was a descendant of John Cotton of Boston, grandfather of Cotton Mather. Parkman attended Gideon Thayer's renowned private school at Chauncey Place and entered Harvard College in 1840. Even while studying trigonometry and Greek history, Parkman exercised his passion for outdoor life. Ironically, his recurrent ill health influenced his skill as a woodsman. As a young sickly child, he was sent to his grandfather's farm near Medford. For five years Parkman lived there and acquired a keen interest in woodlore. As a Harvard student, he frequently hiked and hunted in his favorite domain, the Five Mile Woods. During his senior year, nervous exhaustion forced Parkman to suspend his studies for nine months, and he toured Europe to regain his health. Actually Parkman was plagued with poor health during his entire lifetime. He suffered from a medley of afflictions, including poor eyesight, arthritis, chronic stomach disorders, and severe headaches. By his graduation from Harvard in late 1844, Parkman had repeatedly interrupted his studies for forays into the wilderness areas of New York and New England, where he nurtured an ever-growing interest in Indian culture and the French-Indian War. Also, during his European convalescence, Parkman exhibited his capacity as a diarist by compiling a journal of some 50,000 words. Though his main interest was historical lore and nature, Parkman continued his studies in law, and in 1846 took his degree from Harvard. Ill health and a love for the outdoors moved him to undertake a long trip to the West with his cousin, "Quin" Shaw. Parkman's journey along the Oregon Trail furnished the inspiration for his first important publication, *The California and Oregon Trail* (1849), which three years later was reissued as *Prairie and Rocky Mountain Life: or, The California and Oregon Trail*. Parkman's subsequent writing on the Anglo-French struggle for North America reflected not only his love for the outdoors, but his commitment to both the new German history and his New England Protestant heritage. Like George Bancroft and William Prescott, Parkman espoused the Germanic notion that history was not limited by

the boundaries of national states, but was a continuing saga of the evolutionary development of civil liberties. And because of his New England religious heritage, Parkman viewed the struggle in the western hemisphere as between individual freedom and Catholic autocracy. Hence the struggle for the New World between France and England was viewed by Parkman as a contest between a New France representative of Old World monarchy and the freedom loving instincts of the Anglo-Saxon in North America. Such was the tone of his first work on the Anglo-French struggle, *The History of the Conspiracy of Pontiac* (1851), and remained thus until the publication of *A Half-Century of Conflict* (1892), which was issued the year before his death in Boston. —*Thomas L. Connelly*

Principal Works: *The California and Oregon Trail* (New York: Putnam's, 1849); *The History of the Conspiracy of Pontiac* (Boston: Little & Brown, 1851); *Pioneers of France in the New World* (Boston: Little, Brown, 1865); *The Jesuits in North America in the Seventeenth Century* (Boston: Little, Brown, 1867); *The Discovery of the Great West* (Boston: Little, Brown, 1869); *Count Frontenac and New*

France under Louis XIV (Boston: Little, Brown, 1877); *Montcalm and Wolfe*, 2 vols. (Boston: Little, Brown, 1884); *A Half-Century of Conflict*, 2 vols. (Boston: Little, Brown, 1892).

Principal References: *The Marcus W. Jernegan Essays in American Historiography*, ed. William T. Hutchinson (Chicago: University of Chicago Press, 1937); Howard Doughty, *Francis Parkman* (New York: Macmillan, 1962); Robert L. Gale, *Francis Parkman* (New York: Twayne, 1973).

ELIZABETH PALMER PEABODY (16 May 1804-3 January 1894), friend and associate of the leading figures in the Transcendentalist movement, is remembered for her various educational interests, for her publication of the *Dial* (1842-1843) and *Aesthetic Papers* (1849), and for her founding of the West Street Book Shop and publishing house (1840-1850), which became the Boston gathering place for intellectuals and reformers.

Born in Billerica, Massachusetts, she was the oldest of seven children of Nathaniel Peabody, a physician and pioneer dentist, and Elizabeth Palmer, schoolteacher, both of whom came from solidly established New England families. After being educated in her mother's home school, Peabody herself began her career as a teacher at the age of sixteen, when the family had moved to Lancaster in the hope of improving her father's practice. She shared her responsibilities with her sister Mary, the future Mrs. Horace Mann, and took a lively, if somewhat imperious, interest in the education of her younger sister, Sophia, who would in 1842 become the bride of Nathaniel Hawthorne.

The year 1822 found Peabody teaching in Boston and revelling in its cultural opportunities. She took Greek lessons with Ralph Waldo Emerson, then newly graduated from Harvard, and listened with rapt attention to the sermons of the Reverend William Ellery Channing. Both men were to have a lasting impact on her intellectual life. Privately, she undertook a course of reading in theology equal to that of a Harvard divinity student. After two years, she went to Maine as governess to the affluent Vaughans and Gardiners, making constant use of their extensive libraries and improving her French with the resident Parisian tutor. In 1825 she returned to found a school with her sister Mary. Boston was to remain her home center until the 1860s, when

Concord became the place to which she returned, and where Sleepy Hollow Cemetery became the place of her final rest after her death in Jamaica Plain, near Boston, in 1894.

The pattern of her life was characterized by great intellectual energy and by unfailing concern for human need wherever she observed it. However, these very qualities led her to dissipate her forces in the pursuit of a succession of "worthy causes"—whether of educational theory or of social justice. In consequence, while she was both admired and esteemed by her contemporaries, she was also regarded with a certain indulgent amusement. More seriously, her lack of focus prevented her from contributing major works in the fields of theology, history, language, and education, which were her perennial interests. However, the works that she did publish reveal a capacious mind steeped in the scholarship of both Europe and America.

Record of A School, Exemplifying the Principles of Spiritual Culture, which was published in three editions (1835, 1836, 1874), contains her transcripts of A. Bronson Alcott's inductive lessons given in the Temple School while she was his assistant (1834-1835). It is a document of great importance for any student of Transcendentalism, for it demonstrates the most self-consistent of all applications of the belief that the source of truth is to be found within the child's own consciousness. By the 1860s, Peabody had moved away from Alcott's radically idealist position, and had come under the influence of Friedrich Froebel, the German founder of the kindergarten, whose method was empirical. During the years 1873-1877, she edited the *Kindergarten Messenger*, for which she wrote numerous articles defining purpose, method, and controlled activities for the kindergarten. In 1888 she published her *Lectures in Training Schools for Kindergartners*. Although there is a shift toward learning through the senses, she retained her transcendentalist view of the soul as active, and continued to insist that "inspiration is the universal principle of education."

Also akin to Emersonian Transcendentalism was her emphasis on the significance of language as essentially symbolic. However, this concept was imperfectly blended with influences from Herder's controversial work on the origins of language and the identification of language universals attempted by the Hungarian, Dr. Charles Kraitsir, whose work Peabody was issuing from her publishing house. Her own writing on the subject, which to some extent anticipates twentieth-century linguistic theory in phonetics, includes a long essay entitled "Language" (1848), and several books of exercises for language arts in the schools, notably, *After Kindergarten—What?* (1877) which she coauthored with her sister, Mrs. Mann.

Although Peabody's interest in history somewhat sets her apart from her mentors, Emerson and Channing, her work in this field, too, is dependent on the scholarship of others, such as George Bancroft in American history and Karl Ottfried Muller in early Western history. Her aim in promoting the study of America appears to be largely to foster patriotic pride and to find moral *exempla*. In such essays as "The Dorian Measure" (1848) and "Essay on the Earliest Ages" (1850), myth, history, and religion are interwoven to provide vistas on both historical fact and universal truth. For her the study of history holds the place that Nature holds for Emerson and Thoreau: it provides a means to that self-awareness which enables one to live life deliberately.

Among Peabody's most admired works in her own time were her personal recollections of famous men and women she had known. Chief among these were three essays which form the nucleus of the collection *Last Evening with Allston* (1886), the tribute "Emerson as Preacher," included in F. B.

RECORD OF A SCHOOL:

EXEMPLIFYING

THE GENERAL PRINCIPLES

OF

SPIRITUAL CULTURE.

He that receiveth a little child in my name, receiveth me.—*Jesus Christ.*

BOSTON:
PUBLISHED BY JAMES MUNROE AND COMPANY.

NEW YORK:
LEAVITT, LORD AND CO. 180, BROADWAY.

PHILADELPHIA:
HENRY PERKINS.

1835.

Title page of Peabody's account of Bronson Alcott's Temple School.

Sanborn's *Genius and Character of Emerson* (1885), and the book-length *Reminiscences of Rev. Wm. Ellery Channing* (1880). In these writings she fulfilled Theodore Parker's observation that her rare qualities of mind and heart fitted her to be the "Boswell" of the day.

Like Margaret Fuller, Elizabeth Peabody was a member of the Transcendental Club, standing at the center of New England Transcendentalism. She exemplifies in her life and writings both the strengths and weaknesses of that movement: her diffuseness and casual inconsistencies are obvious, but they are offset by an intense moral purpose, a lively intellectual curiosity, and an unflagging energy for pursuing new fields of knowledge. In addition, she had the true educator's gift of spending herself for others. It is here, perhaps, that her greatest honor lies. —*Margaret Neussendorfer*

ÆSTHETIC PAPERS.

EDITED BY

ELIZABETH P. PEABODY.

" Beautie is not as fond men misdeeme,
An outward show of things that only seeme.
. . . .
Vouchsafe, then, O Thou most Almightie Spright!
From whom all gifts of wit and knowledge flow,
To shed into my breast some sparkling light
Of thine Eternall Truth, that I may show
Some little beames to mortall eyes below
Of that immortall Beautie, there with Thee,
Which in my weake distraughted mynd I see."
Spenser.

BOSTON:

THE EDITOR, 13, WEST STREET.

NEW YORK: G. P. PUTNAM, 155, BROADWAY.

1849.

PRINTED BY JOHN WILSON, 21, SCHOOL STREET, BOSTON.

Front wrapper for Aesthetic Papers *(1849).*

TABLE OF CONTENTS.

POETRY.

Contents page for Aesthetic Papers *(1849).*

Principal Works: *Key to History: First Steps to the Study of History* (Boston: Hilliard, Gray, 1832); *The Hebrews* (Boston: Marsh, Capen & Lyon, 1833); *The Greeks* (Boston: Marsh, Capen & Lyon, 1833); "Spirit of the Hebrew Scriptures," *Christian Examiner*, 16 (May, July, September 1834): 174-202, 305-320, 78-92; *The Polish-American System of Chronology, Reproduced, with some Modifications from General Bem's Franco-Polish Method* (Boston: Putnam's, 1850); *Chronological History of the United States, Arranged with Plates on Bem's Principle* (New York: Sheldon, Blakeman, 1856); *Moral Culture of Infancy and Kindergarten Guide* (Boston: T. O. H. Burnham, 1863); "Industrial Schools for Women," *Harper's New Monthly Magazine*, 40 (May 1870): 885-891; *The Piutes: Second Report of the Model School of Sarah Winnemucca* (Cambridge: John Wilson, 1887).

Principal References: Louise Hall Tharp, *The Peabody Sisters of Salem* (Boston: Little, Brown, 1950)—for corrections applying to this biography, see Robert Straker, "A Gloss Upon Glosses," typescript, Antioch College, 1956; Gladys Brooks, *Three Wise Virgins* (New York: E. P. Dutton, 1957); Ruth M. Baylor, *Elizabeth Palmer Peabody: Kindergarten Pioneer* (Philadelphia: University of Pennsylvania Press, 1965)—this source has the most complete bibliography, although there are occasional errors.

WILLIAM HICKLING PRESCOTT (4 May 1796-28 January 1859), early Victorian historian of the Spanish empire, was born in Salem, Massachusetts. Prescott possessed the typical characteristics of the Brahmin caste of New England. He was of old New England Scotts: his ancestor John Prescott settled in Middlesex County, Massachusetts, about 1640. In 1796 William Prescott married Catherine Hickling, daughter of a wealthy Boston merchant. In 1808 Prescott's father moved to Boston, where he invested successfully in industry, railroads, and insurance. Prescott entered the sophomore class at Harvard College in 1811, intending to follow his father's career in the practice of law, but drastic physical maladies soon forced a change of direction. During his junior year, Prescott lost the sight of his left eye when struck by a hard crust of bread during a brawl in the college dining hall. He continued his studies, and had earned membership in Phi Beta Kappa by the time of his graduation in 1814. After graduation, Prescott began several months of study in his father's law office. In 1815 he suffered a seizure of acute rheumatism, and for extended periods of time could neither see nor walk. The acute inflammation of his right eye steadily worsened, and Prescott was never able to use his remaining eye except for short periods of time and at great discomfort. In September of 1815, Prescott embarked upon a two-year convalescence in the Azores, the British Isles, and Europe. His gentlemanly tour stimulated a desire to write European history. Despite the warning of his physician, Prescott decided to pursue a literary career. Prescott employed assistants to read aloud to him. At first Prescott worked with German sources, but found the script too taxing for the limited use of his frail eye, and by 1822 had switched to an intensive study of the languages and literature of England, France, and Italy. By 1825 Prescott had concentrated his efforts upon the history of Spain. The previous year, George Ticknor, a professor of Spanish and French literature at Harvard, began reading to Prescott his lectures on Spanish literature. Prescott thereafter concentrated his major research upon a history of the Spanish empire. Already in 1821 Prescott had launched his writing career with a series of essays and articles for the *North American Review*. Even after he became engrossed in the history of Spain, Prescott continued to write essays on American literary and historical subjects. His most important were later collected as *Biographical and Critical Miscellanies* (1845). For over three decades Prescott toiled on several volumes of Spanish history. His writing was centered in Boston, and except for occasional forays to New York,

Principal Works: *History of the Reign of Ferdinand and Isabella the Catholic*, 3 vols. (Boston: American Stationers' Company, 1838); *History of the Conquest of Mexico, with a Preliminary View of the Ancient Mexican Civilization and the Life of Cortes*, 3 vols. (New York: Harpers, 1843); *History of the Conquest of Peru, with a Preliminary View of the Civilization of the Incas*, 2 vols. (New York: Harpers, 1847).

Principal References: C. Harvey Gardiner, *William Hickling Prescott: A Biography* (Austin: University of Texas Press, 1969); Donald G. Darnell, *William Hickling Prescott* (Boston: Twayne, 1975).

Washington, and elsewhere, Prescott rarely ventured outside of his Brahmin world. Instead the romance of the Spanish empire was conveyed to his desk in Boston. The wealthy Prescott family procured the needed manuscripts and books from libraries in Europe and Mexico. In 1838 Prescott's first major work was published, a three-volume study entitled *The History of the Reign of Ferdinand and Isabella the Catholic*. Though plagued by a renewal of his eye malady, Prescott worked intently upon his next project, to write exhaustive studies of the conquests of Peru and Mexico. In 1843 he published his three-volume *History of the Conquest of Mexico*, and followed in 1847 with a two-volume *History of the Conquest of Peru*. In these and subsequent volumes on the Spanish empire, Prescott demonstrated the craft of the narrative historian of the early Victorian era. Constitutional and economic problems scarcely interested him; the romance of court life, the excitement of battle, and the saga of colonial empires were the themes stressed by Prescott. Such were his interests until 1859, when he died in Boston, hours after being striken with apoplexy.

—*Thomas L. Connelly*

SAMPSON REED (10 June 1800-8 July 1880), druggist and proponent of Swedenborgianism in the United States, was born in West Bridgewater, Massachusetts. After graduation from Harvard College in 1818, Reed entered the Divinity School where his roommate, Thomas Worcester, introduced him to the mystical writings of Emanuel Swedenborg. Reed was so taken with Swedenborg's thought that the resulting conflict with rational Unitarianism forced him to leave the Divinity School. After receiving a Master of Arts degree in 1821, Reed became a clerk in the shop of a Boston apothecary, later opened his own shop, and eventually built one of the largest wholesale drug businesses in New England. But Reed's foremost concern was the establishment of the Swedenborgian Church in the United States. He supported his beliefs with his prolific writings which appeared in the Swedenborgian *New Jerusalem Magazine* and in a children's magazine he founded in 1843, *The New Church Magazine for Children* (later the *Children's New-Church Magazine*). He died in Boston. Reed is primarily remembered today for the influence two of his compositions had upon Ralph Waldo Emerson. The oration on "Genius" (which circulated in manuscript and was belatedly printed in Elizabeth Peabody's *Aesthetic Papers* in 1849), delivered by Reed upon receiving his Master's degree, is one of the first indictments of Lockean sensualism in the Unitarian Church. *Observations on the Growth of the Mind* (Boston: Cummings, Hilliard, 1826) remains Reed's single most important work because its ideas serve as the basis of the Transcendental aesthetic theory. In this work Emerson found the ideas that each person has his own "peculium" or "use" and may develop his character by exercising that use, that the power of poetry is moral and, most important, the doctrine of correspondences which holds that the universe is an external manifestation of the soul and, therefore, every natural truth corresponds to a spiritual truth. Even the cryptic style of Reed and his optimistic tone have some bearing upon Emerson's development as a writer and thinker. REFERENCES: James Reed, "Biographical Preface" in *Observations on the Growth of the Mind* (Boston: Houghton, Mifflin, 1889); C. P. Hotson, "Ralph Waldo Emerson and Swedenborg," Ph.D. dissertation, Harvard University, 1929; Carl F. Strauch, "Introduction" in *Observations on the Growth of the Mind with Remarks on Some Other Subjects (1838)* (Gainesville, Fla.: Scholars' Facsimiles & Reprints, 1970).

—*Robert E. Burkholder*

GEORGE RIPLEY (3 October 1802-4 July 1880), who first gained national prominence as a Transcendentalist and the founder of the Brook Farm community, had a secondary but significant journalistic career and his greatest fame during the last quarter century of his life. As the dean of literate journalism, known across the country for his book reviews, articles, and essays in Horace Greeley's *New-York Tribune*, Ripley became both the arbiter of taste for many educated Americans and an oracle of culture for a mass audience. Over the years between the 1850s and Ripley's death, millions of readers followed his ideas and opinions in the *Tribune*, in leading periodicals such as *Putnam's Magazine* and *Harper's New Monthly Magazine*, and in the most important reference work of the Civil War era, *The New American Cyclopedia* (16 vols., 1858-1863), coedited with Charles A. Dana.

The most significant work in Ripley's life, however, can be traced to the two decades between 1827 and 1847 when he served as a Unitarian minister, a Transcendentalist, a reformer, the founder of Brook Farm, and a Utopian socialist. A native of Greenfield, Massachusetts, and a graduate of Harvard College and Harvard Divinity School, Ripley served in his first career as Unitarian minister in Boston at the Purchase Street Church for fifteen years until his disillusionment and resignation in 1840. During the years in the pulpit he gained a considerable reputation among religious readers as a result of his theological pamphlets and his editing and writing for the *Christian Register* and the *Christian Examiner*. During the 1830s Ripley and his Boston Brahmin wife (born Sophia Dana) became increasingly involved in the exciting cultural life of Boston and Concord. A friend and an associate of Emerson, Theodore Parker, Bronson Alcott, George Bancroft, Orestes A. Brownson, and other leading Massachusetts writers and intellectuals, Ripley played a role in the creation of Transcendentalism second only to that of Emerson and Thoreau. He served as a founder and a pillar of the Transcendental Club, an editor and contributor for the *Dial*, a major transmitter of contemporary European thought as the editor of the ambitious *Specimens of Foreign Standard Literature* (14 vols., 1830-1842) and the chief protagonist in the angry controversy with Andrews Norton of the Harvard Divinity School which marked the independence of the Transcendentalists from their Unitarian intellectual fathers.

By 1840, however, Ripley had broken with Emerson and Thoreau on the issue of ultra-individualism. The panic of 1837, the results of

which could be seen in the misery of expanding slums around the Purchase Street Church, the arrogance of capitalist wealth, and the isolated irresponsibility of the intellectual, pulled him away from the Emersonian belief that "one man is stronger than a city" and toward the Brook Farm communal experiment (1841-1847) at West Roxbury, Massachusetts. Observers, who chose to see Ripley's enterprise as a high-minded but essentially escapist "room at the Astor House reserved for the Transcendentalists," stressed the diversions and the intellectual life of a community with residents and frequent visitors such as Nathaniel Hawthorne, Margaret Fuller, Parker, Emerson, and Alcott. Nevertheless, Ripley began with "an authentic rage against poverty and injustice" and an interpretation of the communitarian ideal which proposed to alter American society through one shining example. The Brook Farmers wished to abolish both poverty and wealth, bridge the chasm between the social classes, end the alienating elements in modern factory work and commercial life, and unite the worker, the manager, and the thinker in every single person within the context of cooperative socialism rather than competitive capitalism. From the beginning the thought of the French Utopian socialist Charles

Fourier influenced Ripley and his associates, and in 1843 the Brook Farm leaders reorganized the community as a Fourierist "Phalanx." As the communal president, the editor and a major contributor to the best radical journal in America, the *Harbinger*, an officer of the Fourierist "American Union of Associationists," and a New England labor leader, Ripley became one of the most influential radical reformers of the 1840s.

The economic collapse of Brook Farm in 1847 and the dramatic decline of the Fourierist movement in America left a drifting and impoverished man struggling in New York City for a new life and economic survival for himself and his wife. During the 1850s life under slum conditions, the violence of the street gangs, the need to produce large quantities of newspaper copy for pitifully small wages, the painful adjustments of a middle-aged man starting as a novice, and the growing disillusionment with radical and reform causes, all transformed Ripley. The radical and the ideologue perished, but the man survived and, in his own way, triumphed. Very slowly and painfully the starving hack became the successful, influential, and affluent leader of scholarly journalism in America. He died in New York City in 1880, a greatly respected man.

Looking back across Ripley's life, we can see him as a journalist with high intellectual standards and as an antebellum radical reformer of the first magnitude. If he does not belong to the rank of Emerson and Thoreau in literature, he did serve major and minor Transcendentalists extremely well as essayist, editor, translator, pamphleteer, organizer, intellectual gadfly, and useful companion.

—*Charles Crowe*

Principal Works: *Discourses on the Philosophy of Religion* (Boston: James Munroe, 1836); *The Latest Form of Infidelity Examined* (Boston: James Munroe, 1839); with George P. Bradford, "Philosophic Thought in Boston," in *The Memorial History of Boston*, ed. Justin Windsor (Boston: James R. Osgood, 1881), 4:294-330.

Principal References: Octavius Brooks Frothingham, *George Ripley* (Boston: Houghton, Mifflin, 1882); Charles Crowe, *George Ripley, Transcendentalist and Utopian Socialist*—includes bibliography (Athens: University of Georgia Press, 1967).

FRANKLIN BENJAMIN SANBORN (15 December 1831-24 February 1917), teacher, author, abolitionist, and social reformer, was born in Hampton Falls, New Hampshire, and educated at Phillips Exeter Academy and Harvard College. In November 1854 a ten-minute call Sanborn had paid on Emerson the previous spring was rewarded by Emerson's request that Sanborn take over the school once kept by John and Henry Thoreau. Living with William Ellery Channing, the younger, Sanborn grew increasingly interested in abolitionism. After meeting John Brown in the summer of 1857, Sanborn became a zealous disciple of Brown and a member of the "Secret Six"—the only men to know in advance of the Harper's Ferry raid. After the raid, Sanborn fled to Canada and, at Emerson's request, returned to Concord under an assumed name. On the night of 3 April 1860 deputies of the United States Senate attempted to kidnap Sanborn, but a crowd of Concord citizens, including Emerson, ran the deputies out of town, and a subsequent court decision freed Sanborn from any obligations to testify before the Senate. In 1856 Sanborn became the "Boston correspondent" for the Springfield *Republican*, and later was a resident editor of the *Republican*

from 1868 to 1872. He also edited the Boston *Commonwealth* from 1863 to 1867. Increased interest in social reform led to Sanborn's aiding in the founding of the American Association for the Promotion of Social Science and his establishment of the first college course in Social Science at Cornell University, where he was special lecturer from 1884 to 1887. With the aid of William Torrey Harris, Sanborn also founded the Concord School of Philosophy, a summer school which featured the lectures of Bronson Alcott. Between two extended trips to Europe, Sanborn convinced the aged and ailing Ellery Channing to move in with him in 1891. During this period Sanborn regularly questioned Channing in order to get all the information he could about Channing's friendships with Emerson and Thoreau. Always known for his stubborn inability to accept any opinion but his own, Sanborn suffered a decline in popularity in the 1880s which, perhaps, contributed to his being the only member twice dropped from the membership rolls of the elite Social Circle in Concord, a club which Sanborn helped found. Stubborn until the end, at the age of eighty-three Sanborn defended in court his right to use sewage from his own home to fertilize his garden. He lost his court battle, but was ultimately allowed to do as he pleased because he refused to comply with the court's decision. He died in 1917, five weeks after being struck by a baggage wagon on a train platform in Plainfield, New Jersey.

Sanborn's literary reputation is at best paradoxical: he is often given credit for single-handedly establishing the value of the works of Thoreau, Alcott, and Channing, and condemned for the editorial vagaries he committed in publishing those works. Sanborn's three biographies of Thoreau—*Henry D. Thoreau, The Personality of Thoreau*, and *The Life of Henry David Thoreau*—are characterized by Sanborn's ability to speak as an insider about Thoreau and contemporary Concord, his emphasis on Thoreau's college essays rather than what might be called major works, long genealogical digressions, and transcriptions of Thoreau's poems so inaccurate that they might better be termed paraphrases. Editorial problems also occur in Sanborn's edition of *The Familiar Letters of Henry David Thoreau*, where Thoreau's sentences are emasculated by changes in wording and structure; and *Poems of Nature*, which Sanborn edited with Henry S. Salt. Somewhat typical of Sanborn's work as an editor is his edition of *Walden*. Being alerted that there were 12,000 words in manuscript scraps (which Thoreau apparently culled-out during eight years of revision) Sanborn determined to include them in his text. The resulting edition of *Walden* is really *Walden* rewritten, with chapters rearranged by Sanborn so his new-found material would fit. In 1873 Bronson Alcott expressed a desire to have Sanborn do his biography. *A. Bronson Alcott: His Life and Philosophy* by Sanborn and Harris was criticized by reviewers for failing to flesh-out Alcott, the man. Sanborn attempted to remedy this flaw with *Bronson Alcott at Alcott House, England, and Fruitlands, New England (1842-1844)*, but in both cases Sanborn barely consulted Alcott's private Journals, the single most authoritative source, and often misquoted or altered what he did use. Sanborn's two biographies of Emerson are actually as much about Sanborn as Emerson. Like his biographies of Thoreau, Sanborn's *Ralph Waldo Emerson* places undue emphasis on Emerson's youth and Sanborn's recollections of incidents and conversations, while *The Personality of Emerson* is a rambling and sometimes repetitious narrative, with a chronological structure based upon Sanborn's own autobiographical revelations. Sanborn also edited several works by Ellery Channing, wrote a biography of Hawthorne, and might have edited Theodore Parker's papers (since Parker stipulated in his will that he wished Sanborn to perform that task), but for the opposition of Mrs. Parker, who refused Sanborn access to her husband's papers until after her own death. Perhaps the best source for capturing the ambience in Concord in the last half of the nineteenth century as well as a sense of Sanborn, the man, is his memoir, *Recollections of Seventy Years.* —Robert E. Burkholder

Principal Works: *Henry D. Thoreau* (Boston: Houghton, Mifflin, 1882); with William Torrey Harris, *A. Bronson Alcott: His Life and Philosophy*, 2 vols. (Boston: Roberts Brothers, 1893); *The Familiar Letters of Henry David Thoreau*, ed. Sanborn (Boston: Houghton, Mifflin, 1894); Thoreau, *Poems of Nature*, ed. with Henry S. Salt (Boston: Houghton, Mifflin, 1895); *The Personality of Thoreau* (Boston: Charles E. Goodspeed, 1901); *Ralph Waldo Emerson* (Boston: Small, Maynard, 1901); Channing, *Poems of Sixty-five Years*, ed. Sanborn (Philadelphia: J. H. Bentley, 1902); *The Personality of Emerson* (Boston: Charles E. Goodspeed, 1903); *Bronson Alcott at Alcott House, England, and Fruitlands, New England (1842-1844)* (Cedar Rapids, Iowa: Torch Press, 1908); *Hawthorne and His Friends: Reminiscence and Tribute* (Cedar Rapids, Iowa: Torch Press, 1908); Parker, *The Rights of Man in America*, ed. Sanborn (Boston: American Unitarian Association, 1909); *Recol-*

lections of *Seventy Years*, 2 vols. (Boston: Richard G. Badger, 1909); Thoreau, *Walden, or Life in the Woods*, 2 vols., ed. Sanborn (Boston: Bibliophile Society, 1909); *The Life of Henry David Thoreau* (Boston: Houghton Mifflin, 1917).

Principal References: Benjamin Blakely Hickock, "The Political and Literary Careers of F. B. Sanborn," Ph.D. dissertation, Michigan State University, 1953; John W. Clarkson, Jr., "A Bibliography of Franklin Benjamin Sanborn," *Papers of the Bibliographical Society of America*, 60 (First Quarter 1966): 73-85; Clarkson, "An Annotated Checklist of the Letters of F. B. Sanborn (1831-1917)," Ph.D. dissertation, Columbia University, 1971.

CATHARINE MARIA SEDGWICK (28 December 1789-31 July 1867), novelist, was born and lived most of her life at the family estate in Stockbridge, Massachusetts. She was educated both in schools and at home, though her early life was devoted to social pleasures and religious training, the latter greatly influenced by the Reverend William Ellery Channing. Her first novel, *A New-England Tale* (New York: Bliss & White, 1822), was typical of her other five: it accurately described and recreated a native American setting while promoting the virtues of domesticity. *Hope Leslie* (New York: White, Gallaher & White, 1827), an historical romance set in colonial Massachusetts, is her most famous work. She died in West Roxbury, Massachusetts. Sedgwick, though the most popular female novelist before Harriet Beecher Stowe, is of value today primarily because of her pioneering attempt to create a realistic background for her fiction, acting as a midpoint between the romanticism of the past and the realism of the future.
REFERENCES: Mary E. Dewey, *Life and Letters of Catharine M. Sedgwick* (New York: Harpers, 1872); Sister Mary Michael Welsh, *Catharine Maria Sedgwick*—includes bibliography (Washington: Catholic University of America, 1937).

BENJAMIN PENHALLOW SHILLABER (12 July 1814-25 November 1890), journalist and humorist, left his Portsmouth, New Hampshire, home to become a printer's helper in Boston. He joined the Boston *Post* and in 1847 catapulted to literary fame by his creation, "Mrs. Partington." The forte of this widow lady was poetry—bad poetry—and her prose was sprinkled with numerous malapropisms. The "Mrs. Partington" sketches appeared in newspapers and magazines, including his own short-lived comic weekly, the *Carpet Bag* (1852), and "her" first book appeared in 1854 as *The Life and Sayings of Mrs. Partington* (New York: J. C. Derby), quickly selling 30,000 copies. In subsequent years Shillaber edited magazines, wrote juveniles, and published his own humorous verse. He died in Chelsea, Massachusetts. Mark Twain, whose first published sketch appeared in the *Carpet Bag*, is thought to have been influenced by the "Mrs. Partington" character in writing *Tom Sawyer*.
REFERENCES: Shillaber, "Experiences During Many Years," *New England Magazine*, n.s. 9 (September 1893-January 1894): 88-95, 153-160, 529-533, 625-631; n.s. 10 (March-May 1894): 29-36, 247-256, 286-294; Cyril Clemens, "Benjamin Shillaber and His 'Carpet Bag,'" *New England Quarterly*, 14 (September 1941): 519-537.

LYDIA HOWARD (HUNTLEY) SIGOURNEY (1 September 1791-10 June 1865), author, known at the height of her fame as "the sweet singer of Hartford" and "the American Mrs. Hemans," has not sustained her popularity or her reputation. Born in Norwich, Connecticut, the only child of Ezekial and Zerviah (Wentworth) Huntley, she was educated in local schools before teaching young ladies at Norwich and Hartford. Her first book, whose title would have been appropriate for most of her writings, was *Moral Pieces, in Prose and Verse* (1815). In 1819 she married Charles Sigourney, a widower with three children, and she continued writing to support her favorite causes—peace and war relief, temperance and missionaries—and, later on, to augment the family income. In this she was eminently successful. Her verse and prose were moral, sentimental, and pious, concerned principally with death; her style was euphemistic and at times affected; her rhythms were conventional. Her writings appealed to mid-nineteenth-century America as strongly as they fail to appeal to twentieth-century America. Mrs. Sigourney was an omnipresent contributor to the annuals, gift books, and periodicals of her time, from the *North American Review* to *Graham's Magazine*, from the *Southern Literary Messenger* to the *Pioneer: or, California Monthly Magazine*, from the *Ladies' Wreath* to the *Ladies' Repository*. She herself commented at the end of her life: "I think now with amazement, and almost incredulity, of the number of articles I was induced by the urgency of editors to furnish. Before I ceased to keep a regular catalogue they had amounted to more than two thousand." In a steady stream the indefatigable author produced more than sixty-five books, at first anonymously—poetry and essays, historical sketches, travel, fiction. Louis Godey paid her $500 a year for the mere use of her name in his *Lady's Book* (1840-1842) and although Poe considered her style too imitative, he requested a monthly article from her for *Graham's Magazine*. When she went abroad in 1840 she was received by Maria Edgeworth, William Wordsworth, and Thomas Carlyle, as she recorded in her *Pleasant Memories of Pleasant Lands*. At the start of her career the May 1815 *North American Review* pronounced her poems "exquisitely beautiful and pathetick. . . if not sublime." At the height of her popularity the June 1850 *Western Literary Messenger* considered that her poems were "laid on a million of memory's shelves. Children in our infant schools lisp her mellow canzonets; older youths recite her poems for riper minds in our grammar schools and academies; mothers pore over her pages of prose for counsel, and the aged of either sex draw consolation from the

inspirations of her sanctified muse in their declining years." The very attributes that made her so popular in her day—the politeness of her muse, the nobility of her theme, the pseudo-elegance of her manner—fail to connect with readers today. The small, plump, flaxen-haired "lady of letters" with her pious sentimentalities catered to a taste for poetry "more like the dew than the lightning." With the sumptuously bound gift book in which she was ubiquitous, Mrs. Sigourney has gone out of fashion and now merely recalls a taste and a style that have become historic. —*Madeleine B. Stern*

Principal Works: *Moral Pieces, in Prose and Verse* (Hartford, Ct.: Sheldon & Goodwin, 1815); *Traits of the Aborigines of America. A Poem* (Cambridge: Hilliard & Metcalf, 1822); *Sketch of Connecticut, Forty Years Since* (Hartford, Ct.: Oliver D. Cooke, 1824); *Poems* (Philadelphia: Key & Biddle, 1834); *Pocahontas, and Other Poems* (New York: Harpers, 1841); *Pleasant Memories of Pleasant Lands* (Boston: James Munroe, 1842); *The Voice of Flowers* (Hartford, Ct.: H. S. Parsons, 1846); *The Weeping Willow* (Hartford, Ct.: H. S. Parsons, 1847);

Illustrated Poems (Philadelphia: Carey & Hart, 1849); *Whisper to a Bride* (Hartford, Ct.: H. S. Parsons, 1850); *Past Meridian* (New York: D. Appleton, 1854); *The Daily Counsellor* (Hartford, Ct.: Brown & Gross, 1859); *Letters of Life* (New York: D. Appleton, 1866).

Principal Reference: Gordon S. Haight, *Mrs. Sigourney: The Sweet Singer of Hartford* (New Haven: Yale University Press, 1930).

E. Oakes Smith

ELIZABETH OAKES (PRINCE) SMITH (12 August 1806-15 November 1893), popular author and reformer, was born in North Yarmouth, Maine. She was self-educated and wished to pursue a teaching career but, on her mother's wishes, at sixteen she married Seba Smith, a newspaper editor in Portland. Smith managed their family of five sons well and her husband became successful with his humorous "Major Jack Downing Letters." But the Smiths went bankrupt in the panic of 1837 and moved to New York. There, both Smiths wrote for a living: Seba for the dailies; Elizabeth, poetry, sketches, and juveniles. Her *The Sinless Child, and Other Poems* (New York: Wiley & Putnam, 1843) won praise, including that of Edgar Allan Poe. Smith became a regular contributor to *Godey's Lady Book*, *Graham's Magazine*, and the *Southern Literary Messenger*; published juveniles; wrote plays; and joined the New York literary coterie that included Poe, Horace Greeley, and Margaret Fuller. She became an active reformer and her series on woman's rights in the *New-York Tribune* was published as *Woman and Her Needs* (New York: Fowler & Wells, 1851). In 1851 she joined the lyceum circuit to talk on the woman question. Her reform novel, *The Newsboy* (New York: J. C. Derby, 1854), created public interest in the plight of New York's street children. In the 1860s, she published a series of popular novels and, after her husband's death in 1868, retired to Hollywood, North Carolina. REFERENCES: *Selections from the Autobiography of Elizabeth Oakes Smith*, ed. Mary Alice Wyman (Lewiston, Maine: Lewiston Journal Co., 1924); Mary Alice Wyman, *Two American Pioneers: Seba Smith and Elizabeth Oakes Smith* (New York: Columbia University Press, 1927).

Seba Smith.

SEBA SMITH (14 September 1792-28 July 1868), journalist and humorist, taught school around his home in Buckfield, Maine, before entering Bowdoin College in 1815. After he graduated in 1818, Smith taught briefly, travelled through New England and to England, and, upon his return in 1820, joined the staff of the Portland *Eastern Argus*. Smith became editor and part owner, married Elizabeth Oakes

Prince, and settled down to an established family life. In 1826 he sold his share in the paper, only to start two other papers in 1829. One, the Portland *Courier*, carried his humorous letters by "Major Jack Downing of Downingville" after 1830 and brought him national attention. The Smiths lost their money in the panic of 1837 and moved to New York, where Smith contributed to and edited various newspapers and magazines until he retired to Long Island in 1860. Smith's *Life and Writings of Major Jack Downing of Downingville* (Boston: Lilly Wait, 1833) and *My Thirty Years Out of the Senate* (New York: Oaksmith, 1859) are considered among America's first political satires, examining the problems and squabbles of Jacksonian democracy, and are among the first portraits of the "Yankee type" in American literature. Smith also wrote *'Way Down East* (New York: Derby & Jackson, 1854), a series of tales about New England life.
REFERENCE: Mary Alice Wyman, *Two American Pioneers: Seba Smith and Elizabeth Oakes Smith* (New York: Columbia University Press, 1927).

Jared Sparks

Jared Sparks [signature]

JARED SPARKS (10 May 1789-14 March 1866), biographer and historian, overcame his illegitimate birth in Willington, Connecticut, and, by educating himself, entered Harvard College, graduating in 1815. Sparks became a divinity student and was ordained in Baltimore in 1819. He served as chaplain of the House of Representatives and returned to New England in 1823. After buying the *North American Review*, Sparks edited it with such success that in 1829 he sold the magazine for a 100% profit. His first marriage, in 1832, ended when his wife died three years later. His second marriage, in 1839, to a wealthy Bostonian, enabled him to devote the rest of his life to his historical writings and to Harvard, which had named him McLean Professor of Ancient and Modern History in 1838, and which he served as president of from 1849 to 1853. He died in Cambridge. Sparks's fame rests upon his editions of the papers of George Washington (1834-1837) and Benjamin Franklin (1836-1840), his own biographies of famous Americans, and his series, "Library of American Biography" (25 vols., 1834-1838, 1844-1848). Although Sparks did save valuable manuscripts from loss, his editions of them are untrustworthy and his own biographies are too formal and proper to be of use today.

REFERENCES: Herbert B. Adams, *Life and Writings of Jared Sparks*, 2 vols. (Boston: Houghton, Mifflin, 1893); John Spencer Bassett, *Correspondence of George Bancroft and Jared Sparks* (Northampton, Mass.: Department of History of Smith College, 1917).

and *Poems* (Boston: Little & Brown, 1856) were common New England fare which brought him little acknowledgement. His later poems, especially those of *Graffiti d'Italia* (Edinburgh: Blackwood & Sons, 1868) are partially liberated from the restrictive atmosphere of New England, but are pervaded by a European flavor and the influence of Story's neighbor in Rome, Robert Browning. *Roba di Roma* (London: Chapman & Hall, 1862), the most popular of Story's collections of essays, is a rambling guide to contemporary Rome with Story's comments on Roman art, history, and culture. His one novel, *Fiametta; A Summer Idyl* (Edinburgh: Blackwood & Sons, 1885), is overly romantic and sentimental, and features the death of the heroine from unrequited love. Although his popularity and nearly all of his literary acquaintances were European by the 1860s, Story demonstrated his concern over the American Civil War with a series of letters to the London *Daily News* beginning in 1861. REFERENCES: Mary E. Phillips, *Reminiscences of William Wetmore Story* (New York: Rand, McNally, 1897); Henry James, *William Wetmore Story and His Friends*, 2 vols. (Boston: Houghton, Mifflin, 1903).

—*Robert E. Burkholder*

WILLIAM WETMORE STORY (12 February 1819-7 October 1895), lawyer, sculptor, poet, essayist, and novelist, was the son of the eminent jurist Joseph Story. He was born in Salem, Massachusetts. After receiving his Bachelor of Laws degree from Harvard College in 1840, Story settled briefly into the practice of law and published several legal treatises. With the death of his father in 1845, Story was commissioned to design a statue for his tomb. This commission led Story to Italy in 1847. There he was received by a small community of American artists which included Margaret Fuller and Horatio Greenough, and by 1856 Story had abandoned the law and settled permanently in Rome. In 1862, with the acclaim given his statue of *Cleopatra* (which is described in detail by Story's friend Nathaniel Hawthorne in *The Marble Faun*), Story received the recognition as a sculptor he desired. But by this time he was already redirecting his energies into belletristic writing. Story had attempted poetry while still practicing law, but his *Poems* (Boston: Little & Brown, 1847)

HARRIET BEECHER STOWE (14 June 1811-1 July 1896), prolific novelist, is remembered today for *Uncle Tom's Cabin*. She was born in Litchfield, Connecticut, the daughter of the distinguished Congregational minister Lyman Beecher and Roxanna Foote. The family included eight children, among them Catharine, Isabella, and Henry Ward Beecher. When Harriet was four, her mother died. Harriet's father remarried and had three more children by his second wife, Harriet Porter. During this period Harriet and Henry Ward were closely attached. Under her father's pervasive influence, she grew up in "a kind of moral heaven, replete with moral oxygen—full charged with intellectual electricity." Much of that "moral oxygen" and "intellectual electricity" would be injected into *Uncle Tom's Cabin*. The guiding principles of life in the Calvinist parsonage were self-abnegation and spiritual regeneration, principles that were to filter into Harriet's writings. After five years at Miss Sarah Pierce's school in Litchfield, she attended the Hartford Female Seminary opened by her oldest sister Catharine, and subsequently taught there. In 1832 the family moved to Cincinnati where Lyman Beecher became president of Lane Theological Seminary and Catharine founded the Western Female Institute. There Harriet taught and in 1834 won first prize for a sketch in the *Western Monthly Magazine*. Two years later, the shy, thin, plain Harriet Beecher married a widower, Calvin Ellis Stowe, Professor of Biblical Literature at Lane. Five children were born during the first seven years of their marriage. Strongly imbued with Christian purpose, Harriet took charge of the family finances as well as the drudgeries of housekeeping. She also dashed off a tale now and then so that she could hire household help, and in 1843 a collection of her stories, *The Mayflower*, was published by Harpers. A few years later, after the birth of two additional children, Calvin Stowe became a professor at Bowdoin College, Brunswick, Maine. Harriet continued her writing, her early sentimental and conventional sketches reflecting her high-minded interest in social reform, the sanctity of the home, and woman's place in it. She had read of the atrocities of slavery, and when the Fugitive Slave Law spurred her to action she was finally metamorphosed into the instrument of the Lord who created an "epic of Negro bondage," a powerful narrative of damnation and salvation. *Uncle Tom's Cabin* was begun early in 1851 and sold for $300 to the *National Era*, where the first of forty installments appeared in June. At the suggestion of Mrs. John P. Jewett, wife of the Boston publisher, it was published in book form in 1852, the writer accepting a 10% royalty in lieu of half share of expenses and profits. *Uncle Tom's Cabin* was issued first in a two-volume set and later as a single volume priced at 37½ cents. Within a year total sales topped 300,000. Before the Civil War sales reached 3,000,000 and more than double that figure up to 1972. Eventually the book reached "the top flight of the list of American best sellers." With dramatizations, reprints, and foreign translations, its popularity soared. *Uncle Tom's Cabin* made its author famous overnight, inspired a spate of anti-*Uncle Tom* novels, and won the praise of such diverse critics as Henry Wadsworth Longfellow and Henry James. Ralph Waldo Emerson stressed its universality in "Success": "We have seen an American woman write a novel of which a million copies were sold in all languages, and which had one merit, of speaking to the universal heart, and was read with equal interest to three audiences, namely, in the parlor, in the kitchen, and in the nursery of every house." According to one reviewer, "The mightiest princes of intellect, as well as those who have scarcely harbored a stray thought . . . friends of slavery equally with the haters of that institution . . . all . . . bend with sweating eagerness over her magic pages." Though its characters are sometimes symbols and some of its incidents stylized, this domestic novel was also a forceful, vital, original, and daring moral instrument. Its author exercised tact but did not shrink from realism, and her message—that slavery destroys both the master and the slave—rang boldly across the nation. Simon Legree, Eliza, Mr. St. Clare, little Eva, and Uncle Tom joined a parade of unforgettable literary characters, and Mrs. Stowe's timely propaganda stirred the national conscience. She replied to objectors in 1853 with *A Key to Uncle Tom's Cabin*. In 1856 she returned for the last time to the anti-slavery theme in *Dred*. Between 1862, when she reworked her New England childhood into *The Pearl of Orr's Island*, and 1884, Mrs. Stowe produced at least a book a year, providing for her family, educating her children, sustaining an alcoholic son. From her tireless pen flowed essays on the home, domestic novels, stories of death and redemption, as well as a defense of Lady Byron. After her husband's retirement in 1864, the family moved to Hartford, where Mrs. Stowe built a villa, Oakholm. Despite the independence her pen had won her, she continued to sermonize against the emancipated woman who indulged in tobacco. Harriet Beecher Stowe was accurately described by one biographer as a "Crusader in Crinoline." Her crinolines have become period pieces, her crusade historic. Yet she

helped to document and advance that crusade. James Baldwin's attribution of racial prejudice to *Uncle Tom's Cabin* has been effectively rebutted, and recent evaluations of Mrs. Stowe as a writer tend to reveal in her work not less but more literary craftsmanship. Although *Uncle Tom's Cabin* is no longer widely read, it is still being critically examined, and it is unlikely that it will ever be forgotten. —*Madeleine B. Stern*

Principal Works: *The Mayflower; or, Sketches of Scenes and Characters among the Descendants of the Puritans* (New York: Harpers, 1843); *Uncle Tom's Cabin; or, Life Among the Lowly*, 2 vols. (Boston: John P. Jewett, 1852); *A Key to Uncle Tom's Cabin; Presenting the Original Facts and Documents upon which the Story is Founded* (Boston: John P. Jewett, 1853); *Dred; A Tale of the Great Dismal Swamp* (Boston: Phillips, Sampson, 1856); *The Minister's Wooing* (New York: Derby & Jackson, 1859); *The Pearl of Orr's Island: A Story of the Coast of Maine* (Boston: Ticknor & Fields, 1862); *Oldtown Folks* (Boston: Fields, Osgood, 1869); *Lady Byron Vindicated. A History of The Byron Controversy, from its Beginning in 1816 to the Present Time* (Boston: Fields, Osgood, 1870); *Pink and White Tyranny. A Society Novel* (Boston: Roberts Brothers, 1871); *My Wife and I; or, Harry Henderson's History* (New York: J. B. Ford, 1871); *Palmetto-Leaves* (Boston: James R. Osgood, 1873); *Poganuc People: Their Loves and Lives* (New York: Fords, Howard & Hulbert, 1878).

Principal References: Charles Edward Stowe, *Life of Harriet Beecher Stowe compiled from Her Letters and Journals* (Boston: Houghton, Mifflin, 1889); *Life and Letters of Harriet Beecher Stowe*, ed. Annie A. Fields (Boston: Houghton, Mifflin, 1897); Charles Edward Stowe and L. B. Stowe, *Harriet Beecher Stowe, the Story of Her Life* (Boston: Houghton Mifflin, 1911); John R. Adams, "The Literary Achievement of Harriet Beecher Stowe," Ph.D. dissertation, University of Southern California, 1939; Forrest Wilson, *Crusader in Crinoline: The Life of Harriet Beecher Stowe* (Philadelphia: J. B. Lippincott, 1941); Charles Foster, *The Rungless Ladder: Harriet Beecher Stowe and New England Puritanism* (Durham: Duke University Press, 1954); Alice A. Cooper, "Harriet Beecher Stowe: A Critical Study," Ph.D. dissertation, Harvard University, 1964; Edward Charles Wagenknecht, *Harriet Beecher Stowe: The Known and the Unknown* (New York: Oxford University Press, 1965); Alice C. Crozier, *The Novels of Harriet Beecher Stowe* (New York: Oxford University Press, 1969).

Henry David Thoreau

Walter Harding
State University of New York, College at Geneseo

BIRTH: Concord, Massachusetts, 12 July 1817.

UNMARRIED.

DEATH: Concord, Massachusetts, 6 May 1862.

MAJOR WORKS: *A Week on the Concord and Merrimack Rivers* (Boston: James Munroe, 1849); "Resistance to Civil Government" (later known as "Civil Disobedience") in *Aesthetic Papers* (Boston: E. P. Peabody, 1849); *Walden* (Boston: Ticknor & Fields, 1854); *Journal* (Boston: Houghton Mifflin, 1906).

Life and Career:

Generally unrecognized in his own day or, worse, dismissed as a second-rate imitator of his friend and mentor Ralph Waldo Emerson, Henry David Thoreau, in the twentieth century, has emerged as one of America's greatest literary figures. *Walden*, his account of two years spent living in a cabin on the shore of a pond in his native Concord, is universally recognized as the preeminent piece of American nature writing, though it is far more than simply a nature book. "Civil Disobedience," the account of and justification for his night spent in jail in Concord in protest against slavery, particularly through its influence on such activists as Mahatma Gandhi and Martin Luther King, has had wider political impact around the world than any other American literary document. As a prose stylist, Thoreau has been acknowledged by writers as disparate as Robert Louis Stevenson, Marcel Proust, Sinclair Lewis, and Henry Miller to be their master. As the apostle of the simple life, and the advocate of "listening to a different drummer," Thoreau is the hero of many of today's younger generation.

Henry David Thoreau was born on 12 July 1817 in Concord, Massachusetts, eighteen miles northwest of Boston, the only member of the so-called "Concord School of Writers" to be a native of that town. Although both his paternal and maternal ancestors had once been prosperous, the family patrimony had dwindled away and, thanks to his father John Thoreau's financial ineptness, Thoreau himself was brought up in an atmosphere of genteel poverty. The family, with its four children—Helen (born 1812), John (born 1815), Henry, and Sophia

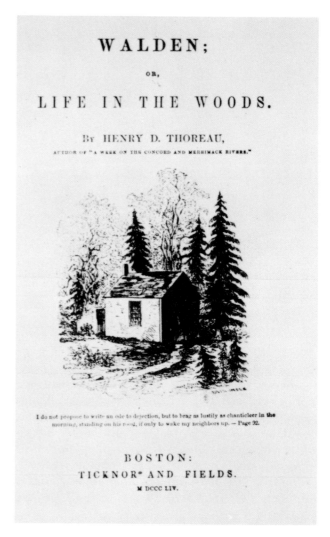

WALDEN;

OR,

LIFE IN THE WOODS.

BY HENRY D. THOREAU,

AUTHOR OF "A WEEK ON THE CONCORD AND MERRIMACK RIVERS."

I do not propose to write an ode to dejection, but to brag as lustily as chanticleer in the morning, standing on his roost, if only to wake my neighbors up. — Page 92.

BOSTON:
TICKNOR AND FIELDS.
M DCCC LIV.

(born 1819)—moved frequently from house to house (for a time living in nearby Chelmsford and in Boston), and the father from job to job, until in 1823 they returned to Concord and established a moderately successful pencil-making business. The children were educated in the Concord public schools and later, at their mother's insistence and at some financial sacrifice, in the more adequate and prestigious private Concord Academy. Henry, a shy and quiet youth, spent much time by himself wandering in the woods and fields of Concord, a proclivity encouraged by his mother, who often took the family on long walks to observe the wonders of nature.

Life.

My life is like a stately warrior horse,
That walks with fluent pace along the way,
And I the upright horseman that bestrides
His flexuous back, feeling my private thoughts.—
Alas, when will this rambling head and neck
Be welded to that firm and brawny breast?—
But still my steady steed goes proudly forth,
Mincing his stately steps along the road;
The sun may set, the silver moon may rise,
But my unresting steed holds on his way.
He is far gone ere this, you fain would say,
He is far going. Plants grow and rivers run;
You ne'er may look upon the ocean waves,
At morn or eventide, but you will see
Far in the horizon with expanded sail,
Some solitary bark stand out to sea,
Far bound—— well so my life sails far,
To double some far cape not yet explored.
A cloud ne'er standeth in the summer's
The eagle sailing high, with outspread wings,
Cleaving the silent air, resteth him not
A moment in his flight, the air is not his perch.
Nor doth my life fold its unwearied wings,
And hide its head within its downy breast,
But still it plows the shoreless seas of time,
Breasting the wave with an unsanded bow.

H. D. Thoreau

By 1833 the family was somewhat more prosperous and with the financial help of his older brother and sister and of his maiden aunts, Thoreau entered Harvard College. Spending a good deal of his time reading in the college library, the first good collection of books he had had access to, he did become gregarious enough to join a fraternity (apparently chiefly to have access to *its* library) and take part in debates and colloquiums. In the winter of 1835-1836, to solve his financial problems, he dropped out for a time and taught school in Canton, Massachusetts, and again in the spring of 1836, he dropped out because of what was apparently an early attack of the tuberculosis that was to plague his life. Despite these absences, he maintained a better than average scholastic record and at his graduation in 1837 was chosen as one of the honor students to speak on the "Commercial Spirit," at the commencement exercises wherein he startled his audience by suggesting, "The order of things should be somewhat reversed; the seventh should be man's day of toil, wherein to earn his living by the sweat of his brow; and the other six his Sabbath of the affections and the soul,—in which to range this widespread garden, and drink in the soft influences and sublime revelations of nature"—a program of life which he himself was soon to adopt.

Although the country was in the midst of a deep depression with a high unemployment rate, Thoreau was fortunate in being hired immediately by the Concord school committee to teach in the same one-room school he had attended as a child. However, within two weeks he had resigned rather than fulfill the committee's insistence on using corporal punishment and for nearly a year searched fruitlessly for another teaching position. Finally in the early summer of 1838 he established a private school in his home, with out-of-town pupils boarding with his mother. The school quickly prospered even though he used educational techniques that anticipated the "progressive education" of a century later. His brother soon joined him in the teaching and they rented the Concord Academy building to accomodate larger classes. The school eventually came to an end in 1841, when John's poor health forced him to drop out and Henry did not wish to continue the teaching alone.

While Thoreau had been away to college, Ralph Waldo Emerson moved to Concord to live. Just when they first became acquainted is problematical, but by October of 1837 Emerson had asked Thoreau if he kept a daily journal, a practice which Emerson himself had long followed, and Thoreau embarked on that project which was to last to within a few

Recreation of Thoreau's room at Walden.

months of his death a quarter of a century later and which was to fill nearly forty manuscript volumes with one of the most complete records of man's life and thought that we have. Begun primarily, as was Emerson's, as a source book for literary works, it eventually became, as we will see, a work of art in itself.

Emerson, thirteen years older and already nationally famous, took an immediate interest in his young friend, encouraging him to develop his literary talents, introducing him to his fellow Transcendentalists and to men and women of prominence in literary and publishing circles. After the closing of the Thoreau school, Emerson invited Thoreau to live in his home, helping thus to free him for further literary endeavors, and with the establishment of the *Dial* in 1840, providing him with an outlet for publication. Later this friendship was to wear thin, particularly when critics began charging Thoreau with being an imitator of Emerson (a charge which Emerson vigorously denied but which nonetheless embarrassed and annoyed Thoreau), and when Emerson's radicalism waned as Thoreau's waxed. But the rupture was never complete, and it was Emerson who gave the eulogy at Thoreau's funeral.

In the summer of 1839 Thoreau met Ellen Sewall of Scituate, Massachusetts, the sister of one of his school pupils and granddaughter of his mother's star boarder, Mrs. Joseph Ward. Henry fell in love with her, only to discover his brother John was in love with her too. John eventually proposed marriage and was rejected. Henry then too proposed and although Ellen was obviously attracted to him, she deferred to her father's wishes (he, a conservative Unitarian minister, was horrified at the thought of an associate of the "radical" Emerson for a son-in-

Where Thoreau lived at Walden.

law) and rejected him too. Although on his deathbed, Thoreau professed that he had always loved her, the whole "romance" has, as Henry Seidel Canby once suggested, the air of "an experiment in the philosophy of love" on Thoreau's part about it. It was the only "romance" of his life.

In the spring of 1843, anxious to further Thoreau's position in the literary world, Emerson made arrangements for Henry to become the tutor of his brother William's sons on Staten Island. Thoreau did get to know a number of the New York City literati, most notably Horace Greeley, the editor of the *New-York Tribune*, then the nation's leading newspaper. Greeley was sufficiently impressed that he volunteered to be Thoreau's literary agent and not only over the years placed a number of his essays in leading journals of the time, but touted him frequently in the pages of the *Tribune*. But Thoreau was not happy on Staten Island. William Emerson had little of his brother's warmth or idealism and Thoreau was chronically homesick for Concord. After only six months he returned home and never left Concord again for any extended period of time.

In his early days as a writer, Thoreau thought of himself as primarily a poet and over the years he turned out a considerable body of verse. But others failed to share his enthusiasm for his poetic product. Emerson, to his later regret, was so discouraging about it that at one point Thoreau destroyed a great deal of the poetry he had written. Enough remains however so that the *Collected Poems* (enlg. ed., 1964) runs to more than 200 pages of text. Yet virtually all he could get published in his lifetime were the fragments he inserted here and there in his prose, such as in *Walden*. And such is their quality that few others than Thoreau have ever regretted that he did not succeed in publishing more.

Brother John Thoreau's tragic death by lockjaw in 1842 had a traumatic effect on Henry. For some weeks thereafter he himself experienced all the symptoms of lockjaw sympathetically, but eventually recovered, though he was never to hear John's name mentioned thereafter without tears coming to his eyes. In the later summer of 1839, he and John had taken a vacation rowboat trip on the Concord and Merrimack Rivers and now he determined to write an elegaic account of that trip as a tribute to his brother. To give himself the necessary time, in the spring of 1845 he persuaded Emerson to let him build a cabin on some newly acquired land on the shores of Walden Pond, a small glacial pond two miles south of Concord village, and there for two years, two months, and two days, he devoted himself to writing that book, observing the circling of the seasons, and living the simple life. His cabin (contrary to popular opinion, a sturdy, well-built structure, plastered and shingled) cost him $28.12½ and his living expenses 27¢ a week. Six weeks of work a year covered all his needs; the rest of his time was his own to live, to write, and to observe. The resulting book, *A Week on the Concord and Merrimack Rivers*, however, found little favor with publishers and did not reach print until in 1849 he guaranteed James Munroe and Company of Boston to reimburse any loss. One thousand copies were printed but when in 1853 Munroe found only 200 copies had been sold (and seventy-five given away), they shipped the remainder to Thoreau to clear their shelves. (Thoreau that night wrote in his Journal, "I have now a library of nearly nine hundred volumes, over seven hundred of which I wrote myself.") Viewed as a travel narrative, *A Week* is a pleasant pastoral glimpse of mid-nineteenth-century New England, but unfortunately, either to add to the length of the book or to get material on hand into print, Thoreau scattered through the narrative a series of digressions on such varied subjects as friendship, cattle shows, Chaucer, Oriental religion, and local history, which as James Russell Lowell said, "We come upon . . . like snags, jolting us headforemost out of our places as we are rowing placidly up stream or drifting down." The best of these digressions, the one on Friendship in the "Wednesday" chapter, is important both for its expression of Transcendentalist notions on the subject and for its insights into some of Thoreau's own personal relationships. But on the whole the book would be vastly improved by a deletion of the digressions—and, indeed, the book has several times been published in that shortened form.

Concord, appropriately enough since it was the site of the first battle of the American Revolution, was a hotbed of anti-slavery agitation. Thoreau's mother and sisters were active members of the Concord Female Anti-Slavery Society and their house was an active station on the Underground Railroad aiding slaves in their flight to freedom in Canada. Thoreau himself both approved and assisted in these activities. In 1843 his friend and fellow-Concordian Amos Bronson Alcott (father of the Louisa May Alcott of *Little Women* fame), who too was an ardent Abolitionist, refused to pay his poll tax in Concord as a protest against the legality of slavery in the South. Alcott was arrested but freed before he could be jailed because a neighbor insisted on paying the tax over his protest. The incident provoked Thoreau's thought: Was serving in the Underground Railroad doing enough? Why not directly confront the government that legalized slavery? So he too refused to pay his poll tax. The local tax collector, constable, and jailer Samuel Staples delayed taking action until one evening late in July of 1846, meeting Thoreau on the main street of Concord (Thoreau had come in from Walden Pond to take a shoe to the cobbler), Staples inquired when Thoreau would pay the tax and even offered to pay it for him if Thoreau was short of funds. Thoreau replied that he was not paying it as a matter of principle. When Staples in turn replied that he would eventually have to arrest him, Thoreau said, "You might as well do it right now," and Staples led him off to jail. Late that evening someone (it is generally thought to have been Thoreau's maiden aunt Maria Thoreau who, though an Abolitionist herself, was shocked to find a nephew in jail) paid his tax for him, and the next morning Staples went to the jail to release him. To Staples's amazement, Thoreau objected strenuously, and left the jail only when Staples threatened to throw him out bodily; it had been his intent to challenge the legality of slaves in the courts and his release from jail effectively deprived him of that opportunity. (It is generally believed that Aunt Maria paid his tax in advance in

following years depriving him of any *later* opportunity.) When curious neighbors pestered him with questions as to why he *wanted* to go to jail, Thoreau finally wrote out an explanation of his position and delivered it to his fellow townsmen as a two-part lecture at the local Concord Lyceum on 26 January and 16 February 1848 on "The Rights and the Duties of the Individual in Relation to Government." A year later, when Elizabeth Peabody was preparing her first (and only) issue of *Aesthetic Papers*, a periodical she hoped would carry on the tradition of the deceased *Dial*, she persuaded Thoreau to let her print the lecture there and it appeared under the title "Resistance to Civil Government." (It was not until 1866, four years after Thoreau's death, when it was gathered into one of his posthumous collections of essays, *A Yankee in Canada, with Anti-Slavery and Reform Papers*, that it was given the title "Civil Disobedience" by which it is best known.)

"Civil Disobedience" is pure Transcendentalism. It argues that when civil law and "higher law," the dictates of one's conscience, come into conflict, it is the duty of the good citizen to disobey the civil law, even though it means going to jail. Such is not a negative, but a positive action, it argues, for it will draw the attention of men of good will to the evil law and thus help to bring about its repeal. Or, if enough men go to jail, they will clog the machinery of the state, and thus make the objectionable law unenforceable. "Civil Disobedience" carries the philosophy of the "Founding Fathers" of this country to its logical conclusion and thus it is sometimes referred to as the "Declaration of Independence for the Conscience."

Thoreau had long been active in the Concord Lyceum, which sponsored a series of lectures in Concord each winter. He attended it as a boy and after returning to Concord from college both occasionally served as its "curator" or secretary and read his own lectures from its platform. As we have seen with "Civil Disobedience," it often served as a trying out place for his essays. Later, as he became better known, he was invited to read his lectures at other lyceums, eventually going as far abroad as Philadelphia and Portland, Maine. His lectures received a mixed reception. When his remarks were chiefly philosophical, he often met indifference or even annoyance at his unconventional ideas. When, however, he read his "excursions," the accounts of his travels in Maine or Cape Cod, their wit won over his audience and he enjoyed a real popularity. Lecturing also produced for him an additional, though small, source of income.

The Rowse portrait of Thoreau at thirty-seven.

When on 4 February 1846, while living at Walden Pond, he delivered a lecture on Thomas Carlyle at the Concord Lyceum, some in his audience told him that they would rather hear about his life at the pond than about an obscure Englishman. A year later, heeding that advice, he delivered a lecture on "The History of Myself," and it was so well received that he followed it with further accounts of his life at Walden, a series of lectures that eventually grew into his masterwork, *Walden*. A first version of the book was completed by the time he left the pond in the fall of 1847, and when he published *A Week* in 1849, he announced therein the forthcoming publication of *Walden*. But *A Week*'s failure was so complete that no publisher would risk issuing a second book by Thoreau. Thoreau, however, was not daunted; he simply went to work revising and revising again his new book. By 1854 when it was finally published, it had gone through seven complete revisions and was a very different book. Had not *A Week* been such a failure, it is conceivable that Thoreau would never have done the revising

and rewriting that eventually made *Walden* the great book it is.

Ostensibly an account of his two years at Walden Pond, *Walden* has much deeper and broader implications. It achieved its first popularity as a "Nature" book. His contemporaries, in general, delighted in his account of his "Life in the Woods," as he originally subtitled the book. (That subtitle was dropped with the second printing of the book, for Thoreau apparently felt it gave his work a wrong emphasis.) They complained whenever he became philosophical and skipped over such chapters as "Economy" and "Higher Laws," preferring the pastorality of such chapters as "Brute Neighbors" and "Winter Animals." *Walden* is indeed still looked upon as America's best piece of nature writing and is the standard by which all nature books since have been judged. But later generations found much more to the volume than simply an idyllic account of life among the birds and trees. *Walden* can, in fact, be approached from many angles, each with its own values and significances. Many see it as a do-it-yourself guide to the simple life, a handbook for those Robinson Crusoes who wish to "get away from it all." (It should be remembered, however, that Thoreau himself at Walden was only a little over a mile from home, visited friends in the village nearly every day, and remained at the pond only a little over two years; he very specifically in the book warned against his readers imitating him and urged them to live their own lives, not his.) He saw the simple life, not as an end in itself, but as a means to living more fully the life he really wanted—in his case, giving him the time to devote himself to writing and to observing nature.

Walden is also a biting criticism of the follies and foibles of mankind. Thoreau is, as he says in the book's epigraph: "brag[ging] as lustily as chanticleer in the morning, standing on his roost, if only to wake [his] neighbors up." There are few popular fashions or customs that he does not question. Because he delights in hyperbole and irony, his jibes often hit close to home. Many of his contemporaries thought him a misanthrope, but that was because they failed to perceive his saving grace of humor. Thoreau may laugh regularly at his neighbors, but he laughs just as hard at himself. If one sees no humor in *Walden*, he can be certain he is missing some of Thoreau's major points.

In recent years critics have become particularly interested in Thoreau's style. *Walden* is often cited as the earliest example of modern American prose. It is concrete, clear, straightforward, and precise, particularly in comparison with the periphrastic

Henry David Thoreau

Sketch of Thoreau by Daniel Ricketson (1854).

all of the leading Transcendentalists from Elizabeth Peabody to Bronson Alcott, from Orestes Brownson to Margaret Fuller, and from Jones Very to Ellery Channing. Thoreau attended some of the later sessions of the Transcendental Club and wrote for the *Dial* and *Aesthetic Papers*. Although Transcendentalism began to fade away as early as the mid-1840s, Thoreau, perhaps more than any of his fellows, remained true to its principles to the very end, and *Walden* is one of the supreme products of the movement. Read as a Transcendentalist document, *Walden* is a plea for the higher life and its central chapter is, appropriately, "Higher Laws." "If one listens to the faintest but constant suggestions of his genius, which are certainly true," Thoreau says therein, "he sees not to what extremes, or even insanity, it may lead him; and yet that way, as he grows more resolute and faithful, his road lies. The faintest assured objection which one healthy man feels will at length prevail over the arguments and customs of mankind. . . . If the day and the night are such that you greet them with joy, and life emits a fragrance like flowers and sweet-scented herbs, is more elastic, more starry, more immortal,—that is your success. All nature is your congratulation, and you have cause momentarily to bless yourself."

Walden is a book about rebirth, spiritual rebirth, and symbols of renascence permeate the book. By basing the whole work on the cycle of the year, he is able to bring it to a dramatic climax with the rebirth of nature in the spring. He tells us of the purification ceremonies of the Indians and the Mexicans, of his farmer neighbors who go down to the pond to wash themselves (though not often enough), and of the mysterious insect buried for sixty years in an apple-tree table that hatched and achieved maturity. He is convinced that would we only try we could reach a higher life right on earth than we ever dreamed of. "The sun," he tells us in the closing words of the book, "is but a morning star. There is more day to dawn."

Walden was published in 1854 by Ticknor & Fields in Boston in an edition of 2,000 copies. It was more widely and generally more favorably reviewed than *A Week*, though at least one reviewer denounced him as "a rural humbug." It took five years however to sell out that first edition and it was not reprinted until after his death in 1862.

While living at Walden Pond in 1846, Thoreau took an "excursion," as he liked to call it, to the wilds of the Maine Woods with his cousin George Thatcher, canoeing its rivers and, by himself, climbing Katahdin, Maine's highest mountain—in fact, being one of the first ever to reach its summit.

abstractions of most of his contemporaries. Although Thoreau never succeeded in writing memorable poetry, in *Walden* he produced some of the most poetic prose in our language.

But it is as a document of American Transcendentalism that *Walden* reaches its apex. Thoreau reached intellectual maturity at the very flowering of Transcendentalism. It was the central topic of debate in his years at Harvard. His friend Emerson was universally recognized as its leader. The reading of Emerson's *Nature* when it first appeared in 1836 was one of the turning points in Thoreau's life. Thanks in part at least to Emerson's efforts, Thoreau became acquainted with virtually

Again in 1853 and in 1857 he made further trips to the Maine Woods, to Chesuncook and to the Allegash River respectively. In 1849 he walked a good part of Cape Cod with his closest friend, Ellery Channing, and returned there again in 1850, 1855, and 1857. In 1850, again with Channing, he made an extended tour of the St. Lawrence River valley of Quebec. On each occasion he made extensive studies of the flora, the fauna, and the history of the area. Then on his return visit to Concord he wrote up an account in his journal. Revising, expanding, and polishing these accounts, he eventually delivered most of them from the lecture platform of his local lyceum, and, as his reputation grew, at the lyceums of other towns. They were unquestionably his most popular lectures. Still later he revised the lectures into essays and published them in such magazines as *Putnam's*, *Sartain's*, and *Graham's*. In the last years of his life he attempted to revise them once again, this time for book publication, but died before he was able to complete the task. Nonetheless, his posthumous editors (particularly his sister Sophia and his friend Channing) were able, in a fashion, to complete his work and these essays, along with similar but shorter "excursions," such as "Walking," "A Winter Walk," and "A Walk to Wachuset," reached print in book form as *Cape Cod*, *The Maine Woods*, and *A Yankee in Canada*, within five years of his death. These travel essays and books lack the profundity of *Walden*, but generally have in its stead a light, witty humor and a perception of the landscape and of the people that have made them favorite guide books ever since.

When in the late summer of 1847 Emerson accepted an invitation to give a lengthy series of lectures in England, he was in a quandary about leaving his ailing wife and three small children at home alone. Lidian Emerson suggested that would Thoreau but leave Walden and come back to live with them, their problem would be solved. Thoreau, who was beginning to fear he was in a rut at the pond, particularly since he had completed first drafts of both *A Week* and *Walden*, accepted their invitation and abandoned his cabin. He remained in the Emerson household for a year and then, on Emerson's return from England, went back to living with his parents, where he remained for the rest of his life. He did not, however, in principle abandon the life he had led at Walden. He continued to devote his mornings to writing, his afternoons to nature, and he still lived a simple enough life that six weeks of work a year covered all his expenses. Surveying became probably his major source of income, but he still worked occasionally in his father's pencil factory, and was not above doing almost any sort of menial labor if and when he needed the cash.

More and more his journal became the center of his creative interest. Daily entries became more extensive and more finished. Less and less did he chop out passages to use as grist for his lecture and essay mill. Although he was having little success in getting his writing into print or winning recognition as a literary artist, he nonetheless somehow developed the faith in his own writings and the conviction that even his massive journal would someday reach print. That goal was not achieved until more than forty years after Thoreau's death, when Houghton Mifflin of Boston published the journal in fourteen volumes. Connoisseurs of Thoreau now consider this huge work his real masterpiece, and, although its very length prevents its ever achieving the widespread reading that *Walden* has won, it is one of the great monuments in American literature. Here we can watch the growth of an inquiring mind; here we can revel in an unmatched account of the joys and beauties of a life close to nature; and here we can find a superb and comprehensive portrait of life in nineteenth-century America.

With the passage of the Fugitive Slave Law in 1850 and the approach of the Civil War, the controversy over slavery became more and more embittered. When in 1854, a fugitive slave, Anthony Burns, was captured in Boston and forced to return to slavery in the South, Thoreau felt impelled to strike out. He attended an anti-slavery gathering in nearby Framingham and there delivered his "Slavery in Massachusetts," a scathing attack not only on the slave-owners in the South but on those in the North who, through their inertia and willingness to go along, enabled slavery to continue in the South. "My thoughts are murder to the State," he cried out in this, perhaps his most polemical, essay. Five years later, when John Brown led his attack on Harper's Ferry, hoping thereby to instigate a mass revolt of the slaves, many of Thoreau's friends were appalled at the audacity of his act, but not Thoreau. He saw Brown as a man who was willing to sacrifice his own life for a principle. Against the advice of even the Abolitionists, Thoreau called a public meeting in Concord Town Hall, rang the bell himself when the selectmen of the town refused to announce the meeting, and in an impassioned voice read his "Plea for Captain John Brown," winning over to his viewpoint a primarily hostile audience. Later he repeated the lecture at Boston and Worcester. On the day of Brown's hanging, he, with friends, conducted a memorial service in Concord where he read "The

Last Days of John Brown," and when Brown was buried in North Elba, New York, the next summer, sent another memorial paper, "After the Death of John Brown," to be read there. But the John Brown incident paradoxically marked the end of Thoreau's anti-slavery activities. A little more than a year later, Thoreau was a seriously ill man. Although he survived through the first year of the Civil War, he was too ill to arouse any further interest in the anti-slavery cause.

Thoreau's surveying activities of the early 1850s, since they were often concerned with the laying-out of wood-lots, led him into a particular interest in the growth and replacement of native trees. Stumbling across the fact that in New England when a pine woods was cut, it was usually replaced naturally by oaks, and vice versa, he refused to accept the local folklore that the new growth was the result of "spontaneous generation," and after intensive research was able to prove that the alternation of species was brought about by a transmission of seeds by birds, animals, and the wind, and by chemical changes in the soil. The resulting essay, "The Succession of Forest Trees," his one major contribution to natural science, was read before the Middlesex County Agricultural Society annual meeting in Concord in 1860. But this paper served to increase his interest and he embarked on a complex series of studies of tree growth and plant succession. Two lecture-essays, "Wild Apples" and "Autumnal Tints," were somewhat side-products of this study, but the great bulk of his researches (they amount to a manuscript of more than 800 pages) remained incomplete and unpublished at his death.

In early December of 1860, Thoreau caught a bad cold and when, against doctor's orders, he refused to cancel a lecture engagement in Waterbury, Connecticut, it worsened into bronchitis. He had been plagued from college days with recurring flare-ups of tuberculosis (or "consumption" as it was then called). The bronchitis brought on a recurrence of the tuberculosis and doctors told him his only hope for recovery was to remove to a drier climate. In May of 1861 he set out for Minnesota with Horace Mann, Jr., son of the famed educator, but it was soon obvious that he had waited too long and after two months of desultory wandering in the upper Middle West, including a visit to a Sioux tribal gathering on the upper reaches of the Minnesota River, he returned to Concord reconciled to an early death. He spent the last months of his life revising old papers (thus many of Thoreau's essays exist in two versions, an original and a revised text) and piecing together unfinished works. The major accomplishment of

The Maxham daguerreotype of Thoreau (1856).

this period perhaps was the conversion to essay form of a lecture he had been delivering for a number of years under various titles and which is now known as "Life Without Principle." It is the capstone of his writing career and in highly concentrated form presents the most significant aspects of his philosophy of life. Too intense, perhaps, to make a good introduction to Thoreau, it does make a superb summing up and is one of the favorite essays of most ardent Thoreauvians.

Thoreau faced death with a remarkable cheerfulness (said by some medical authorities to be characteristic of those dying of tuberculosis). When a more orthodox aunt asked if he had made his peace with God, he replied that he had never quarreled with Him. When a deacon asked him about "that other world," he replied, "One world at a time." When he became too weak to write, he dictated to his sister Sophia. In his last few days he made an heroic effort to complete his Maine Woods papers. When he died on the morning of 6 May 1862 his last words were "moose" and "Indian." He is buried in Sleepy Hollow Cemetery in Concord, on "Authors' Ridge" close to the graves of his friends Emerson, Alcott,

The Dunshee ambrotype of Thoreau (1861).

Hawthorne, and Ellery Channing.

In his own lifetime Thoreau was always overshadowed by his friend and mentor Emerson and achieved comparatively little recognition. Most thought of him as little more than a second-rate imitator of Emerson. At the time of his death he had published only two books, *Walden* and *A Week*, and both were out of print. But *Walden* was reissued within a month and has never been out of print since. *A Week* appeared again shortly thereafter. A collection of his natural history essays and shorter travel works, *Excursions*, appeared in 1863; *The Maine Woods* in 1864; *Cape Cod* and *Letters to Various Persons*, edited by Emerson, in 1865; and *A Yankee in Canada, with Anti-Slavery and Reform Papers*, a catch-all of most of his remaining works, in 1866. The accumulated impact of all these volumes sparked a wider interest in Thoreau than he had enjoyed in his lifetime. Unfortunately, Emerson, working under the conviction that Thoreau's major claim to fame was as a latter-day stoic, had not only over-emphasized Thoreau's negative attributes in a

eulogy he wrote for him and published in 1862, but also in his editing of *Letters to Various Persons*, he had eliminated, over the Thoreau family's protest, any warmth and friendliness in his letters. As a result, a legend grew that Thoreau was a cold, austere, negative person that few if any could warm to. That legend did much to postpone Thoreau's winning a wide reputation for nearly a century and still has a marked effect on the popular image of the man today. Interestingly enough, the most incisive repudiation of that stoic image of Thoreau has been made by, of all persons, Emerson's own son, Edward Emerson, who in a centennial tribute, *Henry Thoreau as Remembered by a Young Friend* (1917), reveals the warm memories he and his fellow townsmen held of Thoreau.

Further damage to Thoreau's reputation was caused by two widely circulated essays of the second half of the nineteenth century: James Russell Lowell's "Thoreau," published in the *North American Review* for October 1865, ostensibly as a review of Thoreau's posthumous books, and Robert Loüis Stevenson's "Henry David Thoreau: His Character and Opinions," published in *Cornhill Magazine* for June 1880. Lowell repeated the charge of Thoreau's imitation of Emerson and dismissed him as "unhealthy" and lacking in humor; Stevenson described him as a "skulker." It made little difference that Lowell was carrying beyond the grave (Thoreau's grave, that is) a longstanding personal feud between the two men, and that Stevenson was later to retract his charges against Thoreau, saying they had been based on false and limited information; the two essays, like the Emerson eulogy, drastically postponed widespread appreciation of Thoreau.

There were, however, a small group of dedicated disciples of Thoreau who were determined to keep his reputation alive. His closest friend, Ellery Channing, published in 1873 his first biography, *Thoreau, the Poet-Naturalist*. H. G. O. Blake, who had inherited Thoreau's manuscripts from the family, began publication of a series of excerpts from the voluminous journals with *Early Spring in Massachusetts* in 1881, to be followed shortly thereafter with volumes for the other three seasons. Blake concentrated almost entirely on natural history in his selections, thus giving a rather restricted view of the breadth of Thoreau's journals, but his volumes were published at a time when there was a great surge in this country of interest in nature writing, and so his efforts to spread the word of Thoreau were surprisingly and pleasingly successful. Meanwhile in England, in 1890 Henry Salt published the first really scholarly and balanced biography, *Henry David Thoreau*, in which, as in subsequent essays, he did not hesitate to chide Thoreau's countrymen for failing to recognize one of their great geniuses. For some years to follow, Thoreau received wider recognition in England than in his own country. The British Labour Party members took a particular interest in him, reprinted some of his works, and often named their local organizations Walden Clubs. It was Salt who introduced Gandhi to Thoreau's writings, when Gandhi was a student at Oxford University. Later, as is well known, Gandhi made effective use of Thoreau's principles of civil disobedience in South Africa and later in his native India in fighting unjust laws, and made Thoreau's name famous around the world.

In America, the major event was the publication in 1906 of the twenty-volume *Writings of Henry David Thoreau* by Houghton Mifflin of Boston, thus for the first time making available the bulk of the journal. To the publisher's surprise, the edition (admittedly a limited one) sold out prior to publication. Then, in 1917, in celebration of the centennial of Thoreau's birth, there was flurry of books and articles. But Thoreau did not really begin to come into his own in his home country until the depression years of the 1930s, when people began to read him not as a nature writer but as a philosopher of the simple life. It is not without significance that the establishment of a Thoreau Society came at the end of the depression.

Immediately after World War II came a sudden surge of interest in Thoreau around the world. Although there had been scattered translations of some of his works earlier, now *Walden* began to appear in virtually every major modern language. The Indian government alone sponsored translation of *Walden* into fifteen different languages of the country—a tribute to Thoreau's impact on Gandhi. In America, books about and editions by Thoreau began to flow from the presses. For the first time he became a household name. No longer did one have to identify his source when he referred to "a different drummer" or "lives of quiet desperation." Thoreau was elected to the Hall of Fame and a postage stamp was issued in his honor. Residents of Concord began to note that more tourists were coming there to visit Walden Pond than to see the homes of all their other famous authors combined. When an over-ambitious park superintendent bulldozed down some trees at Walden Pond to "modernize" the parking lot, editorials appeared in newspapers around the world and he was forced out of office.

When the Reverend Martin Luther King began his fight against segregation laws in the South in the late 1950s, he cited Thoreau's "Civil Disobedience" as his source of inspiration. And a decade later, in the protests against the war in Vietnam, Thoreau became the hero of hippies and war protestors alike. Translations of "Civil Disobedience" appeared on newstands around the world as the "manual of arms" of the day.

Today Thoreau is universally recognized as one of America's greatest writers and his influence reaches out far beyond the portals of college libraries. People as diverse as Frank Lloyd Wright, the prime minister of India, Gene Tunney, Man Ray, John Fitzgerald Kennedy, N. C. Wyeth, Charles Ives, Robert Frost, John Cage, Jack Kerouac, and Diego Rivera have acknowledged their debt to him. The man who a century ago "traveled much in Concord" with little recognition now receives the homage of the world.

Other Writings:

"The Service," a youthful effusion; "Paradise (to be) Regained," a review of a proposed Utopia; "Herald of Freedom," a tribute to Nathaniel Rogers, a fellow anti-slavery worker; "Wendell Phillips Before the Concord Lyceum," a defense of Phillips's freedom of speech in the anti-slavery cause; "Thomas Carlyle and His Works," Thoreau's only extended piece of literary criticism; "Natural History of Massachusetts," ostensibly a review of some natural history reports; "The Landlord," an attempt at the "familiar essay"; "Night and Moonlight" and "The Moon," two abortive attempts by posthumous editors to publish an incomplete essay; several rather routine translations from the Greek; forty college essays; "Love" and "Chastity & Sensuality," two rather Transcendental essays on the sex relation; "Sir Walter Raleigh," a brief biographical study of one of Thoreau's heroes; and "Reform and Reformers," a recently published adaptation of an unfinished essay. Most of these will be found in *The Writings of Henry David Thoreau*, 20 vols. (Boston: Houghton Mifflin, 1906), the standard edition which is being superseded by *The Writings of Henry D. Thoreau* (Princeton: Princeton University Press, 1971-) as new volumes appear. (It should be noted that the Princeton Edition collects many writings not included in the 1906 edition and notes carefully all textual variants.) Particularly helpful annotated editions include *Collected Poems of Henry Thoreau*, ed. Carl Bode, enlg. ed. (Baltimore: Johns Hopkins University Press, 1964), *The Variorum Walden*, ed.

Walter Harding (New York: Twayne, 1962), *The Annotated Walden*, ed. Philip Van Doren Stern (New York: Clarkson Potter, 1970), and *The Variorum Civil Disobedience*, ed. Walter Harding (New York: Twayne, 1967). *Huckleberries*, ed. Leo Stoller (Iowa City: Windhover Press, 1970), is the first publication of one of the essays Thoreau was working on at the time of his death.

Bibliographies:

Francis H. Allen, *A Bibliography of Henry David Thoreau* (Boston: Houghton Mifflin, 1908); William White, *A Henry David Thoreau Bibliography* (Boston: Faxon, 1939); J. S. Wade, "A Contribution to a Bibliography from 1909 to 1936 of Henry David Thoreau," *Journal of the New York Entomological Society*, 47 (June 1939): 163-203; Walter Harding, "A Bibliography of Thoreau in Poetry, Fiction, and Drama," *Bulletin of Bibliography*, 18 (May 1943): 15-18; Philip E. Burnham and Carvel Collins, "Contribution to a Bibliography of Thoreau, 1938-1945," *Bulletin of Bibliography*, 19 (September 1946, January 1947): 16-18, 37-39; Walter Harding, *A Centennial Check-list of the Editions of Henry David Thoreau's Walden* (Charlottesville: University of Virginia Press, 1954); Christopher A. Hildenbrand, *A Bibliography of Scholarship About Henry David Thoreau 1940-1967* (Hays, Kansas: Fort Hayes State College, 1967). Walter Harding, "Additions to the Thoreau Bibliography" has appeared quarterly in the *Thoreau Society Bulletin* since 1941 and has been cumulated in *A Bibliography of the Thoreau Society Bulletin Bibliographies 1941-1969* (Troy, N.Y.: Whitston, 1971). See also, Walter Harding, *Thoreau's Library* (Charlottesville: University of Virginia Press, 1957).

Biographies:

William Ellery Channing, *Thoreau: the Poet-Naturalist* (Boston: Roberts, 1873; rev. ed., Boston: Charles E. Goodspeed, 1902); F. B. Sanborn, *Henry D. Thoreau* (Boston: Houghton, Mifflin, 1882); H. S. Salt, *The Life of Henry David Thoreau* (London: Bentley, 1890; rev. ed., London: Walter Scott, 1896); Annie Russell Marble, *Thoreau: His Home, Friends and Books* (New York: Thomas Y. Crowell, 1902); Edward Emerson, *Henry Thoreau as Remembered by a Young Friend* (Boston: Houghton Mifflin, 1917); F. B. Sanborn, *The Life of Henry David Thoreau* (Boston: Houghton Mifflin, 1917); Henry Seidel Canby, *Thoreau* (Boston: Houghton Mifflin, 1939); Sherman Paul, *The Shores of America:*

Thoreau's Inward Exploration (Urbana: University of Illinois Press, 1958), a biography of Thoreau's intellectual development; Milton Meltzer and Walter Harding, *A Thoreau Profile* (New York: Thomas Y. Crowell, 1962), a "picture" biography; Walter Harding, *The Days of Henry Thoreau* (New York: Alfred A. Knopf, 1965); Joel Porte, *Emerson and Thoreau* (Middletown: Wesleyan University Press, 1966), the best study of the relationship of the two men; Richard Lebeaux, *Young Man Thoreau* (Amherst: University of Massachusetts Press, 1977), a psychological study.

Letters and Journals:

The Correspondence of Henry David Thoreau, ed. Walter Harding and Carl Bode (New York: New York University Press, 1958), will be shortly superseded by the *Correspondence* volume, edited by Walter Harding, in the Princeton Edition of *The Writings*. For extensive annotations, see Kenneth Walter Cameron, *Companion to Thoreau's Correspondence* (Hartford, Ct.: Transcendental Books, 1964), and his *Over Thoreau's Desk: New Correspondence* (Hartford, Ct.: Transcendental Books, 1965). Thoreau's *Journal* appeared as vols. 7-20 in the 1906 edition of *The Writings*. A more complete edition, restoring many "lost passages," will appear in the Princeton Edition. *Consciousness in Concord*, ed. Perry Miller (Boston: Houghton Mifflin, 1958), gives the text of the 1840-1841 so-called "lost journal" not included in the 1906 edition. Thoreau's "Notes on the Journey West" is included in *Thoreau's Minnesota Journey: Two Documents*, ed. Walter Harding (Geneseo, N.Y.: Thoreau Society, 1962). A number of Thoreau's "commonplace books" have been edited by Kenneth Walter Cameron: *Thoreau's Literary Notebook (1840-1848)* (Hartford, Ct.: Transcendental Books, 1964); *Thoreau's Fact Book*, 2 vols. (Hartford, Ct.: Transcendental Books, 1966); and "Thoreau's Reading on Canada" and "Field Notes of Surveys Made by Henry D. Thoreau Since November, 1849," in *Transcendental Climate* (Hartford, Ct.: Transcendental Books, 1963), 2:310-411, 413-549. *The Indians of Thoreau*, ed. Richard F. Fleck (Albuquerque, N.M.: Hummingbird Press, 1974), contains selections from Thoreau's Indian Notebooks.

Criticism:

Joseph Wood Krutch, *Henry David Thoreau* (New York: William Sloane, 1948); Reginald L. Cook, *Passage to Walden* (Boston: Houghton Mifflin,

1949); Ethel Seybold, *Thoreau: The Quest and the Classics* (New Haven: Yale University Press, 1951); James Lyndon Shanley, *The Making of Walden* (Chicago: University of Chicago Press, 1957); Leo Stoller, *After Walden: Thoreau's Changing Views on Economic Man* (Stanford: Stanford University Press, 1957); J. Golden Taylor, *Neighbor Thoreau's Critical Humor* (Logan: Utah State University Press, 1958); *Thoreau: A Collection of Critical Essays*, ed. Sherman Paul (Englewood Cliffs, N.J.: Prentice-Hall, 1962); *The Thoreau Centennial*, ed. Walter Harding (Albany: State University of New York Press, 1964); John Aldrich Christie, *Thoreau as World Traveler* (New York: Columbia University Press, 1965); *Thoreau in Our Season*, ed. John H. Hicks (Amherst: University of Massachusetts Press, 1966); Charles R. Anderson, *The Magic Circle of Walden* (New York: Holt, Rinehart & Winston, 1968); *Twentieth Century Interpretations of Walden*, ed. Richard Ruland (Englewood Cliffs, N.J.: Prentice-Hall, 1968); *The Recognition of Henry David Thoreau*, ed. Wendell Glick (Ann Arbor: University of Michigan Press, 1969); Robert Stowell, *A Thoreau Gazetteer*, ed. William L. Howarth (Princeton: Princeton University Press, 1970); *Studies in Walden*, ed. Joseph J. Moldenhauer (Columbus, Ohio: Charles E. Merrill, 1971); *Thoreau Abroad*, ed. Eugene Timpe (Hamden, Ct.: Archon Books, 1971); Stanley Cavell, *The Senses of Walden* (New York: Viking, 1972); James McIntosh, *Thoreau as Romantic Naturalist* (Ithaca: Cornell University Press, 1974); William J. Wolf, *Thoreau: Mystic, Prophet, Ecologist* (Philadelphia: Pilgrim Press, 1974); Michael Meyer, *Several More Lives to Live: Thoreau's Political Reputation in America* (Westport, Ct.: Greenwood Press, 1977); Walter Harding, *A Thoreau Handbook* (New York: New York University Press, 1959) is a general guide to Thoreau scholarship; it will be superseded shortly by Walter Harding and Michael Meyer, *A New Thoreau Handbook*, to be published by New York University Press.

Concordances:

J. Stephen Sherwin and Richard C. Reynolds, *A Word Index to Walden with Textual Notes* (Charlottesville: University of Virginia Press, 1960); Sarah McEwen Miller, "A Concordance to the Collected Poems of Henry Thoreau," M. A. thesis, University of Toledo, 1966; James Karabatsos, *A Word-Index to A Week on the Concord and Merrimack Rivers* (Hartford, Ct.: Transcendental Books, 1971). Quotations from Thoreau arranged

topically are found in *Thoreau Today*, ed. Helen Barber Morrison (New York: Comet, 1957), and *The Thoughts of Thoreau*, ed. Edwin Way Teale (New York: Dodd, Mead, 1962).

Papers:

The major collections of Thoreau manuscripts may be found at the Pierpont Morgan Library in New York City; the Berg Collection at the New York Public Library; the Houghton Library at Harvard University; the Henry E. Huntington Library; the C. Waller Barrett Library at the University of Virginia; the Abernethy Library at Middlebury College; and the Concord Free Public Library. A comprehensive calendar of his papers is William L. Howarth, *The Literary Manuscripts of Henry David Thoreau* (Columbus: Ohio State University Press, 1974).

GEORGE TICKNOR (1 August 1791-26 January 1871), teacher, philanthropist, scholar, and author, was born in Boston. His father, Elisha Ticknor, was a strict Federalist and Calvinist whose conservative values became his greatest legacy to his son. Ticknor was technically admitted to Dartmouth College at the age of nine, although he did not officially begin attending classes until he was fourteen, when he entered as a member of the junior class. In 1807 he graduated from Dartmouth and returned to Boston to study the classics with a private tutor. By 1810 Ticknor had begun reading law, but in the same year he was invited to join the Anthology Society, a literary and social club which published *The Monthly Anthology and Boston Review*. In the company of these gentlemen of letters George Ticknor learned the Bostonians' ideal of a cosmopolitan scholar who, supported by a strong moral sense, refused to dabble in politics or write for financial reward. Perhaps it was the Anthologists' scorn of financially remunerative employment which led Ticknor to abandon law one year after being admitted to the bar in 1813 and to plan a European trip to further his literary education. From 1815 to 1819 Ticknor toured the continent, spending two years as a student at the University of Gottingen, and visiting Spain, France, and Italy to learn the languages. He returned to the United States to accept two concurrent professorships at Harvard College, one in belles lettres and the Smith Professorship of Modern Languages. Almost immediately upon assuming his place on the Harvard faculty, Ticknor began crusading for disciplinary and academic reforms, including advancement by merit rather than class standing, and division of the college into autonomous departments. Although most of Ticknor's reforms were thwarted before he resigned from the faculty in 1835, his students, including Ralph Waldo Emerson, remembered Ticknor as an effective, if stern, teacher. After his retirement, and a second trip to Europe, Ticknor channeled his energy and intellect into philanthropic ventures, serving on the Boston Primary School Board, and playing an instrumental role in the foundation of the Boston Public Library in the 1850s. But chief among Ticknor's concerns was fulfilling the role of gentleman scholar. In 1829 Ticknor purchased the southeast portion of one of the largest homes on Beacon Hill. There he presided as chief proselyte of civilization and social autocrat for Brahmin Boston, ostracizing those, like George Bancroft and Charles Sumner, whose opinions were tainted with social democracy or abolitionism, and welcoming the great and near-great, including

Charles Dickens, William M. Thackeray, Nathaniel Hawthorne, Daniel Webster, and William Hickling Prescott. Long after his death in Boston in 1871 Ticknor remained a symbol of the order and civilization of antebellum Boston society to young Brahmins like Charles Eliot Norton and Henry Adams.

Ticknor's major literary achievement is his three-volume *History of Spanish Literature* which is almost entirely based upon his Harvard lectures of the early 1820s. The *History of Spanish Literature* was greeted enthusiastically on both sides of the Atlantic, and became somewhat popular because Ticknor's belief that the state of a nation and its literature mirrors the character of its people made the *History* a comprehensive study of the Spanish people and their culture. Also typical of Ticknor's conservative philosophy is his appreciation of the moral tone of Spanish literature and his view of the writer's role as that of a stabilizing force in society. Ticknor's other writings are largely either tracts for causes he espoused or biographies of friends. *Remarks on Changes Lately Proposed or Adopted in Harvard University* is perhaps the fullest expression of Ticknor's educational views, and *Union of the Boston Athenaeum and the Public Library* is representative of Ticknor's desire to build the finest library in the country in Boston. In his *Life of William Hickling Prescott,* Ticknor delineates his view of the importance of the scholar to society, but we are never allowed to forget that Prescott was a Brahmin scholar who wrote because he wanted to and not for material gain. Likewise, Ticknor's *Remarks on the Life and Writings of Daniel Webster of Massachusetts* presents his political ideal in an extremely partisan portrait of the neo-Federalist demogogue whom Ticknor saw as the only true representative of the American character. It is clear that Ticknor's moral and political dogmas affected his taste in contemporary literature. Refusing to notice the importance of Emerson, Thoreau, Hawthorne, or Herman Melville, Ticknor lauded Washington Irving, Henry Wadsworth Longfellow, the Reverend William Ellery Channing, and Webster as the greatest writers of his age. Perhaps because of his conception of the gentleman scholar Ticknor failed to publish many works which remain in manuscript today, including translations of Sophocles, Aristophanes, and Goethe, and studies of Dante and Milton. —*Robert E. Burkholder*

Principal Works: *Syllabus of a Course of Lectures on the History and Criticism of Spanish Literature* (Cambridge: Hilliard & Metcalf, 1823); *Remarks on Changes Lately Proposed or Adopted in Harvard University* (Boston: Cummings, Hilliard, 1825); *Remarks on the Life and Writings of Daniel Webster of Massachusetts* (Philadelphia: Carey & Lea, 1831); *History of Spanish Literature,* 3 vols. (New York: Harpers, 1849); *Union of the Boston Athenaeum and the Public Library* (Boston: Dutton & Wentworth, 1853); *Life of William Hickling Prescott* (Boston: Ticknor & Fields, 1864).

Principal References: *Life, Letters, and Journals of George Ticknor,* ed. George S. Hilliard, Mrs. Anna Ticknor, and Anna Eliot Ticknor, 2 vols. (Boston: James R. Osgood, 1876); Orie William Long, "George Ticknor," in *Literary Pioneers: Early American Explorers of European Culture* (Cambridge: Harvard University Press, 1935), pp. 3-62; David B. Tyack, *George Ticknor and the Boston Brahmins* (Cambridge: Harvard University Press, 1967).

Jones Very

JONES VERY (28 August 1813-8 May 1880), Transcendentalist poet and friend of Emerson and Hawthorne, is today best known for his intensely pious religious sonnets describing the nature of the "will-less existence" which he attempted to live and popularize in the late 1830s. He was born in Salem, Massachusetts, to a long line of seafarers, his father a ship's captain; but his early inclination proved to be intellectual. He entered Harvard as a sophomore in 1834, and quickly distinguished himself there as an essayist and classical scholar, winning the coveted Bowdoin Prize for his essays two consecutive years. The second of these, an essay on Epic Poetry, came to the attention of Elizabeth Palmer Peabody, who in turn brought it to the attention of Ralph Waldo Emerson in 1838. Thus began a close but at times turbulent friendship between the two men, with Emerson pushing Very toward a more professional literary career, and Very trying to convert Emerson to his own religious vision. While Very's critical essays gained him immediate attention, Emerson soon discovered that his poetic talent was even greater. His poems grew out of an increasingly intense mysticism, which began to develop in his college years, culminating in a bout of near insanity in the period immediately after college. He remained at Harvard as a Greek tutor and Divinity student after his graduation in 1836, and in the fall of 1838 he apocalyptically told his students to "Flee to the mountains, for the end of all things is at hand." He returned later to Salem to convince people that he embodied the Second Coming of Christ. Very spent some time in 1838 in the McLean Asylum, his "insanity" proving to be closer to nervous exhaustion, but he retained the respect of those who knew him best. "Such a mind cannot be lost," Emerson remarked. Public recognition for his poetry began to grow in these years, with James Freeman Clarke publishing many of his sonnets in the *Western Messenger* in 1839, and Emerson overseeing the publication of *Essays and Poems* the same year. Working almost exclusively in the difficult form of the Shakespearean sonnet, Very returned repeatedly to the theme of a spiritual life guided by the complete submergence of the individual will into the nature of God. Such a conception of "will-less existence," which has much in common with both mysticism and with other traditional Christian forms of quietist moralism, accounts for what readers have noted as the burning intensity of Very's better poems, and his unusual technique of assuming the voice of God or the Spirit in some of them. Very's career at Harvard ended with his breakdown of 1838, but in 1843 he was licensed to preach as a Unitarian minister. Returning to his family home in Salem, he lived with his sisters Lydia (herself a minor poet) and Frances, preaching occasionally at various churches in the area, and continuing to write verse as an unofficial laureate of Salem, though not of the quantity or the quality of that written during his period of religious excitement. His retirement into self-effacing quiet to Salem after 1840 is somewhat puzzling, but it hints at a man devoted to the cultivation of his spiritual life. Very's poetic reputation has grown to an extent with the increasing importance of the Transcendentalist movement, even though he is in many ways closer to earlier Christian and Unitarian thinking than Transcendentalism. His narrow range of poetic material, consisting almost exclusively of religious poems or nature poems tinged with religious overtones, has hampered his wider recognition, as has his tendency to use well-worn forms of Christian terminology and phrasing, which Emerson criticized in the July 1841 *Dial*. But he made a much-needed contribution to Transcendentalism—a number of poems of stylistic excellence and technical polish which embodied a unique and forceful religious vision. —*David Robinson*

Principal Works: *Essays and Poems* (Boston: Little & Brown, 1839); *Poems by Jones Very*, ed. William P. Andrews (Boston: Houghton, Mifflin, 1883); *Poems and Essays*, ed. James Freeman Clarke (Boston: Houghton, Mifflin, 1886); *Jones Very: Selected Poems*, ed. Nathan Lyons (New Brunswick: Rutgers University Press, 1966).

Principal References: William I. Bartlett, *Jones Very: Emerson's "Brave Saint"* (Durham: Duke University Press, 1942); Warner Berthoff, "Jones Very: New England Mystic," *Boston Public Library Quarterly*, 2 (January 1950): 63-76; Edwin Gittleman, *Jones Very: The Effective Years, 1833-1840* (New York: Columbia University Press, 1967); David Robinson, "Jones Very: An Essay in Bibliography," *Resources for American Literary Study*, 5 (Autumn 1975): 131-146.

WILLIAM WARE (3 August 1797-19 February 1852), novelist and miscellaneous writer, was born in Hingham to a distinguished Massachusetts family. His father was Hollis Professor of Divinity at Harvard College. Ware graduated from Harvard in 1816, taught for a few years, and was ordained a minister in New York, where he settled in 1821. But ill health (which later was diagnosed as epilepsy) and a distaste for pastoral duties plagued him and he resigned in 1836 to devote his full time to writing. Ware is best known for his historical novels about classical and biblical times: *Letters of Lucius M. Piso From Palmyra to His Friend Marcus Civitius at Rome*, 2 vols. (New York: C. S. Francis, 1837), later titled *Zenobia; or, The Fall of Palmyra* (1838); *Probus: or, Rome in the Third Century* (New York: C. S. Francis, 1838), later called *Aurelian* (1848); and *Julian: or, Scenes in Judea*, 2 vols. (New York: C. S. Francis, 1841), his most popular work. He also owned and edited the influential *Christian Examiner* from 1839 to 1844. In later life, Ware lectured, and his series on European capitals was published in 1851 and that on Washington Allston appeared posthumously in 1852. He died in Cambridge. REFERENCE: [William B. Sprague], "William Ware," in *Heralds of a Liberal Faith*, ed. Samuel A. Eliot (Boston: American Unitarian Association, 1910), 2:250-258.

DAVID ATWOOD WASSON (14 May 1823-21 January 1887) was among the most radical of the post-Theodore Parker generation and an early advocate of nondenominational churches for free thinkers. As a contemporary of Octavius Brooks Frothingham and Thomas Wentworth Higginson, he promoted ideas that resulted in the Free Religious Association in 1867. Though never a member, he was a frequent speaker at its meetings and was considered a brilliant and witty man. Born on Penobscot Bay, Maine, of seagoing, shipbuilding people, he attended Phillips Andover Academy, Bowdoin College, and Bangor Seminary, where he was graduated in 1851. After a brief ministry at Groveland, Massachusetts, where he established an independent church, he briefly filled Higginson's pulpit in Worcester, Massachusetts. In 1865 he was called to replace the deceased Theodore Parker at the Twenty-Eighth Congregational Society in Boston. His health forced him to resign within a few months. Virtually the rest of his life was spent in New York, at menial jobs, in declining health and with impending blindness. His aversion to Calvinism and the work ethic of his times strengthened his Unitarianism and rationalized Transcendentalism.

As a political elitist he believed in a humane society led by secularized intellectuals. His contribution is the influence of his ideas upon his contemporaries who are still well known today. His writings include: *Poems* (Boston: Lee & Shepard, 1887); *Essays, religious, social, political*—fragments and a memoir by O. B. Frothingham (Boston: Lee & Shepard, 1889); *Beyond Concord*, ed. Charles Foster (Bloomington: Indiana University Press, 1965).

REFERENCE: Frank Preston Stearns, *Sketches from Concord and Appledore* (New York: Putnam's, 1895). —*J. Wade Caruthers*

NOAH WEBSTER (16 October 1758-28 May 1843) is a name that Americans have regarded as synonymous with "dictionary" for over a century. Popular opinion of Webster not only exaggerates his influence on lexicography, but fails to understand that his real contribution was not to form and direct the course of the language itself but to mold and rationalize the attitudes Americans have toward their language. Websterian zeal for reform, specifically authoritarian linguistic reform, has embued us with a reverence for dictionaries, grammars, and the printed word unparalleled in civilization. Webster's experience during his life in Connecticut as a lawyer, teacher, journalist, lobbyist, and essayist shaped his career as a lexicographer. He felt that the survival of the new nation depended critically on the establishment of a universal and practical system of education, for which there were neither adequate teachers nor suitable textbooks. Webster set out to combine pedogogy and patriotism, drawing on native cultural resources for a grammar, reader, and speller. The latter was first published as *The American Spelling Book* (Hartford, Ct.: Hudson & Goodwin) in 1783, retitled *The Elementary Spelling Book* in 1829, but best known as "The Blue-Back Speller." Despite many pirated editions, it was Webster's only commercial success; estimates of its sales exceed 100 million. Webster's first dictionary, *A Compendious Dictionary of the English Language* (Hartford, Ct.: Hudson & Goodwin), appeared in 1806. The preface acknowledges that the work was "an enlargement and improvement" of John Entick's *A New Spelling Dictionary*, but Webster did make a full display of his notions of reformed spelling, and he did include a substantial number of American contributions to the word stock. But neither the *Compendious* nor Webster's masterpiece, his 1828 *American Dictionary of the English Language* (New York: S. Converse), represented any substantial advance in lexocographical method. Indeed, Webster's chief virtue was in the application, advocacy, and aggressive defense of his principles; his judgment, linguistic or otherwise, often bears little scrutiny. Though by 1828 less convinced of the necessity for justifying American linguistic independence, Webster nonetheless followed Samuel Johnson's sentiment that "The chief glory of a nation is its authors," and liberally, but haphazardly, satisfied his patriotism by selecting illustrative quotations from American writings. He also continued to enter the characteristically American vocabulary, though in retrospect his coverage must be judged uneven. While retreating from his more radical spelling reforms, he retained his passionate dislike for silent letters; on the whole his spelling was still too innovative for the taste of even moderate contemporaries. Though eager to promote American pronunciations in place of what he felt were English or Anglophile affectations, Webster was often overtaken by provincialism: he lent his authority to his New England dialect at the expense of pronunciations at least as well sanctioned by contemporary usage. In etymology, Webster was abysmally ignorant of the philological advances being made by his European colleagues, and held to the already discredited Biblical account of the diversification of tongues. Though he claimed to know more than twenty languages, his puerile interpretations reveal his knowledge of some as quite rudimentary. The *American Dictionary* underwent several substantial modifications during the next generation, the first being the 1829 abridgement by Joseph E. Worcester. The two-volume format and the high price of the 1828 edition had met strong sales resistance, and the abridgment did little better. The subsequent commercial success of Worcester's own dictionary (1830) opened a permanent breach between the two lexicographers. After a bitter dispute over Webster's literary estate, George and Charles Merriam obtained the rights to the dictionaries and carried on an intense rivalry with Worcester until the 1864 Royal Quarto Edition of the *American Dictionary* (Springfield, Mass.: Merriam) appeared. The Royal Quarto dominated the market for the next quarter century, but it was a work from which everything characteristic of Webster himself had been systematically eliminated. The Merriam firm continues to publish dictionaries, and until the early 1950s retained commercial rights to the name Webster.

REFERENCES: Ervin C. Shoemaker, *Noah Webster: Pioneer of Learning* (New York: Columbia University Press, 1936); Thomas Pyles, *Words and Ways of American English* (New York: Random House, 1952); Joseph H. Friend, *The Development of American Lexicography 1798-1864* (The Hague; Mouton, 1967); Raven I. McDavid, Jr., "Noah Webster," *Encyclopaedia Britannica*, 15th ed. (1974), 19: 720-721. —*Raymond K. O'Cain*

JOHN WEISS (28 June 1818-9 March 1879) was a radical Unitarian clergyman who wrote *The Life and Correspondence of Theodore Parker*, 2 vols. (New York: D. Appleton, 1864). He held pulpits in New Bedford and Watertown, Massachusetts, during which time he translated and interpreted for the American audience the major works of Schiller and Goethe. A product of Harvard College and Harvard Divinity School, he helped found the Free Religious Association and gave a major address at its first meeting in Boston in 1867. As a free religionist, he attempted to push the Free Religious Association into social action and a more clear-cut creed. Militant and outspoken, Weiss was, in the words of Octavius Brooks Frothingham, a "flame of fire," a warrior "with his sword constantly unsheathed." Nevertheless he was a man of refined literary taste and a member of the "Town and Country Club," founded by Bronson Alcott. He was known for his wit, practical jokes, and flaming oratory. His biography, to be written by Frothingham, never appeared, due to objections by the Weiss family. His main contribution was his stimulating and abrasive influence on his contemporaries who left more of a written record than Weiss himself. In addition to numerous articles in *Index* and other journals, he wrote *American Religions* (Boston: Roberts Brothers, 1871) and *The Wit and Humor of Shakespeare* (Boston: Roberts Brothers, 1876). He was born and died in Boston. REFERENCES: Cyrus A. Bartol, "The Genius of Weiss" in *Principles and Portraits* (Boston: Roberts Brothers, 1880), pp. 386 ff.; O. B. Frothingham, *Recollections and Impressions* (New York: Putnam's, 1891). —*J. Wade Caruthers*

Charles S. Wheeler

CHARLES STEARNS WHEELER (19 December 1816-13 June 1843), editor and travel writer, was born at Lincoln, Massachusetts, near Concord. In 1833 he and his classmate, Henry David Thoreau, were recommended for Harvard College, and in August the two enrolled as roommates. At Harvard, Wheeler financed his education by helping Jared Sparks on his *Library of American Biography*, teaching, editing, copying, and indexing. He also contributed to the *Christian Examiner*, coedited the undergraduate magazine, *Harvardiana*, and won the Bowdoin Prize in his senior year. Wheeler stayed in Cambridge and pursued his literary interests by helping Emerson edit and publish American editions of Carlyle's *Sartor Resartus* (1836), *French Revolution* (1836), and *Critical and Miscellaneous Essays* (1838-1839). On his own, he edited Macaulay's *Critical and Miscellaneous Essays*, and introduced Tennyson to America when he edited his *Poems* (1842). In 1842 he prepared an annotated edition of Herodotus which was adopted for classroom use at Harvard. An appointment as Greek tutor in 1838 to replace Jones Very was supplemented by an instructorship in history the following year. While at Harvard, Wheeler often vacationed at a hut he built at Flint's Pond, a move which some believe later influenced Thoreau to move to Walden Pond. By 1842 Wheeler had saved enough money to travel to Europe. He spent most of his time in Germany and reported on the local events in travel letters to James Russell Lowell's *Pioneer* and the Transcendentalists' periodical, the *Dial*. Wheeler took ill the next year and died in Leipzig in June. Thoreau commented that Wheeler's death had "left a gap in the community not easy to be filled."

REFERENCE: John Olin Eidson, *Charles Stearns Wheeler: Friend of Emerson* (Athens: University of Georgia Press, 1951). —*Joel Myerson*

EDWIN PERCY WHIPPLE (8 March 1819-16 June 1886), essayist and critic, was born at Gloucester, Massachusetts. He chose banking as a career, but regularly contributed critical essays to newspapers and magazines, and became an accomplished debater. An essay on Thomas Macaulay in 1843, published in the *North American Review*, won him wide recognition, and his *Essays and Reviews*, 2 vols. (New York: D. Appleton, 1848-1849), firmly established him. He received an honorary Master of Arts degree from Harvard University in 1848. Still, Whipple worked in the newsroom of the Merchants' Exchange until 1860, when he devoted all his time to writing and lecturing. Whipple's essays, especially those published in *Recollections of Eminent Men* (Boston: Ticknor, 1887) and *American Literature and Other Papers* (Boston: Ticknor, 1887), are more interpretative than critical, "distributing to the general public the produce of other minds." He died in Boston. REFERENCES: Bliss Perry, "Edwin Percy Whipple," in Edward Waldo Emerson, *The Early Years of the Saturday Club* (Boston: Houghton Mifflin, 1918); Leishman A. Peacock, "Edwin Percy Whipple: A Biography," Ph.D. dissertation, Pennsylvania State University, 1942.

SARAH HELEN (POWER) WHITMAN (19 January 1803-27 June 1878), poet, essayist, and reformer, was born and lived in Providence, Rhode Island, until her marriage in 1828 to a lawyer, John Winslow Whitman. They settled in Boston, but upon her husband's death in 1833 Mrs. Whitman returned permanently to Providence. She had earlier published verses in the magazine her husband edited, and she returned to literature by publishing more poetry and critical essays in a number of major journals. Mrs. Whitman was known as a conversationalist and her salon in Providence attracted many, including George William Curtis and John Neal. While in Boston, she had been caught up by Transcendentalism and continued to support it and other reform movements, including woman's rights, spiritualism, mesmerism, Fourierism, and the progressive educational methods of Bronson Alcott. Her main fame derives from her brief engagement to Edgar Allan Poe in 1848, a confusing and awkward situation soon terminated by mutual consent. In later years she constantly defended Poe against his attackers and provided a constant source of information for his biographers. Her *Edgar Allan Poe and His Critics* (New York: Rudd & Carleton,

1860) is still useful. Both her *Hours of Life, and Other Poems* (Providence: G. H. Whitney, 1853) and *Poems* (Boston: Houghton, Osgood, 1879) are a cut above female poetry of the time. The latter contains a number of poems on Poe and shows his influence on her own verse. The second of Poe's poems "To

Helen" commemorates her. REFERENCES: Caroline Ticknor, *Poe's Helen* (New York: Scribners, 1916); John Grier Varner, "Sarah Helen Whitman: Seeress of Providence," Ph.D. dissertation, University of Virginia, 1940.

John Greenleaf Whittier

Albert J. von Frank
University of Rochester

BIRTH: Near Haverhill, Massachusetts, 17 December 1807.

DEATH: Hampton Falls, New Hampshire, 7 September 1892.

UNMARRIED.

MAJOR WORKS: *Legends of New-England* (Hartford, Ct.: Hanmer & Phelps, 1831); *Justice and Expediency* (Haverhill: C. P. Thayer, 1833); *Poems* (Philadelphia: Joseph Healy, 1838); *Lays of My Home and Other Poems* (Boston: William D. Ticknor, 1843); *Voices of Freedom* (Philadelphia: Thomas S. Cavender, 1846); *The Supernaturalism of New England* (New York: Wiley & Putnam, 1847); *Poems* (Boston: Benjamin B. Mussey, 1849); *Leaves from Margaret Smith's Journal in the Province of Massachusetts Bay* (Boston: Ticknor, Reed & Fields, 1849); *Songs of Labor and Other Poems* (Boston: Ticknor, Reed & Fields, 1850); *The Chapel of the Hermits and Other Poems* (Boston: Ticknor, Reed and Fields, 1853); *The Panorama and Other Poems* (Boston: Ticknor & Fields, 1856); *Home Ballads and Poems* (Boston: Ticknor & Fields, 1860); *In War Time and Other Poems* (Boston: Ticknor & Fields, 1864); *Snow-Bound. A Winter Idyl.* (Boston: Ticknor & Fields, 1866); *The Tent on the Beach and Other Poems* (Boston: Ticknor & Fields, 1867); *Among the Hills and Other Poems* (Boston: Fields, Osgood, 1869); *The Pennsylvania Pilgrim and Other Poems* (Boston: James R. Osgood, 1872); *The Vision of Echard and Other Poems* (Boston: Houghton, Osgood, 1878); *At Sundown* (Boston: privately printed, 1890; Boston: Houghton, Mifflin, 1892).

Life and Career:

Whittier's importance to America's cultural life, and the claim he makes on our remembrance, is at least two-fold. In the first place, his life was and remains a model of dedication to the twin principles of freedom and tolerance. In the long struggle to abolish slavery the Quaker Whittier played an important role as a poet, as a politician, and as a moral force; and yet, though he was an ardent reformer, he was saved from the besetting sin of reformers—a narrowing and self-consuming zeal—by his equal insistence on tolerance, a quality he had come to cherish all the more through his study of the persecution of the Quakers. But if Whittier's life was dramatic for the moral, political, and, on occasion, the physical conflicts it contained, his poetry—the best of it—is of even greater significance. Poets are, first and last, most interesting for their poetry, and whatever else he was, Whittier was a poet. He knew that he had written too much, and that much of what he had written for the abolitionist movement had been hastily composed and for ends that were purely political. Nevertheless, there is in his collected poetry a core of excellent work, at the head of which stands his masterpiece, "Snow-Bound," a lovingly imaginative recreation of the good life in rural New England. This work, together with "Telling the Bees," "Ichabod," "Massachusetts to Virginia," "Skipper Ireson's Ride," "The Double-Headed Snake of Newbury," and a dozen or so others, suggest not only the New England source of Whittier's finest achievements, but also the appeal that folk material had for his imagination.

Whittier's youth—indeed, his whole life—was deeply rooted in the values, history, and traditions of rural Essex County, Massachusetts. Born in a farmhouse that his great-great-grandfather had built in the seventeenth century, Whittier grew up in a poor but respectable household characterized by hard work, Quaker piety, and warm family affection. The region was rich with folklore; tales of witches and ghosts told on winter evenings by the fire exercised the young Whittier's imagination, but it was his discovery of the Scottish poet, Robert Burns, who could speak the beauty of the commonplace circumstances of a rural environment, that made him wish to be a poet.

In 1829, at the age of twenty-two, too frail to be of much help on the farm, too poor to have given himself more than a year at the Haverhill Academy, and beginning already to doubt his abilities as a poet, Whittier accepted the editorship of the *American Manufacturer*, a political weekly in Boston. This position had been secured for him by William Lloyd Garrison, himself a young newspaper editor who was just then beginning his long career as a reformer. It is safe to say that Whittier entered journalism for the opportunity to write; what he learned from the experience, however, were politics and polemics. His editorials, first in the *Manufacturer* and later in the Hartford, Connecticut, *New England Review*, were at least as fierce in their denunciation of the Democrat Andrew Jackson as they were warm in support of the Whig Henry Clay.

In February 1831, while at Hartford, Whittier published a collection of tales and poems entitled *Legends of New-England*. Although the volume received little attention at the time, it is significant as a pioneering effort to render New England folklore, and in some respects it may be said to anticipate Hawthorne. Whittier was never entirely comfortable with the gothic mode, however, and suppressed the book in later life. On one occasion he paid five dollars for the privilege of destroying a copy of this rare early volume.

Toward the end of 1831, Whittier retired in ill health to Haverhill and spent the winter convalescing. He knew that he was at a crossroads in his life and wished to settle finally on a vocation. Poetry hardly paid at all, but he had come to like politics and found that his vociferous public support for Clay had made him a popular man in Massachusetts. In fact, he might well have been elected to Congress in 1832 had he not been just a few months shy of the legal age. The answer to Whittier's dilemma about

his vocation seems to have arrived in the mail on 22 March 1833. His friend and patron, William Lloyd Garrison, who had begun publishing his *Liberator* two years before, wrote to Whittier urging him to enlist in the gathering struggle against slavery. "Your talents, zeal, influence," he told Whittier, "all are needed." He knew that to enlist in this cause, unpopular as it then was in New England, would be tantamount to giving up all hope of gaining elective office. To form such an alliance would also exclude him from influential literary circles and make it difficult if not impossible for him to publish his poetry. Still, Whittier had been slowly coming to the very conclusion that Garrison now sought to force on him—that the evil of slavery had to be resisted actively.

He responded in June 1833 with a privately-printed pamphlet called *Justice and Expediency*, a closely reasoned and carefully documented attack on the Colonization Society. Widely supported by Northern and Southern churches, the Colonization Society was a conservative reform group that proposed to resolve the issue of slavery by sending American blacks, both slave and free, back to Africa. It was, at the time of Whittier's pamphlet, headed by Henry Clay. An abolitionist group in New York

*If, for the age to come this hour
Of trial hath vicarious power,
And, blest by Thee, our present pain
Be Liberty's eternal gain,
Thy will be done!*

*Strike, Thou the Master, we Thy keys,
The anthem of the destinies!—
The minor of Thy loftier strain,
Our hearts shall breathe the old refrain,
Thy will be done!*

Amesbury, Mÿ. 12 2 mo 1864

John G. Whittier

reprinted the work and distributed hundreds of copies. Whittier's commitment to the cause was now sealed; as he expressed it many years later, he

> Had left the Muses' haunts to turn
>   The crank of an opinion-mill,
> Making his rustic reed of song
>   A weapon in the war with wrong,
> Yoking his fancy to the breaking-plow
>   That beam-deep turned to the soil for truth
>   to spring and grow.

On the basis of this pamphlet and as a friend of Garrison, Whittier was chosen a delegate to the Philadelphia convention that in December 1833 founded the American Anti-Slavery Society. It was an important moment in his life, and though his identification with the movement entailed many sacrifices throughout his career, he was far from ever regretting his decision. "I set a higher value on my name as appended to the Anti-Slavery Declaration of 1833," he later said, "than on the title-page of any book."

Though he could no longer hope to fulfill his dream of winning important elective office, he was able, in 1835, to gain a seat in the state legislature from his small home district of Haverhill. There he was an effective spokesman for his cause, winning over many to his views on the slavery question, sending petitions to the Congress, trying to get a bill through the state house granting trial by jury in cases involving the return of runaway slaves, and even organizing opposition to the death penalty. Whittier served only one term, again jeopardizing his health by hard work. He continued all the while to express his abolitionism in poems published in Garrison's *Liberator* and in the editorial columns of the *Gazette*, but opposition to his moral stand was mounting. He was forced out of the *Gazette* for failing to toe the orthodox Whig line, and was threatened with violence in September 1835 by a mob in Concord, New Hampshire.

In 1836 Whittier sold the 148-acre family farm and moved with his mother and sister a few miles away to Amesbury in order that he and they might be closer to the Friends' meetinghouse. He was, however, frequently away. In 1837 he was in New York helping in the offices of the Anti-Slavery

John Greenleaf Whittier

Society, and in 1838 moved to Philadelphia to edit the *Pennsylvania Freeman,* which he succeeded in turning into a vigorous organ of the abolitionist movement.

Poems Written During the Progress of the Abolition Question in the United States, Between 1830 and 1838—the first collection of Whittier's poetry—was brought out in 1837 without the poet's knowledge by some of his anti-slavery associates in Boston. In 1838 Whittier authorized an expanded and corrected edition, called *Poems,* which was published in Philadelphia. Included in these collections are some of his most heartfelt polemics, such as "Clerical Oppressors," a poem attacking the hypocrisy of the Southern clergy in lending the support of Christianity to the slave system:

> Feed fat, ye locusts, feed!
> And, in your tasselled pulpits, thank the Lord
> That, from the toiling bondman's utter need,
> Ye pile your own full board.

In such poems as "Stanzas" (later called "Expostulation") Whittier noted the irony of America's apparent commitment to slavery in light of her historic dedication to freedom. He appealed to the

regional pride of New England in "The Yankee Girl" and "Stanzas for the Times," but in these, as in most of the anti-slavery poems of the period, Whittier's anger swept everything before it, often including artistic control. The poems were meant to be, and indeed were, effective propaganda.

During the late 1830s a split developed within the ranks of the abolitionists: some, such as Whittier, preferred to work through the political system for change and hoped to preserve the Union; others, such as Garrison, were less concerned with the Union and believed that slavery could not be abolished without also destroying the Constitution. While Garrison worked with the extreme "non-resistants," Whittier was busy helping to organize the Liberty Party. He retired to Amesbury in 1840, but continued to work actively for Liberty Party candidates and for the election of others, regardless of party, who favored emancipation.

The publication in 1843 of Whittier's *Lays of My Home* marked his return to the poetic treatment of regional materials. Included in this collection are poems like "The Merrimack," treating the local scenery with the touch of the pastoral landscape artist; poems like "The Ballad of Cassandra Southwick," exploring New England history; and poems like "The Funeral Tree of the Sokokis," based on Indian lore. The near relation of Whittier's regional and abolitionist poetry is indicated not only in the consistent advocacy of tolerance and brotherhood in the regional poems, but also in the appeal to New England pride that so often forms the basis of his anti-slavery expressions. The finest poem of this sort, "Massachusetts to Virginia," makes its appearance in this volume. After the overwhelming enthusiasm of the 1830s had dissipated in division and recrimination within the anti-slavery ranks, Whittier was able, during the next two decades, to maintain a healthier, maturer balance between his twin commitments to poetry and reform.

In 1846 Whittier published his last collection of anti-slavery poems, *Voices of Freedom,* and in 1847 brought out a collection of prose sketches entitled *The Supernaturalism of New England.* A caustic review of the latter volume by Hawthorne, who pointed out its author's fundamental lack of sympathy with gothic themes, may have contributed to Whittier's decision to suppress the book. In the same year, 1847, he became a contributing editor with the *National Era,* a Washington-based anti-slavery journal which, until the founding of the *Atlantic Monthly* ten years later, served as his main publishing outlet. The most significant of Whittier's works to appear in the *Era* was *Leaves from Margaret*

Smith's Journal (1848-1849). His only novel, the *Journal* is cast in the form of the letters and diary of a seventeenth-century New England Quakeress, Margaret Smith. The story is sprightly and realistic, and the character of Margaret—"among the first of our native heroines," as Lewis Leary has observed—is carefully and sensitively portrayed.

Whittier's library.

The decade of the 1850s opened with a shock. On the seventh of March, 1850, Daniel Webster affirmed his support of compromise with the Southern slave power. Whittier, shocked and saddened by the unexpected defection, responded with his powerful protest, "Ichabod." The poem is one of Whittier's very best, its invective tightly controlled and ironically deepened by the poet's acknowledgment of the frailties of all men, even the greatest:

> So fallen! so lost! the light withdrawn
>   Which once he wore!
> The glory from his gray hairs gone
>   Forevermore!
>
> Revile him not, the Tempter hath
>   A snare for all;
> And pitying tears, not scorn and wrath,
>   Befit his fall!
>
> . . . .
>
> Then, pay the reverence of old days
>   To his dead fame;
> Walk backward, with averted gaze,
>   And hide the shame!

Meanwhile Whittier was busy trying to get a reluctant Charles Sumner to run for the Senate from Massachusetts. His maneuverings were successful and, with Whittier's advice and encouragement, Sumner became perhaps the most outspoken abolitionist in Washington.

Whittier's books of poetry were appearing at fairly regular intervals now that he had settled on the Boston publishing firm of Ticknor, Reed and Fields (later Houghton, Mifflin). Sales, however, continued to be moderate at best. In 1850 appeared *Songs of Labor, and Other Poems*, which, besides "Ichabod," included "Calef at Boston," "On Receiving a Quill. . .," and the series of occupational poems which gives the volume its title. *The Chapel of the Hermits, and Other Poems* was published in 1853, and *The Panorama, and Other Poems* followed in 1856. The popular "Barefoot Boy," a sentimental tribute to the naturally free and unspoiled life of poor New England children, was collected in the latter volume together with a fine anti-slavery poem entitled "The Haschich."

Whittier's house at Amesbury.

An important turn in Whittier's career occurred in 1857. The founding of the *Atlantic Monthly* in that year gave him a forum where he appeared regularly with all the most prominent writers of New England. His contributions to the earliest issues—including "Skipper Ireson's Ride" and "Telling the Bees"—were better poems than he had ever written. Symbolic of Whittier's entry into Boston's literary establishment was the publication, also in 1857, of the "Blue and Gold Edition" of his poetry in a format to match Longfellow's. Toward the end of the year, Whittier's mother died and the poet himself turned fifty.

The poetry of this period shows Whittier's increasing disengagement from broadly political issues. His attention was turning more and more to his own personal past, as shown in the nostalgic, quasi-autobiographical poems, "Telling the Bees"

Whittier at the age of twenty-two.

and "My Playmate"; he was also increasingly drawn to the larger but still personal past of New England history, as shown in the many fine ballads which he wrote at this time—"Skipper Ireson's Ride," "The Garrison of Cape Ann," "The Prophecy of Samuel Sewall," "The Double-Headed Snake of Newbury," and "The Swan Song of Parson Avery." All of these poems were first collected in *Home Ballads and Poems*, published in 1860. Almost the only hint that the volume contained of the impending Civil War was the poem Whittier wrote in response to the raid on Harper's Ferry, "Brown of Ossawatomie."

Whittier's Quaker pacifism did not prevent him from being an ardent supporter of the Union cause when the War broke out. He admired Lincoln and was particularly proud of having voted for him four times, as a citizen and as an elector in 1860 and 1864. He wrote a number of patriotic poems during the War, of which "Barbara Frietchie" is certainly the most famous. *In War Time and Other Poems*, published in November, 1863, contained several better examples of Whittier's public poetry ("Thy Will Be Done" and "Ein Feste Berg. . . ," for example), in addition to several more "home ballads," including "Cobbler Keezar's Vision," "Amy Wentworth," and "The Countess." This

volume was reissued in 1865 under the title *National Lyrics* and included "Laus Deo," in which Whittier joyously recorded the death-knell of slavery, the moment for which so much of his career had been a preparation.

Whittier in middle age.

With the War over and the Thirteenth Amendment to the Constitution ratified, a part of Whittier's public life came to a close, just as, a year earlier, a part of his personal life had come to a close with the death of his beloved younger sister, Elizabeth. Whittier's whole mood was retrospective as he set to work on the "Yankee pastoral" that he had promised James Russell Lowell he would write. The result was "Snow-Bound," his masterpiece, published in February 1866.

The poem recalls a winter storm at the old Whittier homestead when the poet was a child. A day and a night of driving snow had transformed everything:

> We looked upon a world unknown,
> On nothing we could call our own,
> Around the glistening wonder bent
> The blue walls of the firmament,
> No cloud above, no earth below,—
> A universe of sky and snow!

The threat of isolation, of freezing or starving, is countered by the family at the wood fire on the hearth, the warmth of which is a symbol of life and family affection.

> Shut in from all the world without,
> We sat the clean-winged hearth about,
> Content to let the north-wind roar
> In baffled rage at pane and door,
> While the red logs before us beat
> The frost-line back with tropic heat.

The physical and spiritual sufficiency of this besieged family circle is the subject of the poet's reminiscence precisely because most of those who were then present are now dead. By recalling each of them in turn, Whittier substitutes the light of affectionate memory for the light of the burning oaken log by which that night they gathered together. The effect is to make the poem itself stand witness to "The truth to flesh and sense unknown, / That Life is ever lord of Death, / And Love can never lose its own!"

Unlike many of Whittier's poems, "Snow-Bound" has lost none of its appeal with the passing of time. A large part of its charm is in its presentation of what Whittier called "Flemish pictures of old days," composed of the common detail of rural life in early nineteenth-century New England: the few books, the schoolmaster boarding with the family, the sounds to be heard on windy winter nights ("We heard the loosened clapboards tost, / The board-nails snapping in the frost"), the importance of newspapers in gaining a sense of the larger world outside, and especially the companionship of nature. In 1866 the kind of life that "Snow-Bound" describes was as surely departed in fact as it was present to the memory of thousands of readers. The poem was Whittier's first genuine commercial success as well as his most complete artistic success. He realized $10,000 from the sale of the first edition and was never to want for money again.

The Tent on the Beach and Other Poems, which followed a year later, continued the success, 20,000 copies being sold in three weeks. "The Wreck of the Rivermouth," "The Changeling," "The Dead Ship of Harpswell," and "Abraham Davenport"—all first collected in this volume—show Whittier's abiding fondness for legendary and historical New England material, while "The Eternal Goodness" and "Our Master" indicate the new importance which the liberal religious tradition of the Quakers was coming to assume in his later poetry. If, after the Civil War, anything may be said to have taken on the personal importance that Whittier had before

attached to the fight against slavery, it was certainly his desire to see religion in America liberalized and the last vestiges of repressive Puritanism swept away. Oliver Wendell Holmes, who shared this hope, maintained that Whittier had done as much in America as Robert Burns had done in Scotland toward "humanizing" the hard theology of Calvinism. Whittier's edition of *John Woolman's Journal*, published in 1871, gave new currency to that classic work of Quaker spiritual autobiography.

The remainder of the poet's long life was spent quietly and uneventfully in Amesbury and, after 1876, in a spacious home in Danvers, Massachusetts, called Oak Knoll, which he left only for his regular summer excursions into the lake and mountain region of New Hampshire. He continued to write almost up to the time of his death. *Among the Hills* (1869) is evidence that he knew of the darker and solitary side of rural life in New England. The title poem in *The Pennsylvania Pilgrim* (1872), one of Whittier's more successful long narratives, concerns the seventeenth-century German Pietist, Francis Daniel Pastorius, who founded Germantown near Philadelphia, and who, after formally joining the Quakers, drafted one of the earliest American anti-slavery statements. The volume also contains "The Brewing of Soma," from which the popular hymn, "Dear Lord and Father of Mankind," is taken. *The Vision of Echard* (1878) contains, among other poems, "The Witch of Wenham," "In the 'Old South,' " and a surprisingly good courtly love lyric entitled "The Henchman." Whittier's last book of poems, *At Sundown*, was privately printed in 1890 for close friends, and was reissued for the public, with additions, at about the time of the poet's death on 7 September 1892. The very last poem that Whittier wrote was a tribute to his friend Oliver Wendell Holmes on the occasion of his eighty-third birthday. They had outlived all their generation.

Whittier's reputation was never higher nor more apparently secure than at the time of his death. For years his birthdays had virtually been public holidays and were marked by celebrations throughout New England and the West. Whittier was essentially a public poet, a poet speaking to a large segment of the American people, including many who were not otherwise readers of poetry. They often came to his work to bask in the poet's moral tone, to attend the heroic or prophetic voice in his poems, or to receive comfort from his characteristic optimism. Whittier, for better or worse, rarely challenged his audience. The popularity he enjoyed among his contemporaries seems, unfortunately, to have been based largely on just those poems ("The Barefoot

This Indenture, Made this _First_ day of _February_ in the year of our Lord eighteen hundred and _forty five_ by and between _John G Whittier_ of _Amesbury_ in the County of _Essex_ and State of _Massachusetts_ of the first part, and TICKNOR & FIELDS, of Boston, in the County of Suffolk, and Commonwealth of Massachusetts, Publishers, of the second part,

Witnesseth, That whereas the said party of the first part is author of a work entitled

"Snow Bound"

And whereas the said parties of the second part have proposed to publish the same in book-form, with the title aforesaid, or such other title as may be hereafter given it, which proposal the said party of the first part has accepted; now, therefore, the said parties of the first and second parts have agreed upon the following terms and articles, to the full and faithful performance of which they mutually bind themselves, their heirs, representatives, and assigns, each to the other.

First. The copyright of the said work (in whatever name it may be entered) shall belong to the said party of the first part, _his_ heirs, representatives, and assigns.

Second. The said party of the first part hereby gives, grants, and conveys to the said parties of the second part, their heirs, representatives, and assigns, the sole right to publish the said work during the term of this agreement.

Third. The said parties of the second part shall stereotype or electrotype the said work at their own cost and charge, and the said stereotype or electrotype plates shall belong to them, their heirs, representatives, and assigns, who shall print and publish the said work in good style, and at their own expense and risk, and at all times keep such stock of said work on hand as shall reasonably supply the market for the same. There shall be paid to the said party of the first part, _his_ heirs, representatives, or assigns, as a consideration for the copyright of said work, the sum of _ten cents_ ——————————— per copy on all copies of said work which shall be sold, ~~except the first~~ ——————————— ~~copies~~ ~~printed, upon which said~~ ——————————— ~~copies no payment~~ ~~of any consideration whatever for the copyright aforesaid shall be made.~~ The first payment under this clause shall be made on or before the first day of _July_ now next ensuing, at which time an account of sales of said work shall be rendered. Subsequent payments shall be made on or before the first day of _January_ and the first day of _July_ of each year, at each of which times an account shall be rendered of the number of copies printed and sold during the six months previous.

Fourth. This agreement shall continue in force during the term of copyright of said work, as fixed by law.

IN WITNESS WHEREOF, the parties of the first and second parts have set their hands to two copies of this agreement interchangeably, on the day and year first above mentioned.

Ticknor & Fields

John G. Whittier

Contract for Snow-Bound.

Boy" and "Barbara Frietchie," for example) that modern readers reject as sentimental. A reaction against the kind of soft-focus vision of the world that Whittier too often invoked set in during the early years of the present century when a new, more muscular poetry was establishing itself, in part by overturning the Victorian canons of taste that had elevated the work of Whittier's generation. Most nineteenth-century American poetry—and Whittier's perhaps most of all—suffered by comparison with the works of the modern New Englanders, E. A. Robinson and Robert Frost. Over the years, the basis for an admiration of Whittier's poetry has not eroded; it has merely been identified more clearly and precisely.

Other Writings:

Mogg Megone (Boston: Light & Stearns, 1836); *Narrative of James Williams, an American Slave* (New York: American Anti-Slavery Society, 1838); *Moll Pitcher and the Minstrel Girl* (Philadelphia: Joseph Healy, 1840); *The Stranger in Lowell* (Boston: Waite, Pierce, 1845); *Old Portraits and Modern Sketches* (Boston: Ticknor, Reed & Fields, 1850); *Literary Recreations and Miscellanies* (Boston: Ticknor & Fields, 1854); *Miriam and Other Poems* (Boston: Fields, Osgood, 1871); *Hazel-Blossoms* (Boston: James R. Osgood, 1875); *The King's Missive and Other Poems* (Boston: Houghton, Mifflin, 1881); *The Bay of Seven Islands and Other Poems* (Boston: Houghton, Mifflin, 1883); *Saint Gregory's Guest and Recent Poems* (Boston: Houghton, Mifflin, 1886). The standard collected edition is the seven-volume Riverside Edition of *The Writings of John Greenleaf Whittier* (Boston: Houghton, Mifflin, 1888-1889). Early uncollected poetry is gathered in Frances M. Pray, *A Study of Whittier's Apprenticeship as a Poet* (Bristol, N. H.: Musgrove Printing House, 1930); a number of uncollected prose pieces are gathered in *Whittier on Writers and Writing*, ed. E. H. Cady and H. H. Clark (Syracuse: Syracuse University Press, 1950).

Bibliographies:

Thomas Franklin Currier, *Bibliography of John Greenleaf Whittier* (Cambridge: Harvard University Press, 1937); Albert J. von Frank, *Whittier: A Comprehensive Annotated Bibliography* (New York: Garland, 1976).

Biographies:

Samuel T. Pickard, *Life and Letters of John Greenleaf Whittier*, 2 vols. (Boston: Houghton, Mifflin, 1894; rev. ed., 1907); Thomas Wentworth Higginson, *John Greenleaf Whittier* (New York: Macmillan, 1902); George Rice Carpenter, *John Greenleaf Whittier* (Boston: Houghton, Mifflin, 1903); Albert Mordell, *Quaker Militant: John Greenleaf Whittier* (Boston: Houghton Mifflin, 1933); Whitman Bennett, *Whittier: Bard of Freedom* (Chapel Hill: University of North Carolina Press, 1941); John A. Pollard, *John Greenleaf Whittier: Friend of Man* (Boston: Houghton Mifflin, 1949); Edward Wagenknecht, *John Greenleaf Whittier: A Portrait in Paradox* (New York: Oxford University Press, 1967).

Letters:

The Letters of John Greenleaf Whittier, ed. John B. Pickard, 3 vols. (Cambridge: Harvard University Press, 1975).

Criticism:

Winfield Townley Scott, "Poetry in America: A New Consideration of Whittier's Verse," *New England Quarterly*, 7 (June 1934): 258-275; Louise C. Schaedler, "Whittier's Attitude toward Colonial Puritanism," *New England Quarterly*, 21 (September 1948): 350-367; Joseph M. Ernest, Jr., "Whittier and the American Writers," Ph.D. dissertation, University of Tennessee, 1952; George Arms, *The Fields Were Green: A New View of Bryant, Whittier, Holmes, Lowell, and Longfellow* (Stanford: Stanford University Press, 1953); Donald Hall, "Whittier," *Texas Quarterly*, 3 (Autumn 1960): 165-174; John B. Pickard, "Whittier's Ballads: The Maturing of an Artist," *Essex Institute Historical Collections*, 96 (January 1960): 56-72; Pickard, "Imagistic and Structural Unity in 'Snow-Bound,' " *College English*, 21 (March 1960): 338-343; Pickard, "The Basis of Whittier's Critical Creed: The Beauty of the Commonplace and the Truth of Style," *Rice Institute Pamphlets*, 47 (October 1960): 34-50; Roy Harvey Pearce, *The Continuity of American Poetry* (Princeton: Princeton University Press, 1961); Hyatt H. Waggoner, *American Poets from the Puritans to the Present* (Boston: Houghton Mifflin, 1967); *Memorabilia of John Greenleaf Whittier*, ed.

Pickard (Hartford, Ct.: Transcendental Books, 1968); Robert Penn Warren, "Whittier," *Sewanee Review*, 79 (Winter 1971): 86-135; Donald A. Ringe, "The Artistry of *Margaret Smith's Journal*," *Essex Institute Historical Collections*, 108 (July 1972): 235-243; Leonard B. Trawick, "Whittier's Snow Bound: A Poem About the Imagination," *Essays in Literature* (Western Illinois University), 1 (Spring 1974): 46-53.

Papers:

The largest collection of Whittier manuscripts and correspondence is the Oak Knoll Collection at the Essex Institute, Salem, Massachusetts. Other notable collections include the Samuel T. Pickard-John Greenleaf Whittier Papers in the Houghton Library at Harvard University, and the Roberts Collection located at the Haverford College Library.

Joseph Worcester.

JOSEPH EMERSON WORCESTER (24 August 1784-27 October 1865) was Noah Webster's foremost rival in the field of lexicography. After Webster's death Worcester carried on the rivalry with the firm of G. & C. Merriam for some twenty years, during which many of Worcester's ideas were adapted to the scheme of the Webster dictionaries. His most important contribution to the development of the dictionary was his introduction of the practice of carefully discriminating among words closely related in meaning. In contrast to Webster, who could not resist the temptation to reform language according to his own inspirations, Worcester saw his role as modern lexicographers do, to dispassionately and systematically gather, sift, and weigh the best available evidence from actual usage. As such, Worcester continued to influence lexicographical practice well into the twentieth century. A native of Bedford, New Hampshire, and educated at Yale, he settled in Cambridge and first applied himself to teaching and preparing texts in geography and history. By the time his first dictionary, the *Comprehensive Pronouncing and Explanatory Dictionary* (Boston: Hilliard, Gray) appeared in 1830, he thoroughly understood the merits and defects of his competitors, for he had not only abridged Webster's *American Dictionary*, but had made his own revision of Samuel Johnson's (Boston: Charles Ewer & T. H. Carter, 1827). Worcester's dictionary underwent steady refinements and improvements in subsequent editions, culminating in *A Dictionary of the English Language* (Boston: Hickling, Swan & Brown, 1860). The *Comprehensive* was an immediate success, owing as much to the avoidance of Websterian extravagancies perhaps as to its one-volume format and popular price. Because of this success, and because of Webster's less than complete satisfaction with the abridged *American Dictionary*, a fierce rivalry arose between the two lexicographers. Moreover, Worcester's 1846 edition was reprinted in London in 1853 with Webster's name prominently on the title page, an attempt by an unscrupulous publisher to exploit the reputation of both men. The Merriam firm took grave offense at this, and stepped up its already extensive campaign of advertising and pamphleteering. Yet this rivalry would have amounted to little had not dictionaries found an ever-expanding market in the growing public school movement. The aggressive competition for an ever-increasing market summoned up every gimmick of high pressure salesmanship. Webster ultimately prevailed with the Merriam edition of 1864. The Merriam firm had effectively institutionalized lexicography, while upon Worcester's death no successor was forthcoming. Moreover, the firm's superior commercial acumen parlayed Webster's name and authority, already known nationwide because of "The Blue-Back Speller," into a tidy profit; Webster himself had already fanned the smoldering American linguistic insecurity into a burning desire for an authoritative word book. Yet without the catalytic effect of Worcester's patient and sober scholarship, a truly modern American dictionary would have been considerably delayed. REFERENCES: James H. Sledd and Gwin J. Kolb, *Dr. Johnson's Dictionary* (Chicago: University of Chicago Press, 1955); Harold Whitehall, "The English Language," *Webster's New World Dictionary of the American Language*, College ed. (Cleveland: World Publishing Co., 1958), pp. xv-xxxiv. —*Raymond K. O'Cain*

Appendix I
Publications and Social Movements

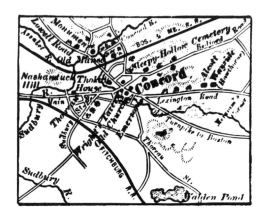

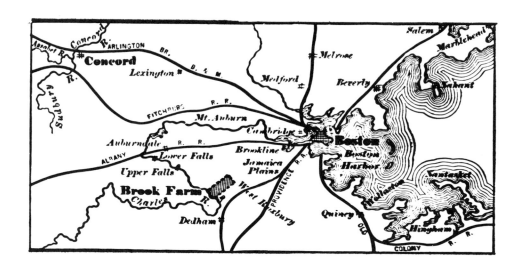

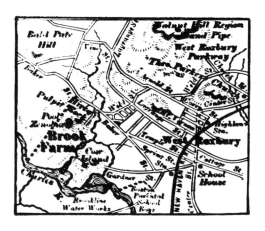

Brook Farm and Concord (1899).

AESTHETIC PAPERS, edited and published by Elizabeth Palmer Peabody, lasted only one issue in 1849 but its contents would have made any editor proud. Among the twelve articles and six poems, ranging on topics from the vegetation of Salem to pure philosophic musings, were: Ralph Waldo Emerson's lecture on "War"; Sampson Reed's "Genius," a Swedenborgian text that had circulated in manuscript since 1821 and which had influenced Emerson early in his career; John Sullivan Dwight's philosophical discussion of the nature of "Music"; Nathaniel Hawthorne's "Main-Street"; Peabody's examination of "Language"; and Henry David Thoreau's "Resistance to Civil Government," which Peabody probably printed as a favor and which is now famous under the title of "Civil Disobedience." Further numbers were not published for the simple reason that only about fifty copies of the first issue were sold. REFERENCE: Clarence L. F. Gohdes, *The Periodicals of American Transcendentalism* (Durham: Duke University Press, 1931), pp. 143-156.

myself; not that I am certain that the public wants it, but because I want it." Brownson wished an outlet for his opinions, one in which no editorial censorship could be imposed on him. No topic was ignored as Brownson wrote with passion about all the reforms of the day. He warned the Transcendentalists of their foibles and the conservative Unitarians of their dangerous aristocratic attitudes. The *Boston Quarterly Review*'s contributors included Bronson Alcott, George Bancroft, Alexander Hill Everett, Margaret Fuller, Elizabeth Palmer Peabody, and George Ripley, but most of it was written by Brownson. His subscribers were loyal and the journal flourished so that, following the October 1842 number, it was purchased and merged with the *Democratic Review*. Brownson continued to write for the *Democratic Review* but, after numerous editorial disputes, quit and founded *Brownson's Quarterly Review* in January 1844. In this journal he continued his polemical writing, with a brief suspension from 1865 to 1872, until 1875.

THE

BOSTON QUARTERLY REVIEW.

JANUARY, 1838.

ART. I. — INTRODUCTORY REMARKS.

In adding another to the numerous periodicals of our country, I have not much to say by way of introduction, and nothing by way of apology. I undertake the present publication, with a deep feeling of responsibleness, and with the hope of contributing something to the moral pleasure and social progress of my countrymen.

Had I consulted my ability to conduct a periodical as I would see one conducted, or had I listened to the counsels of some of my warmest and most judicious friends, I had not engaged in my present undertaking. But I seem to myself to be called to it, by a voice I dare not and even cannot disobey if I would. Whether this voice, which I have long heard urging me to the work, be merely an illusion of my own fancy, the promptings of my own vanity and self-esteem, or whether it be an indication of Duty from a higher Source, time and the result must determine. It speaks to me with Divine authority, and I must obey.

No man is able to estimate properly the value of his own individual experience. All are prone to exaggerate, more or less, the importance of what has happened to themselves. This it is altogether likely

VOL. I. NO. I.   1

First page of the first number of the
Boston Quarterly Review, *1838.*

BROWNSON'S

QUARTERLY REVIEW.

JANUARY, 1844.

ART. I. — INTRODUCTION. — *The Boston Quarterly Review.* — *Greeting to Old Friends.* — *Design of the Work.* — *Change of Views.* — *Eclecticism.* — *Saint-Simonism.* — *German Philosophy.* — *Philosophy of Life.* — *Theology.* — *The Church.* — *Law of Continuity.* — *Ultraists.* — *Conservatism.* — *Constitutionalism.* — *Moral and Religious Appeals.*

At the close of the volume for 1842, I was induced to merge the Boston Quarterly Review, which I had conducted for five years, in the Democratic Review, published at New-York, on condition of becoming a free and independent contributor to its pages for two years. But the character of my contributions having proved unacceptable to a portion of its ultra-democratic subscribers, and having, in consequence, occasioned its proprietors a serious pecuniary loss, the conductor has signified to me, that it would be desirable for my connexion with the Democratic Review to cease before the termination of the original agreement. This leaves me free to publish a new journal of my own, and renders it, in fact, necessary, if I would continue my communications with the public. I have no fault to find with the conductor of the Democratic Review, Mr. O'Sullivan, — a gentleman for whom I have a very

VOL. I. NO. I.   1

First page of the first number of
Brownson's Quarterly Review, *1844.*

THE BOSTON QUARTERLY REVIEW began in January 1838 with these words from its editor, Orestes Brownson: "I undertake this Review . . . for

REFERENCES: Clarence L. F. Gohdes, *The Periodicals of American Transcendentalism* (Durham: Duke University Press, 1931), pp. 38-82; Minda

Ruth Pearson Dorn, "Literary Criticism in the *Boston Quarterly Review*, the *Present*, and the *Massachusetts Quarterly Review*," Ph.D. dissertation, Southern Illinois University, 1975.

Painting of Brook Farm as it appeared in 1844.

BROOK FARM, a community established by George and Sophia Ripley, lasted from April 1841 to September 1847. It is one of America's most famous communal experiments and the best representation of the social aspect of Transcendentalism. When Ripley began the community, he wrote Ralph Waldo Emerson "Our objects . . . are to insure a more natural union between intellectual and manual labor than now exists; to combine the thinker and the worker, as far as possible, in the same individual; to guarantee the highest mental freedom, by providing all with labor, adapted to their tastes and talents, and securing to them the fruits of their industry; to do away with the necessity of menial services, by opening the benefits of education and profits of labor to all; and thus to prepare a society of liberal, intelligent, and cultivated persons, whose relations with each other would permit a more simple and wholesome life, than can be led amidst the pressure of our competitive institutions." Emerson declined to join the community and his reply shows a basic difference between the two men: "It seems to me a circuitous & operose way of relieving myself of any irksome circumstances, to put on your community the task of my emancipation which I ought to take on myself." That is, while Ripley felt that just laws and good living would produce good people, Emerson believed that the individual must first be reformed and that just people would then—and only then—make just laws.

Ripley had hoped to raise some $50,000 capital, but soon lowered his sights to $30,000. Yet when he purchased the 170-acre Ellis Farm in West Roxbury, Massachusetts, near Boston, for $10,500, he immediately had to take out two mortgages because of a lack of working capital. In September 1841, the "Brook Farm Institute of Agriculture and Education" was chartered, with twenty-four shares at $500 apiece pledged, one-third of that sum in cash. Each shareholder was to receive free tuition for his children in the Brook Farm school or 5% annual interest. Membership in the community was granted by a two-thirds vote after a two-month probationary period. Those who worked received free board; those who did not paid $4 a week.

The early period of Brook Farm went fairly well.

Ripley wanted a community where everyone shared in the work and in the profits, yet had time for contemplation and artistic endeavors. Not everyone found it possible to do all these things and Nathaniel Hawthorne, an original sharcholder, lcft when he discovered that his workload was too heavy to permit him to write. (He later fictionalized Brook Farm in his novel, *The Blithedale Romance*.) Activities were distributed in these areas: teaching in the school, farming, working in the manufacturing shops, such as the shoemaker's, domestic tasks, maintenance of buildings and grounds, and group recreation. Of these, the only unqualified successes were the school and recreation. Life was hard but pleasant, and visitors included Bronson Alcott, Orestes Brownson, Emerson, Margaret Fuller, and Theodore Parker.

"The Nest" at Brook Farm in 1897.

A dramatic change of direction occurred in March 1845 when the community was reorganized as the "Brook Farm Phalanx." Patterned after the ideal community of the French utopian Charles Fourier, the Phalanx structured its life around various "groups." Each person served in a number of groups—Dinner Waiters, Farmers, Washers, and so on—and, in theory, could work in any of them. The strict regimentation brought about by this upset many people and the community's fortunes declined. The death blow was delivered in March 1846, when the new central building being constructed, the Phalanstery, caught fire and was destroyed, at a loss of $7,000. Brook Farm never recovered and collapsed in September 1847.

One reason for the community's demise was the declining public interest in utopian and communitarian ventures in the late 1840s. Another—and more important—reason was Brook Farm's shaky finan-cial base. Immediately after buying the land for Brook Farm, Ripley took out two mortgages, one for $6,000 and another for $5,000; that is, he mortgaged the property for $500 more than he had paid for it. A third mortgage of $1,000 was taken out in April 1843 and a fourth mortgage of $2,500 in August 1845.

The buildings at Brook Farm as they appeared in 1897.

Small wonder, then, that the loss of the Phalanstery—and the money invested in it—signaled the end of the community. Ripley sold his library to help pay off the debts and eventually paid all creditors personally. REFERENCES: Georgiana Bruce Kirby, *Years of Experience: An Autobiographical Narrative* (New York: Putnam's, 1887); John Thomas Codman, *Brook Farm: Historic and Personal Memoirs* (Boston: Arena, 1894); *Early Letters of George Wm. Curtis to John S. Dwight: Brook Farm and Concord*, ed. George Willis Cooke (New York: Harpers, 1898); Amelia E. Russell, *Home Life of the Brook Farm Association* (Boston: Little, Brown, 1900); Lindsay Swift, *Brook Farm: Its Members, Scholars, and Visitors* (New York: Macmillan, 1900); John Van Der Zee Sears, *My Friends at Brook Farm* (New York: Desmond FitzGerald, 1912); Marianne Dwight, *Letters from Brook Farm 1844-1847*, ed. Amy L. Reed (Poughkeepsie, N.Y.: Vassar College, 1928); Zoltan Haraszti, *The Idyll of Brook Farm as Revealed by Unpublished Letters in the Boston Public Library* (Boston: Trustees of the Public Library, 1937); Katherine Burton, *Paradise Planters: The Story of Brook Farm* (London: Longmans, Green, 1939); *Autobiography of Brook Farm*, ed. Henry W. Sams (Englewood Cliffs, N.J.: Prentice-Hall, 1958); Edith Roelker Curtis, *A Season in Utopia: The Story of Brook Farm* (New York: Thomas Nelson, 1961); Charles Crowe, *George Ripley: Transcendentalist and Utopian Socialist*

207

(Athens: University of Georgia Press, 1967); Nathaniel Hawthorne, *The American Notebooks*, ed. Claude M. Simpson (Columbus: Ohio State University Press, 1972); Joel Myerson, *Brook Farm: An Annotated Bibliography and Resources Guide* (New York: Garland, 1978).

day. REFERENCES: Frank Luther Mott, *A History of American Magazines 1741-1850* (Cambridge: Harvard University Press, 1930), pp. 284-292; Frances Pedigo, "Critical Opinions of Poetry, Drama, and Fiction in *The Christian Examiner,* 1824-1869," Ph.D. dissertation, University of North Carolina, 1953.

Front wrapper of the Christian Examiner *for March 1837.*

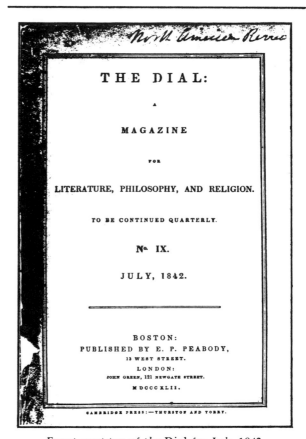

Front wrapper of the Dial *for July 1842.*

THE CHRISTIAN EXAMINER was the most important exponent of the conservative Unitarian viewpoint during the American Renaissance. Published bimonthly, the *Examiner* ran from 1824 to 1869 and at various times had as its editors Jared Sparks (1824-1825), James Walker (1831-1839), William Ware (1839-1844), George Putnam (1849-1857), and Frederic Henry Hedge and Edward Everett Hale (1857-1861). Although it had published pieces by Hedge and George Ripley espousing the Transcendental philosophy in the mid-1830s, during the period of the Unitarian controversy with the Transcendentalists, the *Examiner,* which had solid Harvard connections, toed the conservative line and some of the most negative American reviews of Emerson's writings appeared in it. Overall it was highly respected for the quality of its articles and considered by many as the best American review of its

THE DIAL was a quarterly magazine published from July 1840 to April 1844. Margaret Fuller edited the first eight numbers and Ralph Waldo Emerson the last eight; George Ripley was business manager through the October 1841 number and Henry David Thoreau was in charge of editing the April 1843 number in Emerson's absence. Among its important contributors, the magazine counted, in addition to its editors, Bronson Alcott, James Elliot Cabot, Ellery Channing, Lydia Maria Child, James Freeman Clarke, Christopher Pearse Cranch, George William Curtis, Charles A. Dana, John Sullivan Dwight, Frederic Henry Hedge, James Russell Lowell, Theodore Parker, Elizabeth Palmer Peabody, and Jones Very. The *Dial* provided Fuller and Thoreau with an opportunity to test their writings in print; gave Parker and Ripley an outlet for their religious writings after the pages of the conservative

Unitarian journals were closed to them; and featured some of Emerson's best poetry, sketches, and lectures. It was, in short, the most visible gathering point for the Transcendentalists.

The *Dial* grew out of a meeting of the Transcendental Club on 18 September 1839 at which it was proposed that a journal "designed as the organ of views more in accordance with the Soul" be started. Alcott gave the magazine its title, named after the heading he had given his thoughts which he had been assembling from his journals over the past few years. Fuller volunteered to be editor and tried for two years to fairly present "all kinds of people" in her journal. The *Dial*'s contributors indeed had, in Fuller's words, "freedom to say their say, for better, for worse," but the reviewers, choosing the *Dial*— and especially Alcott's "Orphic Sayings"—as a

convenient scapegoat for all the unpopular aspects of Transcendentalism, abused the new journal, and the public, unable to grasp or digest the varied articles, declined to buy the *Dial*, whose subscription list never rose above 300. In March 1842, hampered by ill health and upset that none of her promised salary had been paid, Fuller resigned. Despite Emerson's assuming the editorship, the *Dial* failed in 1844. REFERENCES: George Willis Cooke, *An Historical and Biographical Introduction to Accompany THE DIAL*, 2 vols. (Cleveland: Rowfant Club, 1902); Joel Myerson, "A History of the *Dial*," Ph.D. dissertation, Northwestern University, 1971; Donald F. Warders, " 'The Progress of the Hour and the Day': A Critical Study of the *Dial*," Ph.D. dissertation, University of Kansas, 1973.

The buildings at Fruitlands.

FRUITLANDS, a Utopian experiment begun by Bronson Alcott at Harvard, Massachusetts, near Concord, lasted from June 1843 to January 1844. Alcott first conceived of such a venture while in England in the summer of 1842 and was decided upon it when he returned to Concord that fall with two English reformers, Charles Lane and Henry G. Wright. In May 1843 Lane bought the ninety-acre Wyman Farm at Harvard for $1,800, receiving the house and barn rent-free for a year. The Alcotts, Lane, Wright, and a few others moved there on 1

June, with Alcott proposing to "take charge of the agricultural and educational departments, assist too in household labours, and carry forward the literary work with Mr. Lane, as far as I have time." As summer wore on, though, the project started falling apart. No one, especially Alcott and Lane, knew much about agriculture, and their farming habits were erratic at best. Mrs. Alcott had early developed a strong dislike for Lane, an egotistical and overbearing man, who held his financial backing of the community—Alcott had had no money of his own to put up—over the Alcotts' heads, whose attempt to convert Alcott to his own belief in celibacy drove a wedge between him and Mrs. Alcott, and who strictly enforced a vegetarian dietary regimen of fruit, nuts, bread, and water that made Mrs. Alcott ill. Things became worse when, in September, the

The small dining room at Fruitlands.

harvesting season, Lane and Alcott left on a lecture trip, leaving the women to bring in the crops. Alcott, too, began to have his doubts. The lack of privacy bothered both him and his wife. More important, Lane wanted a true communitarian organization, one where the individual's own needs and desires were placed second to the good of the group, and this contrasted sharply with Alcott's Transcendental belief in individualism. By the end of the year, open dissent broke out and Lane left to join a Shaker community. On 16 January 1844, Alcott, ill and depressed, called it quits and returned to Concord with his family. The failure nearly broke him— never again would he risk so much on his beliefs— and he wrote his brother after arriving at Concord: "... the ways of God, are less clear to me, at times, than at former periods ... Such a disproportion between my desires and deeds!" Louisa May Alcott's "Transcendental Wild Oats," first published in 1873, is a thinly-veiled fictional account of Fruitlands. REFERENCES: Alcott and Lane, "Fruitlands," *Dial*, 4 (July 1843): 135-136; Ednah D. Cheney, *Louisa May Alcott: Her Life, Letters, and Journals*—prints part of Louisa's Fruitlands journal (Boston: Roberts Brothers, 1889); Annie M. L. Clark, *The Alcotts in Harvard* (Lancaster, Mass.: J. C. L. Clark, 1902); Clara Endicott Sears, *Bronson Alcott's Fruitlands* (Boston: Houghton Mifflin, 1915); *The Journals of Bronson Alcott*, ed. Odell Shepard (Boston: Little, Brown, 1938); Odell Shepard, *Pedlar's Progress: The Life of Bronson Alcott* (Boston: Little, Brown, 1938); David Palmer Edgell,

"The New Eden: A Study of Bronson Alcott's Fruitlands," M.A. thesis, Wesleyan University, 1939; Roger William Cummins, "The Second Eden: Charles Lane and American Transcendentalism," Ph.D. dissertation, University of Minnesota, 1967; Robert Howard Walker, "Charles Lane and the Fruitlands Utopia," Ph.D. dissertation, University of Texas, 1967; *The Letters of A. Bronson Alcott*, ed. Richard L. Herrnstadt (Ames: Iowa State University Press, 1969); Louisa May Alcott, *Transcendental Wild Oats and Excerpts from the Fruitlands Diary* (Harvard, Mass.: Harvard Common Press, 1975). The original buildings of Fruitlands have been restored and are open to the public.

First page of the Harbinger *for 7 November 1846.*

THE HARBINGER was the official paper of the Brook Farm community. Eight volumes were published between 14 June 1845 and 10 February 1849, the last three volumes by the American Union of Associationists in New York as Brook Farm collapsed. George Ripley was its primary editor. Unfortunately for students of the history of Brook Farm, the *Harbinger* was more interested in promoting associationism—the organization of men into harmonious working groups—than it was in promoting Brook Farm, and articles on the community itself are scarce. Of the many articles on associationism, perhaps the best brief statement is Albert Brisbane, "The American Associationists," 2 (7 March 1846): 200-203. The *Harbinger*'s literary reviews were characterized by an optimistic idealism which saw the artist as a prophet of a better life and literature as constructive social criticism.

REFERENCES: Clarence L. F. Gohdes, *The Periodicals of American Transcendentalism* (Durham: Duke University Press, 1931), pp. 101-131; Marjorie Ruth Kaufman, "The Literary Reviews of the *Harbinger* During Its Brook Farm Period 1845-1847," M.A. thesis, University of Washington, 1947; Sterling F. Delano, *"The Harbinger:* A Portrait of Associationism in America," Ph.D. dissertation, Southern Illinois University, 1973.

lasted only from December 1847 to September 1850. Parker wanted "a *Dial* with a beard" and his journal vigorously championed unpopular religions and political causes, from German philosophy to anti-slavery. The journal failed, not from a lack of public support, but because of the publisher's bankruptcy.

REFERENCES: Clarence L. F. Gohdes, *The Periodicals of American Transcendentalism* (Durham: Duke University Press, 1931), pp. 157-193; Minda Ruth Pearson Dorn, "Literary Criticism in the *Boston Quarterly Review*, the *Present*, and the *Massachusetts Quarterly Review*," Ph.D. dissertation, Southern Illinois University, 1975.

THE

MASSACHUSETTS QUARTERLY

REVIEW.

VOL. I.

BOSTON:
PUBLISHED BY COOLIDGE & WILEY,
NO. 12 WATER STREET.
1848.

Title page for the first volume of the
Massachusetts Quarterly Review, *1848.*

SPECIMENS

OF

FOREIGN STANDARD LITERATURE.

EDITED

BY GEORGE RIPLEY.

VOL. I.

CONTAINING

PHILOSOPHICAL MISCELLANIES,

FROM THE FRENCH

OF

COUSIN, JOUFFROY, AND BENJAMIN CONSTANT.

BOSTON:
HILLIARD, GRAY, AND COMPANY.
M.DCCC.XXXVIII.

Half-title for the first volume in
Specimens of Foreign Standard Literature.

THE MASSACHUSETTS QUARTERLY REVIEW, despite its impressive roster of contributors—including Ralph Waldo Emerson, Richard Hildreth, Julia Ward Howe, Samuel Gridley Howe, Henry James, Sr., James Russell Lowell, and Wendell Phillips—under the editorial direction of Theodore Parker,

SPECIMENS OF FOREIGN STANDARD LITERATURE, a fourteen-volume series published between 1838 and 1842 under the general editorship of George Ripley, was a significant attempt to make available accurate translations of French and German authors to a general American audience. "The word 'standard' was a deliberate assertion," as Perry Miller noted, "as against [Andrews] Norton and [Francis] Bowen, that what they still regarded as the 'new' and suspect literature of Europe had already become, in the capitals of culture, 'standard.'" The volumes are: *Philosophical Miscellanies . . . from the French of Cousin, Juoffroy, and B. Constant*, trans. George Ripley, 2 vols. (Boston: Hilliard, Gray, 1838); *Select Minor Poems . . . from the German of Goethe and Schiller*, trans. John S. Dwight (Boston: Hilliard, Gray, 1839); *Conversations with Goethe in the Last Years of His Life . . . from the German of Eckermann*, trans. S. M. Fuller (Boston: Hilliard, Gray, 1839); *Introduction to Ethics, Including a Critical Survey of Moral Systems . . . from the French of Jouffroy*, trans. William H. Channing, 2 vols. (Boston: Hilliard, Gray, 1840-1841); *German Literature . . . from the German of Wolfgang Menzel*, trans. C. C. Felton, 3 vols. (Boston: Hilliard, Gray, 1840); *Theodore; or, The Skeptic's Conversion. History of the Culture of a Protestant Clergyman. . . . from the German of De Wette*, trans. James F. Clarke, 2 vols. (Boston: Hilliard, Gray, 1841); *Human Life or Practical Ethics . . . from the German of De Wette*, trans. Samuel Osgood, 2 vols. (Boston: James Munroe, 1842); *Songs and Ballads . . . from Uhland, Korner, Burger, and Other German Lyric Poets*, trans. Charles T. Brooks (Boston: James Munroe, 1842).

THE TRANSCENDENTAL CLUB and the *Dial* were the two focal points of Transcendentalism, places where the members of the "new school" of literature, philosophy, and religion could meet and discuss their views among friends. The Club had its beginning in June 1836, when Frederic Henry Hedge, a minister at Bangor, Maine, sent Ralph Waldo Emerson a letter proposing the formation of a "symposium" to discuss the mood of the times. Hedge had talked with two Boston ministers, George Putnam and George Ripley, and all wished to assemble "certain likeminded persons of our acquaintance for the free discussion of theological & moral subjects." Emerson agreed, and they used the Harvard College bicentennial celebration in September as the occasion of their first meeing. On 8 September they met at Willard's Hotel in Cambridge and agreed that the present state of philosophy and theology was "very unsatisfactory" and they wished to discuss what, if anything, could be done "in the way of protest and introduction of deeper and broader views." The tone of the discussion was encouraging and Ripley volunteered his home for the next meeting on 19 September, when eleven people gathered. During the four years that followed, the Club met nearly thirty times,

discussing matters of mutual religious and philosophic interest. Among those who attended the Club's meetings were Bronson Alcott, George Bancroft, Cyrus Bartol, Orestes Brownson, the Reverend William Ellery Channing, William Henry Channing, James Freeman Clarke, Christopher Pearse Cranch, John Sullivan Dwight, Convers Francis, Margaret Fuller, Theodore Parker, Elizabeth Palmer Peabody, Henry David Thoreau, Jones Very, and Charles Stearns Wheeler. After meeting in September 1840, the Club disbanded. What had originally been organized for informal discussion among a small influential group of dissidents now found itself containing some very important and very opinionated members who wielded real power. With other forums and careers to occupy its members, who were beginning to differ sharply and often harshly among themselves, the Club wisely and silently drifted apart. The contemporary impact of the Club cannot be denied. In an era of "Conversations," such as those made by Alcott and Fuller, the opportunity to freely discuss and exchange ideas was important. In addition, the Club was a major force behind the founding of the *Dial*. REFERENCES: Clarence Gohdes, "Alcott's 'Conversation' on the Transcendental Club and *The Dial*," *American Literature*, 3 (March 1931); 14-27; Joel Myerson, "A Calendar of Transcendental Club Meetings," *American Literature*, 44 (May 1972): 197-207; Myerson, "A History of the Transcendental Club," *ESQ: A Journal of the American Renaissance*, 23 (I Quarter 1977): 27-35.

TRANSCENDENTALISM was a Boston-centered movement flourishing between 1836 and 1844. It reached its period of greatest influence with the publication of Ralph Waldo Emerson's *Nature* on 9 September 1836 and with the first meeting of the Transcendental Club one day earlier. By 1844 whatever unity had existed among the Transcendentalists was no longer present and formal recognition of this came when the semi-official journal of the movement, the *Dial*, ceased publication in April. Most Transcendentalists were Harvard-educated Unitarian ministers dissatisfied with the conservative Unitarians who led their faith, and all were dissatisfied with the general conservative tenor of the time. This conservatism is best described by Henry Adams who, though educated at Harvard in the 1850s, had many of the conservative Unitarians as his teachers: "For them, difficulties might be ignored, doubts were waste of thought; nothing exacted solution. Boston had solved the universe; or had

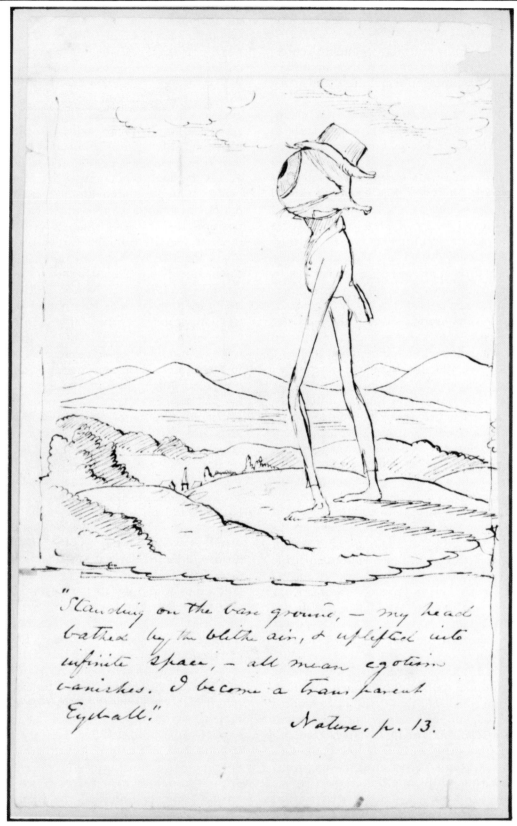

"Standing on the bare ground, — my head bathed by the blithe air, & uplifted into infinite space, — all mean egotism vanishes. I become a transparent Eyeball."

Nature, p. 13.

Christopher Pearse Cranch's caricature of lines from Emerson's Nature *(by permission of the Houghton Library).*

offered and realized the best solution yet tried. The problem was worked out."

Between the Transcendentalists and the conservative Unitarians, there were four particular areas of conflict: literature, philosophy, religion, and man's place in society.

In literature, the Transcendentalists championed English and continental writers such as Thomas Carlyle and Goethe. Emerson published Carlyle in America and George Ripley introduced continental authors in his series of *Specimens of Foreign Standard Literature*. Yet dissension existed within the ranks of the Transcendentalists. Some, led by Emerson, believed that a few "representative men" should set an example and lead the way; others, led by Orestes Brownson, felt that literature should "appeal to the mass, wake up just sentiments, quicken elevated thoughts in them, and direct their attention to great and noble deeds; the literature will follow as a necessary consequence."

In philosophy, the Transcendentalists followed Immanuel Kant in believing that man had an innate ability to perceive that his existence transcended mere sensory experience, as opposed to the prevailing belief of John Locke that the mind was a blank tablet at birth which then registered only those impressions perceived through the senses and experience. From the writings of Sampson Reed came the idea of correspondence, that every object was a microcosm—or world in miniature—of the vast spiritual force later named by some the Oversoul, and an early formulation of the concept of organic style, that the artist produces his work by giving expression to the forms of nature rather than by imposing an artificial arrangement upon nature. The Transcendentalists also took much from the idealism of Victor Cousin. And because man was basically good, evil, to some Transcendentalists, did not exist; in Emerson's words, "Evil is merely privative, not absolute; it is like cold, which is the privation of heat."

In religion, the Transcendentalists were holding dangerous ground. In 1828, the Reverend William Ellery Channing had said that "man has a kindred nature with God, and may bear the most important and ennobling relations with him." Now, less than a decade later, Channing and his fellow Unitarians were being accused of perpetrating a monstrous duplicity, centering on the question of the accuracy or believability of the miracles which Christ is said to have performed. William Henry Furness proposed in 1836 that if all nature were truly seen as miraculous, then no specific phenomenon could be more so; hence, to believe in miracles was to deny the

miraculous everywhere and was also a mere skepticism based upon Locke's ideas. In response, Orville Dewey described man as too fallible a creature to discern the truth of Christianity without the evidences provided for by miracles. The conservative Unitarians were now caught in the middle: they had, in denying Calvinism, with its acceptance of depravity, belief in original sin, and ideas of predestination, dedicated themselves to a lofty concept of man, but they refused to glorify him as did the Transcendentalists by believing that he could attain religion without miracles or supernatural assistance. By placing their elders in this position, the Transcendentalists were also accusing them of literally robbing man of his dignity even more shamefully, because more slyly, than the Calvinists had. The Unitarian response was circumspect: Andrews Norton loftily announced that the Transcendentalists, many of whom had taken his courses in the Harvard Divinity School, were simply not competent to speak on such matters, and that their movement was characterized by "the most extraordinary assumption, united with great ignorance, and incapacity for reasoning"; Francis Bowen called Transcendentalism an un-American fad, and its adherents arrogant and dogmatic. Ripley led the counterattack by responding to Norton with a plea for intellectual freedom, and by answering Bowen that Harvard itself was so isolated that it failed to see Transcendentalism was indeed the sentiment of the land. Brownson carried the idea of Harvard's isolation one step further, saying that the battle was social as well as religious, the aristocratic institutions of the Unitarian church arrayed against the democratic principles of the Transcendentalists; the Unitarians were now themselves accused of being anti-American. The battle then raged, lasting into the 1840s, when Theodore Parker summed up the Transcendentalists' position thus: "Their [miracles] connection with Christianity appears accidental: for if Jesus had taught at Athens, and not at Jerusalem; if he had wrought no miracle, and none but the human nature had ever been ascribed to him; if the Old Testament had forever perished at his birth,—Christianity would still have been the word of God; it would have lost none of its truths. . . . So if it could be proved—as it cannot—in opposition to the greatest amount of historical evidence ever collected on any single point, that the Gospels were the fabrication of designing and artful men, that Jesus of Nazareth never lived, still Christianity would stand firm, and fear no evil." In short, the word and spirit—the teachings—of Christ gave Christianity its validity, and not any mere, and unprovable "supernatural" actions.

In viewing man's position in society, the Transcendentalists also challenged accepted beliefs. Attacking the religious and social formalism of the day, they wished to have freedom and spontaneity in all ways of life. Commercialism, too, disturbed them, and they countered the traditional view of "success" as measured by monetary or materialistic standards with a belief that individual moral insights should supersede the dollar as the standard of conduct. Finally, in opposition to what they saw as a false democracy that had legislation enacted through the will of the majority, the Transcendentalists held that the individual should oppose laws he feels are unjust. As Thoreau put it, the government "is not armed with superior wit or honesty, but with superior physical strength," and "It costs me less in every sense to incur the penalty of disobedience to the state, than it would to obey."

REFERENCES: Charles Mayo Ellis, *An Essay on Transcendentalism* (Boston: Crocker & Ruggles, 1842); Emerson, "The Transcendentalist," in *Nature: Addresses, and Lectures* (Boston: James Munroe, 1849), pp. 319-348; Octavius Brooks Frothingham, *Transcendentalism in New England* (New York: Putnam's, 1876); Harold Clarke Goddard, *Studies in New England Transcendentalism* (New York: Columbia University Press, 1908); Walter Leighton, *French Philosophy and New England Transcendentalism* (Charlottesville: University of Virginia Press, 1908); Clarence L. F. Gohdes, *The Periodicals of American Transcendentalism* (Durham: Duke University Press, 1931); Arthur E. Christy, *The Orient in American Transcendentalism* (New York: Columbia University Press, 1932); F. O. Matthiessen, *American Renaissance: Art and Expression in the Age of Emerson and Whitman* (New York: Oxford University Press, 1941); Henry A. Pochmann, *New England Transcendentalism and St. Louis Hegelianism* (Philadelphia: Carl Schurz Foundation, 1948); *The Transcendentalists: An Anthology*, ed. Perry Miller (Cambridge: Harvard University Press, 1950); Alexander Kern, "The Rise of Transcendentalism, 1815-1860," in *Transitions in American Literary History*, ed. Harry Hayden Clark (Durham: Duke University Press, 1954), pp. 245-314; Stanley M. Vogel, *German Literary Influences on the American Transcendentalists* (New Haven: Yale University Press, 1955); William R. Hutchison, *The Transcendentalist Ministers* (New Haven: Yale University Press, 1959); *Selected Writings of the American Transcendentalists*, ed. George Hochfield

(New York: New American Library, 1966); *Transcendentalism and Its Legacy*, ed. Myron Simon and Thornton H. Parsons (Ann Arbor: University of Michigan Press, 1966); *American Transcendentalism: An Anthology of Criticism*, ed. Brian M. Barbour—includes bibliography (Notre Dame: University of Notre Dame Press, 1973); Lawrence Buell, *Literary Transcendentalism: Style and Vision in the American Renaissance* (Ithaca: Cornell University Press, 1973); Paul F. Boller, Jr., *American Transcendentalism, 1830-1860: An Intellectual Inquiry* (New York: Putnam's, 1974); Donald M. Koster, *Transcendentalism in America* (New York: Twayne, 1975).

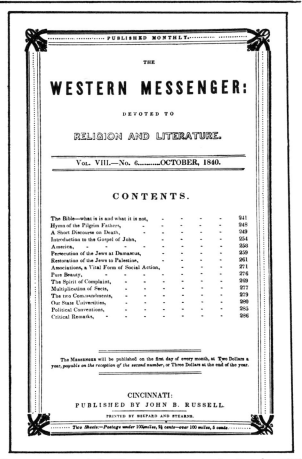

Front wrapper of the Western Messenger *for October 1840.*

THE WESTERN MESSENGER was the voice of New England liberal Unitarianism in the Ohio Valley. Published monthly in Cincinnati and Louisville from June 1835 to April 1841, the *Messenger* was mostly edited by transplanted New Englanders: James Freeman Clarke (1836-1839), Christopher Pearse Cranch (1837-1839), and William Henry Channing (1839-1841). Among the Transcendentalists published in the *Messenger* were John Sullivan Dwight, Ralph Waldo Emerson, Margaret

Fuller, Theodore Parker, Elizabeth Palmer Peabody, and Jones Very. Although it began as a religious journal, one that defended the Transcendentalists from the attacks of the conservative Unitarians, the *Messenger* in its later years became primarily a literary journal. It wholeheartedly supported Emerson against those who called his works "the latest form of infidelity," defended Jones Very against those who called him insane, and endorsed the English Romantic poets, especially Percy Bysshe Shelley, at a time when Americans considered them atheists. Besides supporting unpopular literary causes, the *Messenger* consistently came out in favor of abolitionism. The magazine ceased publication because its sales were dwindling and because its editors returned to New England. REFERENCES: Clarence L. F. Gohdes, *The Periodicals of American Transcendentalism* (Durham: Duke University Press, 1931), pp. 17-37; Charles E. Blackburn, "James Freeman Clarke: An Interpretation of the Western Years (1833-1830)," Ph.D. dissertation, Yale University, 1952; Blackburn, "Some New Light on the *Western Messenger*," *American Literature*, 26 (November 1954): 320-336.

Appendix II
Books for Further Reading

The following selective list should be of value to those wishing to read further in the American Renaissance. Additional information may be obtained from Clarence Gohdes, *Bibliographical Guide to the Study of the Literature of the U.S.A.,* 4th ed. (Durham: Duke University Press, 1976), Lewis Leary, *Articles on American Literature, 1900-1950* (Durham: Duke University Press, 1954), Leary, *Articles on American Literature, 1950-1967* (Durham: Duke University Press, 1970), the annual *PMLA* bibliography, and *American Literary Scholarship: An Annual* (Durham: Duke University Press, 1965-). Journals regularly publishing articles about the American Renaissance include: *American Literature, American Transcendental Quarterly, ESQ: A Journal of the American Renaissance, Emerson Society Quarterly (1955-1971), New England Quarterly,* and *Studies in the American Renaissance.*

Adams, Grace, and Edward Hutter. *The Mad Forties.* New York: Harpers, 1942.

Ahlstrom, Sydney E. "The Middle Period (1840-1880)," in *The Harvard Divinity School: Its Place in Harvard University and in American Culture,* ed. George Huntston Williams, pp. 78-147. Boston: Beacon, 1954.

Ahlstrom, Sydney E. *A Religious History of the American People.* New Haven: Yale University Press, 1972.

Allen, Joseph Henry. *Our Liberal Movement in Theology.* Boston: Roberts Brothers, 1882.

Allen, Joseph Henry. *Sequel to "Our Liberal Movement".* Boston: Roberts Brothers, 1897.

Anagnos, Julia R. *Philosophiæ Quæstor; or, Days in Concord.* Boston: D. Lothrop, 1885.

Ando, Shoei. *Zen and American Transcendentalism.* Tokyo: Hokuseido, 1970.

Bacon, Edwin M. *Literary Pilgrimages in New England.* New York: Silver, Burdett, 1902.

Baker, Paul R. *The Fortunate Pilgrims: Americans in Italy 1800-1860.* Cambridge: Harvard University Press, 1964.

Barbour, Brian M., ed. *American Transcendentalism: An Anthology of Criticism.* Notre Dame: University of Notre Dame Press, 1973.

Bartlett, George B. *Concord: Historic, Literary and Picturesque,* 3rd ed. Boston: D. Lothrop, 1885.

Bartlett, Irving H. *The American Mind in the Mid-Nineteenth Century.* New York: Thomas Y. Crowell, 1967.

Baym, Max I. *A History of Literary Aesthetics in America.* New York: Frederick Ungar, 1973.

Bercovitch, Sacvan. *The Puritan Origins of the American Self.* New Haven: Yale University Press, 1975.

Blau, Joseph L. *Men and Moments in American Philosophy.* Englewood Cliffs, N.J.: Prentice-Hall, 1952.

Blumenthal, Henry. *American and French Culture, 1800-1900: Interchanges in Art, Science, Literature, and Society.* Baton Rouge: Louisiana State University Press, 1975.

Boas, George, ed. *Romanticism in America.* Baltimore: Johns Hopkins University Press, 1940.

Boller, Paul F., Jr. *American Transcendentalism, 1830-1860: An Intellectual Inquiry.* New York: Putnam's, 1974.

Branch, Douglas E. *The Sentimental Years 1836-1860.* New York: D. Appleton-Century, 1934.

Brooks, Van Wyck. *The Dream of Arcadia: American Writers and Artists in Italy 1760-1915.* New York: E. P. Dutton, 1958.

Brooks, Van Wyck. *The Flowering of New England 1815-1865.* New York: E. P. Dutton, 1936.

Brown, Herbert Ross. *The Sentimental Novel in America 1789-1860.* Chapel Hill: University of North Carolina Press, 1940.

Brown, Jerry Wayne. *The Rise of Biblical Criticism in America, 1800-1870: The New England Scholars.* Middletown, Ct.: Wesleyan University Press, 1969.

Brown, Mary Hosmer. *Memories of Concord.* Boston: Four Seas, 1926.

Buell, Lawrence. *Literary Transcendentalism: Style and Vision in the American Renaissance.* Ithaca: Cornell University Press, 1973.

Burton, Katherine. *Paradise Planters: The Story of Brook Farm.* London: Longmans, Green, 1939.

Calverton, V. F. *The Liberation of American Literature.* New York: Scribners, 1932.

Carpenter, Frederic I. *American Literature and the Dream.* New York: Philosophical Library, 1955.

Carter, Everett. *The American Idea: The Literary Response to American Optimism.* Chapel Hill: University of North Carolina Press, 1977.

Charvat, William. *Literary Publishing in America: 1790-1850*. Philadelphia: University of Pennsylvania Press, 1959.

Charvat, William. *The Origins of American Critical Thought 1810-1835*. Philadelphia: University of Pennsylvania Press, 1936.

Charvat, William. *The Profession of Authorship in America, 1800-1870*, ed. Matthew J. Bruccoli. Columbus: Ohio State University Press, 1968.

Chase, Richard. *The American Novel and Its Tradition*. Garden City, N.Y.: Doubleday, 1957.

Christy, Arthur. *The Orient in American Transcendentalism*. New York: Columbia University Press, 1932.

Conrad, Susan P. *Perish the Thought: Intellectual Women in Romantic America 1830-1860*. New York: Oxford University Press, 1976.

Cooke, George Willis, ed. *The Poets of Transcendentalism: An Anthology*. Boston: Houghton, Mifflin, 1903.

Cooke, George Willis. *Unitarianism in America*. Boston: American Unitarian Association, 1902.

Cowie, Alexander. *The Rise of the American Novel*. New York: American Book Company, 1948.

Crawford, Mary Caroline. *Romantic Days in Old Boston*. Boston: Little, Brown, 1910.

Cunliffe, Marcus. *The Literature of the United States*. London: Penguin, 1954.

Curtis, Edith Roelker. *A Season in Utopia: The Story of Brook Farm*. New York: Thomas Nelson, 1961.

Day, Martin S. *History of American Literature from the Beginning to 1900*. Garden City, N.Y.: Doubleday, 1970.

Dickens, Charles. *American Notes for General Circulation*. London: Chapman and Hall, 1842.

Douglas, Ann. *The Feminization of American Culture*. New York: Alfred A. Knopf, 1977.

Duyckinck, Evert A. and George L., eds. *Cyclopaedia of American Literature*. 2 vols. New York: Charles Scribner, 1856.

Ekirch, Arthur A., Jr. *Man and Nature in America*. New York: Columbia University Press, 1963.

Eliot, Samuel A., ed. *Heralds of a Liberal Faith*. 4 vols. Boston: American Unitarian Association, 1910.

Emerson, Edward Waldo. *Early Years of the Saturday Club 1855-1870*. Boston: Houghton Mifflin, 1918.

Falk, Robert. *The Victorian Mode in American Fiction*. East Lansing: Michigan State University Press, 1965.

Feidelson, Charles, Jr. *Symbolism and American Literature*. Chicago: University of Chicago Press, 1953.

Fellman, Michael. *The Unbounded Frame: Freedom and Community in Nineteenth Century American Utopianism*. Westport, Ct.: Greenwood Press, 1973.

Fenn, William W. *The Religious History of New England*. Cambridge: Harvard University Press, 1917.

Fiedler, Leslie A. *Love and Death in the American Novel*. New York: Criterion, 1960.

Fish, Carl Russell. *The Rise of the Common Man 1830-1850*. New York: Macmillan, 1927.

Floan, Howard R. *The South in Northern Eyes 1831 to 1861*. Austin: University of Texas Press, 1958.

Foerster, Norman. *American Criticism*. Boston: Houghton Mifflin, 1928.

Foster, Edward Halsey. *The Civilized Wilderness: Backgrounds to American Romantic Literature, 1817-1860*. New York: Free Press, 1975.

Freidel, Frank, ed. *Harvard Guide to American History*. Rev. ed. 2 vols. Cambridge: Harvard University Press, 1974.

Frothingham, Octavius Brooks. *Transcendentalism in New England*. New York: Putnam's, 1876.

Fussell, Edwin. *Frontier: American Literature and the American West*. Princeton: Princeton University Press, 1965.

Gardiner, Harold C., ed. *American Classics Reconsidered: A Christian Appraisal*. New York: Scribners, 1958.

Gelpi, Albert. *The Tenth Muse: The Psyche of the American Poet*. Cambridge: Harvard University Press, 1975.

Goddard, Harold Clarke. *Studies in New England Transcendentalism*. New York: Columbia University Press, 1908.

Gohdes, Clarence. *American Literature in Nineteenth Century England*. New York: Columbia University Press, 1944.

Gohdes, Clarence. *The Periodicals of American Transcendentalism*. Durham: Duke University Press, 1931.

Green, Martin. *The Problem of Boston: Some Readings in Cultural History*. New York: W. W. Norton, 1966.

Green, Martin. *Re-appraisals: Some Commonsense Readings in American Literature*. London: Hugh Evelyn, 1963.

Greer, Louise. *Browning and America*. Chapel Hill: University of North Carolina Press, 1952.

Griffin, C. S. *The Ferment of Reform, 1830-1860*. New York: Thomas Y. Crowell, 1967.

Gross, Theodore L. *The Heroic Ideal in American Literature*. New York: Free Press, 1971.

Haraszti, Zoltan. *The Idyll of Brook Farm as Revealed by Unpublished Letters in the Boston Public Library*. Boston: Trustees of the Public Library, 1937.

Hart, James D. *The Popular Book: A History of America's Literary Taste*. New York: Oxford University Press, 1950.

Hendrick, George, ed. *The American Renaissance: The History and Literature of an Era*. Berlin: Verlag Moritz Diesterweg, 1961.

Herreshoff, David. *American Disciples of Marx*. Detroit: Wayne State University Press, 1967.

Higginson, Thomas Wentworth, and Henry Walcott Boynton. *A Reader's History of American Literature*. Boston: Houghton, Mifflin, 1903.

Hochfield, George, ed. *Selected Writings of the American Transcendentalists*. New York: New American Library, 1966.

Hoffman, Daniel G. *Form and Fable in American Fiction*. New York: Oxford University Press, 1961.

Horton, Rod W., and Herbert W. Edwards. *Backgrounds of American Literary Thought*. New York: Appleton-Century-Crofts, 1952.

Howard, Leon. *Literature and the American Tradition*. Garden City, N.Y.: Doubleday, 1960.

Howe, Daniel Walker. " 'At Morning Blessed and Golden Browed,' " in *A Stream of Light: A Sesquicentennial History of American Unitarianism*, ed. Conrad Wright, pp. 33-61. Boston: Beacon, 1975.

Howe, Daniel Walker. *The Unitarian Moral Conscience: Harvard Moral Philosophy, 1850-1861*. Cambridge: Harvard University Press, 1970.

Hutchison, William R. *The Transcendentalist Ministers: Church Reform in the New England Renaissance*. New Haven: Yale University Press, 1959.

Huth, Hans. *Nature and the American: Three Centuries of Changing Attitudes*. Berkeley: University of California Press, 1957.

Jones, Howard Mumford. *American and French Culture 1750-1848*. Chapel Hill: University of North Carolina Press, 1927.

Jones, Howard Mumford. *Belief and Disbelief in American Literature*. Chicago: University of Chicago Press, 1967.

Jones, Howard Mumford. *The Theory of American Literature*. Ithaca: Cornell University Press, 1965.

Kaplan, Harold. *Democratic Humanism and American Literature*. Chicago: University of Chicago Press, 1972.

Kaufman, Paul. "The Romantic Movement," in *The Reinterpretation of American Literature*, ed. Norman Foerster, pp. 114-138. New York: Harcourt, Brace, 1928.

Kern, Alexander. "The Rise of Transcendentalism, 1815-1860," in *Transitions in American Literary History*, ed. Harry Hayden Clark, pp. 245-314. Durham: Duke University Press, 1954.

Knight, Grant C. *American Literature and Culture*. New York: Ray Long and Richard R. Smith, 1932.

Kolb, Harold H., Jr. *A Field Guide to the Study of American Literature*. Charlottesville: University Press of Virginia, 1976.

Koster, Donald N. *Transcendentalism in America*. Boston: Twayne, 1975.

Kreymborg, Alfred. *Our Singing Strength: An Outline of American Poetry, 1620-1930*. New York: Coward-McCann, 1929.

Lader, Lawrence. *The Bold Brahmins: New England's War Against Slavery: 1831-1863*. New York: E. P. Dutton, 1961.

Leary, Lewis. *American Literature: A Study and Research Guide*. New York: St. Martin's, 1976.

Lehmann-Haupt, Hellmut, et al. *The Book in America: A History of the Making and Selling of Books in the U.S.* 2nd ed. New York: R. R. Bowker, 1952.

Leighton, Walter L. *French Philosophy and New England Transcendentalism*. Charlottesville: University of Virginia, 1908.

Leisy, Ernest Erwin. *American Literature: An Interpretative Survey*. New York: Thomas Y. Crowell, 1929.

Leisy, Ernest Erwin. *The American Historical Novel*. Norman: University of Oklahoma Press, 1950.

Lewis, R. W. B. *The American Adam: Innocence, Tragedy and Tradition in the Nineteenth Century*. Chicago: University of Chicago Press, 1955.

Lewisohn, Ludwig. *Expression in America*. New York: Harpers, 1932.

Lieber, Todd M. *Endless Experiments: Essays on the Heroic Experience in American Romanticism*. Columbus: Ohio State University Press, 1973.

McKinsey, Elizabeth R. *The Western Experiment: New England Transcendentalists in the Ohio Valley*. Cambridge: Harvard University Press, 1973.

McWilliams, Wilson Carey. *The Idea of Fraternity in America*. Berkeley: University of California Press, 1973.

Madden, Edward H. *Civil Disobedience and Moral Law in Nineteenth-Century American Philosophy*. Seattle: University of Washington Press, 1968.

Martin, Terrence. *The Instructed Vision: Scottish Common Sense Philosophy and the Origins of American Fiction*. Bloomington: Indiana University Press, 1961.

Marx, Leo. *The Machine in the Garden: Technology and the Pastoral Ideal in America*. New York: Oxford University Press, 1964.

Matthiessen, F. O. *American Renaissance: Art and Expression in the Age of Emerson and Whitman*. New York: Oxford University Press, 1941.

Maxwell, D. E. S. *American Fiction: The Intellectual Background*. New York: Columbia University Press, 1963.

Mead, David. *Yankee Eloquence in the Middle West: The Ohio Lyceum, 1850-1870*. East Lansing: Michigan State College Press, 1951.

Miller, Perry. *Nature's Nation*. Cambridge: Harvard University Press, 1967.

Miller, Perry, ed. *The Transcendentalists: An Anthology*. Cambridge: Harvard University Press, 1950.

Minnegerode, Meade. *The Fabulous Forties 1840-1850*. Garden City, N.Y.: Garden City Publishing Company, 1924.

Minter, David L. *The Interpreted Design as a Structural Principle in American Prose*. New Haven: Yale University Press, 1969.

Mitchell, Donald G. *American Lands and Letters: Leather-Stocking to Poe's "Raven"*. New York: Scribners, 1899.

More, Paul Elmer. *Paul Elmer More's Shelbourne Essays on American Literature*, ed. Daniel Aaron. New York: Harcourt, Brace, and World, 1963.

Mott, Frank Luther. *Golden Multitudes: The Story of Best Sellers in the United States*. New York: Macmillan, 1947.

Mott, Frank Luther. *A History of American Magazines*. 5 vols. Cambridge: Harvard University Press, 1938-1968.

Mumford, Lewis. *The Golden Day: A Study in American Experience and Culture*. New York: Boni and Liveright, 1926.

Newton, Annabel. *Wordsworth in Early American Criticism*. Chicago: University of Chicago Press, 1928.

Nilon, Charles H. *Bibliography of Bibliographies in American Literature*. New York: R. R. Bowker, 1970.

Nye, Russel Blaine. *Society and Culture in America 1830-1860*. New York: Harpers, 1974.

Nye, Russel Blaine. *The Unembarrassed Muse: The Popular Arts in America*. New York: Dial, 1970.

Orians, G. Harrison. "The Rise of Romanticism, 1805-1855," in *Transitions in American Literary History*, ed. Harry Hayden Clark, pp. 161-244. Durham: Duke University Press, 1954.

Papasvily, Helen Waite. *All the Happy Endings*. New York: Harpers, 1956.

Parrington, Vernon Lewis. *The Romantic Revolution in America 1800-1860*. New York: Harcourt, Brace, 1927.

Parrington, Vernon Lewis, Jr. *American Dreams: A Study of American Utopias*. Providence: Brown University Press, 1947.

Pattee, Fred Lewis. *The Development of the American Short Story*. New York: Harpers, 1923.

Pattee, Fred Lewis. *The First Century of American Literature 1770-1870*. New York: D. Appleton-Century, 1935.

Payne, Edward F. *Dickens Days in Boston*. Boston: Houghton, Mifflin, 1927.

Pearce, Roy Harvey. *The Continuity of American Poetry*. Princeton: Princeton University Press, 1961.

Pease, Jane H. and William H. *Bound Them in Chains: A Biographical History of the Antislavery Movement*. Westport, Ct.: Greenwood Press, 1972.

Perry, Bliss. *The American Spirit in Literature*. New Haven: Yale University Press, 1918.

Persons, Stow. *American Minds: A History of Ideas*. New York: Holt, Rinehart, and Winston, 1958.

Persons, Stow. *Free Religion: An American Faith*. New Haven: Yale University Press, 1947.

Pochmann, Henry A. *German Culture in America*. Madison: University of Wisconsin Press, 1956.

Pochmann, Henry A. *New England Transcendentalism and St. Louis Hegelianism*. Philadelphia: Carl Schurz Foundation, 1948.

Poirier, Richard. *A World Elsewhere: The Place of Style in American Literature*. New York: Oxford University Press, 1966.

Power, Julia. *Shelley in America in the Nineteenth Century*. Lincoln: University of Nebraska Press, 1940.

Pritchard, John Paul. *Criticism in America*. Norman: University of Oklahoma Press, 1956.

Quinn, Arthur Hobson. *American Fiction: An Historical and Critical Survey*. New York: Appleton-Century, 1936.

Quinn, Arthur Hobson, ed. *The Literature of the American People: An Historical and Critical Survey*. New York: Appleton-Century-Crofts, 1951.

Rayapati, J. P. Rao. *Early American Interest in Vedanta: Pre-Emersonian Interest in Vedic Literature and Vedantic Philosophy*. London: Asia Publishing House, 1973.

Rees, Robert A., and Earl N. Harbert, eds. *Fifteen American Authors Before 1900: Bibliographic Essays on Research and Criticism*. Madison: University of Wisconsin Press, 1971.

Riegel, Robert E. *Young America 1830-1840*. Norman: University of Oklahoma Press, 1949.

Riley, Woodbridge. *American Thought from Puritanism to Pragmatism and Beyond*. New York: Henry Holt, 1915.

Rourke, Constance. *American Humor: A Study of the National Character*. New York: Harcourt, Brace, 1931.

Sams, Henry W., ed. *Autobiography of Brook Farm*. Englewood Cliffs, N.J.: Prentice-Hall, 1958.

Schlesinger, Arthur M., Jr. *The Age of Jackson*. Boston: Little, Brown, 1945.

Schneider, Herbert W. *A History of American Philosophy*. New York: Columbia University Press, 1946.

Scudder, Townsend. *Concord: American Town*. Boston: Little, Brown, 1947.

Seldes, Gilbert. *The Stammering Century*. New York: John Day, 1928.

Simon, Myron, and Thornton H. Parsons, eds. *Transcendentalism and Its Legacy*. Ann Arbor: University of Michigan Press, 1966.

Slotkin, Richard. *Regeneration through Violence: The Mythology of the American Frontier, 1600-1860*. Middletown, Ct.: Wesleyan University Press, 1973.

Smith, Bernard. *Forces in American Criticism: A Study in the History of American Literary Thought*. New York: Harcourt, Brace, 1939.

Smithline, Arnold. *Natural Religion and American Literature*. New Haven: College and University Press, 1966.

Spencer, Benjamin. *The Quest for Nationality: An American Literary Campaign*. Syracuse: Syracuse University Press, 1957.

Spiller, Robert E. *The Cycle of American Literature*. New York: Macmillan, 1956.

Spiller, Robert E. *The American in England During the First Half Century of Independence*. New York: Henry Holt, 1926.

Spiller, Robert E., et al. *Literary History of the United States*. 4th ed., rev. New York: Macmillan, 1974.

Stapleton, Laurence. *The Elected Circle: Studies in the Art of Prose*. Princeton: Princeton University Press, 1973.

Stauffer, Donald Barlow. *A Short History of American Poetry*. New York: E. P. Dutton, 1974.

Stern, Madeleine B. *Imprints on History: Book Publishers and American Frontiers*. Bloomington: Indiana University Press, 1956.

Stewart, Randall. *American Literature and Christian Doctrine*. Baton Rouge: Lousiana State University Press, 1958.

Stovall, Floyd. *American Idealism*. Norman: University of Oklahoma Press, 1943.

Stovall, Floyd, ed. *The Development of American Literary Criticism*. Chapel Hill: University of North Carolina Press, 1955.

Swayne, Josephine Latham. *The Story of Concord Told by Concord Writers*. 2nd rev. ed. Boston: Meador, 1939.

Swift, Lindsay. *Brook Farm: Its Members, Scholars, and Visitors*. New York: Macmillan, 1900.

Tanner, Tony. *The Reign of Wonder: Naivety and Reality in American Literature*. Cambridge, England: Cambridge University Press, 1965.

Taylor, Walter Fuller. *The Economic Novel in America*. Chapel Hill: University of North Carolina Press, 1942.

Trent, William P. *A History of American Literature 1607-1865*. New York: D. Appleton, 1903.

Turner, Lorenzo Dow. *Anti-Slavery Sentiment in American Literature Prior to 1865*. Washington, D.C.: Association for the Study of Negro Life and History, 1929.

Unitarianism: Its Origin and History. Boston: American Unitarian Association, 1890.

Van Nostrand, A.D. *Everyman His Own Poet: Romantic Gospels in American Literature*. New York: McGraw-Hill, 1968.

Vogel, Stanley M. *German Literary Influences on the American Transcendentalists*. New Haven: Yale University Press, 1955.

Wagenknecht, Edward. *A Pictorial History of New England*. New York: Crown, 1976.

Wager, Willis. *American Literature: A World View*. New York: New York University Press, 1968.

Waggoner, Hyatt H. *American Poets from the Puritans to the Present*. Boston: Houghton Mifflin, 1968.

Webber, Everett. *Escape to Utopia: The Communal Movement in America*. New York: Hastings House, 1959.

Welter, Barbara. *Dimity Convictions: The American Woman in the Nineteenth Century*. Athens: Ohio University Press, 1976.

Welter, Rush. *The Mind of America 1820-1860*. New York: Columbia University Press, 1975.

Wendell, Barrett. *A Literary History of America*. New York: Scribners, 1900.

White, Morton. *Science and Sentiment in America*. New York: Oxford University Press, 1972.

Whiting, Lilian. *Boston Days*. Boston: Little, Brown, 1911.

Williams, Stanley T. *The Beginnings of American Poetry (1620-1855)*. Upsala, Sweden: Almquist & Wiksells, 1951.

Wilson, Rufus Rockwell. *New England in Letters*. New York: A. Wessels, 1904.

Wright, Conrad. *The Beginnings of Unitarianism in America*. Boston: Starr King Press, 1955.

Wright, Conrad. *The Liberal Christians: Essays on American Unitarian History*. Boston: Beacon, 1970.

REFERENCES.

1 Antiquarian Society House.
2 Armory.
3 Prichard Arboretum.
4 Home of Jane Austin.
5 Bates House.
6 Battle Lawn. Tablet.
7 Battle Monument.
8 John Beaton House.
9 Home of Frank Bigelow.
10 Site of Old Block.
11 Old Block House.
12 Home of George M. Brooks.
13 Site of House of Rev. Peter Buckley. Tablet.
14 Hill Burying Ground.
15 Main Street Burying Ground.
16 Major John Buttrick House.
17 Canoe Club House.
18 St. Bernard's Cemetery.
19 Sleepy Hollow Cemetery.
20 William Ellery Channing House.
21 Trinitarian Church.
22 Trinity Church.
23 Norwegian-Danish M. E. Church.
24 St. Bernard's Church. R. C.
25 Colonial Hotel.
26 Court House and Christian Science Rooms.
27 The Dove-Cote.
28 Egg Rock.
29 Emerson House.
30 Central Fire Station.
31 Home of Allen French.
32 Studio of Daniel C. French.
33 Memorial Fountain.
34 Grounds of Golf Club.
35 Grapevine Cottage.
36 Grave of British Soldiers.
37 Hawthorne Tablet.
38 Home of Samuel Hoar.
39 Home of E. R. Hoar.
40 Home for the Aged.
41 Edmund Hosmer House.
42 Adj. Joseph Hosmer House.
43 Site of Hubbard House.
44 Home of Frederic Hudson.
45 Elisha Jones House.
46 Tablet, Liberty Street.
47 Public Library.
48 Minute Man.
49 Horace Mann House.
50 Old Manse.
51 Masonic Building.
52 First Parish Meeting House.
53 Meriam's Corner.
54 Meriam House.
55 Site of Middlesex Hotel.
56 Monument Hall.
57 Home of William Munroe.
58 Nashawtuc Bridge.
59 Site of the Old North Bridge.
60 Orchard House.
61 Prichard Park.
62 School of Philosophy.
63 Public School Playground.
64 Minott Pratt House.
65 Dr. Samuel Prescott House; home of John H. Moore.
66 Reservoir.
67 Home of Frank B. Sanborn.
68 Emerson School.
69 High School.
70 Home School.
71 Manual Training School.
72 Ripley School.
73 Concord Power Station.
74 B. & M. R. R. Station Fitchburg Division.
75 B. & M. R. R. Station Southern Division.
76 Simmons House.
77 Soldiers' Monument.
78 Wright Tavern.
79 Jones' Tavern.
80 Thoreau-Alcott House.
81 Scene of "The Village Tragedy."
82 Town House.
83 Site of the Old Town House.
84 Wayside.
85 Home of William Whiting.
86 Willard Common.
87 Willard Farm. Tablet.

A First Position of the American forces on the morning of April 19, 1775
B Second Position of the American forces on the morning of April 19, 1775
C Third Position of the American forces on the morning of April 19, 1775
D Fourth Position of the American forces on the morning of April 19, 1775
E Route of the Americans to intercept the British at Meriam's corner.

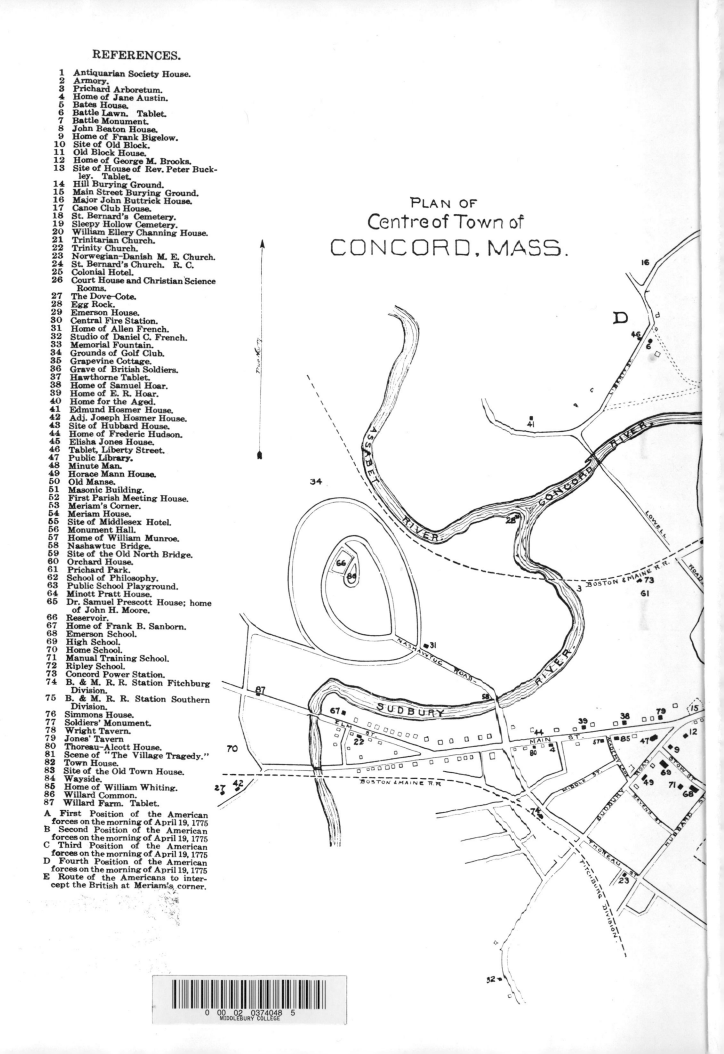

PLAN OF
Centre of Town of
CONCORD, MASS.